R
917.8043
HART
TOUR GUIDE
TO OLD WESTERN
FORTS

TOUR GUIDE TO OLD WESTERN FORTS

TOUR GUIDE TO OLD WESTERN FORTS

HERBERT M. HART

MAP
showing the Location of
MILITARY POSTS, INDIAN RESERVATIONS & PRINCIPAL ROUTES
in the
States & Territories comprising the
MILITARY DIVISION OF THE MISSOURI,
Lieut General P.H. SHERIDAN, COMMANDING.
Indicates the Boundaries of the Division.
Departments within the Div.
Indian Reservations.

BRITISH POSSESSIONS
WASHINGTON
OREGON
NEVADA
UTAH
WYOMING
COLORADO
NEBRASKA
KANSAS
NEW MEXICO
TEXAS
MEXICO
LOWER CALIFORNIA
FT. COLVILLE
FT. BUFORD
FT. PEMBINA
FT. VANCOUVER
WALLAWALLA
FT. LAPWAI
CAMP BAKER
FT. ELLIS
NEW POST
FT. RICE
FT. RANSOM
FT. ABERCROMBIE
FT. WADSWORTH
FT. KLAMATH
FT. BOISE
FT. BIDWELL
FT. M^c.DERMITT
CAMP BROWN
FT. FETTERMAN
FT. HALLECK
CAMP DOUGLAS
FT. M^c.PHERSON
FT. LEAVENWORTH
FT. RILEY
FT. HARKER
FT. HAYS
FT. WALLACE
FT. LYON
FT. REYNOLDS
FT. DODGE
FT. LARNED
FT. UNION
CAMP SUPPLY
FT. GIBSON
CAMP CADY
CAMP MOHAVE
CAMP WHIPPLE
CAMP VERDE
CAMP APACHE
CAMP McDOWELL
CAMP LOWELL
CAMP BOWIE
FT. CRITTENDEN
FT. WINGATE
FT. CRAIG
FT. STANTON
FT. TULAROSA
FT. BAYARD
FT. SELDEN
FT. CUMMINGS
FT. BLISS
FT. QUITMAN
FT. DAVIS
FT. STOCKTON
FT. CONCHO
FT. M^c.KAVETT
FT. GRIFFIN
FT. RICHARDSON
FT. CLARK
FT. DUNCAN
FT. M^c.INTOSH
RINGGOLD BKS.
FT. BROWN
FT. YUMA
DRUM BKS.
Santa Fe
Denver
Salt Lake City
Austin
San Diego
Los Angeles

PRUETT PUBLISHING CO.
Boulder, CO

THE OLD ARMY PRESS
Ft. Collins, CO

ISBN: 0-87108-568-2

Library of Congress Cataloging in Publication Data

Hart, Herbert M
Tour guide to old western forts.

Bibliography: p.
1. Fortification—The West—Guide-books. 2. The West—History, Local. 3. The West—Description and travel—1951- Guide-books. I. Title.
F591.H27 917.8'0433 80-14782
ISBN 0-87108-568-2

PHOTO CREDITS:

1. The National Archives
2. The Thomas Gilcrease Institute of American History and Art
3. George Eastman House, Rochester, N.Y.
4. Oregon Historical Society
5. State Historical Society of North Dakota
6. Minnesota Historical Society
7. Nebraska State Historical Society
8. Joslyn Art Museum, Omaha, NE
9. Wyoming State Archives & Historical Dept.
10. State Historical Society of Colorado
11. Nevada Historical Society Quarterly
12. Colonel George Rulen
13. Kansas State Historical Society
14. Society of California Pioneers
15. Kern County Museum, Calif.
16. State of California Dept. of Natural Resources
17. Bancroft Library, University of Calif. Berkeley
18. Harold G. Schutt, Calif.
19. *Harper's Weekly,* Oct. 28, 1865
20. *Harper's Weekly,* March 23, 1861
21. Ralph W. DeMoro
22. Yale University Western Collection
23. Dr. F.E. Shovlain, superintendent, Western State Hospital
24. Fort Columbia, Wash. Museum
25. University of Washington Library
26. Washington State Historical Society
27. Colonel Fred Rogers Collection
28. Oklahoma Historical Society
29. Fort Smith Museum Board
30. South Dakota Historical Society
31. American Pioneer Trails Assoc.
32. from Davis, "El Gringo", 1857
33. Montana Historical Society
34. Idaho State Historical Society
35. Merle Wells, Idaho Historical Society
36. David A. Simmons Estate and Michael J. Becker, NPS

Please send all orders to:
Pruett Publishing Company
3235 Prairie Avenue
Boulder, Colorado 80301

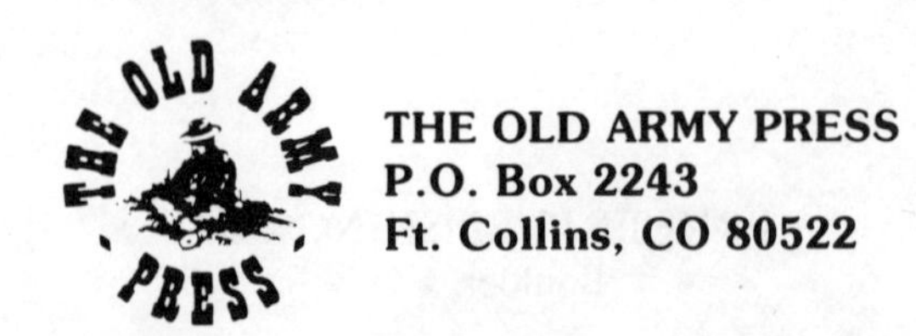

THE OLD ARMY PRESS
P.O. Box 2243
Ft. Collins, CO 80522

CONTENTS

Dedicated to
Megan, Michael, and Patrick
The newest Harts.

FOREWORD

It is with a great deal of uneasiness that I submit *Tour Guide to Old Western Forts.* I know only too well that I am risking the future of each fort site to the hazards of the treasure hunter, the souvenir collector and the just plain vandal.

Hopefully, my concern will be unfounded and the user of this book will observe the rules which I have proposed in the *Forts of the Old West* series and elsewhere. The most important rule is, of course, that private property must be respected. Most of these fort sites belong to someone; before stepping foot on the property, permission must be obtained. Preferably, advance permission should be requested by letter or telephone. Once permission is in hand, simple courtesy should include closing all gates, observing all fences and barriers and, most important, leaving the area clean, undisturbed and exactly as it was found.

My treasure- and souvenir-hunting friends notwithstanding, I have no truck with the individual who considers any untended location as fair game for his mine detector, shovel and axe. In my 160,000 miles of traveling to about two thousand fort sites, I have been shown an amazing amount of clutter by these souvenir hunters — clutter so valued by them that usually it was piled in a cardboard box in a rear closet with no record of why it was obtained. To the treasure hunters, whom I hold responsible for a lot of the hollowed-out walls, dug-out floors, and dismantled chimneys, I say right now: I know of no tale of buried treasure at any site in this book. Please leave the sites as you find them. Do not accelerate the deterioration that nature is accomplishing at a great speed unaided.

To all who read this book, I ask that heed be given to warnings about rattlesnakes, weather, heavy duty vehicles and isolated sites. Although most of the sites can be reached by the family car, there are some for which I recommend four-wheel drive, a minimum of two persons, spare fuel and water, tire chains, a shovel and some boards and gunny sacks, special maps from the U.S. Geological Survey, and the forethought to brief someone at the jumpoff point so that help can be sent if you do not return on time.

The total of more than a thousand entries in this book represent fort sites for which I could find reasonable directions. As reference to the directions in the *Forts* series can confirm, this does not include every military and civilian fort in the West before 1900. It does, however, include every one for which directions can be provided. I have visited almost all of these sites in person and these are the directions that I would use if I were to return to a site. Some directions may not agree with current maps, but I found that the actual access to some sites did not agree, either.

The directions are current as of 1978. Those which appeared along with more detailed coverage in the *Forts* series have been updated to agree with new construction and the interstate system, based on the official maps supplied by each Western state and three major oil companies. The oil companies and their representatives who provided advice and the latest maps were J.W. Scherer, Texaco, New York; M.H. Boeger, Shell Oil Company, New York; and the Advertising Travel Department of Standard Oil of California, San Francisco. It is because of this updating that some directions in the earlier volumes of the *Forts* may seem in error; actually, the original directions usually are adequate but those in this guide are more current for 1978 and beyond.

Any contradictions between the data in this book and in the regular series should be resolved in favor of this *Guide.* I have had no qualms in using this as the vehicle to correct errors that crept into the series. The few significant errors are pointed out, in fact.

Each fort is listed by the name for which it was best known. Its alternate names are included and cross referenced. The dates of activity usually reflect the opening and closing of the fort. They should not be considered as reflecting continuous occupancy in every case. The sites are those of 19th century significance in most cases but some of later periods are included for completeness.

Only a line or two is provided about each site in order to give an idea of something significant, perhaps an incident in its history or an indication of the post's layout.

Rand McNally's Railroad Map of 1876 is the base map for the fort locations, and has been used with their permission. The fort sites have been overprinted at the approximate locations, considering the inaccuracies of these early maps. An eagle eyed reader may notice that some overprinted locations do not agree with those on the basic map, and that some forts on the map are not included in this guide, again because of inaccuracies of that map. Solid stars are used for military posts, or those places that owe their inclusion here to military use (such as garrisoned stage stations). Trading posts, settler forts, and other non-military sites are marked with hollow stars.

As an aid to locating the many coast defense batteries of the forts of Texas, California, Oregon and Washington, these are listed with that of the parent fort and then, in most cases, as separate entries. Because dates are difficult to establish firmly—between authorization, construction start or completed or suspended, or whatever—only the era is usually given. In most cases this will be that of the Endicott Board between 1890 and 1910 or the Taft Board, 1907-1920. Because of the nature of their construction, most of these batteries are still in evidence, but with conditions ranging from almost museum mint with mounted guns to overgrown and trash filled.

Many of the illustrations have not appeared before in the *Forts* series; some of them have never been published at all and are presented here for national distribution for the first time. Most illustrations were made from originals purchased from dealers or borrowed from the U.S. Army Military History Institute, Carlisle Barracks, Pennsylvania; the Army libraries at the Pentagon and Fort Leavenworth; the National Archives, and various participating libraries of the Interlibrary Loan Service.

In addition to the contributor of each illustration as shown with it, I must express my appreciation for the help of the historians of the National Archives, the National Park Service, the Heritage Conservation and Recreation Service, the state and local historical societies, my fellow members of the Westerners, the Western History Association, the U.S. Cavalry Memorial Association, the Company of Military Historians, the Council on Abandoned Military Posts, the Association of the U.S. Army, and the many, many kind persons who are mentioned with thanks in the *Forts* series.

Without minimizing the efforts of others, I must acknowledge by name thirteen persons who helped throughout every step of this project, even to the point of incurring personal expenses and making available to me virtually the entire contents of their own files and libraries. Words are inadequate to express my thanks to Sara D. Jackson and Robert M. Utley of Washington, D.C.; retired Colonels George Ruhlen and Fred B. Rogers, late of San Diego, California; retired Major General George Ruhlen of San Antonio, Texas; Dr. Robert Frazer of Long Beach, California; Lee Myers of Las Cruces, New Mexico; the late Marvin King of Arenas Valley, New Mexico; Fred Greguras of Omaha, Nebraska; and coast artillery experts Robert Zink, King George, Virginia, Glen Williford, Longwood, Florida, and Alfred Chiswell, Falls Church, Virginia. Number 13 is my wife Teresa, who somehow found time to have babies number 6 and 7 while this project was being born.

As the first listing of its kind, to a certain extent this guide is a first draft. Readers are asked to send me their corrections and recommended changes via the publisher so that any future revisions of this guide will reflect them and thus more accurately contribute to the story of the development of the American West.

Herbert M. Hart

ARIZONA

FORT GRANT *(1)*

Apache wars and Arizona seem almost synonymous and the posts and camps of the thirty years of campaigns against the Apache dot most of the state. These are especially numerous in the southeastern portion. The posts listed are but a few of the many camps used by the military, representing the major sites with a few of the lesser, more temporary locations.

The Civil War camps of the California Column also are included, if they attained any status in the permanent record and some agreement has been reached on the sites.

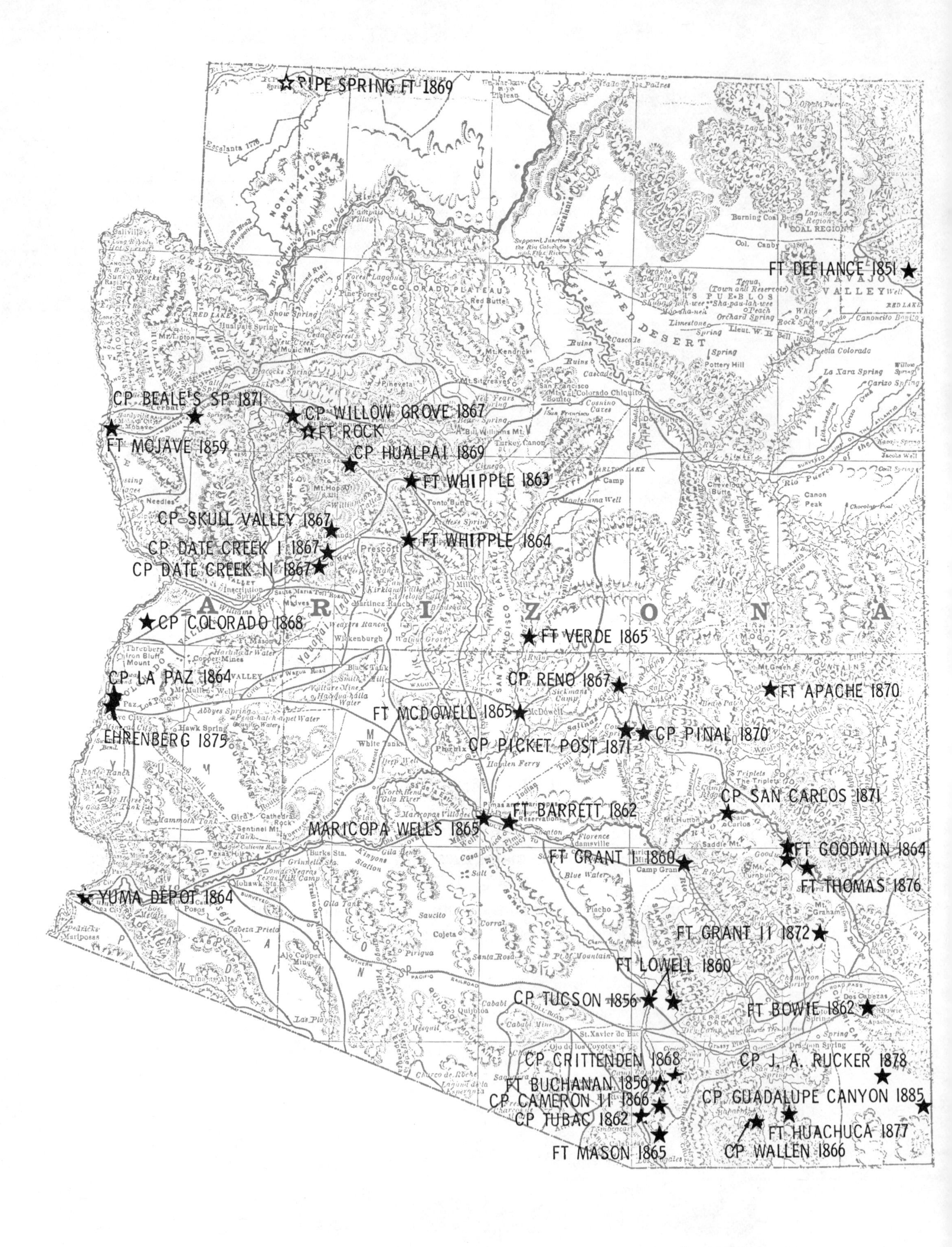
PIPE SPRING FT 1869
FT DEFIANCE 1851
CP BEALE'S SP 1871
CP WILLOW GROVE 1867
FT ROCK
FT MOJAVE 1859
CP HUALPAI 1869
FT WHIPPLE 1863
CP SKULL VALLEY 1867
FT WHIPPLE 1864
CP DATE CREEK I 1867
CP DATE CREEK II 1867
A R I Z O N A
CP COLORADO 1868
FT VERDE 1865
CP LA PAZ 1864
CP RENO 1867
FT APACHE 1870
FT MCDOWELL 1865
EHRENBERG 1875
CP PINAL 1870
CP PICKET POST 1871
CP SAN CARLOS 1871
FT BARRETT 1862
MARICOPA WELLS 1865
FT GOODWIN 1864
FT GRANT I 1860
FT THOMAS 1876
YUMA DEPOT 1864
FT GRANT II 1872
FT LOWELL 1860
CP TUCSON 1856
FT BOWIE 1862
CP CRITTENDEN 1868
CP J. A. RUCKER 1878
FT BUCHANAN 1856
CP CAMERON II 1866
CP GUADALUPE CANYON 1885
CP TUBAC 1862
FT HUACHUCA 1877
FT MASON 1865
CP WALLEN 1866

Fort Apache. 1870-1922. *Camp Ord, Camp Mogollon, Camp Thomas.* One of the headquarters for General George Crook's Apache expeditions, this post was under seige after the nearby Battle of Cibicu. The parade ground still is flanked by Army buildings, now used by the Indian Agency. From Globe, take US 60 northeast 66 miles to right turn on Arizona 73, arriving in 27 miles after turn at town of Fort Apache; fort buildings are next to town.

FORT APACHE
Officer's Quarters & Administration Bldg. *(1)*

New Post at Babocomari Ranch. *Camp Wallen.*

Fort Barrett. 1862. The California Column headquartered here enroute to secure Arizona and New Mexico in the early days of the Civil War. The Confederates were here first, at the Ammi White mill, and burned the mill so that the Federals could not use it. Regardless, it was in the vicinity of the mill that the Californians camped. From Phoenix, take I-10 south about 25 miles to Bapchule turnoff, turn west, go 5 miles to dirt road 2 miles beyond Public Health Service buildings (on left, southern side of road). At dirt road, turn right and continue north on road until it reaches Gila river, near which is site of White's mill. Guide advisable.

Camp Beale Spring. 1871-74. A trail-protecting post, this short-term camp had 12 buildings of adobe with shingle roofs plus a 3-tent hospital. The barracks was 60 feet long, 20 wide. The bare site is now marked on the outskirts of Kingman on Arizona 93.

Fort Bowie. 1862-94. Apache fights swirled around this remote sentinel at bloody Apache Pass, but it was from here that in 1886 Geronimo and his followers were sent to Florida to end the Apache wars. From Bowie, on I-10 about 26 miles west of Willcox, follow the signs south to the National Park Service's historic site. The Park Service has stabilized the ruins of the many adobe buildings, and a ranger is resident at the site. From the parking area, it is a picturesque mile-long hike to the fort.

Fort Buchanan. 1856-61. *Camp Moore.* Hardly anything remains at this once critical outpost of the pre-Civil War Indian battles, burned when it was abandoned at the start of the war. It was outposted periodically until the end of the war. The United States' first Medal of Honor was awarded to the surgeon of Fort Buchanan for heroism against the Apaches. The site, and some of its excavated building outlines, can be reached from Sonoita, going west on Arizona 82 one mile to Crown C Ranch; site is on west side of road on privately owned property.

Camp Cameron I. *Fort Mason.*

Camp Cameron II. 1866-67. This site is approximately 45 miles south of Tucson. There are remains of two buildings at the site.

Fort Canby. Despite many official and semi-official records, this post never existed as an independent command "28 miles from Fort Defiance." In actuality, it was the official name of the Army garrison located at the Fort Defiance site during the Civil War.

Camp Clark. *Fort Whipple.*

Camp Colorado. *Fort Mojave.*

Camp Colorado. 1868-71. This was a tent and hut camp west of the city of Parker on the Colorado river. The site is now covered by irrigation projects.

Camp Crittenden. 1868-73. The post-Civil War successor of Fort Buchanan, Crittenden now has

FORT BOWIE *(1)*

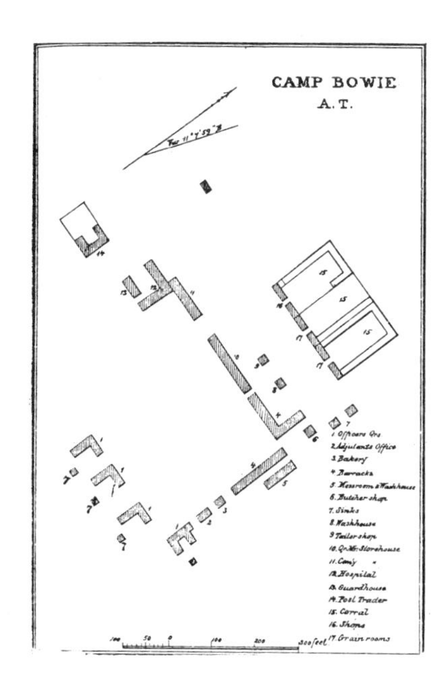

a scattering of deteriorating adobe ruins. From Sonoita, go west on Arizona 82 about 1 mile. Ruins of post are on high ground above Buchanan site several miles west of road on privately owned Crown C ranch.

Camp Date Creek. 1867-73. *Camp McPherson, Camp Skull Valley.* The first Date Creek (1867) was three miles north of Date Creek. The third camp (1867-73) (*Camp McPherson*), one of the several sites at which General George Crook narrowly escaped death, is dotted with man-high adobe and rock walls. From Phoenix, go north on US 89 for 69 miles to side road 1.4 miles beyond Congress. Turn left (west) and continue north for 9.1 miles to Hawkins Ranch. After obtaining permission, take gravel road 1.2 miles to turnoff; in 0.2 miles stop and continue on foot for 200 yards across creek to adobe ruins directly south. See *Camp Skull Valley* for the second Date Creek site.

Fort Defiance. 1851-64. *Fort Canby.* The Navajo Indians who were the targets of Fort Defiance operations until the Civil War occasionally kept this place under siege. Abandoned in 1861, the fort was revived as Fort Canby in 1863-64 for Kit Carson's Navajo expeditions. Some traces of the post still remain at what is now a modern Indian Agency. From Gallup, N.M., go north on US 666 for 8 miles to left turn on Arizona 68 to intersection with Navajo 7 at Arizona border east of St. Michaels. Take this past Window Rock to agency of Fort Defiance, 7 miles, the site of the fort.

Camp Devin. *Camp Hualpai.*

Detachment at Ehrenberg. c. 1875. Here on the Mojave river, the Army kept tiny details to handle supply shipments arriving for the posts of California and Arizona. Army buildings included rented quarters and a quartermaster warehouse; turn-of-the-century flooding washed away all traces but a picturesque cemetery remains at the town site. The town is at the western terminus of I-10 in Arizona north of the Colorado river bridge.

Fort Garrett. This site is marked on Snap Canyon, Arizona, quadrangle of the U.S. Geological Survey maps of Arizona but the 12x14 foot rock "fort" is probably only a sheepherder's shelter. The area is included in a 1976 addition to Grand Canyon National Park.

Field Camp in Guadalupe Canyon. 1885. A supply depot used by the 4th U.S. Cavalry during the Geronimo campaign, this camp was attacked by Apaches when most of the garrison was on patrol. Three troopers were killed. The approximate site can be reached via a rough jeep road from Douglas which goes past the Slaughter Ranch at San Bernadino and from there through the canyon. There is some possibility that the exact site is just over the New Mexico border.

New Post on the Gila. *Fort Thomas.*

FORT DEFIANCE *(1)*

FORT HUACHUCA *(1)*

Fort Goodwin. 1864-71. Sometimes the Indians protected by Fort Goodwin outnumbered the garrison, much to the concern of the commanding officer as he desperately tried to feed and shelter the Indians who accepted the Army offers of peace. The first post, *Camp Goodwin,* was north of Geronimo in 1864; the garrison moved that year to a location west of Geronimo. From Globe, take US 70 about 48 miles east to Geronimo. Take dirt road to west about ½ mile to ranch-house. Cotton field west of ranchhouse was site of post and adobe mounds are under trees across field. Permission must be requested.

Fort Grant. There were two Grants in Arizona. The first, 1860-72, known also as *Forts Arivaypa, Breckenridge* and *Stanford* and *Camp Wright,* was the site of the 1871 Camp Grant massacre. A total of 85 Apache Indians at the post were killed by Tucson civilians and Papago Indians.

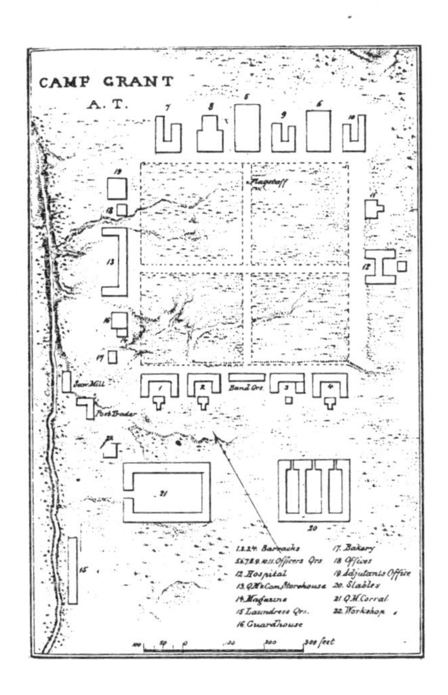

The post was moved soon after to a second site (1872-1907), the base of operations for many expeditions during the Apache campaigns.

The Old Camp Grant site has been obliterated 40 miles northeast of Tucson. From Tucson, take US 80-89 north to Arizona 77. Go north about 10 miles beyond Mammoth where a dirt road enters from right. Fifty yards southeast of this intersection is the privately owned site of the first fort.

New Camp Grant is 45 miles to the southeast. From Safford, go south on US 666 about 17 miles to Arizona 266. Go west 22 miles to Arizona State Industrial School, user of the site and some of the old Army buildings. Permission to visit must be requested.

Fort Huachuca. 1877- –. The only active Army post in modern Arizona, Fort Huachuca's electronics and communications missions are not far removed from its nineteenth century use of Indian scouts and the heliograph in settling the Apache wars. Many old buildings and an active post museum memorialize the tradition of this post. From Tucson, take I-10 to Arizona 90 turnoff. Go south on Arizona 90 for 30 miles to Sierra Vista. Fort Huachuca's main gate is 3 miles west.

Camp Hualpai. 1869-73; 1881. *Camp Devin, Camp Toll Gate.* Situated on a gravelly mesa, this post was established to protect the wagon road. Hardly a trace is left of the tent-and-hut camp except for some rock foundations and occasional square nails. From Prescott take Forest Road 95 for about 35 miles northwest to the mesa above Walnut Creek. This is 2 miles west of the junction with Forest Road 6. Stop at the Forest Service sign erected by the Prescott chapter of the Daughters of the American Revolution in 1953, that specifies that this is the site of Camp Hualpai.

Camp Ibis. This was a World War II desert training camp north of Needles, Calif., where Arizona, Nevada, and California intersect. Lake Havasu City, Ariz., residents continually unearth artifacts from the vast area.

Infantry Camp, Pinal Mountains. *Camp Pinal.*

Camp John A. Rucker. 1878-80. *Camp Supply, Camp Powers.* First located under its initial name on a stream off of the White river in Cochise county, the post was moved in 1878 to its permanent site six miles from White river. From here its troopers fought the second and final Apache war. Some buildings still remain, having been used as a ranch headquarters. From I-10 at the Arizona-New Mexico border, go southwest on US 80 at Road Forks, N.M. At Chiracahua, 50 miles, turn right into Coronado National Forest. At 15.2 miles, turn right, continue for .7 mile to ranch, privately owned site of Camp Rucker.

Camp Lake Carleton. This post was to be built in the 1860's in honor of General James H. Carleton, commander of the California Column, in the vicinity of Mormon Lake. It never was built but appears on several period maps.

Camp La Paz. 1864; 1874-75. *Camp Lincoln.* Actually the Lincoln name came first as the Civil War site of a short-lived Army detachment. Later, soldiers occupied the abandoned adobes of La Paz town in trying to keep peace between Indians and miners. Only a few hard-to-distinguish adobe mounds and a well are left of this ghost town. From Ehrenberg, at the Arizona end of I-10, go north about 10 miles to site of La Paz, a ghost town now in the Colorado River Indian Reservation. The Indian Agency should be contacted for permission and a guide.

Camp Lincoln. *Camp La Paz.*

Camp Lincoln. *Fort Verde.*

Fort Lowell. 1860-91. The first Fort Lowell, also known as *Camp Tucson* or the *Post* or *Depot of Tucson,* belonged to the Union before the Civil War and to the Confederates in the early days of the War. It was mainly a 13-building supply depot and headquarters until moved to a site east of Tucson in 1873.

The new post was a quarter mile long parallelogram of buildings designed for a 300-man garrison. The downtown Tucson site is now generally the location of the Santa Rita Hotel. The Arizona Historical Society, 949 East 2nd street, has an excellent diorama of this first post.

To get to the Fort Lowell post-Civil War location, take Broadway from downtown east 55 blocks to Craycroft road. Turn left (north), go 30 blocks to Fort Lowell Park. Visitor's Center, museum, ball playing, picnic and parking areas are available to visitors amidst the ruins. A restoration project has intermingled recreation facilities with historical remnants to insure permanent care along with civic appreciation of the site.

Post at Maricopa Wells. 1865-67. The Army maintained detachments here to protect the mail and supply lines. After the Gila river inundated the town several times, the location was moved several miles eastward to the present site of Maricopa. There are some adobe ruins, speedily being destroyed by souvenir and treasure hunters, at the Maricopa Wells site. To get there from Maricopa, a guide should be requested as the route involves numerous back roads and rough trails.

Fort Mason. 1865-66. *Fort McKee, Post at Calabasas, Camp Calabasas No. 1.* Once expected to become the largest post in Arizona, Fort Mason lasted but a short time—partly because of unhealthful conditions but mainly because it was no longer necessary. There are no remains but archaeological research has exposed foundations. From Tucson, go south on US 89 for 56 miles to the marker for Calabasas town. The site of the fort was between the highway and the town site, 2 miles east of the road. In 1978, the site was scheduled for housing development.

Fort McDowell. 1865-90. *Camp Verde.* General O. O. Howard tried without success to make Fort McDowell an Indian preserve; the habits of the intended wards militated against such a project.

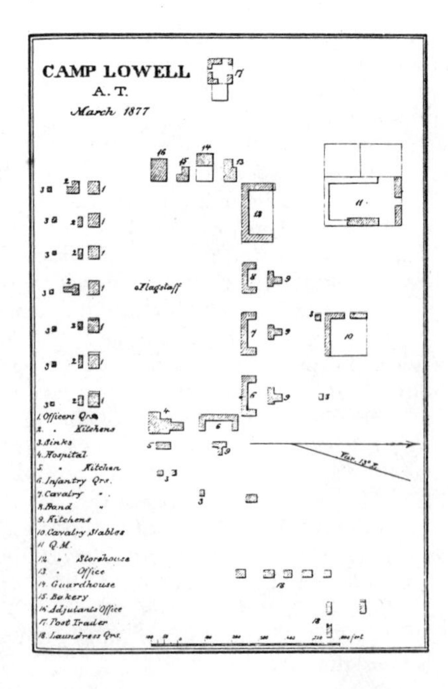

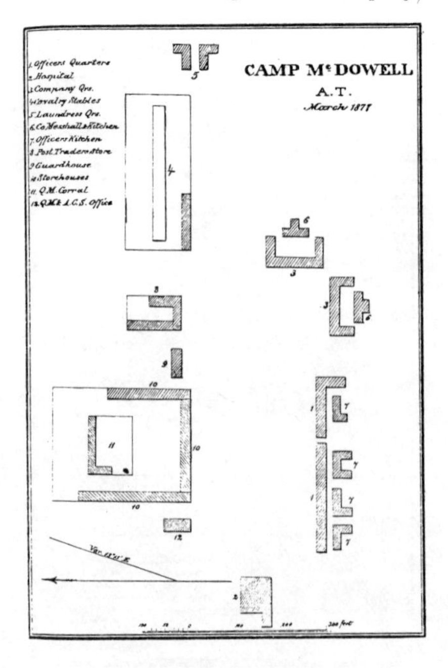

This post was the headquarters of the District of the Verde during the post-Civil War period. Two buildings are left but the entire site is scheduled to be inundated by reclamation projects.

From Phoenix, take Arizona 87 northeast. About 12 miles from intersection with US 80-89-60-70, this highway crosses an improved road that heads straight north; by taking this road, the route will go through McDowell Pass, a favorite ambush point. Both this road and Arizona 87 pass entrance to Fort McDowell Indian Reservation, left turn. Follow road to dead end at site, about 2 miles. A reconstruction of Fort McDowell is being built at Pioneer Arizona, an outdoor museum north of Phoenix.

Camp McPherson. *Camp Date Creek.*

Camp Mogollon. *Fort Apache.*

Fort Mojave. 1859-90. *Camp Colorado, Fort "Navajo."* The official Arizona spelling is Mohave, but the Mojave spelling was official in the War Department, crica 1859, when the Army first established itself at the site by defeating the Indians. The lesson was learned and few Indian troubles took place in the later days of the garrison—which was more concerned with battling the unseemingly hot weather.

After a post-Army career as an Indian School, the post was dismantled in 1941. From Las Vegas, Nevada, go southeast on US 95 for 78 miles to Nevada 77 east across Colorado river and Davis Dam until it intersects with Arizona 68 about 1.5 miles. Turn back to west toward Davis Dam town and Bullhead City. One mile south of Bullhead City, at fork of dirt road labelled "Rogers Landing," jog right.

Follow main course of dirt road as it curves around the river bend, cuts southward down small peninsula, and then comes to river again. About 8 miles south of Rogers Landing, road has a fork, one route going directly south, the other straight west. Follow west fork until it disappears in rolling bluffs overlooking river, possibly marked by small signs indicating that this is site of "Fort Mohave." Private property.

Camp Moore. *Fort Buchanan.*

Fort Navajo. This was the name used in 1862 by General James H. Carleton in pre-California Column dispatches to mislead Confederate spies. He probably meant Fort Mojave, covered elsewhere in this section.

Camp Newell. 1916-21. Border post established for upwards of 900 men and 1,500 horses during the border war period, using leased site on John J. Newell ranch. Numerous buildings are left, rented to workers; owner Tom Newell lives in former hospital. The post site is near Naco on the border.

Camp Ord. *Fort Apache.*

Camps Pinal and **Picket Post.** 1870-71. *Camp Infantry.* The story of these two posts is so intermixed as to be almost impossible to separate. As Camp Infantry and then Camp Pinal the post was founded in 1870 to protect the miners.

A year later the camp was moved and renamed to a site that is in the shadow of Picket Post Butte, a heliograph station in the days of the Apache campaigns. This site became the town of Pinal, once a mining camp of 2,500 persons. Now only a few ranches dot the area.

From Miami, go west on US 60-70 for 11 miles, turn left on gravel road. This is the site of Camp Pinal. To get to Picket Post site, from Superior go west of US 60-70 for 1.6 miles to left turn below Picket Post Butte at Apache Tears road.

Pipe Spring Fort. 1869-75. This was an important Mormon settlers' fort that consisted of two double-story redstone buildings enclosed by sandstone walls and heavy gates. Firing platforms, loopholes in the walls, and a well within the enclosure assured that a good defense could be put up against any Indian attack. This is now Pipe Spring National Monument, on Arizona 389 about 15 miles southwest of Fredonia.

Camp Pomeroy. *Fort Whipple.*

Prescott Barracks. *Fort Whipple.*

Camp Powers. *Camp John A. Rucker.*

Camp Reno. 1867-70. After the Army established posts around the fringes of Tonto Basin northeast of Fort McDowell, the next step was to move into the Basin. Camp Reno, an adobe and frame post surrounded by a stockade, was this step.

This was an active camp during its existence, hardly reflected in the fact that modern remains consist of only two small disappearing adobe rectangles and the cemetery site.

From Phoenix, take Arizona 87 north for 73 miles to turnoff marked for "Jake's Corner." Turn right (east). Proceed on the gravel road past Jake's Grocery through Pumpkin Center to the Tonto Basin Forest Ranger Station, right turn.

Request permission from ranger. He can provide directions to dirt road and site 3 miles from the ranger station. This is a fair weather, rough duty vehicle road only.

Fort Rock. *Fort Rock Springs.* Although several maps show this location with one or the other name, this was not an Army post. Midway between Mojave and Prescott, this was a stage stop at which more than 100 Hualpais were held off in 1866 by three soldiers, the mail carrier and a boy, the latter doing most of the shooting because he had the only operable rifle. See Camp Willow Grove directions and go 2 miles further south.

Camp San Carlos. 1871-1900. The Army provided protection for reservation Indians and the Indian Agent and sometimes served as Agent, too, at this once hot, sandy site now inundated by San Carlos Lake behind Coolidge Dam. From Globe, go south on US 70 to the turnoff to Peridot. This road heads north to the new town and agency of San Carlos; it heads south to San Carlos Lake and overlooks the fort site.

Camp Skull Valley. 1867. *New Camp Date Creek.* This was the site to which and from which Camp Date Creek's garrison moved, in the trace of the movements of the Indians. The name comes from a story that after one Indian skirmish the dead were not buried, resulting in bleaching skulls and bones in the dry Arizona sun. From Prescott, go northwest on the road to Iron Springs which intersects with the southerly road to Skull Valley settlement, the post site.

Camp Supply. *Camp John A. Rucker.*

Camp Thomas. *Fort Apache.*

Fort Thomas. 1876-92. *New Post on the Gila.* Although Fort Thomas was a center from which Indian operations were fielded, two other problems were present. Unhealthy climate caused much sickness in its early years; banditry extended throughout its later period. The latter included an 1889 ambush of a 12-man paymaster detachment, resulting in the loss of $28,000 and the wounding of eight soldiers. The town of Fort Thomas is on US 70 about 55 miles south of Globe. The fort site is covered by plowed fields north of the town and beside the highway.

Camp Toll Gate. *Camp Hualpai.*

Camp Tubac. 1862-68. Troops periodically outposted this historic town—site of Spanish and Mexican presidios—but there were no Army buildings. The soldiers lived in various houses in the town, the protection that they provided being considered sufficient rent by the grateful citizens. Remnants of the presidio are preserved. From Tucson, take US 89 south for 45 miles to the turn-off to Tubac, ½ mile to the east.

Camp near Tucson. 1856-59. (Also see *Fort Lowell.*) Captain Richard S. Ewell, the commander of the Army here, divided his time between fighting Indians, trying to get money for his camp, and managing a herd of cows—until the Indians drove off the herd. The site of the camp is in the vicinity of downtown Tucson. A half mile from downtown is the site of the first *Camp Tucson* where the Mormon Battalion encamped for a short time in 1846 after the surrender of the *Presidio of Tucson.*

Presidio of Tucson. 1776-1828; 1840-46. The 75 Spaniards who garrisoned this post calculated that they could keep the Indians under control by making them dependent on Spanish friendship and liquor. Mexicans replaced the ineffective

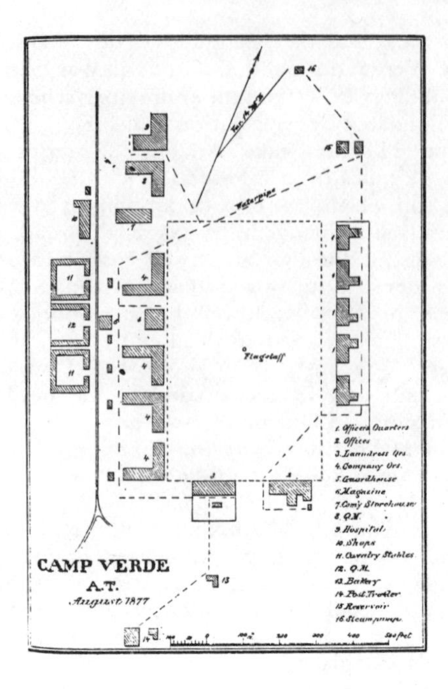

garrison but upon the arrival of the Mormon Battalion in 1846, they, too, withdrew. The site of the Presidio is in downtown Tucson, bounded by Washington, Main, Pennington and Church streets.

New Post on the Upper San Pedro. *Camp Wallen.*

Campo Verde. *Fort McDowell.*

Fort Verde. 1865-90. *Camp Lincoln.* Founded one mile north of the present-day town of Camp Verde, the first post was on the site of a civilian stone stronghold, so-called *Camp Lincoln.* The Army arrived in 1865 and the post became official in 1866 under the Lincoln name. The Army moved to the final site in 1871; two years later General George Crook's first Apache campaign ended with a surrender ceremony on the Fort Verde parade ground. Several buildings of the

CAMP SAN CARLOS *(1)*

second post are maintained by the State Parks Board and are open to visitors. The town of Camp Verde is 36 miles directly east of Prescott and 2 miles east of the turnoff from Arizona 79. The post site covers the northern half of the hamlet.

Camp Wallen. 1866-69. *New Post at Babocomari Ranch, New Post on the Upper San Pedro.* The Army located a detachment after the Civil War at this so-called "Fort Babocomari," a ruined adobe hacienda that dated from before 1800. Apache troubles were so great that the post was still an adobe ruin when the Army left three years later. Some adobe walls are left on the privately owned Babocomari Ranch in the vicinity of Elgin. It is closed to the public; permission to visit must be obtained in advance from the headquarters in Phoenix.

Fort Whipple. 1863-1913. *Camp Pomeroy, Camp Clark, Prescott Barracks, Whipple Depot/ Barracks.* The Army started a post at Del Rio Springs in order to protect the Government of

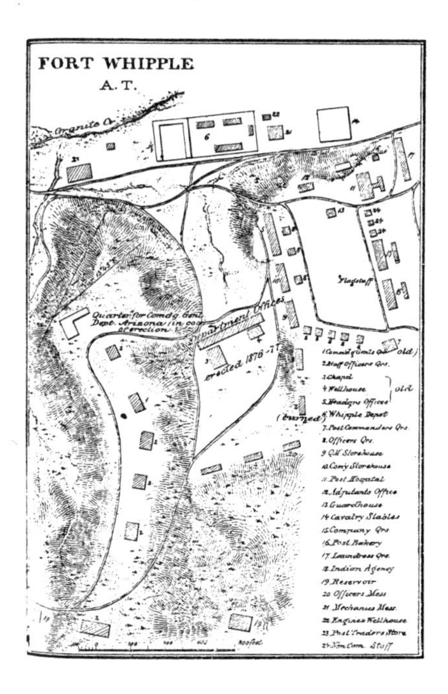

Arizona in 1863 and a year later the troops moved next to Prescott, the site selected as a capital by the first governor. Whipple was headquarters or supply depot for almost every campaign in the later Apache Wars. The first post was at Del Rio Springs, 18 miles northeast of Prescott; the second site and many old buildings from Army days are now occupied by the Veterans Administration Hospital, 1 mile east of Prescott on US 89 and Arizona 69.

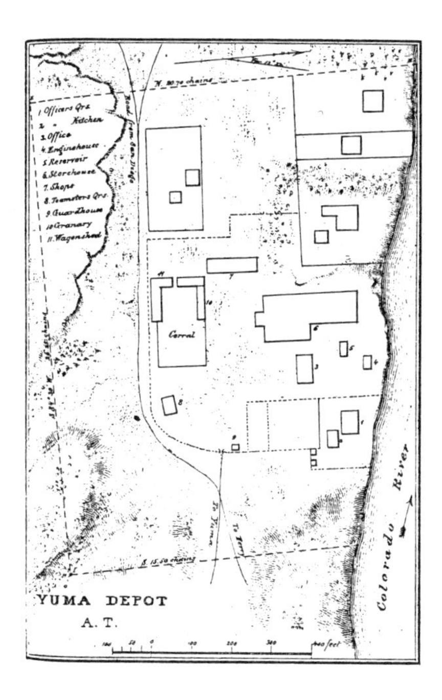

Camp Willow Grove. 1867-69. Protection of the Mohave road was the mission of the 90 troopers housed in tents and shanties at this make-shift post. The site is a peninsula-like flat bordered on the north and west by Willow creek and the south by an erosion channel. Remnants of several rooms and fireplaces were excavated by the Museum of Northern Arizona in 1966 and these can still be seen at the gradually eroding site. Take I-40 for 40 miles east of Kingman to interchange. This is about 2 miles north of the site; 2 miles further south is so-called Fort Rock.

Yuma Depot. 1864-85; 1911-13; 1915-22. *Post at Yuma.* This is not the fabled Fort Yuma, which is across the Colorado river in California, but this post provided supply support for the fort and the other forts up-river. A detachment of troops garrisoned the place in 1885 and in the later years. Rebels escaping from the Mexican Revolution were imprisoned here in 1884, as bars on the windows of the supply depot attest. After the rebels had been pleasantly housed and fed by the depot detachment, they were returned to Mexico—and were wiped out to the last shortly after. The buildings are in a park and maintained by the Arizona Historical Society and local groups. The site is at the north end of North 2d avenue on the Yuma side of the river.

CALIFORNIA

CAMP YERBA BUENA ISLAND *(17)*

Spanish, Mexicans, Russians, the Bear Flag Republic, and the United States all contributed to the military and civilian forts of California's nineteenth century and before. The camps of the Mexican War usually were temporary until a so-called permanent line was established in mid-nineteenth century.

Many Civil War camps were set up to counter secessionist activities and to prepare and then support the California Volunteers who manned almost all of the forts of the state during the period (the only exception was Alcatraz and even this was garrisoned by them for short periods). Most were merely camps of short duration and, especially those in the Northern California back-country, are impossible to locate precisely.

CP LINCOLN 1862
CP SUPPLY 1873
FT BIDWELL 1865
CP LAVA BEDS 1873
FT TERWAW 1857
FT JONES 1852
FT WOOL 1855
FT GASTON 1858
FT CROOK 1857
CP CURTISS 1862
CP BURNT RANCH 1864
FT ANDERSON 1862
CP LYON 1862
CP BOYNTON'S PRAIRIE 1864
CP IAQUA 1863
FT BAKER 1862
FT READING 1852
FT SEWARD 1861
CP CASS 1859
FT HUMBOLDT 1863
FT LIPPITT 1862
CP NOME LACKEE 1855
FT WRIGHT 1862
CP BIDWELL 1863
FT BRAGG 1857
FT WELLER 1859
CT FAR WEST 1849
FT SUTTER 1846
CP UNION 1861
CP J.W. ANDERSON 1849
FT ROSS 1812
CP MERCHANT 1863
CP DOWNEY 1861
FT SONOMA 1846
BENICIA 1851
CP STANFORD 1863
CP HALLECK 1862
CP MCDOUGALL 1861
CP GILMORE 1863
CP REYNOLDS 1863
FT BAKER 1897
FT POINT 1853
CP BARRETT 1898
CP WRIGHT 1861
CP MILLER 1898
CP SUMNER 1861
CP HOOKER 1862
FT VIGILANCE 1856
CP ALCATRAZ 1859
CP YERBA BUENA IS 1860
FT MASON 1863
CP ALERT 1861
PRESIDIO SAN FRANCISCO 1776
FT MONTGOMERY 1846
CP ADOBE MEADOWS 1862
FT YOSEMITE 1886
FT MILLER 1851
CP INDEPENDENCE 1862
CP SEQUOIA NATL PK 1886
POOLE'S FT
FT MERVINE 1770
CP BABBITT 1862
CP RESTING SP 1859
FT SODA 1860
CP BITTER SP 1859
FT PIUTE 1860
CP MARL SP 1866
CP ROCK SP 1859
CP CADY 1859
FT TEJON 1854
CP MORRIS 1863
CP BANNING 1859
NEW CP CARLETON 1862
CP CAJON 1847
EMERGENCY CP 1862
FT SAN BERNARDINO 1852
CP FITZGERALD 1861
CP CARLETON 1861
FT MOORE 1846
FT BENSON 1856
CP KELLOGG 1862
CP RANCHO DEL JURUPA 1852
CP LATHAM 1861
DRUM BKS 1862
CP WRIGHT 1861
CP SANTA CATALINA IS 1864
CP MN SAN LUIS REY 1846
FT YUMA 1849
CP CALHOUN 1849
FT GUIJARROS 1779
PT MISSION SAN DIEGO 1847
FT ROSECRANS 1898
PRESIDIO SAN DIEGO 1769
NEW SAN DIEGO BKS 1850
CP RILEY 1849

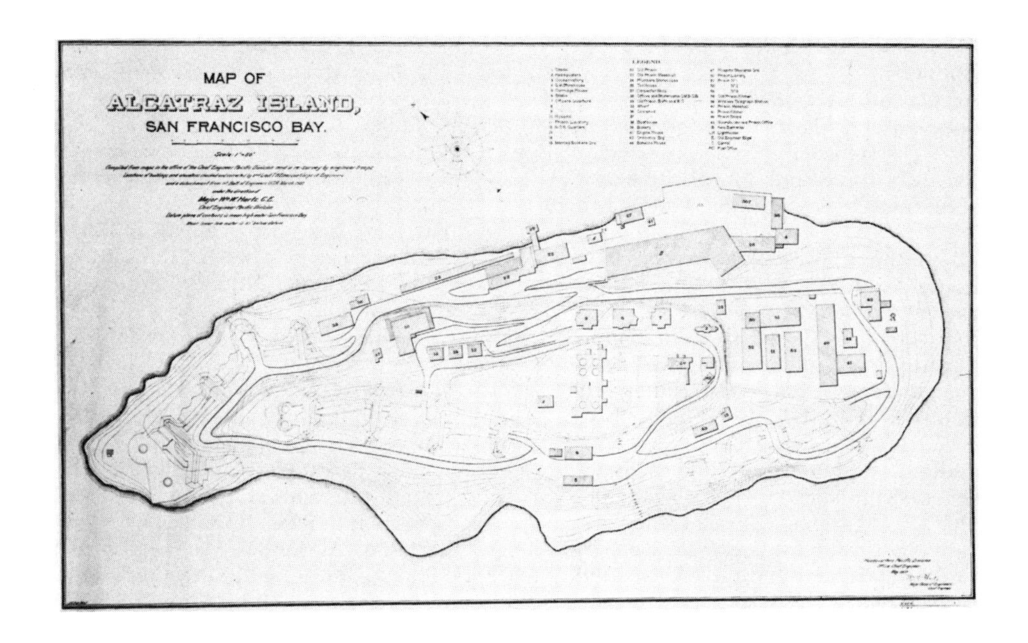

Camp at Adobe Meadows. 1862. This June-August Volunteer camp was in Adobe Valley, 15 miles east of Mono Lake.

Battery Alexander. This was an Endicott period 12-inch gun position at Fort Barry.

Camp Alcatraz. 1859-1934. *Prison Post at Alcatraz Island, "Fort" Alcatraz.* Until 1895 this post was an artillery key to the defense of San Francisco bay; in 1895 it became a military prison. A number of buildings dating from Army days remain, mixed in with the abandoned cell blocks of the former federal penitentiary. Both suffered during the Indian occupation, 1970-71, when damage was considerable. The island is now operated by the National Park Service's Golden Gate National Recreation Area, encompassing much of San Francisco Bay, and boat trips to it leave regularly from Fisherman's Wharf in San Francisco.

POST AT ALCATRAZ, barracks

ALCATRAZ

Camp Alert. 1861. California Volunteers trained here at the Pioneer Race Track before moving to Salt Lake City. The race track was between Mission and Folsom, and 24th and 26th streets in San Francisco.

Camp J. W. Anderson. 1849. This short-time post was occupied by two companies of the 2d Infantry until the founding of Cantonment Far West. It was at Sutterville, three miles south of Sutter's Fort on the east bank of the Sacramento river.

Fort Anderson. 1862-66. The log huts that comprised this post have completely disappeared from this peaceful pasture site. Indian depredations once were so great in this area that the Anderson troopers were hard-pressed to establish that peace. From Eureka, go north on US 101 through Arcata to California 299. Turn right (east), go through Blue Lake, 7 miles. About 12 miles further east, gravel road branches off to left (north). Follow this for 4 miles to Redwood creek, site of Fort Anderson.

Post at Angel Island. *Camp Reynolds.*

Avila Adobe. 1847. This was Commodore Stockton's headquarters when he was commander-in-chief of American forces in California. It is now a state historic monument in Old Town, Los Angeles.

Arizona, Department of Headquarters. 1887-88. After Nelson A. Miles captured Geronimo to end the Apache campaign he decided Arizona was not as comfortable as California so he moved headquarters here to a building that had been Saint Vincent's College at Sixth and Hill streets in downtown Los Angeles. This would be Pershing Square today.

Camp Babbitt. 1862-66. *Post at Visalia.* Secessionists rather than Indians were the main opponents of this Civil War post. The ill-feeling was so great that in 1865 the post was moved out of town to put more space between the civilians and the soldiers. The original site is occupied by the Visalia Ice Plant where there is a historical sign at the corner of Race and Santa Fe streets in Visalia. The second site is unmarked in the vicinity of Ben Maddox way and Houston avenue.

CAMP BABBITT *(18)*

Fort Baker. 1897-—. *Fortification at Lime Point.* This semi-active post is at the north side of the entrance to San Francisco Bay and can be reached by following the turnoff signs from Golden Gate Bridge. The original plan called for Batteries Point Bonita, Point Diablo, Gravelly Reach, Lime Point Ridge, Cavallo, and Point Cavallo. The Endicott period batteries became Spencer, Kirby, Duncan, Wagner, and Yates.

Fort Baker. 1862-66. On a small flat from one and a half to two miles long and a half mile wide, Fort Baker lasted only a short time until it was abandoned in 1863. It was outposted frequently until 1866. From Eureka, go south on US 101 about 20 miles to California 36. Turn left (east) about 25 miles to Bridgeville; about 14 miles past Bridgeville is Van Duzen creek, the general site of Fort Baker which has been obliterated by frequent flooding.

Battery Baldwin. This was an Endicott period 3-inch gun position at Fort Winfield Scott.

Fort at Ballast Point. *Fort Rosecrans.*

Camp Banning. 1859. *Camp Prentiss, Camp Dolores (1851).* Rest camp and supply depot for the 1859 Mojave Expedition, this temporary post also kept an eye on the San Bernardino Mormons. The same site was occupied in 1851 by California Rangers. The post was at the southwest corner of Mill street and Mount Vernon avenue in San Bernardino.

Camp Barbour. *Fort Miller* (Millerton).

Battery Barlow. This was a 12-inch gun position at Fort MacArthur.

Camp Barrett. 1898. This mobilization camp was at Fruitvale between Oakland and Alameda.

Fort Barry. 1904-1965. Originally a part of Fort Baker, this San Francisco coast defense became a fort in 1904. It had seven Endicott period batteries: Alexander, Mendel, Rathbone, McIndoe, Smith, Guthrie, and O'Rorke. Casemated Battery Wallace was added in World War I. Barry is at the north end of the Golden Gate Bridge next to Fort Baker.

Fort Beale. *Fort Piute.*

Benicia. 1851-1964. This post served as a depot, barracks and arsenal for 113 years and many historic buildings still remain—including the Arsenal, the oldest brick building in California, and the stone stables that housed camels of the pre-Civil War experiment. Benicia is a city north of San Francisco and west of San Pablo Bay. The post is a park adjacent to the city.

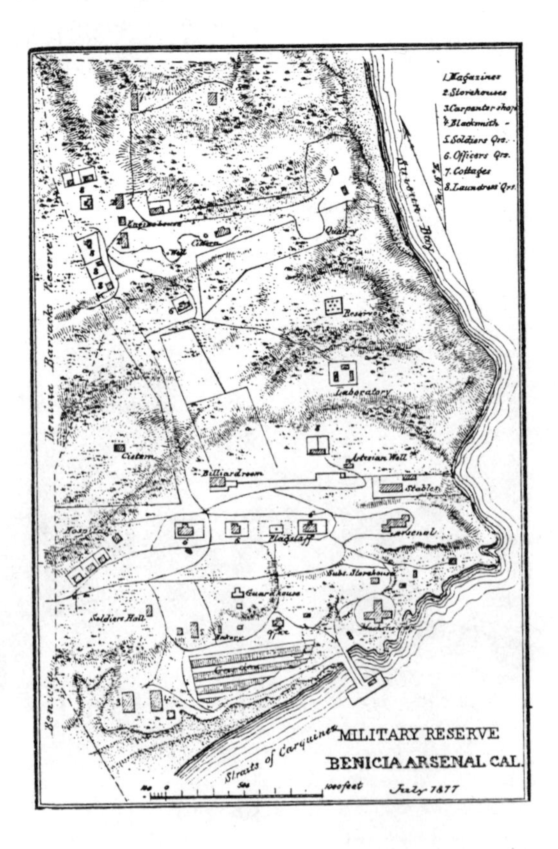

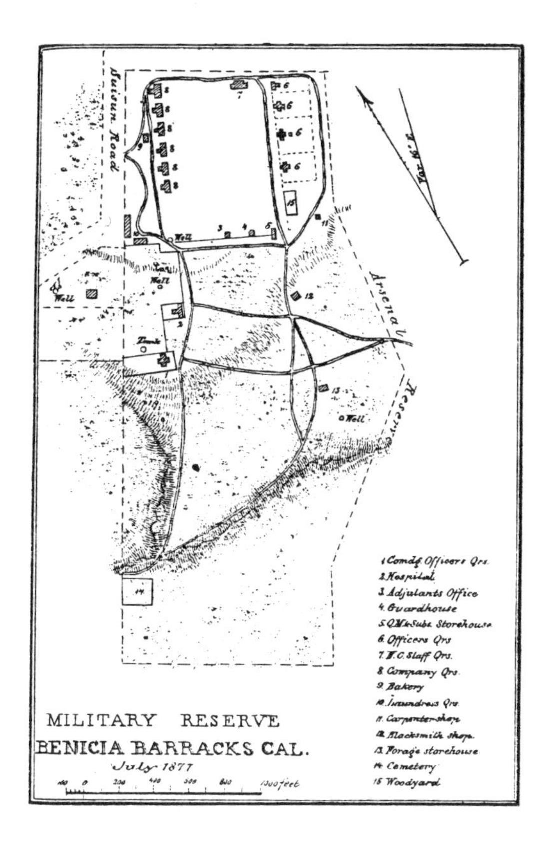

Fort Benson. 1856-57. A settler earthwork that included an old brass cannon, this "fort" was the work of Jerome Benson during land ownership problems in early-day San Bernardino. From San Bernardino, go south on I-15 to the cloverleaf with I-10. The site of Fort Benson is near the cloverleaf, between the I-10 and the Southern Pacific tracks, on the west side of Hunt's lane were a marker for State Registered Landmark 617 is located.

Fort Bidwell. 1865-93. *Detachment at Surprise Valley.* Not to be confused with the Civil War post at Chico, also called *Fort Bidwell,* this post supplied troops for the Battle of Infernal Caverns (1867), the Modoc War of 1872-73, and the Bannock and Nez Perce campaigns. Many fort buildings are left. The Town of Fort Bidwell is in Surprise Valley in northeastern California, reached by US 299 from the west. In the center of the town turn left at Lowell's Store, go west 300 yards to the fort site.

Camp Bidwell. 1863-65. As many as four companies of California Volunteers were at this temporary post to protect peaceful settlers and Indians against attacks by warlike Indians and whites. It was on the Arroyo Chico ranch of John Bidwell, one mile from Chico.

Camp Bitter Springs. 1859-60. This desert outpost was built by Major James Carleton on the stage route between Los Angeles and Las Vegas. It is 20 miles west northwest of Baker on the Fort Irwin military reservation. Permission to visit and directions to the site must be obtained from the Army authorities at Fort Irwin.

Black Point. *Fort Mason.*

Battery Blaney. This was an Endicott period 3-inch gun position at Fort Winfield Scott.

Fort Blanco. *Fort Point.*

Blunt Point. *Camp Reynolds.*

Battery Boutelle. This was an Endicott period 5-inch gun position at Fort Winfield Scott.

Boyle's Camp. *New Supply Camp.*

Camp at Boynton's Prairie. 1864. This was a Civil War tent camp that has completely disappeared but the name is still used at this farming site southeast of Arcata. From Arcata take Fickle Hill road south for 9.8 miles to the approximate site.

Fort Bragg. 1857-64. *Fort at Mendocino.* This post was a peace keeper before the Civil War, watching over both the Indian and the settler. It was manned by California Volunteers at the start of the war. The name lives on in the name of this northern California city which grew up on the Army site after the area was opened to settlement in 1867. In the town of Fort Bragg, 150 miles north of San Francisco on California 1, the fort parade ground site is bounded by modern Laurel street on the north between Franklin and McPherson. The point about 100 feet south of Redwood street was the parade ground's southern boundary. The state marker for the fort is on a stone near the hospital site at 321 Main street.

Battery Burnham. This was an Endicott period 8-inch gun position at Fort Mason.

Camp Burnt Ranch. 1864. California Volunteers occupied this site while moving Indians to Fort Humboldt between May and November,

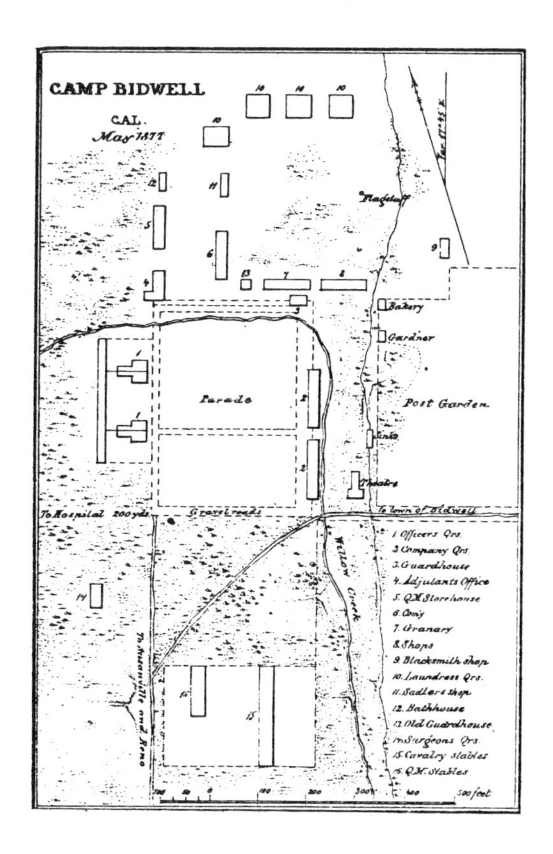

CAMP CADY *(17)*

1864. The location is at the town on the south side of the Trinity river.

Camp Cady. 1859-71. *Depot on the Mojave.* John Fremont rested here before a desert expedition in 1841 and the Mojave Expedition used the site as a depot in 1859. The permanent adobe post was started in 1860 as a 40-foot square fortress. Cady guarded the western end of the Government Road across the Mojave Desert. Except for a few huts used as ranch outbuildings, nothing is left of this once important post. From Barstow, take I-15 east 21 miles to Harvard Station, nothing but a signpost alongside the railroad track. Turn right (south). Local directions and permission should be obtained in order to visit the Cady site between this point and the mountains. The area is so crisscrossed by jeep tracks through loose sand that a guide and a 4-wheel drive vehicle are necessary.

Camp Cajon. 1847; 1857-59. *Camp at Martin's.* Outposted to guard Cajon Pass, 15 miles to the north, this site saw varied sentinel-type activity but never was more than a temporary troop shelter. From San Bernardino, take I-15 north to Devore turnoff. Go west at the turnoff for 1.2 miles to the pasture which is the site of the camp.

Battery Calef. This was an Endicott period 10-inch gun battery at Fort Rosecrans.

Camp Calhoun. 1849. The U.S. Boundary Commission occupied this camp from October to December, 1849. The same location was later occupied by Fort Yuma.

Battery Call. This was an Endicott period 5-inch gun position at Fort Miley.

Fort Capell. 1856. This was a temporary camp of the 4th Infantry during the summer, 1856, at Cappell Bar, 10½ miles below the mouth of the Trinity river.

Fort Cape of Pines. *Fort Mervine.*

New Camp Carleton. 1862. *Camp at El Monte.* This post was the site to which the troops moved after their San Bernardino site was flooded. It is only vaguely located 10 miles east of Los Angeles.

Camp Carleton. 1861-62. *Old Camp Carleton.* California cavalrymen, less their horses, manned this tent camp while they watched over secessionist activities in nearby San Bernardino. From downtown San Bernardino, take Tippecanoe avenue east to where it crosses the Santa Ana river just past the Norton Air Force Base entrance. The site is to the left of the road in the river bottom from which it was washed out in 1862.

Camp Cass. 1859. The vague site of the 6th Infantry summertime post is at Red Bluff.

El Castillo. *Fort Mervine.*

Castillo de San Jose. *Fort Point.*

Fort Castillo Guijarros. *Fort Guijarros.*

Post on Clear Lake. 1850. This temporary post was established after an engagement with Indians at Clear Lake on an island known as "Bloody Island." Water reclamation projects have obliterated the site one mile south of the town of Upper Lake.

Battery Cavallo. This was an early gun position at Fort Baker, San Francisco Bay.

Battery Chamberlin. This was an Endicott period 6-inch gun position at Fort Winfield Scott. The National Park Service reinstalled one 6-inch disappearing carriage, obtained from West Point through the Smithsonian Institution, in 1977 and this weapon can be seen in position behind a chainlink fence at the battery.

Battery Chester. This was an Endicott period 12-inch gun position at Fort Miley.

Battery Cranston. This was an Endicott period 10-inch position at Fort Winfield Scott.

Fort Crook. 1857-69. *Camp Hollenbush.* George Crook was a lieutenant at this Northern California post that initially was named after the camp surgeon. Once one of the most active in keeping the peace, there is nothing left of this log and frame establishment. From Redding, go northeast on California 299 about 70 miles to Fall River Mills. Turn left (north) on Farm Road 1220 to Glenburn, 6 miles. At Glenburn post office, turn left (north) on road A19. Follow it around 3.2 miles to marker which is on the right side of the road.

Battery Crosby. This was an Endicott period 6-inch position at Fort Winfield Scott.

Camp Curtiss. 1862-65. *Camp on the Janes Farm.* This tent camp was manned by California Volunteers during the Civil War on a site occupied periodically by citizen-soldiers as early as 1858. The solitary remainder is a towering redwood tree at the site. From Arcata, go north on US 101 for 7.4 miles. A marker on the right (east) side of the highway identifies the site which is across the highway.

Fort Defiance. 1849. This settler camp guarded the ferry across the Colorado river on the west bank of the river four miles below the site of Fort Yuma.

Fort Defiance. *Roop's Fort.*

Fort Dick. This was a log house built for defense against the Indians eight miles north of Crescent City.

Camp Dolores. *Camp Banning.*

Camp Downey. 1861. A Civil War recruit training camp, this tent camp stood at East 12th and 17th avenues, Oakland.

Camp Dragoon Bridge. 1860-61. A building, 18 by 30 feet, and a stone corral were built by soldiers of the 3d Artillery to protect the nearby bridge across the Susan river and the settlements of Honey Lake Valley. The site is a half mile south of Litchfield.

Battery Drew. This was an Endicott period 8-inch position at Fort McDowell on Angel Island.

Battery Duncan. This was an Endicott period 8-inch gun position at Fort Baker, San Francisco Bay.

Fort DuPont. *Fort Stockton,* near the Presidio of San Diego.

Battery "Dynamite." Although never operational, this was to be a 15-inch position at Fort Winfield Scott from the Endicott period.

Battery Farley. This was a 14-inch gun position at Fort MacArthur.

Cantonment Far West. 1849-1852. Tents and huts comprised this lonely outpost that tried to protect the gold diggers who usually outnumbered the size of the garrison. A tiny graveyard and marker are on the site. From San Francisco take I-80 to the Roseville turnoff, 14 miles past Sacramento. Continue north on California 65 for 22 miles to Wheatland. Turn right in center of town toward the east, go 1.5 miles to the E. Clemens Horst ranch. Ask permission to enter private property. At a dirt road follow signs to right toward "Camp Far West Reservoir," a recreation area. At the first fork in the dirt road, veer right. This road leads in about 1 mile to the site of the post.

Battery Fetterman. This was an Endicott period 3-inch gun position at Fort Rosecrans.

Camp Fitzgerald. 1861. A training camp established near the Army corral in "downtown" Los Angeles in May, 1861, Camp Fitzgerald was moved in August because of the dust and absence of water. The site is at the intersection of 3d and Main streets in Los Angeles.

Fontana Barracks. 1898. It appears that troops used this warehouse enroute to the Philippines; it was on the northeast corner of Taylor and Francisco streets, San Francisco, and was owned by the Fontana company.

Camp at Forks of Salmon. 1864. A company of Mountaineers was stationed at this site at the junction of the north and south forks of the Salmon river February-June, 1864, as protection against the Indians.

Camp Fremont. 1917-1919. Army trained at this World War I camp for France and wound up in Siberia. The site is in San Mateo.

Fort Fremont. This is the name incorrectly attached to *Camp Rancho del Jurupa,* probably on the erroneous idea that Fremont once was stationed here.

Fort Fremont. *Fort Mervine.*

Camp at Fremont's Peak. 1846. Captain John Fremont erected a hasty fortification of logs and earth surrounding a flagpole flying the American flag at this location atop Gabilan Peak in defense against an attack by the Spanish that never came. The site is in Fremont Peak State Park.

Fort Gaston. 1859. This site on the Colorado river probably was occupied by the Hoffman Expedition enroute to establish Fort Mojave. Sixty miles north of Fort Yuma, it was in the vicinity of Palo Verde.

Fort Gaston. 1858-92. California's redwoods come right to the edge of this center of operations for most of the Indian wars of Northern California. Many of the buildings from the fort still line the

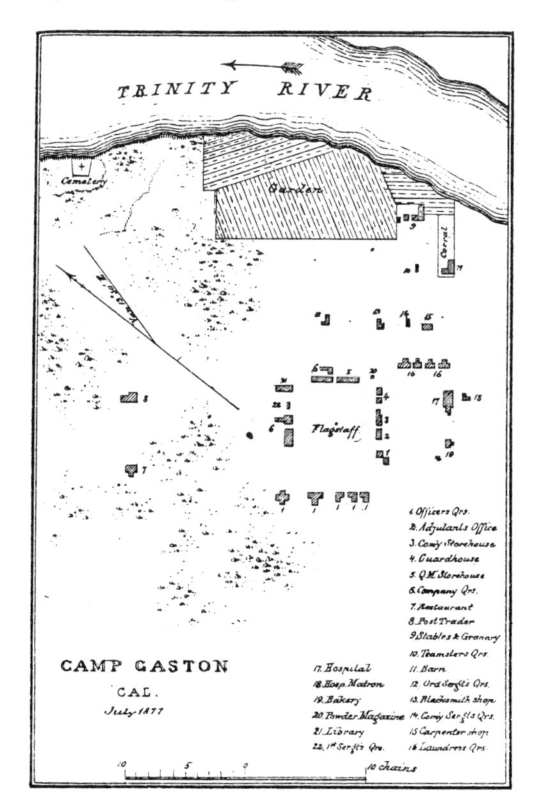

parade ground, now the location of the Hoopa Indian Agency. From Eureka, take US 101 north to US 299. Follow US 299 for 41 miles to Willow Creek. Turn left. The road parallels the Trinity river to Hoopa, 9 miles. Just before arriving at the town, the fort site can be seen to the left next to a modern high school.

General Gillam's Camp. *Camp in the Lava Beds.*

Camp Gilmore. 1863. This was a five-week tent camp in mid-1863 of California militia on the site of *Camp McDougall* south of Stockton.

Camp Gilmore. 1863-64. Only huts were erected at this site to house the 15-man detachment protecting the stage between Trinidad and Gold Bluffs. The site was three and a half miles north of Trinidad.

Military Post at Goat Island. *Camp Yerba Buena Island.*

Camp Grant. 1863-65. Protecting the mail route between Hydesville and Long Valley was the mission of this scouting post two miles southeast of Dyerville on the South bank of the Eel river.

Battery Godfrey. This was an Endicott period 12-inch position at Fort Winfield Scott.

Battery Gravelly Beach. This was a battery at Fort Baker, San Francisco Bay, replaced by Battery Kirby.

Fort Guijarros. 1779-1849 (?). *Fort Castillo Guijarros, Fort Pio Pico.* Built of adobe and cobblestones, this work included an artillery battery that commanded the entrance to San Diego Bay. Its only naval action was against a Yankee fur smuggler—the smuggler won by forcing the fort's garrison to take cover from broadside fire as the ship sped by. The site is now used by the Naval Piers immediately south of Fort Rosecrans at the entrance to San Diego Bay.

Battery Guthrie. This was an Endicott period 6-inch gun position at Fort Barry.

Camp Halleck. 1862. A Civil War tent camp in Stockton, Halleck's site is now the location of the Training Center for the Handicapped at the southeastern corner of US 50 (Charter Way) and Airport Way.

Fort Halleck. *Fort Mervine.*

Hancock Redoubt. *Fort Soda.*

Hasting's Barracks. 1843. Supposedly this was a settler fort of huge pine logs built by Lansford W. Hastings and 16 companions at the base of the hill on the north side of the little valley opposite Lower Soda Springs in Shasta Valley.

Fort Hill. *Fort Moore.*

Fort Hill. *Fort Mervine.*

Camp Hollenbush. *Fort Crook.*

Camp Hooker. 1862. A tent camp of the early Civil War period, there is nothing left of Hooker to show Army occupancy along McKinney avenue south of California street on the outskirts of Stockton.

Battery Howe. This was a 12-inch gun position of the Endicott period at Fort Winfield Scott.

Fort Humboldt. 1863-66. The most famous member of Humboldt's garrison was U.S. Grant who resigned from the Army while he was stationed here before the Civil War. Several reconstructed buildings are in a state park at the site on a bluff overlooking US 101 at the southern edge of Eureka.

Fort Humboldt, near Eureka.
Where General Grant, then Captain, was stationed in 1853-4. indicates Grant's quarters.

FORT HUMBOLDT *(17)*

Camp Iaqua. 1863-66. *Camp Juaqua.* A Civil War camp that tried to keep the peace between the settlers and the Indians, there is nothing left at the site of Camp Iaqua. From Eureka, go east on the hard surface road through Freshwater Corners, Eddyville, Freshwater and Kneeland. This winding mountain road passes Iaqua Butte and Iaqua Lookout Station and, about 22 torturous miles from Eureka, the site of the camp at Iaqua Creek.

Camp Independence. 1850-51. There were several sites for this military camping place on, adjacent to, and near to the later location of Fort Yuma, the final one being six miles downriver from the Yuma site.

Camp Independence. 1862-77. The troops spent their first months at Independence in caves along the sides of a ravine. Later a relatively comfortable post was built in a meadow in the shadow of the Sierra Nevada mountains. In addition to routine troubles with Indians and bandits that kept them busy, the garrison also had to cope with damage from an earthquake in 1872. The former commanding officer's quarters has been moved to Independence where the building is at 303 Edwards street (US 395). Continuing north on US 395, proceed to Shabbell lane (Old US 395), 2 miles, and turn east ¼ mile. The ravine, with the original camp's caves, is on the right at this point. Go a few hundred yards further to the post site on the left.

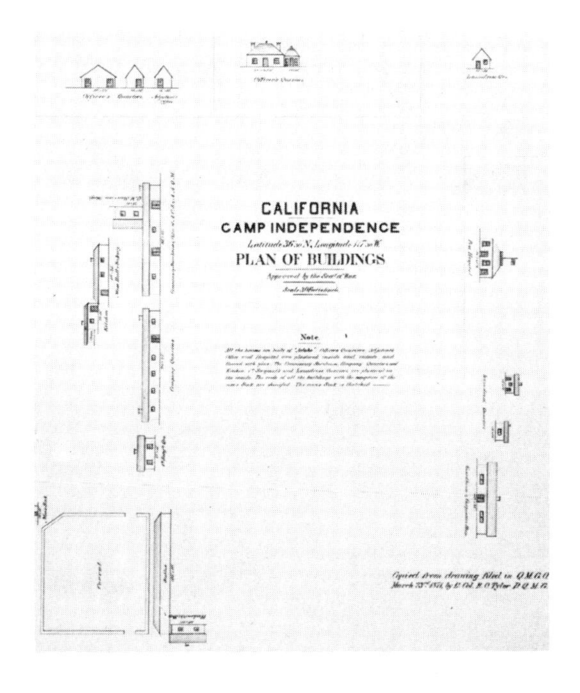

Camp Jackson. 1865. Volunteers were here for three months near Ione City.

Camp on the Janes Farm. *Camp Curtiss.*

Fort Janesville. 1860. Settlers built this stockade, loopholed for rifles with a bastion at the southwest corner, ¾ miles northwest of Janesville after the Battle of Pyramid Lake. The site is a California Historic Landmark.

Camp Johns. 1864. Nevada Volunteers used this temporary camp during an expedition from July to August, 1864. It was located at Susanville near Roop's Fort.

Fort Jones. 1852-58; 1864. George Crook fought Indians from this log cabin-type post, his first duty station after arriving in California. The post also was manned for a short time in 1864 by the California Mountaineer Battalion. The town of Fort Jones is in Scott Valley, 16 miles west of Yreka. From the center of town, go south on California 3 to East Side road; the site of the fort is ½ mile south of town on the left side of East Side Road.

Jones' Fort. *Fort Mervine.*

Camp Juaqua. The correct spelling of this often mis-spelled post is *Camp Iaqua.*

Fort Jurupa. *Camp Rancho del Jurupa.*

Camp Kearny. 1847. This was a temporary camp on the outskirts of Monterey after the New York Volunteers landed in April, 1847.

Camp Kellogg. 1861-62. This was a camp of the 5th California Infantry named for the regimental commander. The site is vaguely described as being in Willow Grove in Culver City, a Los Angeles suburb.

Battery Kirby. This was an Endicott period 12-inch gun position at Fort Baker, San Francisco Bay.

Battery Knox. This was a Civil War emplacement at Camp Reynolds.

Battery Lancaster. This was an Endicott period 12-inch position at Fort Winfield Scott.

Camp Latham. It was to this tent camp that the troops moved when they left downtown Los Angeles and it was from here that the California Column started out for Arizona and the Confederates. The site is on Ballona Creek near Culver City, a Los Angeles suburb.

Camp in the Lava Beds. 1873. *General Gillam's Camp.* The place from which the Army conducted the Modoc War, and near which General Canby's government delegation was assassinated, has probably changed little from its 1873 appearance. Campsites, artillery circles, Indian strongholds and marked sites all make it simple to picture this strange war. The National Park Service maintains Lava Beds National Monument near the Oregon-California border 41 miles south of Klamath Falls, Oregon. The northeast entrance is 6 miles southeast of Tulelake from California 139. The camp site is about 7 miles west of the entrance.

Battery Leary. This was a 14-inch gun position at Fort MacArthur.

Battery Ledyard. This was an Endicott period 5-inch position at Fort McDowell on Angel Island.

Camp Leonard. 1863. Five months in the latter half of 1863 a company from the 2d California Volunteer Cavalry protected the mining camps from this site in the Kern River Valley, on the north bank of the south branch of the Kern river, opposite the mouth of Kelso (Kelsey) creek, 15 miles northeast of Keysville.

Battery Lime Point Ridge. This was a battery

at Fort Baker, San Francisco Bay, replaced by Battery Spencer.

Camp Lincoln. 1862-69. *Long's Fort. Camp Long.* First at the Indian Agency near Crescent City, this post was soon moved to a clearing in the redwoods 6 miles away. Here it could be impartial in its attempts to keep peace between settler and Indian. From Crescent City take US 199 northeast 6 miles. Turn left at Smith's River Valley road which almost parallels the highway. The fort site is about 2 miles north, flanking the road on private property. The crest is on the right hand side behind which the former commanding officer's quarters on a rise: the building directly across the road from the marker was once a duplex officers' quarters.

Fort Lippitt. 1862. This was a temporary camp named in honor of the commander of nearby Fort Humbolt, near Eureka.

Camp Liscom Hill. 1863. This was a log cabin post occupied by a few California Volunteers in the early days of the Civil War. The site is below Liscom Hill and after the Civil War was the location of Scottsville. It is now in the town of Blue Lake, 6 miles east of Arcata, on the Leo Schueman property.

Battery Livingston. This was an Endicott period 12-inch gun position at Fort Miley.

Lockhart's Fort. 1856. This settler fort was where Sam Lockhart fought for his life for five days against hostile Indians. It is on a hill near Fall River Mills.

Battery Lodor. This was a 3-inch gun position at Deadman's Island, Fort MacArthur.

Camp Long and **Long's Fort.** *Camp Lincoln.*

Post at Los Angeles. *Fort Moore.*

Camp Low. 1865. This was a California Volunteer post at San Juan.

Camp Lyon. 1861. Troops mustered here in September, 1861, before moving to the Presidio of San Francisco. The site was near Hunter's Point, San Francisco.

Camp Lyon. 1862. This was a short-lived post designed to protect the settlers about 20 miles east of Arcata in the mountainous Mad river area. A peaceful pasture is all that remains at the site. From Blue Lake, continue on US 299 a half mile east to the gravel road to Korbel and Maple Creek. About 13 miles south of Blue Lake, by a nerve-wracking series of switchbacks and steep slopes is a dirt turnoff at Blue Side. The post site is on the right next to the Mad river.

Fort MacArthur. 1914-1975. This was the only major Taft-era construction in the continental United States with Batteries Merriam, Leary, Farley, Osgood, Barlow, Saxton and Lodor still located at this Los Angeles harbor defense. The post was deactivated in 1975 but quarters and some activities are still in operation. The post is south of Los Angeles on California 11.

Camp Mackall. 1857-58. This was a temporary camp in Round Valley on the Cache Creek near but not on the same site as later Fort Wright.

Detachment Mare Island. 1861-62. For four months in the Civil War 25 soldiers swung hammocks in the USS *Independence* and guarded the shipyard at Mare Island. The ship is gone but many buildings that the Army guarded still remain. Mare Island Naval Shipyard is adjacent to Vallejo in San Francisco Bay, about 25 miles north of San Francisco on I-80. Enter the Navy Yard by Tennessee Avenue. Permission to visit must be obtained prior to arrival due to security reasons.

Camp Marl Springs. 1866-67. Water was the reason that the Mojave Government Road had need for Army protection at this desolate desert site. The stone outlines of several buildings still surround the spring. From Baker, take the private road passing through Rainbow Wells east of Baker from I-15. Two and a half miles south of Rainbow Wells, take the right set of tracks toward the Marl mountains. The site of the camp is at the foot of the Marl mountains, next to Marl Springs, marked by a Geological Survey marker 25 yards away. This is a fair-weather, rough-duty route; guide recomended.

Camp at Martin's Ferry. 1864. Troops were here only two weeks in March, 1864, operating against hostile Indians. The site was at Martin's Ferry on the Klamath river, 13 miles west of Weitchpec.

Camp at Martin's. *Camp Cajon.*

Fort Mason. 1863-. *Fort Point San Jose, Black Point.* John Fremont claimed to own this site even though the Army charged that his was a squatter's title. The outcome of the debate may be indicated by the fact that the Army still occupies many historic buildings dating from the Civil War,

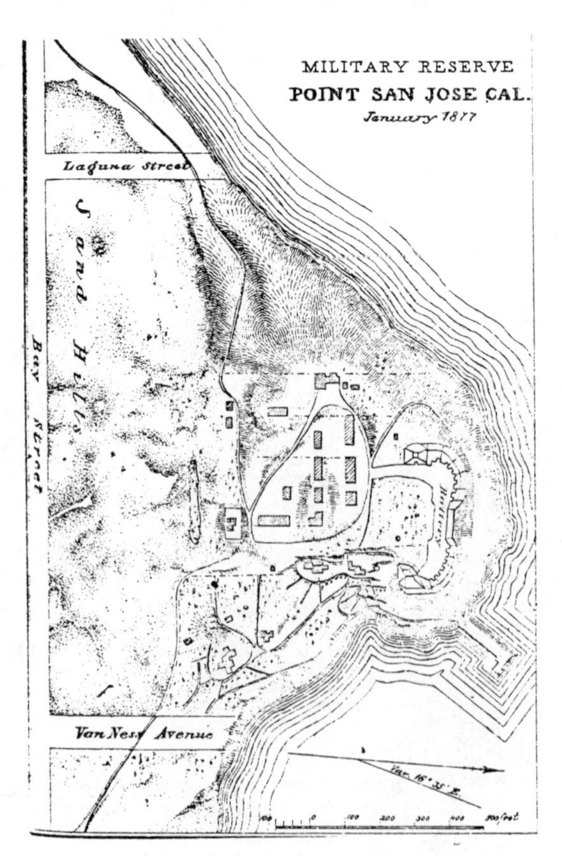

FORT MASON *(1)*

as does the National Park Service. The main entrance is at Bay street and Van Ness avenue in San Francisco. Battery Burnham was an Endicott era coast defense here.

Camp McClellan. 1861. This was a mustering-in camp for Volunteers in the vicinity of Auburn in the fall, 1861.

Camp McDougall. 1861. Recruiting and training were the principal occupations of California Volunteers at this autumn, 1861, camp that included 35 tents for privates, three tents for officers, and hospital and kitchen tents. The site was reoccupied in 1863 as *Camp Gilmore.* From downtown Stockton go south on US 50 about 4 miles to French Camp Slough. The site of Camp McDougall is intersected by the highway to the north of the slough.

Fort McDowell. *Camp Reynolds.*

Battery McGrath. This was an Endicott period 5-inch gun position at Fort Rosecrans.

Battery McIndoe. This was an Endicott period 6-inch gun position at Fort Barry.

Battery McKinnon. This was a 12-inch Endicott period gun battery at Fort Winfield Scott.

Battery Meed. This was an Endicott period 3-inch gun position at Fort Pio Pico.

Battery Mendel. This was an Endicott period 12-inch position at Fort Barry.

Fort at Mendocino. *Fort Bragg.*

Camp Merchant. 1863. *Camp Merritt.* This short-lived tent camp of the Civil War was near Lake Merritt in Oakland.

Camp Merriam. 1898. Troops preparing for the Philippine Expedition camped at this site at the Presidio of San Francisco.

Battery Merriam. This was a 14-inch gun position at Fort MacArthur.

Camp Merritt. *Camp Merchant.*

Camp Merritt. 1898. This was a rendezvous camp for troops enroute to the Phillippines. It was at the race track near Golden Gate Park, between 2d and 3d avenues and Balboa and Fulton streets, San Francisco.

Fort Mervine. 1770-1865. *El Castillo, Presidio of Monterey, Monterey Redoubt, Fort Hill, Fort Halleck, Jones' Fort, Fort Fremont, Fort Cape of Pines, Post of Monterey, Ord Barracks, Fort Savannah.* The hill overlooking Monterey Bay had many military occupants, as the various alternate names suggest. El Castillo and the Presidio of Monterey dated from 1770. The other names came when the Americans took over after the fall of Monterey in 1846. The site of the post is well-marked within the modern Presidio of Monterey Army post overlooking Lighthouse avenue. The house occupied by William T. Sherman, as a lieutenant, is on Main street near Jefferson.

Camp Mettah. 1872. A summer-time camp to prevent a collision between Indians and settlers, this post was at the Metta Indian village below the confluence of Mettah creek with Klamath river.

Fort Miley. 1893-1946. This Veterans Hospital facility was once a Coast Artillery defense of San Francisco bay on Point Lobos at the south side of the entrance to San Francisco Bay. It had Endicott-era Batteries Chester, Livingston, Springer, and Call plus Battery No. 243, built in World War II.

Battery Miller. This was an Endicott period 10-inch position at Fort Winfield Scott.

Camp Miller. 1898. This was a Spanish-American War training camp on the grounds of the Presidio of San Francisco.

Fort Miller. 1851-58; 1863-64. *Camp Barbour.* The Barbour name was the original one for this central California post and, after adoption of the Miller title, was attached to the blockhouse that remained at the post. In 1939 the fort was described as "the best preserved of the forts erected after California became one of the United States" and the sites of most buildings were visible, along with the remains of the blockhouse and the three officers' quarters. The Friant Dam and its resulting Millerton Lake inundated the fort site. From Fresno, take California 41 north for 20 miles, turning right on County 145 to Millerton Lake State Park, 6 miles. The Fort Miller blockhouse reconstruction is at the park.

FORT MILLER, 1864, by C.F. Otto Skobel, Cal. Volunteer

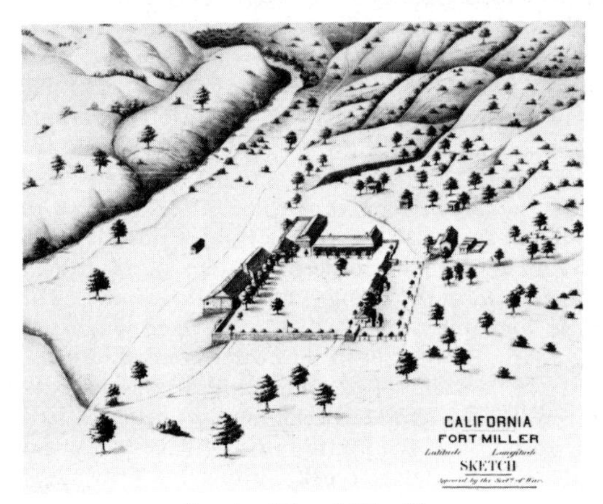

Sketch of Fort Miller *(1)*

Camp at Mineral Spring. *Camp Sequoia National Park.*

Post at Mission San Diego. 1847-1860. The Mormon Battalion under General Philip St. George Cooke camped here in 1847 to find that the mission had been abandoned for 13 years. Cooke set up his troops in the plain below the chapel. Later, the regular Army garrison used the chapel as a barracks. The mission was returned to the church in 1865 and restored in 1934. From downtown San Diego take I-8 east from I-5 about 8 miles; turn north on Murphy road 3/4 mile, east of Friars lane 1/2 mile.

Post at Mission San Luis Rey de Francia. *Camp San Luis Rey.*

Depot on the Mojave. *Camp Cady.*

Fort Monroe. 1891. This was a military check point at the entrance to Yosemite National Park, on the old road.

Presidio, Post and **Redoubt or Monterey.** *Fort Nervine.*

Fort Montgomery. 1846-47. This was where the Marines from the USS *Portsmouth* raised the American flag in what became downtown San Francisco. This site is now Portsmouth Square at Washington and Kearny streets.

Fort Moore. 1846-49. *Fort Hill, Post at Los Angeles.* Marine Captain Archibald H. Gillespie set up a temporary barricade at this so-called Fort Hill in 1846, but was ousted after a short siege. When the Army returned in force a year later, this commanding site was the logical place to build a 400-foot long breastwork that commanded the Plaza below. A towering stone mural on the site commemorates the units that occupied California after the Navy and Marines with Kearny's Dragoons captured it from Mexico. It is on Hill street near Sunset boulevard in downtown Los Angeles.

Mormon Stockade. *Fort San Bernardino.*

Camp Morris. 1863. This was a short-term post that occupied town buildings in San Bernardino.

Fort Mulgrave. The erroneous appearance of this name in 1849 Congressional documents caused this non-existent post to be credited to California. Actually there was a Port (with a P) Mulgrave, Alaska, but no fort by the name.

Camp Nome Lackee. 1855-58. *Fort Vose.* This was a post to protect the Nome Lackee Indian Agency, and was located four miles north of Flournoy.

Old Supply Camp. 1873. This was the initial supply depot for the Modoc War, soon shifted to a site nearer to Newell. The Battle of Scorpion Point took place nearby. The site is 5.5 miles directly south of Newell, reached by a series of agricultural and irrigation roads.

Ord Barracks. *Fort Mervine.*

Camp at Orleans Bar. 1864. A squad of Volunteer Mountaineers guarded the town of Orleans Bar from Indians during the summer of 1864.

Battery O'Rorke. This was an Endicott period 3-inch gun position at Fort Barry.

Battery Osgood. This was a 14-inch gun position at Fort MacArthur.

Post at Pardee's Ranch. 1858-60. Frequently during the pre-Civil War period, and during the

FORT POINT, looking across the Golden Gate before the bridge *(21)*

war, troops camped at this ranch on the old Trinity Trail between Eureka and the Trinity river.

Fort on Pine Creek. 1861. This was a settler fort built by Charles Putnam at Little Pine, later Independence, used as a refuge from Indian attack in the Civil War period.

Fort Pio Pico. *Fort Guijarros.*

Fort Pio Pico. This was an Endicott-era post on North Island that had Battery Meed, two 3-inch guns. There is no trace due to construction at this San Diego harbor island.

Fort Piute. 1860; 1866-68. *Fort Beale, Fort Piute Hill.* After the Mojave travelers ascended Piute Hill and looked westward, they knew that this rock post was the gateway to the sun-beaten deserts of three states which could be seen from here. Several rock ruins are left from Army days.

From Searchlight, Nevada, take US 95 south for 12 miles to a dirt road on the right. Turn right and go 3 miles west to a dead end at the power line. Turn left and go south along the power line about 12 miles to the privately owned George Erwin Ranch on right.

Fort ruins are 2 miles past the ranch in the canyon; permission to visit must be requested. This is a fair-weather, rough-duty vehicle route only.

Fort Point. 1835-1906. *Fort Blanco, Castillo de San Joaquin, Old Fort Scott.* This striking fortification—the earliest of its type on the pacific coast—may be dwarfed by the Golden Gate bridge overhead, but it is still magnificent in its solitude at the entrance to San Francisco Bay.

Lincoln boulevard, at the entrance of the Presidio of San Francisco, goes under the Golden Gate Approach at McDowell avenue. At this point, take the right fork away from Lincoln boulevard, go under the approach and follow

FORT POINT *(1)*

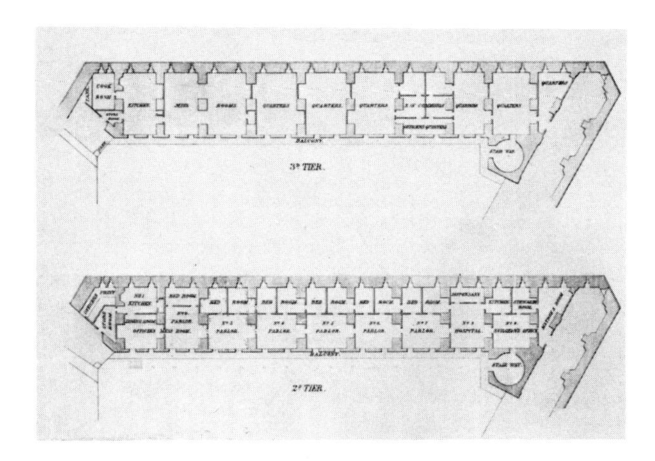

FORT POINT
Plan of Officers' & Soldiers quarters

McDowell and Long avenues past Fort Point Coast Guard Station and Fort Point Mine Dock to the fortress, or National Park Service Historic Site.

Battery Point Cavallo. This was an early gun position at Fort Baker, San Francisco Bay.

Battery Point Diablo. This was planned to be a battery at Fort Baker, San Francisco Bay, but not completed.

Fort Point San Jose. *Fort Mason.*

Camp Pollock. 1864. This was a month-long, early summer base of operations for a reconnaissance of Surprise Valley, by the Nevada Volunteers. It was near Warm Springs.

Poole's Fort. c. 1850. This was a forted-up stage stop owned by John Poole at a ferry crossing on the Kings' river 20 miles southeast of Fresno. The wooden building, purchased in 1968 by a private party in Fresno and moved about 3½ miles from the river site, was to be restored to its appearance of 1850 when it was one of the two permanent-type structures in the Sierra foothills of the San Joaquin valley.

Camp Prentiss. *Camp Banning.*

Camp Prentiss. 1859. The Hoffmann Expedition to establish Fort Mojave camped at this site three miles southwest of San Bernardino, now the location of San Bernardino Valley College.

Post at Rancho del Chino. 1850-52. The 1st Dragoons occupied leased quarters at what is now the George Junior Republic, five miles south of Pomona.

Camp Rancho del Jurupa. 1852-54. *Fort Jurupa, Fort Fremont.* The troops occupied a grist mill at this post while they guarded the "eastern Indian frontier" and now only a mill stone marks the site. From downtown Riverside, take Palm avenue north to 7th street, turn west across Santa Ana river to the community of Rubidoux. Turn at the sign for "Rubidoux Grist Mill Site." This is Fort drive, the only visible suggestion of a military post, which ends at the mill stone monument.

Battery Rathbone. This was an Endicottt period 6-inch gun position at Fort Barry.

Fort Reading. 1852-56. This two-company post had two major disadvantages: the site was unhealthy and it often flooded during the rainy season. It was abandoned in 1856 and used only occasionallly until the buildings were sold in 1867. From Redding—a city that spells its name differently because it is named after a railroad man rather than the fort—take I-5 south 7 miles to the North street exit in Anderson. Go north (left) on North street across the Sacramento river to Dersch road, 2 miles. Site is 5.4 miles directly east of this turn.

Camp at Red Bluff. 1862. This was a summertime post for a company of California Cavalry, at the town of Red Bluffs.

Camp Resting Springs. 1859-60. This desert outpost was manned occasionally to protect a waterhole on the Spanish Trail. From Baker, go north on California 127 to the right (east) turnoff to Tecopa. Pass through Tecopa to the site 5 miles east of the town. It would be best to ask directions locally.

Camp Reynolds. 1863-1946. *Fort McDowell, Post of Angel Island.* Although seemingly far-removed from San Francisco, this island post maintained frequent boats so that it could have the advantage of being near to the city but would have none of the disadvantages. There are several sites under jungle-like growth on this Bay island; when abandoned, there were 235 buildings scattered over the island. Angel Island is part of the California Beaches and Parks System and its picnic grounds can be reached by a daily boat

CAMP REYNOLDS *(1)*

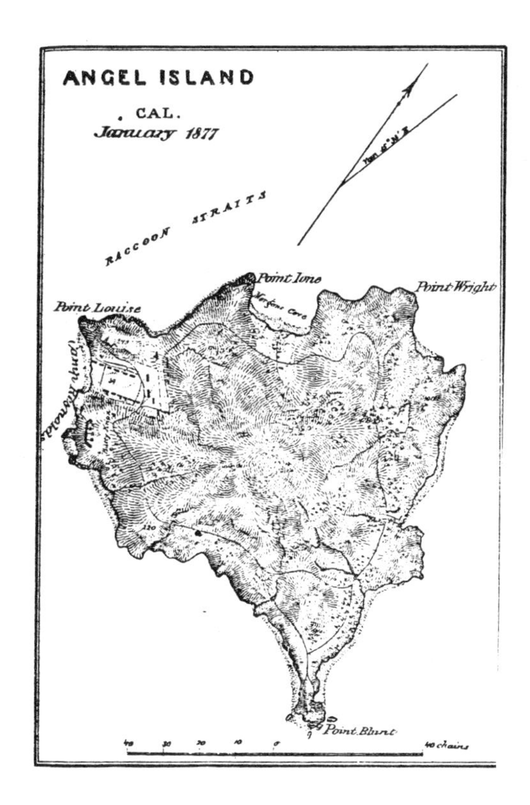

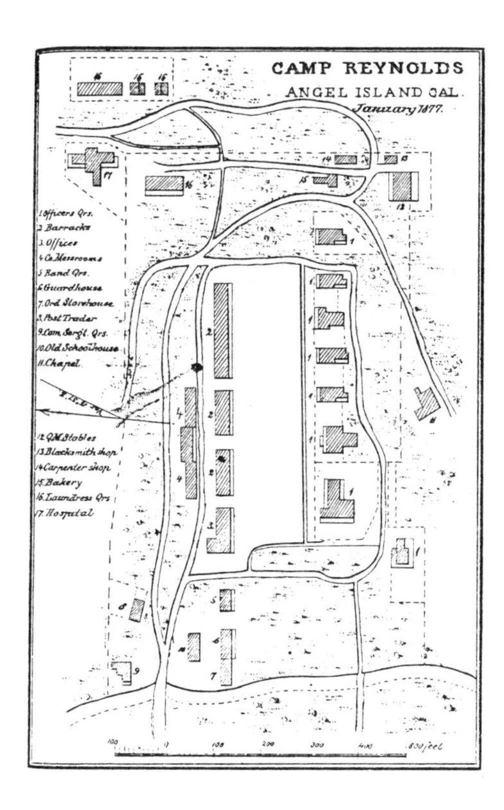

from Fisherman's Wharf or, on weekends and holidays, a more frequent one that leaves from Tiburon. Because of their unsafe condition, the sites of the Army posts may not be visited except through prior arrangement with the park system. Battery Knox was a bashelte emplacement on the west side of the island. At Point Blunt there were three officers quarters and a 75-man barracks. The post was renamed Fort McDowell in 1900 with Batteries Wallace, Drew and Ledgard.

Camp Riley. 1849. The Boundary Commision camped here at the southern end of San Diego Bay where nothing but salt flats are left. From downtown San Diego take I-5 to the Palomar turnoff south of Chula Vista. The camp was along the bay shore.

Roop's Fort. 1854. *Fort Defiance.* This blockhouse, now a museum at Susanville, was a settler protection built by Isaac N. Roop.

Camp Rock Springs. 1859-68. This was the only mid-Mojave desert Government Road post that actually won official status as more than just a way station. Traces at the site attest to its Civil War occupancy. From Baker, take I-15 east for 28 miles to Valley Wells turnoff. Follow this blacktop road south through Cima, 17 miles. Continue south about 4 miles where a gravel road deadends from the east. Turn left up this road, going up Cedar Canyon. In 10 miles, on the right will be the site of Government Holes and in another mile, site of Camp Rock Springs. Unlike the other Mojave desert sites, this is a good road throughout.

Fort Rosecrans. 1898-1950. *Fort at Ballast Point.* Although reserved in 1852, the site of Fort Rosecrans did not have an Army post until the Spanish-American War. Its coastal defense batteries provided protection to San Diego Bay for three wars and the remaining buildings still are used by reserve activities. The post is in north San Diego at the end of Chatsworth boulevard, an extension of Barnett avenue from I-5. The fine Endicott period emplacements included Batteries Wilkeson, Calef, McGrath and Fetterman, while Whistler and White were built during the Taft Board period.

Fort Ross. 1812-41. The Russian tide into California stopped militarily at the fur trading post at this point, a fort bought in 1841 by Captain John Sutter. The post has been restored by the California Beaches and Parks System. Included is the fort's restored chapel, the oldest standing Russian Orthodox church in the United States. The site is almost as isolated today as it was in the ninetheenth century. From Santa Rosa, take California 20 west 30 miles to Jenner and the intersection with California 1. This highway bisects the fort 13 miles north of Jenner.

Fort and Redoubts at Sacramento. *Fort Sutter.*

Battery Saffold. This was an Endicott period 12-inch position at Fort Winfield Scott.

Fort San Bernardino. 1852-57. *Mormon Stockade.* The Mormons built this 12-foot high, 300-by-720-foot stockade during their first year at San Bernardino, but soon expanded far beyond its confines. The Army was here for a short time in 1855. There is nothing left at the site, now occupied by the courthouse on Arrowhead avenue between 3d and 4th streets in downtown San Bernardino.

Fort San Diego. *Presidio of San Diego.*

PRESIDIO OF SAN FRANCISCO *(1)*

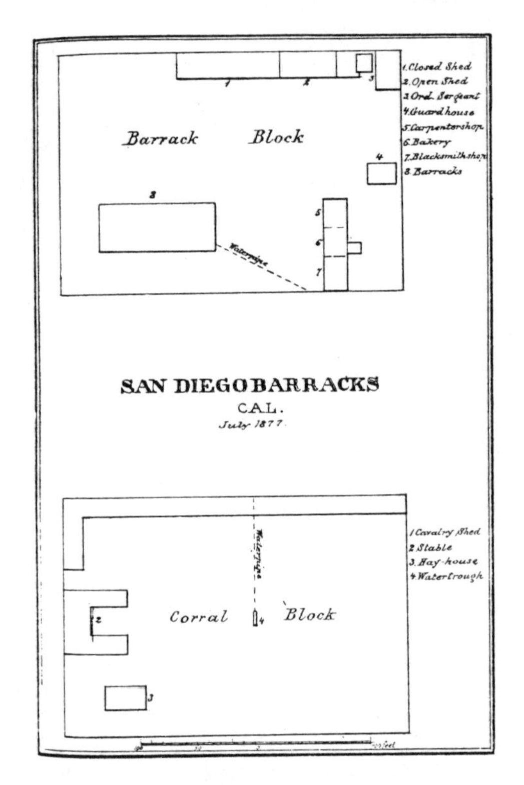

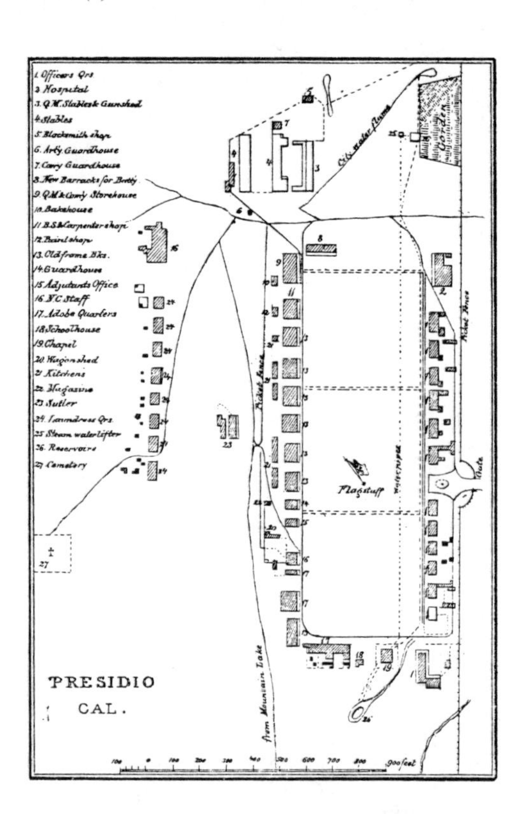

New San Diego Barracks. 1850-1921. This post watched over the ships unloading at the nearby San Diego wharfs, but its downtown site kept it within block-size proportions. This was primarily a supply forwarding center with occasional use as a barracks. The site is marked at Kettner and California streets southwest of downtown.

Presidio of San Diego. 1769-1850. *Fort Stockton, Fort San Diego, Garrison at San Diego.* The dates include the on-again, off-again manning of this adobe post by small Spanish and Mexican Army detachments, and the arrival in 1846 of the Americans who set up Fort Stockton on the hill above the presidio. Mounds and a reconstructed wall are at the presidio site; only a flagpole and cannon mark Fort Stockton where once there was a 60- by 90-foot rectangle formed by casks filled with sand. The sites are in Presidio Park, San Diego, above Old Town and the intersection of I-5 and I-8.

Presidio of San Francisco. 1776-. The American Republic started in the same year as the Presidio of San Francisco, now the oldest active Army post in the West. The installation includes many buildings dating from the span of the 19th century. The officers' club includes portions of the original Commandant's quarters built in 1776, making it the oldest building in San Francisco.

From downtown San Francisco, take US 101 (Van Ness) north and then west (on Lombard) to the main gate west to Graham street.

The southern end of this large parade ground was the original presidio. The officers' club, the former Commandant's quarters, is at the south end of Graham street.

Camp San Luis Rey. 1846; 1850-52. *Post at Mission San Luis Rey de Francia.* The Mormon Battalion camped here in 1846 and later the Army maintained small detachments to protect travelers. Earlier, from 1798 until after the padres left in 1835, Spanish and Mexican troop details stayed here to protect the mission. The restored church and monastery and the stabilized ruins of the soldier barracks are at the site 3.5 miles east of Oceanside on Mission road, California 76. Despite some official records that indicate there were two sites of this post, research has established that only one site existed.

Camp San Miguel. 1849-51. This was the base of operations for escorts of the 2d Infantry; the camp was at the Mission of San Miguel.

Camp near and New Pedro. *Drum Barracks.*

Camps at Santa Barbara. 1846-64. The dates shown bracket the periodic troop encampments at Santa Barbara. The first Americans were part of Fremont's rangers who headquartered at the St. Charles hotel in 1846. This building, then known as Thompson's residence, was used by the New York Volunteers the next year, but their main camp was on the beach at the foot of Cahpala street; the officers were at a site now occupied by the Little Town Club. California Volunteers periodically garrisoned the town in the Civil War.

Presidio of Santa Barbara. 1788-1860. This was a rectangular enclosure with adobe buildings on the four sides, bastions at the east and west corners. It had fallen into neglect by the time U.S. soldiers arrived in 1846. Some restored buildings were destroyed by the 1925 earthquake but two buildings are in place and restored. The old presidio enclosure is bounded by Carrillo, Garden, De la Guerra, and Anacapa streets.

Camp Santa Catalina Island. 1864. The Army outposted this place with the intention of using it as an Indian reservation. When the idea was abandoned, so was the post. The site and one frame building, used as a country club, are at the isthmus in the center of this resort island. The site can be reached by a long boat trip from Avalon, the main resort on the island, or directly by a sea plane flight from Long Beach. Also on the island are the remnants of a World War II radar station, mostly fallen-down frame structures.

Camp at Santa Isabel. 1851-52. Although Kearny used this camp for a night in 1846, it wasn't until 1851 that it became an offical Army location and was used as a depot. It was at the assistencia of Santa Isabel of the San Diego Mission, 60 miles east of San Diego.

Fort Savannah. *Fort Mervine.*

Battery Saxton. This was a 12-inch gun position at Fort MacArthur.

Fort Winfield Scott. 1912-. *Fort Scott, Fort Point.* This name was applied to Fort Point at the time it was condemned and vacated in 1906, and then to the new buildings above the fort – as the western portion of the Presidio of San Francisco–into which the Army moved in 1912. This site had 17 batteries planned or built in the Endicott period: Howe, Wagner, Stotsenburg, McKinnon, "Dynamite," Lancaster, Godfrey, Saffold, Miller, Cranston, Slaughter, Crosby, Chamberlin Boutelle, Sherwood, Blaney, and Baldwin. The batteries are vacant but the fort still is active.

Camp Sequoia National Park. 1886-1916. *Camp at Mineral King.* This is where the Army camped until relieved of the responsibility of protecting the park by the establishment of the National Park Service. It is now the location of the park headquarters.

Fort Seward. 1862-63. *Camp on Del River.* This was a Civil War post that California Volunteers manned to keep peace between the settlers and Indians. Although several old buildings in the area are claimed to have housed U.S. Grant–who left California long before the start of Fort Seward–there is no trace of the Army post in the hamlet of Fort Seward presently at the site. From Eureka take US 101 south about 40 miles to the turnoff to South Fork. Follow this secondary road through South Fork and McCann for 21 miles to a fork, take the left fork for 5 miles to Fort Seward community.

Battery Sherwood. This was an Endicott period 5-inch gun position at Fort Winfield Scott.

Camp Sigel. 1861-62. California Volunteers were mustered in at this site near Auburn.

Battery Slaughter. This was an Endicott period 8-inch position at Fort Winfield Scott.

Battery Smith. This was an Endicott period 6-inch gun position at Fort Barry.

Fort Soda. 1860-68. *Hancock Redoubt, Fort Soda Lake, Camp Soda Springs.* The dry soda lake next to this desert post is an indication of its climate. Regardless, the atmosphere and other conditions here have contributed to the preservation of parts of the original buildings, now a Desert Studies Center. From Baker, go west on I-15 for 6 miles to the turn on road 466 to the south. In 5 miles turn in to Zzyzx Springs, formerly privately owned health and rest resort, the site of the fort where remains of the Army buildings are included in the modern construction.

Post of Sonoma. 1846-51. *Sonoma Barracks.* Not long after this Mexican post fell to the California Bear Flag Republic, the United States took over. Navy Lieutenant Joseph W. Revere, grandson of the American Revolution's Paul Revere, was in command for awhile. The Leese-Fritch house was the headquarters of the Army on the Pacific from 1849 to 1850 at which time Lieutenant William T. Sherman lived at the Ray House (Adler Adobe). Sonoma is 45 miles north of San Francisco via US 101 and California 37 and 121. The barracks is on the plaza at Spain street East and 1st street East. Leese-Fritch house is at 490 1st street West and the Ray house is at 209 Spain street East.

Battery Spencer. This was an Endicott period 12-inch battery at Fort Baker, San Francisco Bay.

Battery Springer. This was an Endicott period 12-inch gun position at Fort Miley.

Camp Stanford. 1863. A Civil War tent camp

near downtown Stockton. The site is now the playground of Annunciation school at Van Buren and Rose streets.

Camp Stanislaus. 1849-50. This camp was at Knight's Ferry on the Stanislaus river 30 miles southeasterly from Stockton.

Camp Steele. 1852. This was a temporary camp of the 2d Infantry between the north and south forks of the Merced river.

Fort Stockton. 1846. This was a blockhouse erected at Monterey, later named Fort Mervine.

Fort Stockton. *Presidio of San Diego.*

Battery Stotsenburg. This was a 12-inch gun position of the Endicott period at Fort Winfield Scott.

Camp Strowbridge. *Fort Wool.*

Camp Sumner. 1861. This was a Civil War rendezvous for mustering troops and watching over secessionist tendencies in San Francisco. It was near the Presidio of San Francisco.

New Supply Camp. 1873. *Boyle's Camp.* This was the supply camp for the Modoc War. From Tulelake go south on California 139 to Newell, location of Tulelake Airport. Camp site is on the left (east) of the highway at the ravine ½ mile south of the center of Newell.

Detachment at Surprise Valley. *Fort Bidwell.*

Camp Susan. 1864. This Nevada Volunteers camp was to protect the roads around Susanville. It was located at Susanville.

Fort Sutter. 1845-50. *Sutter's Fort, Fort Sacramento, Redoubts at Sacramento, Camp at Sutter's Fort.* An irregular parallelogram 330 by 180 feet, this fort was started for trading purposes in 1839 by John Sutter. The arrival of the Army in 1846 and the discovery of gold nearby not long after ended Sutter's empire. The fort has been rebuilt as a California State Historical landmark at 2701 L street, Sacramento.

Camp Swasey. 1862. California Volunteers camped here near Eureka.

Camp Taylor. 1858-59. This post was eight miles southeast of Fort Crook at Fall River Mills.

Fort Tejon. 1854-64. The camel experiment passed through this mountain post and then one of the leaders—Edward Fitzgerald Beale—made this area his headquarters. Frequently more than a thousand Indians were imprisoned here in less than ideal conditions. Fort Tejon is now part of the California State Beaches and Park System and the restored buildings are on the west side of I-5 about 36 miles south of Bakersfield.

Fort Terwaw. 1857-62. The Klamath river continues to flood the site of this post just as it did during the Army's occupation when 17 buildings were inundated. George Crook was the post's founder and frequent commander. From Eureka, go north on US 101 about 70 miles to Klamath. Take Terwaw Valley road east 3.7 miles to Klamath Glen road. Turn right (south) .2 miles to marker in center of community of Klamath Glen, site of the fort.

Camp at Trinidad. 1863. Troops headquartered here from July to October, 1863, until moved to Camp Gilmore four miles northward. This camp was in the town of Trinidad.

Camp Tulare. 1871. This was a temporary camp on the Tulare Indian Farm three miles east of Portersville.

Camp Union. 1861-66. First a training camp for California Volunteers, this post provided men for western camps throughout the Civil War and was a discharge center afterward. The marked site of the second Union is at the northwest corner of Suttersville and Del Rio roads, Sacramento. The first site, from which the troops were flooded in 1861, is on the other side of the Sacramento river at what was once the Yolo race track.

Camp and **Depot Vallecito.** 1850-53. This was an important resupply point even after it was given up officially. The site is Vallecito County Park, 19 miles south of Scissors Crossing on California 78; the old stage station has been restored.

SUTTER'S FORT, 1846
From a drawing by Lt. J.W. Revere, U.S.N. *(16)*

FORT TEJON *(15)*

Fort Vigilance. 1856. *Fort Gunnybags.* This was the sand-bagged warehouse that served the San Francisco Vigilantes as drill hall, armory and headquarters during their near-dictatorship that was begun in order to bring law and order to San Francisco and ended when it was found to be the worst offender. This site is in San Francisco on Sacramento street, bounded by Front, Davis and California streets.

Fort Vose. *Camp Nome Lackee.*

Camp Waite. 1865-66. Troops camped here to prevent Indian disturbances in Tehama County. The site was on Antelope creek west of Red Bluff.

Battery Wallace. This was an Endicott period 8-inch position at Fort McDowell on Angel Island.

Battery Wallace. This was a World War I-era 12-inch battery at Fort Baker.

Battery Wagner. This was an Endicott period 5-inch gun position at Fort Baker, San Francisco Bay.

Battery Wagner. This was a 12-inch gun position of the Endicott period at Fort Winfield Scott.

Camp at Warner's Ranch. 1850. This temporary camp was established by the 2d Infantry to protect the emigrant road; the site became Camp Wright in 1861.

Fort Weller. 1859-60. This was a pre-Civil War short-term camp of which there are no remains. From Calpella, on US 101 about 68 miles north of Santa Rosa, go straight north on County 230 through Redwood Valley town and the Indian reservation of the same name. A total of 5.2 miles north of Redwood Valley town, which is about 1.5 miles after a bridge across the Russian river, the road passes the fort site on the left (west) side of the road.

Battery Whistler. This was a Taft period 12-inch gun position at Fort Rosecrans.

Battery White. This was a Taft period 12-inch gun position at Fort Rosecrans.

Battery Wilkeson. This was an Endicott period battery at Fort Rosecrans, consisting of 10-inch guns.

Wilmington Depot. 1861-1870. This post supplied Drum Barracks and the Mojave desert expeditions and, in 1863, was a stopping place for the camels of the pre-Civil War experiment. The site is a block long and two blocks wide in Wilmington, bordered by C, Front and Canal streets.

Camp A.E. Wood. 1891-1914. The Army occupied this site in Yosemite National Park while protecting it before the start of the National Park Service.

Fort Wool. 1855. *Camp Strowbridge.* Located at the confluence of the Trinity and Klamath rivers, this temporary post kept an eye on the Hoopa Indians in the early days of the bitter and bloody warfare. There is nothing at the site now at the northern boundary of the Hoopa Indian reservation. Follow directions to Fort Gaston but continue north on California 96 for 12 miles beyond Hoopa the Weitchpec, site of Fort Wool.

Camp Worth. 1865. This was the site of an Indian prisoner camp on the peninsula between Humboldt Bay and the Pacific, five miles from Lighthouse Point.

Vigilante headquarters in San Francisco in 1856 was called Fort Gunnybags because of its fortifications *(14)*

Camp Wright. 1861. This was a mustering-in tent camp near San Francisco.

Camp Wright. 1861-62. Crossroads of Southern California branched in three directions from here, toward Los Angeles, San Diego and San Luis Rey. The site was passed by the Army as early as the Kearny and Cooke expeditions of 1846-47. Both forces rested here after crossing the desert.

Actually there were three sites. The first site can be reached from San Diego by taking I-8 east to California 79, about 40 miles. Turn left (north). Stay on California 79 for about 40 miles to the intersection with San Felipe road. To the left (west) of this intersection is the first site of Camp Wright. On the high ground 1/8 of a mile to the west is the second site of Wright to which it moved in November, 1861.

Continue north on California 79 about 16 miles to Oak Grove, the third and most important site of the camp, where there are markers for Camp Wright and the Oak Grove stage station on the left side of the highway.

Fort Wright. 1862-75; 1887. In Northern California's Round Valley, this site first hosted troops as a temporary camp in 1848. After the post was established in 1862, the Army suggested that the main trouble makers were the Indian Agency employees rather than the Indians. At one point, the Army commander invoked martial law and ejected the agent. From Fort Bragg, go southeast on California 20 to US 101 at Willits. Head north on US 101 about 24 miles to Laytonville. Turn right (east) 12 miles to Del Rios, continue 16 more miles to Round Valley. The post was in the northwest corner of the valley, west of the hamlet of Covelo.

Battery Yates. This was an Endicott period 3-inch gun position at Fort Baker, San Francisco Bay.

Camp Yerba Buena Island. 1860-80. *Military Post at Goat Island.* The dates of Army use of Yerba Buena Island—or YBI or Goat Island as it was nicknamed at various times—are irregular.

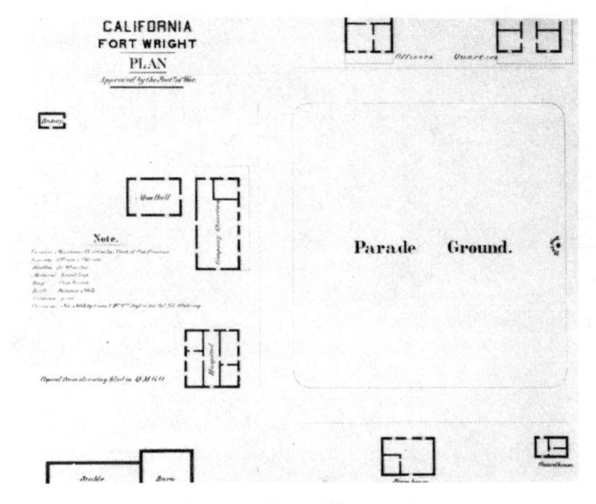

Plan of Fort Wright *(27)*

It was intended to be a site for artillery batteries defending San Francisco Bay, but served instead as an ordinary camp and, ultimately, as a Navy station. From San Francisco or Oakland, take the Bay Bridge to the turnoff for Yerba Buena Island. This flanks the bridge on one side; Treasure Island flanks it on the other side. After leaving the bridge, proceed to road fork. Take lower road after checking for permission at sentry box. The lower road is narrow, steep and winding leading out on small peninsula on which the Army camp once stood.

Fort Yosemite. 1885-1916. *Detachment at Yosemite National Park.* This was where the Army watched over Yosemite Park until the formation of the National Park Service. The Army headquarters is now the park headquarters within view of the famed "fire fall." The park is reached by California 140 about 80 miles east of Merced.

Fort Yuma. 1849-85. This adobe post was often condemned as the hottest, most uncomfortable in the Army. From its earliest days until after the Civil War it was also one of the most active. The fort buildings are now used as an Indian agency. The site overlooks the Colorado river from the California side, across from Yuma, Arizona, above I-8. The site can be reached by various side roads from the highway, all of which cross the Fort Yuma Reservation and permission to visit must be requested from the Tribal Council at the fort.

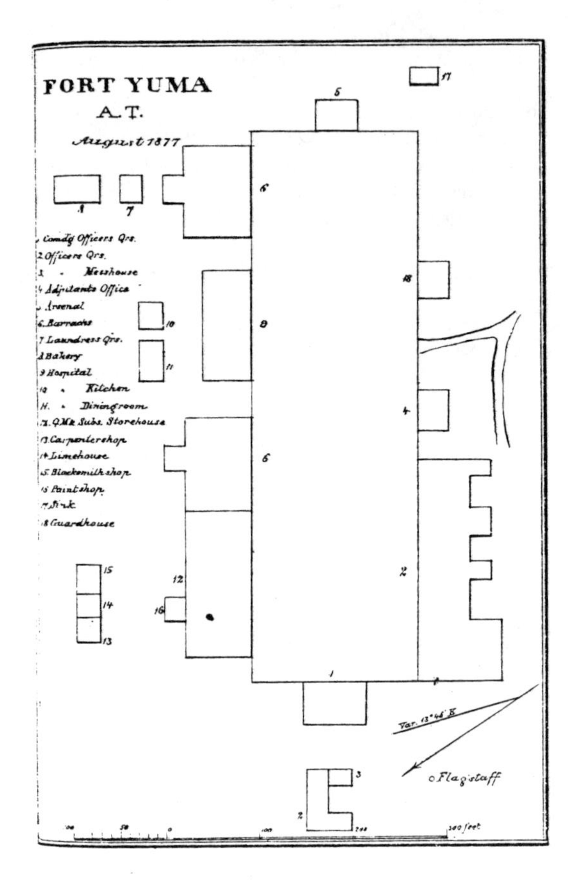

FORT YUMA *(1)*

COLORADO

FORT MASSACHUSETTS *(10)*

Protecting prospectors and travelers seemed to be the two main missions of Colorado's forts; fur trading was the main activity of the trading posts.

This listing includes the bulk of the military posts and camps and most of the trading and settler forts that attained any recognition or permanence. State or locally sponsored markcrs, and more elaborate traces in many cases, are at many of the sites, easing both the matter of cataloging and locating them.

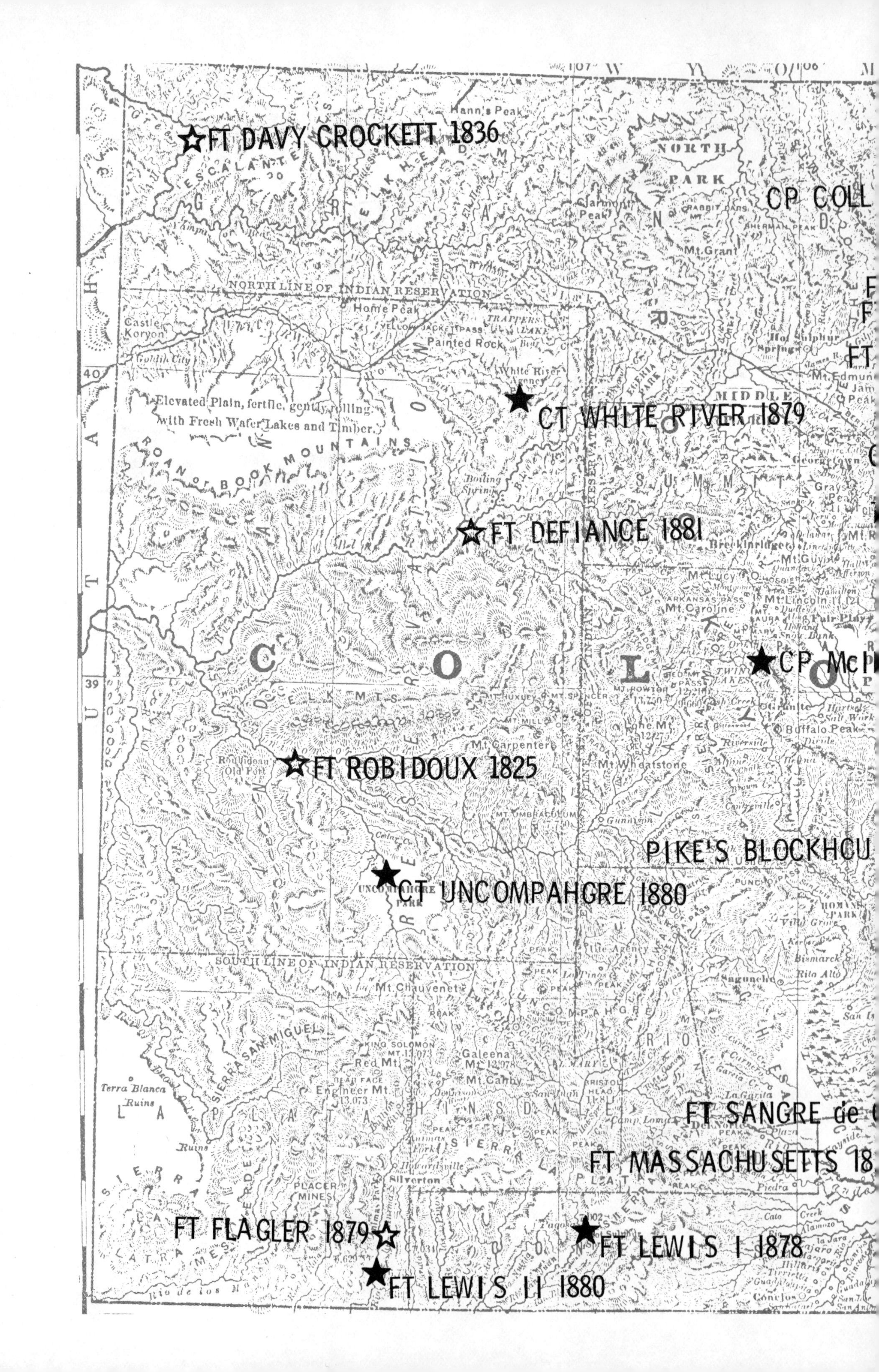

FT DAVY CROCKETT 1836
CP COLL
CT WHITE RIVER 1879
FT DEFIANCE 1881
CP McI
FT ROBIDOUX 1825
PIKE'S BLOCKHOU
CT UNCOMPAHGRE 1880
FT SANGRE de
FT MASSACHUSETTS 18
FT FLAGLER 1879
FT LEWIS I 1878
FT LEWIS II 1880
NORTH PARK
NORTH LINE OF INDIAN RESERVATION
SOUTH LINE OF INDIAN RESERVATION
Elevated Plain, fertile, gently rolling, with Fresh Water Lakes and Timber.
ROAN or BOOK MOUNTAINS
ELK MTS.
SIERRA SAN MIGUEL

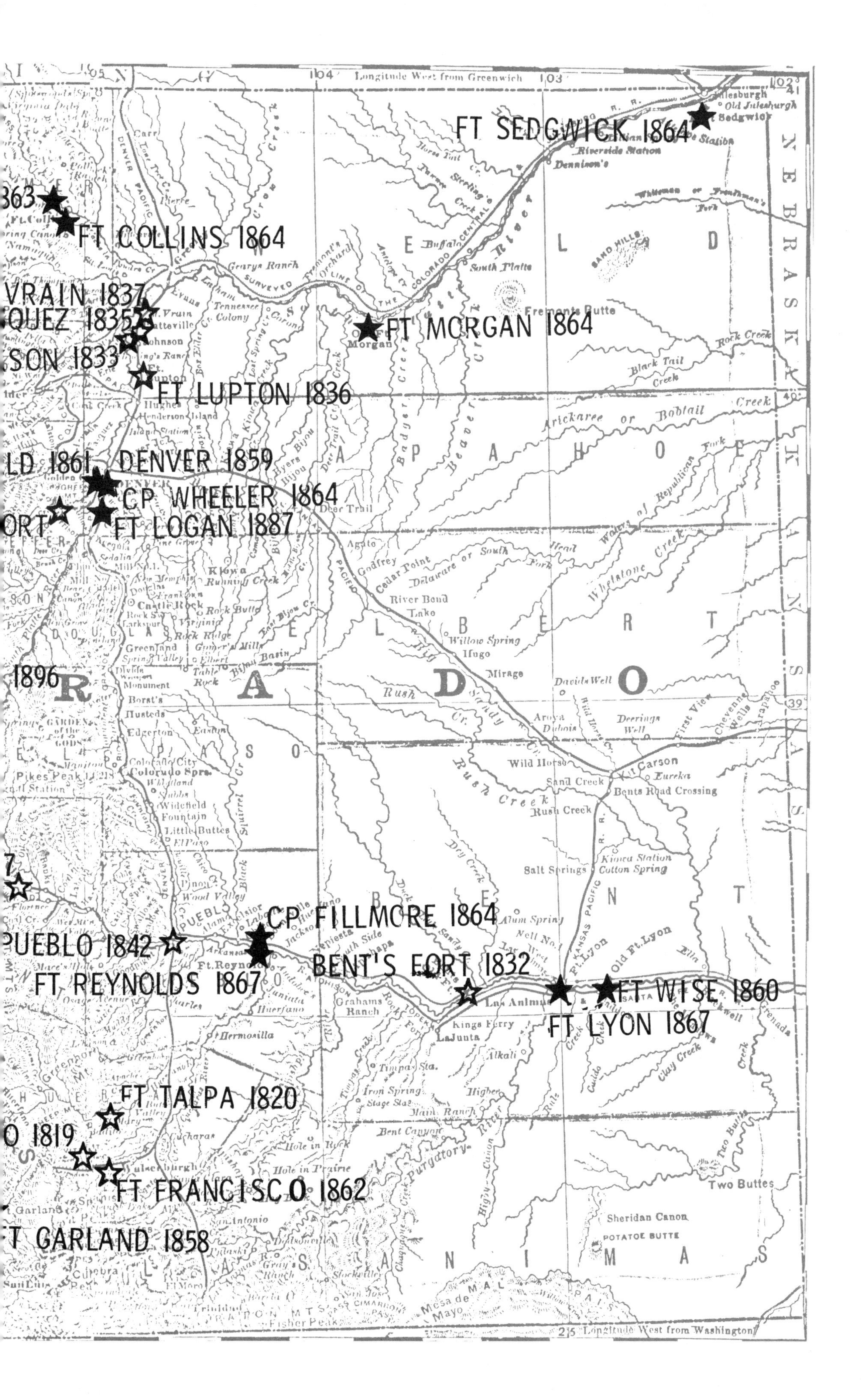

FT SEDGWICK 1864
FT COLLINS 1864
VRAIN 1837
QUEZ 1835
SON 1833
FT LUPTON 1836
FT MORGAN 1864
LD 1861
DENVER 1859
CP WHEELER 1864
ORT
FT LOGAN 1887
1896
CP FILLMORE 1864
PUEBLO 1842
BENT'S FORT 1832
FT REYNOLDS 1867
FT WISE 1860
FT LYON 1867
FT TALPA 1820
O 1819
FT FRANCISCO 1862
T GARLAND 1858
Longitude West from Greenwich
Longitude West from Washington
NEBRASKA
KANSAS
ELD
ARAPAHOE
ELBERT
RADO
EL PASO
BENT
LAS ANIMAS
Fremonts Butte
Two Buttes
Sheridan Canon
POTATOE BUTTE
Kit Carson
Las Animas
La Junta
Kings Ferry
Denver
Colorado Sprs.
Pikes Peak
Hugo
Mirage
Willow Spring
River Bend
Riverside Station
Dennison's
Julesburgh
Old Julesburgh
Sedgwick
Deer Trail
Agate
Godfrey
Cedar Point
Kiowa
Running Creek
Castle Rock
Larkspur
Greenland
Monument
Husteds
Edgerton
Colorado City
Manitou
Wild Horse
Sand Creek
Rush Creek
Bents Road Crossing
Salt Springs
Kiowa Station
Cotton Spring
Alum Spring
Graham's Ranch
Trinidad
Fisher Peak
San Antonio
Big Sandy
Rush Cr.
Republican Fork
Arickaree or Bobtail Creek
Whetstone Creek
Purgatory
Clay Creek
Rock Creek
Black Tail Creek
Bent Canyon
Hole in Rock
Hole in Prairie
Iron Spring Stage Sta.
Timpas Sta.
Higbee
Alkali
Mesa de Mayo
Hermosilla
Huerfano
Walsenburgh
Cuchara
Garland
Culebra
Sun Luis
Ft. Lyon
Old Ft. Lyon
Ft. Reynolds
Ft. Lupton
Ft. Morgan
Ft. Collins

Camp Adams. 1898. Tents housed the National Guard at this site before leaving for the Phillippines. The site is northeast of 26th Avenue and Colorado Boulevard, Denver.

Ben Quick Fort and Ranch. 1868. *Fort Washington.* Stockade was built in 1868 to protect house, 1861. Once entire population of West Plum Creek Valley forted up here for two months. This is at Palmer Lake about 20 miles north of Colorado Springs.

Bent's Fort. 1832-52. *Bent's Old Fort.* The Bent brothers owned this famous trading post that was the first bit of civilization west of Independence, Missouri on the early Santa Fe Trail. Finally William Bent blew it up when the Army – which moved nearby and discouraged Indian visitors – refused to buy it.

From Las Animas take US 50 for 10 miles west to Colorado 194 branching to the northwest. This National Park Service Historic Site now has a reconstruction of the fort.

Note should be taken of "The Fort," a restaurant built as a replica of Bent's Old Fort. Featuring menus of the 1832 era at Morrison, 17 miles west of Denver, builder and owner Sam Arnold operated this realistic representation of the original Bent's Fort until selling it in 1976.

Bent's New Fort. *Fort Wise.*

Camp Collins. 1863-66. This was the first Collins site, at the Overland stage station in Laporte. Troops were stationed here to guard the station, but spent more of their time fending off claimants on the camp site and recovering from floods. For these reasons the Army did not stay long here.

Fort Collins. 1864-67. This was where the troops moved after they decided that the Laporte site was unsatisfactory. Colorado Volunteers and ex-Confederates – the so-called Galvanized Yankees – watched over the Utes and the stage route from here. Fort Collins is now a city 65 miles north of Denver. A museum and the restored "Aunty Stone Cabin" – the unofficial officers' mess – are in Lincoln Park, 219 Peterson Street, east of downtown. The actual fort site is covered by the Union Pacific railroad wards, but a stone marker is next to the power house on College Avenue, north of downtown.

Colorado City, Fort and Stockade. 1864-68. Log settler protection in case of Indian attack, now marked by a stone and plaque at 2824 Pikes Peak Ave., Colorado Springs.

Fort Davy Crockett. 1836-40. *Fort Misery.* A fur post that was the social center of the Rocky Mountains, this post was of logs with a dirt roof and no stockade. The site is vague, but take Colorado 318 northwestward from Maybell about 65 miles (including a left turn onto Colorado 430 after 53 miles) to the intersection of the Green river with Vermilion creek, left side.

Fort Defiance. 1881. This was a blockhouse built by miners to withstand the Indian threat when the lure of rich ore seemed greater than the danger of Indian massacre. The vague site is 6 miles northwest of Glenwood Springs.

Denver Depot and **Arsenal.** 1859-65. This small establishment served as a warehouse throughout the Civil War and as a refuge during the Indian scares of 1864. The site is now a parking lot on the northeast corner of 11th and Larimer streets, Denver.

Camp or **Post near Denver.** *Fort Logan.*

Camp Elbert. *Camp Weld.*

Camp Evans. 1864. The 3rd Colorado Cavalry occupied this temporary camp two and a half miles northeast of Denver on the Platte River.

Fort Faunterloy. *Fort Wise.*

Camp Fillmore. 1864-65. Not to be confused with the New Mexican fort of the same name – this one was named after the paymaster of the Colorado Volunteers – this was the site where the volunteers assembled in 1864 enroute to the Sand Creek Massacre and where Colonel John Chivington assumed command of the expedition. There are no remains. From Pueblo, go east on Bypass US 50 for 18 miles toward Boone (leave the bypass at Colorado 96 a mile west of North Avondale). Fillmore site is on the south (right) side of the highway next to the Arkansas river.

Fort Flagler. 1879. In the aftermath of the Meeker Massacre, the citizens of Animas City organized their own militia and the government provided more than moral support with 600 troopers who outposted a log stockade for a short period. Both the fort and the town have all but disappeared. From Durango go north for 2.5 miles on US 550 to the site of Animas City and Fort Flagler.

Fort Francisco. 1862-66. This was a fortified headquarters that protected the Coucheras Ranch in La Veta. It stood next to the railroad, was a

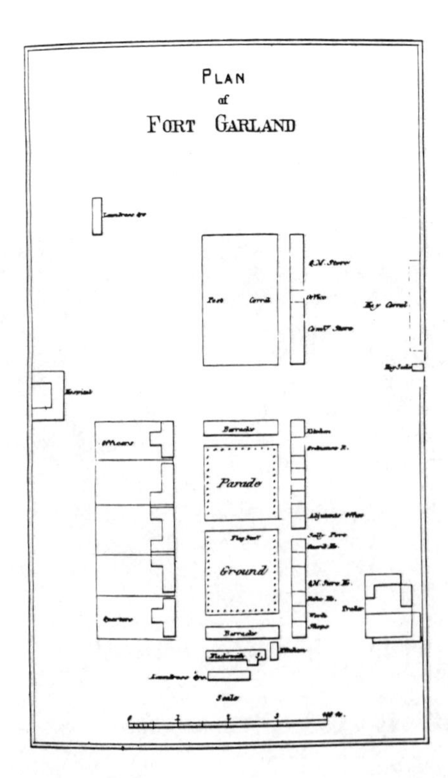

FORT GARLAND *(1)*

single story high, and enclosed three sides of a 100-foot square.

Fort Garland. 1858-83. Brigadier General Kit Carson fought Indians from this post and his luck in keeping the peace lasted for almost 15 years. The fort succeeded Fort Massachusetts, to the north. It is maintained by the Colorado State Historical Society and additions to this excellent restoration are made regularly. From Alamosa, go east on US 160 for 25 miles to the town of Fort Garland. The fort is just south of the intersection with Colorado 159 in the center of town and Colorado 159 passes within 20 yards of the restored fort.

Fort George. *Fort Saint Vrain.*

Fort Jackson. 1833-39. This was a fur trading post founded by Peter Sarpy and Henry Fraeb and bought by Ceran St. Vrain in 1838 and later abandoned. From Platteville, go south on US 85 to Ione for 5 miles. Turn right (west) for 3 miles to the approximate site.

Station and Post at Julesburg. *Fort Sedgwick.*

Post of Junction and Junction City. *Fort Morgan.*

Fort Lancaster. *Fort Lupton.*

Fort Le Duc. 1830s. Octagonal shaped upended pine log trading fort of Maurice Le Duc next to Hardscrabble Trail that failed because of absentee managership and Hardscrabble Trail's minor role. Faint traces and depression marking fort's well are on private property west of a marker on highway 67 near Wetmore (which is 28 miles west of Pueblo at the intersection of Colorado 96 with 67).

Fort Lewis No. 1. 1878-80. *Cantonment Pagosa Springs.* Unlike most Western Army sites, Pagosa Springs was a pleasant, healthful location; in fact the Indian name for the place meant "healing water." More than one wag has suggested that for this reason the garrison was moved after only a short tour here. The site is now a city park southeast of the center of the town of Pagosa Springs in southwestern Colorado.

Fort Lewis No. 2. 1880-91. *Cantonment on the Rio de la Plata.* Troops moved here to protect the settlers from the Ute Indians and after the Army abandoned the post it became an Indian school. In peace the Indians did what they could not do in war – unruly wards of the government soon had burned down many of the buildings, including most of the officers' quarters and barracks. Many buildings still are left, intermingled with the modern construction of the farm experimental campus of Durango's Fort Lewis Agricultural and Mechanical College. From Durango, go west on US 160 for 11 miles to left (south) turn at Colorado 140. Five miles south of the turn on the left (west) side of the road are the remaining buildings of Fort Lewis.

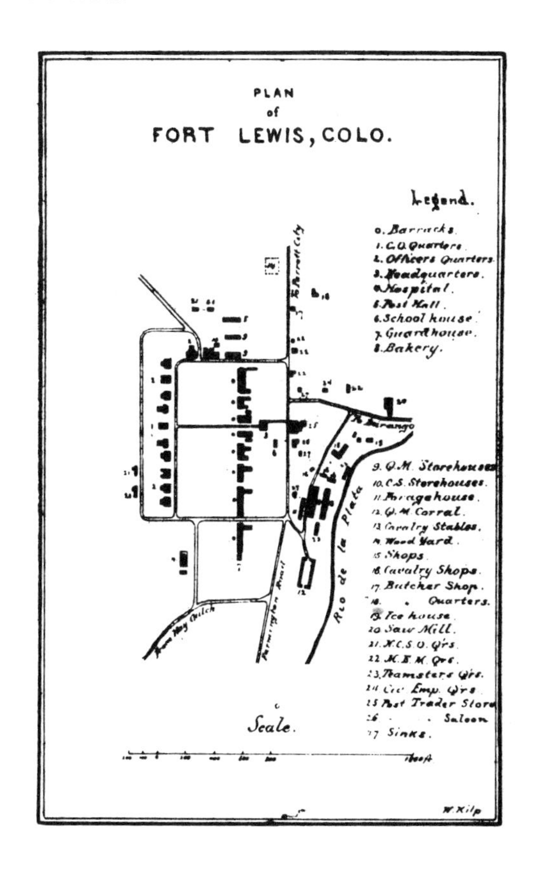

FORT LOGAN *(1)*

FORT LOGAN

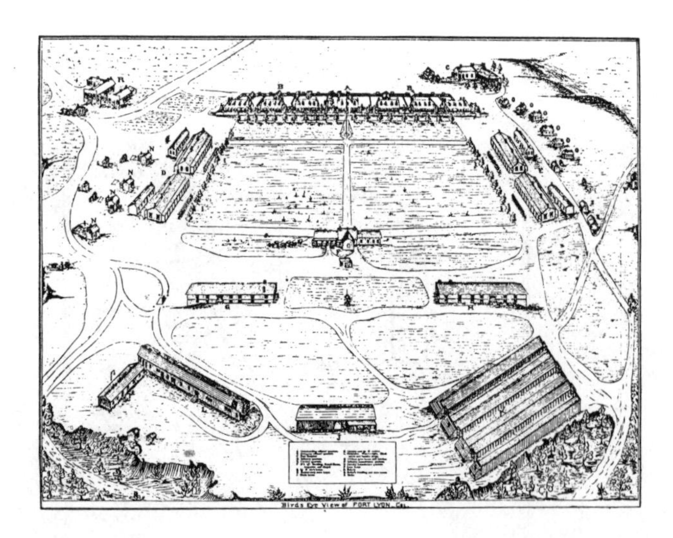

Fort Logan. 1887-1946. *Fort Sheridan, Camp* or *Post near Denver.* After General Phil Sheridan decided that he wanted his name attached to a post near Chicago instead of this new one near Denver, the Logan name was adopted to honor an Illinois politician general who won the Medal of Honor in the Civil War and was a leader in the impeachment attempt against President Johnson. The fort took over the peacekeeping mission for Colorado when the smaller camps were abandoned. Many of the Army buildings still stand, in use by the Fort Logan Mental Health Center. From Denver, go south from downtown on US 85 (Valley and Santa Fe drives) for 8 miles to the suburb of Sheridan. Turn west on W. Oxford avenue which deadends at the fort site.

Fort Lookout. *Fort St. Vrain.*

Fort Lupton. 1836-64. *Fort Lancaster.* Built by Army Lieutenant Lancaster Lupton, this actually was a trading post. It served also as a stop on the Overland Mail and in 1864 the Army maintained a detachment here for a short period. The adobe remains of the walls are now within a barn. From Fort Lupton town, north of Denver on Colorado 3, continue north 1/2 mile. Turn left at marker, west side of road. The barn housing the fort is at end of the road, 1/4 mile, on the privately owned ranch of Mrs. George Ewing.

Fort Lyon. 1867-89. As the successor of Bent's Forts and Fort Wise, this sandstone post was active throughout the years of the Civil War and the later Indians wars. Regulars, state volunteers and so-called "Galvanized Yankees," garrisoned this key post on the Santa Fe Trail. Many of the old buildings, including the one in which Kit Carson died, still are in use at what is now a Veterans Administration Hospital. From Las Animas, go east on US 50 for 1 mile to county road 183 which runs into the hospital in another mile.

Old Fort Lyon. *Fort Wise.*

Marcy's Camp. *Fort Reynolds.*

Fort Massachusetts. 1852-58. When this post was established there was doubt whether it was in Colorado or New Mexico. It was not long before the question became academic because the unhealthy situation (both from Indians and sickness) dictated a move to the site that became Fort Garland. In 1968 there were excavations on the site of this log stockade. From Alamosa, go east on Colorado 160 for 25 miles to the town of Fort Garland. The Massachusetts site can be reached by a dirt road two miles west of town and six miles north of US 160. Private property.

Camp McIntire. 1896 A tent camp of the Colorado National Guard during the 1896 miners' strike, there is nothing left at the site at Leadville.

Fort Misery. *Fort Davy Crockett.*

Fort Morgan. 1864-68. *Camp Tyler, Post of Junction Station, Post of Junction, Fort Wardwell.* This was a sod fort reinforced with logs that withstood Indian ravages against the Overland Trail but, after its abandonment, did not last long against settlers who dismantled the buildings for their own use. The modern town of Fort Morgan is on I-80 northeast of Denver. The post site, with a DAR marker, in a small park, is on Riverview avenue at Prospect street; a model of the fort is in the town's Indian Museum.

Cantonment Pagosa Springs. *Fort Lewis No. 1.*

Pike's Stockade. 1807. *Pike's Blockhouse.* Built of logs by Lieutenant Zebulon Pike, this 36-foot square breastwork had log walls 12 feet high surrounded by a moat, or drainage ditch. Its main claim to fame was that it was the first American construction in what was to become Colorado. The Pike expedition occupied it for less than a week while they tried unsuccessfully to climb what is now known as Pike's Peak. From Alamosa, go south on US 285 for 15 miles to Colorado 136 at Romeo. Take 136 for 5 miles east of Sanford to reconstruction of stockade.

El Pueblo. *Fort Pueblo.*

Fort Pueblo. 1842-54. *El Pueblo.* This was an adobe trading post that was infiltrated on Christmas Day, 1854, by Ute Indians who massacred the occupants. A marker for the fort is south of the City Hall in Pueblo; a replica that is almost full-size is in the El Pueblo Museum on South Prairie in Pueblo.

Camp Rankin. *Fort Sedgwick.*

Fort Reynolds. 1867-72. *Marcy's Camp.* Thirty buildings made up this post, including a 143-foot long adobe barracks that was plastered red both inside and out, but today only a few rock wall lines at surface level are all that remain. From Pueblo take Colorado 231 east for 16 miles to Avondale. One mile further east, on the left (north) side of the highway is a marker for Fort Reynolds; the site and the slight remains are on private property behind the marker.

Cantonment on the Rio de la Plata. *Fort Lewis No. 2.*

Fort Robidoux. 1825-45. *Fort Uncompahgre.* This was Antoine Robidoux' first trading post, established on the Gunnison river in the mid-1820s. All traces were wiped out by ranching operations in the 1880's. From Grand Junction go southeast for 42 miles to a point 3 miles west of Delta. Across the Gunnison river to the right (south) is the approximate site.

Fort Sangre de Cristo. 1819-21. *Spanish Fort.* The official name of this post is unknown, but the Sangre de Cristo title has been attached to it because of its proximity to the pass through which the Taos Trail passed. One story of the fort's activities is that a half dozen members of the Spanish garrison were massacred in 1820 by white men disguised as Indians. From Walsenburg, go west on

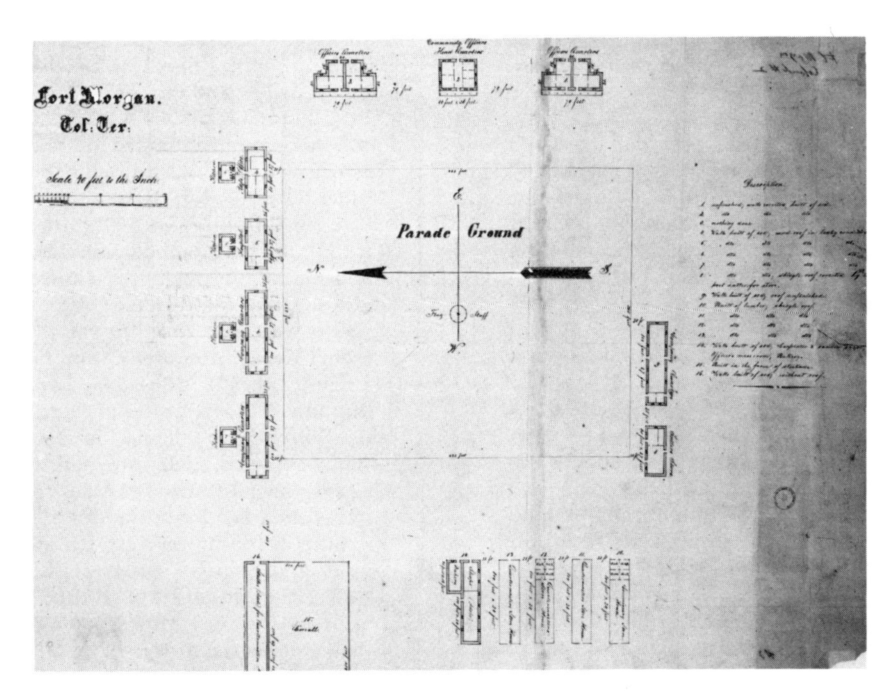

FORT MORGAN

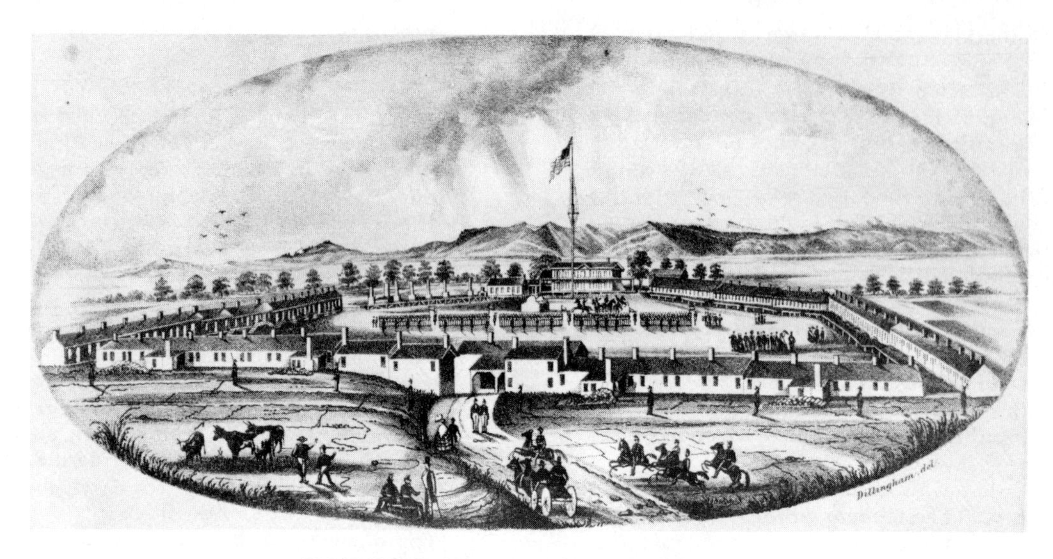

CAMP WELD, from a lithograph made in 1862 *(10)*

US 160 for 29 miles to the north side of La Veta Pass. One half mile west of the summit, go 1.8 miles northeast of the pass in rough terrain to the fort site. This is a fair weather, four-wheel drive vehicle route only.

Fort Sedgwick. 1864-71. *Camp Rankin, Post at Julesburg Station.* At first Fort Sedgwick had everything enclosed with a sod corral 240 by 360 feet. During lulls in the frequent Indian activities, the post was built into the traditional buildings-around-a-parade-ground style. There is nothing at the site but a stone marker. From Julesburg, take the road from the center of town (next to the park). Turn right (west) after passing picnic grounds south of the South Platte river. About 3 miles west, a stone marker is on the north side of the road; the fort site is 1/2 mile north in a privately owned pasture.

Fort Sheridan. *Fort Logan.*

Fort Stevens. 1866. This post had hardly a month to operate before it was ordered abandoned when General Sherman decided that Coloradans were able to protect themselves. Nothing is left at the site of this fort that was never completed on the Apishapa river 20 miles north of Trinidad.

Fort St. Vrain. 1837-44. *Fort Lookout, Fort George.* Founded by traders William Bent and Ceran St. Vrain, this adobe fur post was the first and largest of the South Platte posts. It was 125 feet long, 100 feet wide, and had 2-foot thick walls that were 14 feet high. From the Fort Vasquez replica at Platteville, go north on Colorado 3 for 5 miles to Gilcrest. Turn left (west) to St. Vrains, a sub-station of the Colorado Public Service Company; turn right from St. Vrains .2 miles to a granite marker at the fort site.

Fort Talpa. 1820. This adobe outpost was built by the Spaniards and can be reached by taking Colorado 69 northwest from Walsenburg for 21.1 miles to Farista, where the site is located.

Camp Tyler. *Fort Morgan.*

Cantonment on the Uncompahgre. 1880-90. *Fort Crawford.* The Ute War of 1879 was the reason for this post and it was here that General Ranald Mackenzie started the Utes on their way to Utah. The site is now used for agricultural purposes with no apparent remains of the once elaborate post. From Montrose, go south on US 550 for 8 miles to the ranch of Harold Flowers on the right (west) side. This is the privately owned site of the cantonment; only the stately cottonwoods along a fenceline are reminders of Army days.

Fort Uncompahgre. *Fort Robidoux.*

Fort Vasquez. 1835-41. This 100-foot adobe square was a fur trading post that should not be confused with a log cabin post operated by Louis Vasquez 5 miles north of Denver in 1834 (which was usually known as *"Fort Convenience").* The 12-foot high walls were reconstructed by the WPA and are maintained by the Colorado State Historical Society. A museum outside of the entrance tells the story of the post. From Denver go north on Colorado 3/US 85 through Fort Lupton for 8.5 miles; the reconstructed fort is between the lanes of the highway at this point, about 1.5 miles south of Platteville.

Fort Wardwell. *Fort Morgan.*

Fort Washington. *Ben Quick Fort and Ranch.*

Camp Weld. 1861-65. **Camp Elbert.** The Colorado Volunteers who were instrumental in the Confederate defeat in New Mexico were trained at this elaborate militia post next to Denver. Two fires in 1864 destroyed most of the camp. From the State Capitol in Denver go directly south 6 blocks to West 8th avenue. Turn right (west) and continue on West 8th about 2 miles. Upon going on the 8th avenue overpass, which begins at Mariposa street, look to the right. This is the area of Camp Weld. A marker for the post is on the right at the immediate western end of the overpass where Vallejo street deadends into West 8th.

Camp Wheeler. 1864. This was a tent camp of the Colorado Volunteers for a short period in the Civil War. The site is now Lincoln Park at 13th and Osage streets, Denver.

Cantonment on White River. 1878-83. The Meeker Massacre of 1879 brought 1,500 soldiers to quiet the Utes. This was the headquarters of the Army contingent. After the Army left, the frame and log buildings of the post served as the nucleus of the town of Meeker. Meeker is at the junction of Colorado 64 with Colorado 789 and 13 in northwestern Colorado. The courthouse stands in the center of the former parade ground; three log cabins north of it, all privately owned and occupied, were officers' quarters. One of the cabins also serves as a museum.

Fort Wise. 1860-67. *Bent's New Fort, Fort Faunterloy, Old Fort Lyon.* This was the Civil War post that took over the new trading fort built by William Bent after he left the original *Bent's Fort.* Troops from here participated in many Indian actions, the most famous (or infamous) of which was the Sand Creek Massacre. From Lamar take US 50 west 8 miles to Prowers sign. Turn left 1 mile to a dead end; turn left, go 1/2 mile, turn right for another half mile. Bent's New Fort was on the rise to the right, located by a marker. From this point look to the southwest. Between the marker and the river, on the low ground, is the Fort Wise site. The only remains at either site are the diggings of historians and treasure hunters.

Meeker, Colorado, 1887: "Camp on The White River" *(10)*

IDAHO

OLD FORT HALL *(34)*

Nature still has her way in much of Idaho and visiting the far-flung sites of military and trading posts is no easy matter. There has been no program to mark or preserve the sites, thereby complicating the path of the fort hunter.

Trading posts marked the early history of Idaho and military posts took over along the emigrant trails in the last half of the nineteenth century. Some of the major posts that lasted through the Nez Perces war can be located because cities or government activities now use the sites. A few can be found because they are so isolated that man has not had a chance to tear them down completely.

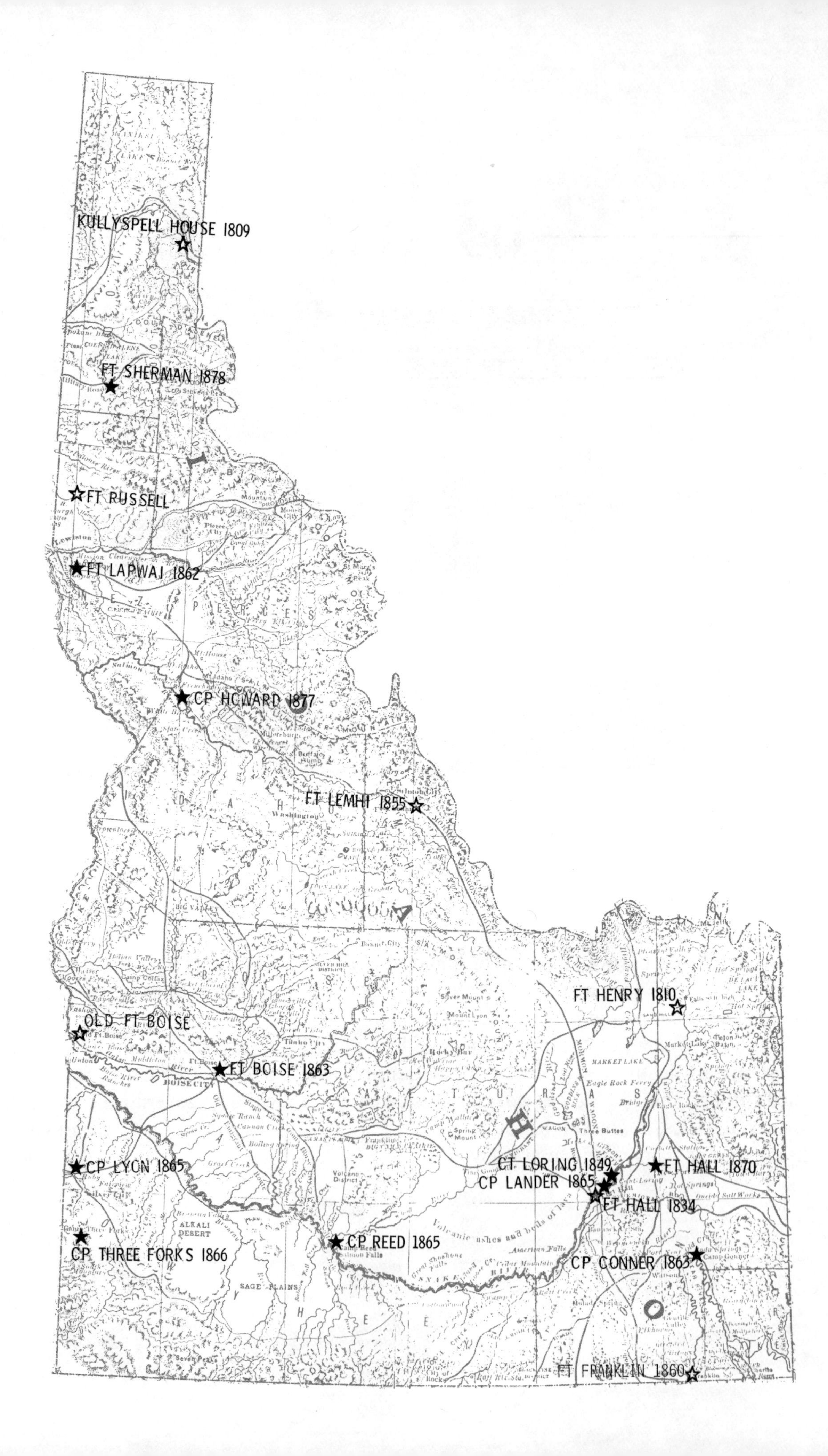

KULLYSPELL HOUSE 1809
FT SHERMAN 1878
FT RUSSELL
FT LAPWAI 1862
CP HOWARD 1877
FT LEMHI 1855
FT HENRY 1810
OLD FT BOISE
FT BOISE 1863
CP LYON 1865
CT LORING 1849
FT HALL 1870
CP LANDER 1865
FT HALL 1834
CP REED 1865
CP THREE FORKS 1866
CP CONNER 1863
FT FRANKLIN 1860

FORT BOISE *(1)*

Fort Boise. 1963-1913. *Boise Barracks.* Centrally located for troops to move quickly to hot spots of activity, between 1863 and 1879 Fort Boise was almost a continual base of operations against the Indians. During the Bannock War of 1876 it was the field headquarters of the troops fighting the elusive Nez Perce. After World War I it was turned over to the Veterans Administration and now is a VA Hospital at which several old buildings still are in use. From Boise, go north from downtown to 5th and Fort streets to the VA Center. Building No. 6 was once the paymaster's office; two of the residences on the hillside to the rear are reminders of the 1890 officers' row.

Fort Coeur d'Alene. *Fort Sherman.*

Camp Connor. 1863-65. This post was started to protect a group of dissident Mormons and at the same time was able to keep peace with the Shoshone Indians. It was a cluster of log buildings dominated by a sky-scraping flagpole. From Soda Springs, on US-north 68 miles southeast of Pocatello, go west on the highway to the edge of town. An inforamtion sign on the left (south) side of the highway identifies the site of Camp Connor.

Fort Franklin. 1860-63. This was a stockade erected by the Mormons amidst their land allocations at what became the town of Franklin. Indian hostility was the reason for the stockade until hostile activities were stilled by the Battle of Bear River, 12 miles north of the fort. There is a marker at the site of the fort in Franklin, a town on US 91 a mile north of the Utah border and 7 miles south of Preston.

Fort Hall. 1834-6 . Also see *Camp Lander* and *Cantonment Loring.* The original Fort Hall was a trading post built by Nathaniel Wyeth. A wooden stockade 80 feet square and 15 feet high, the fort was adobed after the Hudson Bay Company bought it in 1836. The site was inundated by the American Falls Reservoir. There is a marker two miles north of the actual site. This can be reached from the modern hamlet of Fort Hall, headquarters of the Indian reservation, by taking Sheepskin road west at the north edge of town for 7.1 miles. Turn left (north), go 3 miles. Turn right on a dirt road, continue for 1.8 miles to the marker on the right side. A guide is essential.

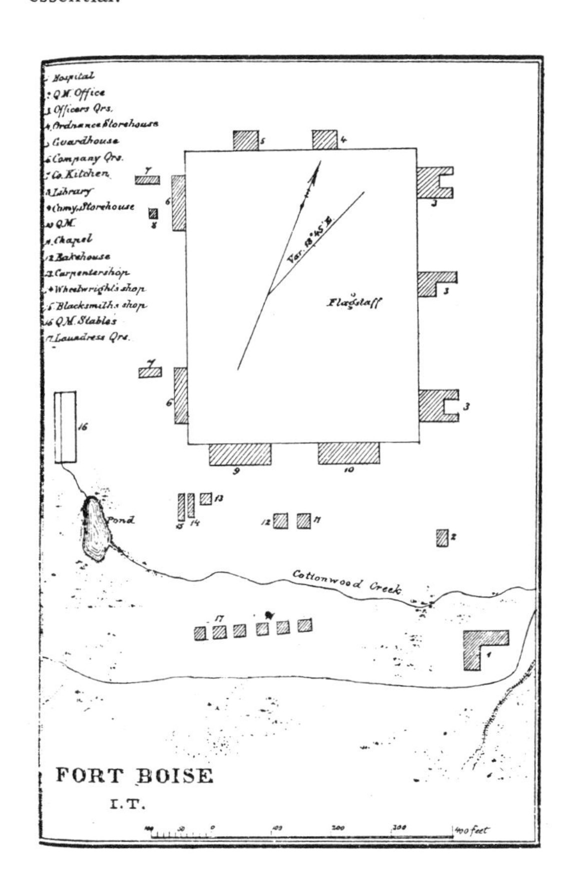

Fort Hall. 1870-83. This was the U.S. military post which was located 25 miles northeast of the trading post of the same name. Consisting of a dozen or so wooden buildings, the post was supposed to guard the Bannock Indian reservation. The only remnants of Army days are rows of trees along the former parade ground. From Blackfoot, go east for 12 miles to Lincoln creek where the parade ground trees indicate the site of the fort.

Fort Henry. 1810-11. Two log cabins and a dirt cellar provided shelter for this unsuccessful fur trading post that lasted for only the winter of 1810-11. In late 1811 the post was the location at which the Astorians built the 15 canoes in which they attempted to navigate the Snake river. A marker is on the site. From St. Anthony, go west 4 miles to Parker. Go south from Parker for 3 miles to Henry's Fort bridge. At .2 mile after crossing the bridge, turn left at the first gate. East of this gate, on private property, is the marker for the site of Fort Henry.

Camp Howard. 1877-79. Keeping an eye on the Nez Perce sub-agency 25 miles away was the mission of this post that included nine sites of officers quarters, two 32-by-25 foot barracks and more than a dozen other buildings, all of logs. There are no traces at the site except for some lead found in the trees near what was once the rifle range. From Grangeville, go south 2.5 miles on the road marked "Snow Haven Ski Hill" to property of John School, owner of the site of the camp.

Kullyspell House. 1809-10. *Thompson Trading Post.* The first trading post of the Pacific Northwest, this two-house log establishment was in business for one year before its founder, David Thompson, moved westward to Spokane House. Until modern times only the piles of two chimney stones remained to mark the site. From Coeur d'Alene, go north on US 95 for 46 miles to Sandpoint. Turn right (east) on US Alternate 10 for 19 miles to Clark Fork. From Clark Fork take the unimproved dirt road westward for 10 miles to the shore of Pend Oreille Lake where a marker is on the site of the post.

Camp Lander. 1865-66. Patrolling of the Oregon Trail near Fort Hall was handled by the Oregon Volunteer Cavalry for a year after the Civil War. Company B of that regiment erected this temporary post "on Snake creek a little north of Fort Hall" using remnants of the trading post for their shelters. Directions to the inundated site are the same as for the Fort Hall trading post.

Fort Lapwai. 1862-84. Despite the efforts of this post, the Army was unable to prevent the Chief Joseph breakout and subsequent 2,000 mile retreat. After the Lapwai Indians surrendered, this post kept the peace of Northern Idaho. From Lewiston, take US 95 east to the town of Lapwai, 25 miles. One mile south of the town is the Lapwai Agency headquarters on the right (west) side of the road. This is the site of Fort Lapwai and several former Army buildings are in use as residences. The former cemetery is a half

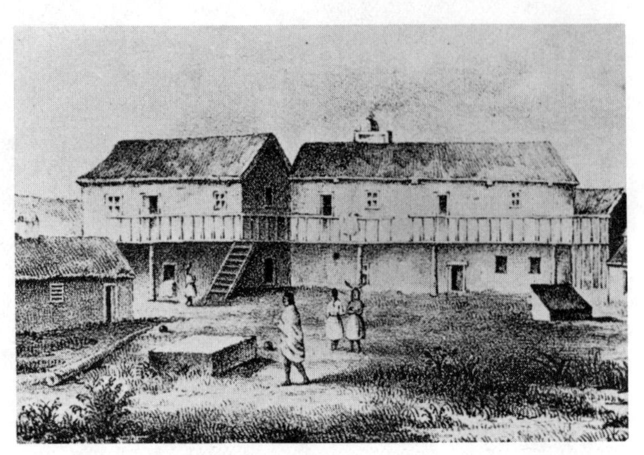

OLD FORT HALL *(34)*

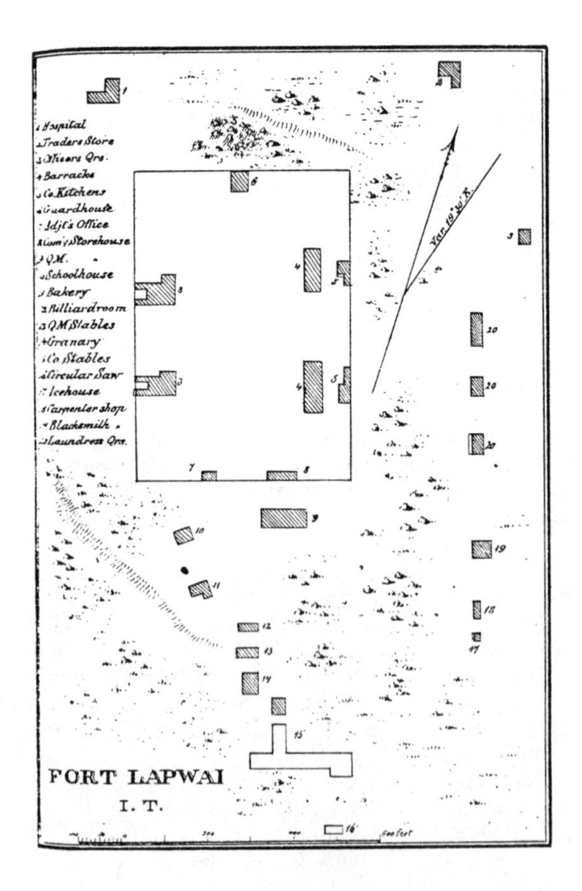

FORT LAPWAI, about the end of the 19th century *(35)*

mile south of the post; metal number stakes show where the graves once were located.

Fort Lemhi. 1855-58. The Mormons built this stockade as protection for an agricultural attempt, but the project was abandoned after three years of Indian troubles. The remnants of the settler fort cannot be separated from other remants at the ghost town of Lemhi which date from later gold rush, but an irrigation ditch built by the Mormons still is in use. From Salmon, go south on Idaho 28 for 29 miles to the site of Lemhi, left (east) side.

Cantonment Loring. 1849-50. Although sometimes known by the Fort Hall name, this Mounted Riflemen post was three miles up the Snake river from the Hall trading post. This was a two-company encampment named after the Mounted Rifle's regimental commander, one-armed Colonel William W. Loring. To get to the area of the inundated site follow the directions to the Fort Hall trading post.

Camp Lyon. 1865-69. Keeping peace along the stage routes of southwestern Idaho and southeastern Oregon was a project considerably hampered by settlers who offered $100 bounties for Indian scalps. This log eight-building post saw considerable activity in countering these policies, including reacting to a nearby ambush of 50 Chinese miners in 1866 and a later engagement with an estimated 500 Indians.

From Boise, go west on US 30 for 36 miles to the junction with US 95 west of Marsing. Follow US 95 south for 37 miles to the northern edge of Sheaville, Oregon. Turn left (east) on a dirt road at this point, following it for 2 miles to the east, bearing right at the dead end.

At the cluster of old town buildings, used as a ranch, turn left, go up the hill and continue on the dirt road to the Oregon-Idaho state border signs, ¼ mile further. Camp Lyon site is directly north of this point in the low ground between the road and the distant hills.

Camp Reed. 1865-66. This Civil War post was manned by Oregon Volunteers. It was near modern Twin Falls.

Fort Russell. This trading post included a stockade that could be seen on the site until after the turn of the 20th century. Now only a marker is left, although some stumps still are underground. The site is in Moscow in the 800 block of B street.

Fort Sherman. 1878-1900. *Fort Coeur d'Alene.* This post was supposed to keep the peace in Northern Idaho, watch the Canadian border and protect the railroad and telegraph crews. It was busy at the first and third tasks but somehow the Canadians never needed much watching, although American Indians kept skipping back and forth across the border to pose mutual diplomatic embarrassment.

Several buildings, including a red frame chapel, remain at the site next to Coeur d'Alene Lake. From Spokane, Washington, go east for 20 miles on I-90 to the western edge of Coeur d'Alene, Idaho. Upon entering the city, turn right toward the city park.

The fort marker is at the western corner of the park; four blocks westward is the site of the fort. The chapel and several former duplex officer quarters remain.

Camp Three Forks of the Owyhee. 1866-71. *Camp Winthrop.* It took only six weeks to build log barracks and other buildings to support 200 men, but the pressures of the Snake War would allow no more time. After the war, the post served as a prison for the Indian captives for another six months.

When the post was given up, the whole place was sold for $90. One building, a survivor of cattle ranch use, is left at this desolate site.

From Jordan Valley, Oregon, on US 95, go east gravel road 4 miles to right (south) turn onto another gravel road. Continue on this road 5.6 miles to fork; take right (west) fork. Continue another 10 miles to wooden bridge over Soldier creek. Take dirt road along north side of creek for 2.5 miles to privately owned site of camp. This is a fair-weather, four-wheel drive route for which a guide is recommended.

Thompson Trading Post. *Kullyspell House.*

Camp Winthrop. *Camp Three Forks.*

FORT SHERMAN *(1)*

Camp Three Forks of the Owyhee *(1)*

KANSAS

FORT HAYS *(1)*

Settler wars, with and without John Brown, gave many fort names to Kansas history, although research reveals that they were forts more in name than in fact.

Some of these fort-type places are included in the following, along with the military posts of the Santa Fe Trail and those of the Civil War and post-war Indian campaigns.

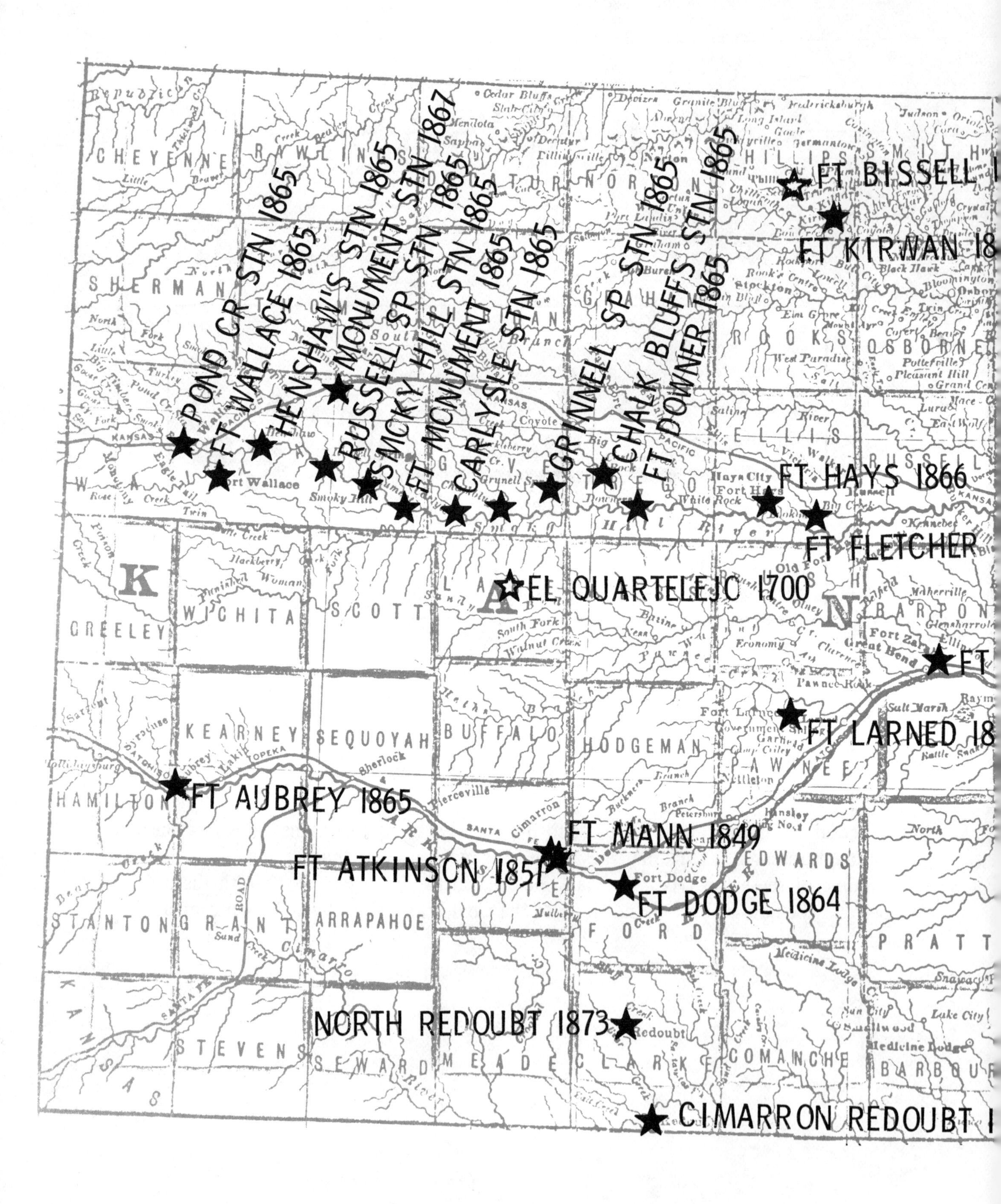

FT BISSELL
FT KIRWAN
POND CR STN 1865
FT WALLACE 1865
HENSHAW'S STN 1865
MONUMENT STN 1867
RUSSELL SP STN 1865
SMOKY HILL STN 1865
FT MONUMENT 1865
CARLYSLE STN 1865
GRINNELL SP STN 1865
CHALK BLUFFS STN 1865
FT DOWNER 1865
FT HAYS 1866
FT FLETCHER
EL QUARTELEJO 1700
FT LARNED
FT AUBREY 1865
FT MANN 1849
FT ATKINSON 1851
FT DODGE 1864
NORTH REDOUBT 1873
CIMARRON REDOUBT

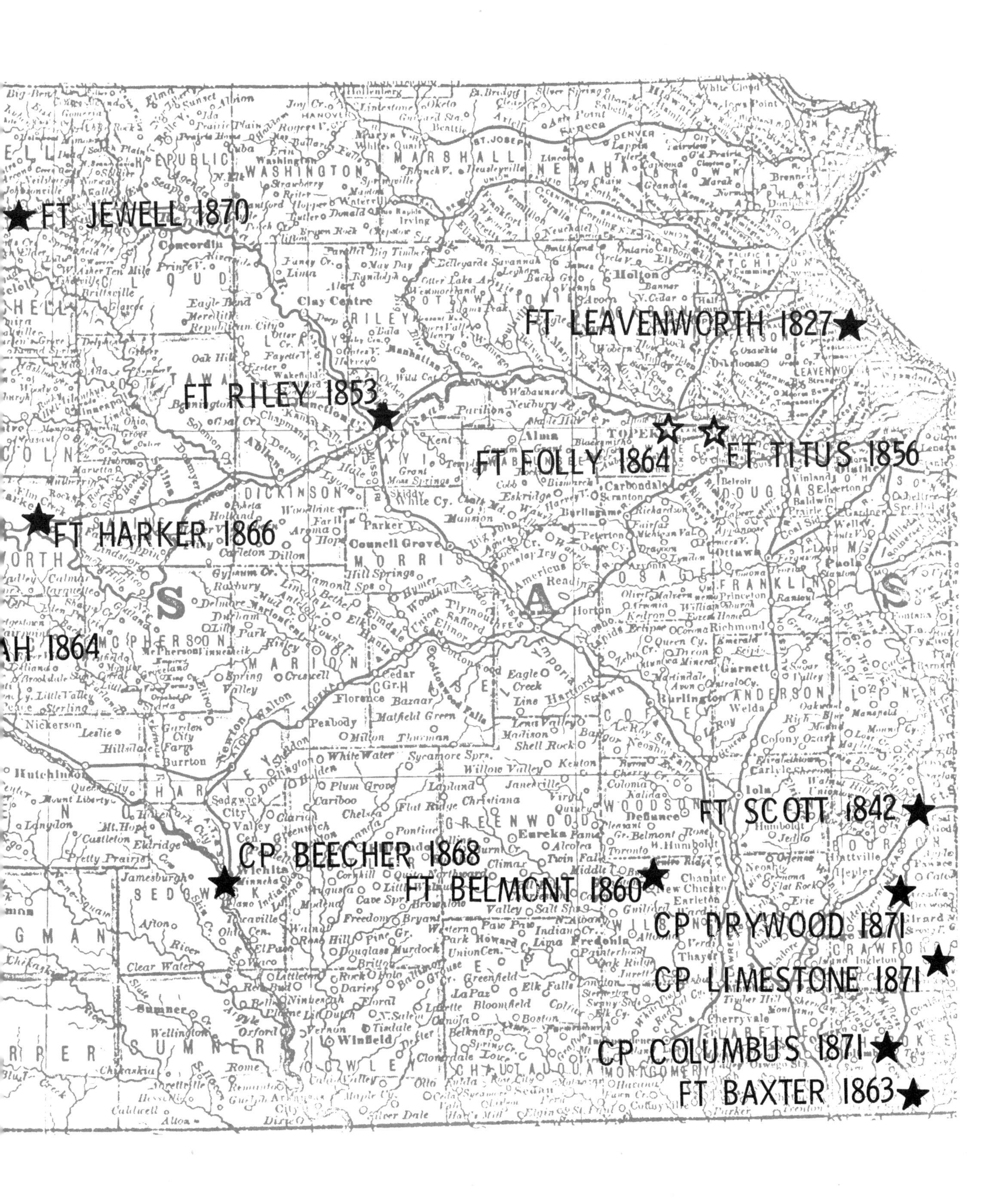
FT JEWELL 1870
FT LEAVENWORTH 1827
FT RILEY 1853
FT FOLLY 1864
FT TITUS 1856
FT HARKER 1866
AH 1864
FT SCOTT 1842
CP BEECHER 1868
FT BELMONT 1860
CP DRYWOOD 1871
CP LIMESTONE 1871
CP COLUMBUS 1871
FT BAXTER 1863

Camp Alert. *Fort Larned.*

Fort Atkinson. 1849-54. *Fort Mann, Camp Mackay, Fort Sod, Fort Sodom, Camp No. 57.* As Fort Mann, this post was a cluster of four log buildings connected by loopholed timber framework. It was abandoned in 1851 and almost immediately succeeded by the log-and-sod Fort Atkinson. The alternate names were attached to the Atkinson post, some apparently in deference to its unsanitary, vermin infested condition. Go west on US 50 for 4 miles from Dodge City. Marker for the fort is on right (north) side of highway; fort site was between road and river, left (south) side. There are no remains.

Fort Aubrey. 1865-66. *Camp Wynkoop.* Once expected to be the most important post on its portion of the Santa Fe Trail, this 300-man dugout-type fort was abandoned before any real construction could occur. Only a few indentations, possibly traces of the Army's dugouts, are left on the site. From Syracuse, go west on US 50 for 4 miles. Turn right (south) on a dirt road; follow this around to the first farmhouse on the right, 1/2 mile. This is the Helms' ranch, privately owned. A Santa Fe Trail marker is in the Helms' yard; the fort site is immediately west of the house.

Fort Baxter. 1863. This log and earth enclosure was being rebuilt by a depleted garrison when Quantrill's Raiders attacked it in October, 1863. After killing nine soldiers, Quantrill turned his attention to an approaching headquarters detachment escorting Major General James G. Blunt. Eighty-seven soldiers were killed in the resultant ambush of Blunt's force – which had mistaken the raiders to be a welcoming detail. The site is at the end of US 66 and 166.

Bear Creek Redoubt. 1870-73. *North Redoubt.* This was one of two defensive works on the Fort Dodge-Camp Supply road. It was similar in size and sandbagged design to its counterpart to the south, Cimarron Redoubt. A square depression enclosed by 3-foot high walls remains at the site in a privately owned meadow north of Ashland; the owner does not desire directions to be given.

Camp Beecher. 1868-69. *Camp Wichita, Camp Davidson, Camp Butterfield.* The most important of the post-Civil War camps, this post was short-lived as it provided protection for the Chisholm Trail and the cottonwood pole huts and dugouts of a trading post that became Wichita in 1870. Troops for the Winter Campaign of 1868-69 stopped here for resupplying; the delay in their departure, while they waited for the supplies, was almost fatal for the expedition. The site of the camp is now occupied by the city of Wichita.

Fort Belmont. c. 1860. Although nothing remains of this obscure Civil War camp, near the site are the unmarked locations of the graves of Osage Chief Hapo and his daughter, both of whom died while the Osages were camped near the fort. Hapo had fought for the North during the Civil War and was attempting to obtain aid for his starving tribe when he died at Fort Leavenworth. His tribesmen brought his body back to Belmont to lie beside the daughter who had succumbed earlier. From Buffalo on US 75 go west on a dirt road for 2 miles to the approximate site of the fort and the Indian graves. There are no traces.

Fort Bissell. 1872-78. This replica of Fort Bissell does not profess to match the original settler stockade, but two of its cabins are from the 1870 period. Many frontier day momentoes are displayed in this Chamber of Commerce museum. The reconstruction of Fort Bissell is 1/2 mile west of Phillipsburg on the south side of US 36. The original site is on the Davis ranch near Phillipsburg. From the center of town go north on 2nd street (US 183) to the dirt road at the city limits immediately south of the refinery. Turn left (west) to the ranch, 2 miles on the left (south) side. The site is a short walk behind the ranch-house on private property.

Fort Blair. 1861. This was the name of a block-house at Fort Scott.

Camp Butterfield. *Camp Beecher.*

Detachment at Carlysle Stage Station. 1865-66. This was one of the small havens of security along the Smoky Hill route, similar to Fort Monument. Cellar holes and trail ruts are visible on private property. From Grainfield, at the intersection of I-70 and Kansas 23, go south on Kansas 23 for 13 miles to Gove and then for 11 miles to the intersection with an improved road. Turn right (west) for 6 miles to dead end, turn left (south) for 5 miles to Smoky river; site is immediately north of river.

Detachment at Castle Rock Creek Station. 1865-67. A stage station on the Smoky Hill stage route, it was not far from here that the Indians attacked a military escort that in 1867 was following General George Custer in the 1867 trip that resulted in his courtmartial. A farm building stands on the station site and hardly any trace of the former occupation is left. From WaKeeney, go west on I-70 for 12 miles to county 198 at Collyer. Go south on state 198 for 12 miles to a hard turn to the west. This point, about 1 mile east of scenic Castle Rock, is the site of the stage station, now privately owned.

Camp Center. *Fort Riley.*

Detachment at Chalk Bluffs Station. 1865-67. The 1867 Plains Expedition was precipitated by numerous Indian incidents including a Cheyenne attack that destroyed this stage station and killed the stocktenders there. Cellar holes and a trench still are visible in a privately owned pasture. From Grainfield, go south on Kansas 23 as if going to Carlysle Station; do not turn off at the improved road intersection, however. Continue south on Kansas 23 for 5 more miles to the Smoky Hill river; station site is on left (east) side of road at the river.

Cimarron Redoubt. 1873. A 50-foot square earthwork midway between Fort Dodge and Camp Supply that was not big enough to be called anything but a "redoubt," this was one of two such places along the supply route. A dozen soldiers were garrisoned in this sandbagged, 10-foot high fortification. There are slight outlines of the earthworks in privately owned farm land. From Main street in Ashland, go west for 1/2 mile to a gravel road and turn left (south) for 12 miles. After road crosses Cimarron river, turn left at the next road to Lewis George ranch. The redoubt is on this ranch.

Camp Columbus. 1871-73. Protection of the Kansas City, Fort Scott and Gulf railroad line was the mission of the company stationed in the temporary buildings at this post. The camp was near Columbus, a thriving town that was founded in 1868. The site of the post is unmarked in the vicinity of Columbus on US 69 in southeastern Kansas.

Fort De Cavagnial. 1744-64. This westernmost of several outposts of Imperial France under Louis XV was for the protection of French fur traders on the Missouri against each other and the depredations of the Indians. It was a stockade of stout piles, 80 feet on the inside square with bastions at each corner, the rear bastions being storied. Inside the stockade were the commandant's house, a guard house and powder house, all with an upper story, and a guard house and trader's house for the trader's employees. All were of logs, covered with mud with chimneys similarly constructed. Troops at the post usually were French Marines, but the garrison had many civilians. The Spanish took over in the waning days of the fort and its last entry was in 1764. The Lewis and Clark journals record finding its remains, principally chimneys, one mile inland from the Missouri river. There are no traces at the site at the present northerly boundary of Fort Leavenworth.

Camp Davidson. *Camp Beecher.*

Fort Dodge. 1864-82. This famous post underwent attack by the Indians and near-riot by the civilians of nearby Dodge City. The post held up well and many of the buildings from Army days are now used by the State Soldiers Home on the south side of US 154 about 4 miles east of Dodge City.

Fort Downer. 1865-68. *Detachment at Downer's Station.* General Custer used this stage station and temporary military post as a base during his 1867 Plains Expedition. His failure to go to the aid of a group of stragglers who had been ambushed nearby by Indians was one of the charges in his 1867 courtmartial. There are cellar holes and the ruins of a stone wall on privately owned pasture land. The site is south of WaKeeney off of I-70.

Camp Drywood. 1871-73. Only the approximate site of this short-term, temporary post can be identified, reflecting the transitory nature of its mission to protect the railroad south of Fort Scott. The post was in the general area of Englevale, a hamlet 1 mile west of US 69 and 16 miles south of Fort Scott.

Fort Ellsworth. *Fort Harker.*

Fort Fletcher. 1866-67. This was the name of the original Fort Hays, a temporary post that was washed out 14 miles southeast of Hays City. Elizabeth Custer tells of her days here in *Tenting on the Plains.* Some crumbling remnants are left at the site. From Hays go (13 miles east on I-70) to the Walker exit. Go south on this road about 5 miles to a dirt road; turn right (west) to the confluence of Victoria and Big Creek. Here, on the site of Fort Fletcher, are some remains and a monument erected in 1931 to Elizabeth Custer.

Fort Folly. 1864. This irreverant name was attached to a roofless log stockade erected in 1864 as protection against General Price's Confederate raiders. The site is marked by a plate in the sidewalk in front of the National Bank building at the northwest corner of 6th street and Kansas avenue, Topeka.

Detachment at Grinnell Springs Station. 1865-67. This was another of the short-lived stage stations on the Smoky Hills route; it was 10 miles west of Castle Rock station and 9 miles east of Chalk Bluffs station. A 34th Infantry soldier was killed in an Indian fight near here in 1867. There are trail ruts and rifle pit remains still visible around the station site. From Grainfield, follow the directions southward on Kansas 23 to Carlysle Station; at the improved road intersection, turn left (east) rather than right (west) proceeding away from Carlysle Station's site. Go east on this road for 8 miles, ignoring any turnoffs, to a deadend; turn right (south) at the deadend and follow this road 2.5 miles to the river and station site.

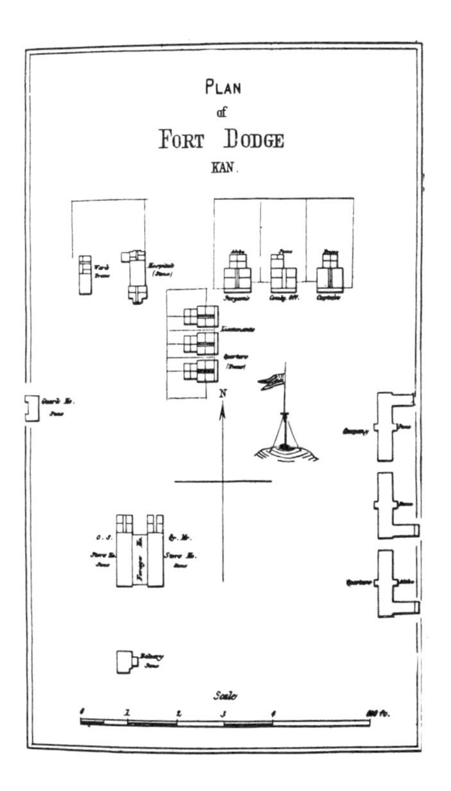

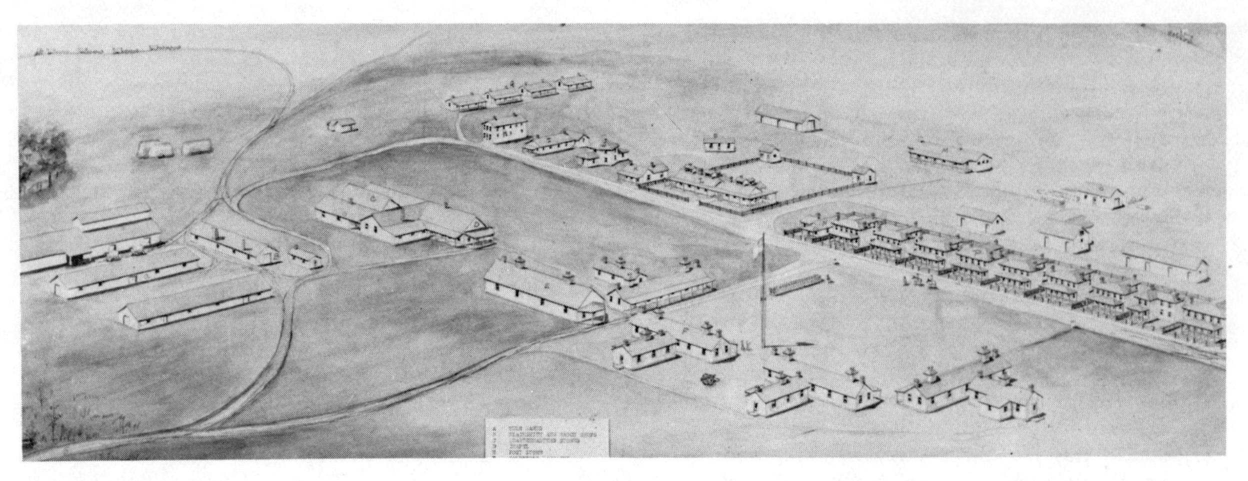

FORT HAYS *(13)*

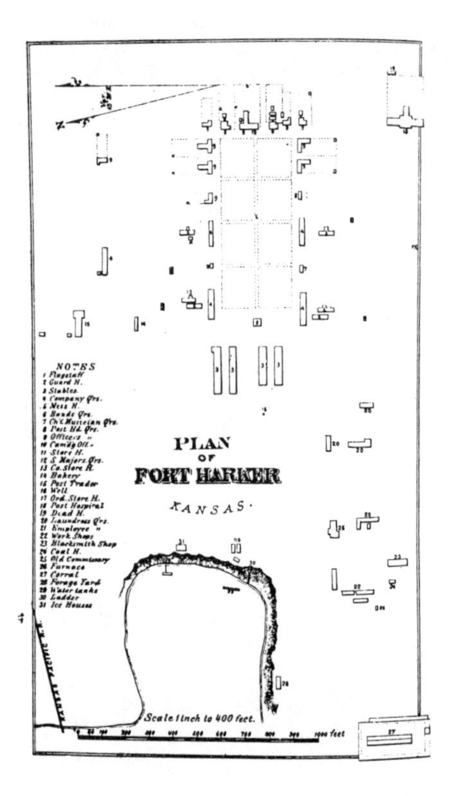

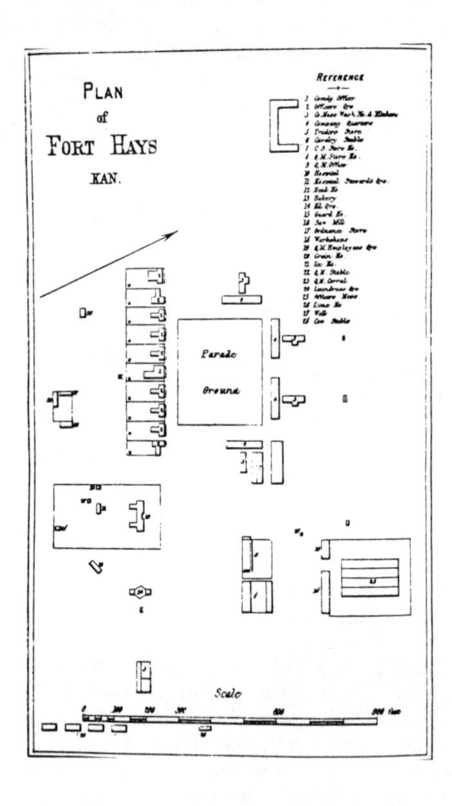

Fort Harker. 1866-73. *Fort Ellsworth.* This post was originally four miles from Ellsworth, a rip-roaring example of a cow town, but moved to the permanent site after the construction of stone buildings. It was an important troop and supply point for the forts of the Western plains. Fort Harker was the destination of General George Custer's 1867 ride that resulted in courtmartial. The fort is now the location of the town of Kanopolis. From Salina, go west on US 40 for 32 miles to the intersection with Kansas 111. Turn south (left) 2 miles. From the center of Kanopolis, the fort site is two blocks to the west (right) where several buildings are private residences and the former guardhouse is a museum.

Fort Hays. 1866-89. *Fort Fletcher.* George Custer, Nelson A. Miles, and Wild Bill Hickock were some of the names that figured prominently in the history of this elaborate post. The guardhouse, magazine and one officers' quarters are maintained as museums. Hays is south of I-70 at the intersection of US 183. The fort site is on a hill immediately south of the city where the old parade ground is now the city golf course.

Fort Henning. 1861. This was a blockhouse at Fort Scott.

Detachment at Henshaw's Station. 1865-67. This was the first stop east of Fort Wallace on the Smoky Hill route. There are some cellar holes visible in privately owned pasture land. The site is 1 mile east of McAllaster on the south side of US 40.

Fort Insley. 1861. This was the largest blockhouse at Fort Scott.

Fort Jewell. 1870. A sod enclosure 50 yards square and seven feet high with four-foot thick walls, this post was built in two days by a hurriedly mustered militia group of settlers during a Cheyenne scare. Regular troops relieved the volunteers after a month of psychological siege and occupied the enclosure during the summer of 1870. There are no remains at the site in the hamlet of Jewell about 11 miles southwest of Mankato on Kansas 14 in northcentral Kansas.

Fort Kirwan. 1865. Troops of the 12th Tennessee Cavalry, under Lieutenant Colonel John S. Kirwan, were based here while they escorted a government survey team. Here for only a summer, the troops built a 90-foot square stockade; six years later the citizens of Kirwin – note that the spelling was changed in the interim – built a 50- by 90-foot stockade right in town when word came of an Indian scare. The site of the temporary post was 1.5 miles southwest of Kirwin, inundated by the Kirwin Dam Reservoir. A marker in the town memorializes the post.

Fort Larned. 1859-78. *Camp Alert, Camp on Pawnee Fork.* The Indians had more than a little success with this garrison. Indian squaws and liquor figured in some of the plots to divert the Civil War Volunteers while the herd was being stolen. It was besieged by Indians at least five times, fielded several expeditions, and, beginning in 1864, provided armed escorts for the Santa Fe Trail trains. The parade ground still is surrounded by many of the original Army buildings, maintained by the National Park Service. From Larned, go west on US 156 for 6 miles. The post is on the left (south) side of the highway, about 100 yards distant.

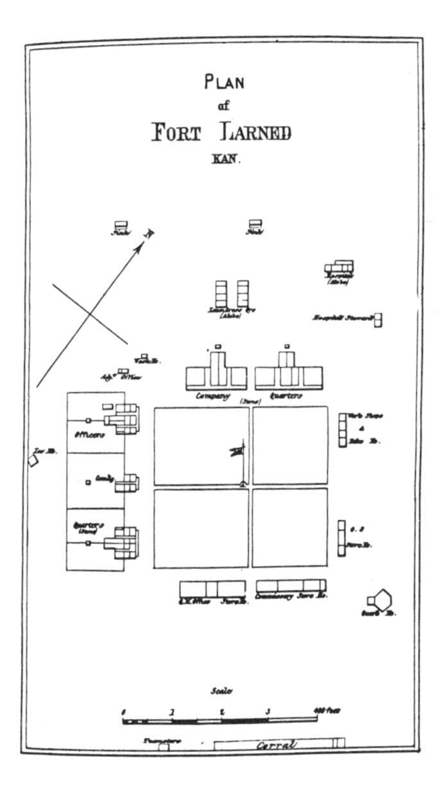

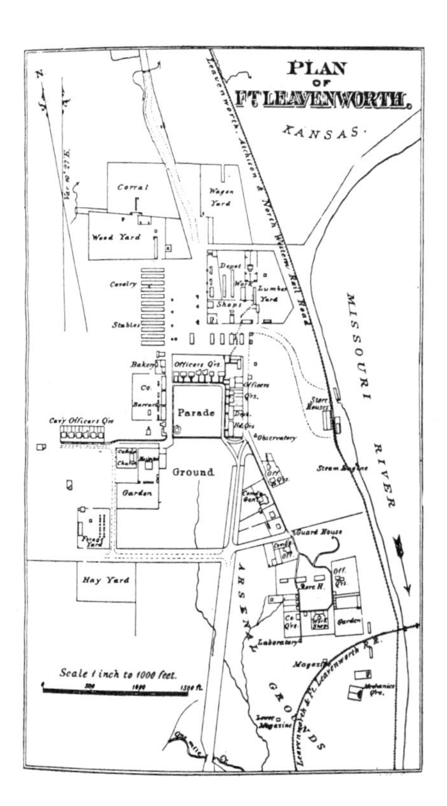

Fort Leavenworth. 1827- . One of the most historic posts in the United States, Fort Leavenworth still fulfills the post-Civil War prediction of General W.T. Sherman: "Fort Leavenworth is the most valuable military reservation in the West. It will always be the most appropriate depot and headquarters for a department, and should have barracks for a battalion of infantry, a regiment, and suitable buildings for headquarters."

Some buildings dating from the 1830's are joined by modern construction at what is now one of the Army's most important posts and the location of the Army Command and General Staff College, one of the world's foremost courses of military instruction.

The fort is immediately north of the town of Leavenworth on US 73; the entrance is at Metropolitan and Grant avenues.

Camp Limestone. 1871-73. "Temporary build-

FORT LEAVENWORTH *(1)*

ings were constructed and the troops made as comfortable as possible where they were not expected to remain permanently," is how the surgeon of this railroad guardian described the post. The site of the post is unmarked on Limestone creek near Pittsburgh on US 69 in southeastern Kansas.

Fort Mann. 1849-51. This is the same site as Fort Atkinson.

Fort Monument. 1865-67. *Fort Pyramid, Fort Monument Station.* This sod redoubt provided protection for the Smoky Hill route of Butterfield's Overland Mail but was given up soon after Butterfield sold out to Ben Holladay and the Smoky Hill route was abandoned. From Oakley, at the intersection of US 40 and 83, go south on US 83 for 21.3 miles to an improved road. Turn left, go east 4 miles to another improved road; turn right, 6 miles; then left for 7 miles; then right to Monument Rocks, 7.5 miles in the valley of the Smoky Hill river. The unmarked site has cellar holes, low wall ruins and ruts and trenches of either the stage station or military post, or both.

Detachment at Monument Station. 1867-68. This post is usually confused with Fort Monument which it succeeded to a certain extent. The mission was different, however: protection of the Kansas Pacific railroad rather than the Smoky Hill stage route. The site is in a pasture and some traces of excavations remain. From Oakley, go west on US 40 for 8 miles to the town of Monument. Continue for 2.5 miles further west; the site was at this point on right (north) side of highway.

North Redoubt. *Bear Creek Redoubt.*

Camp on Pawnee Fork. *Fort Larned.*

Detachment at Pond Creek Station. 1865-66. Not to be confused with Camp Pond Creek, the early name of Fort Wallace, this station was attacked in June, 1867, by 300 Cheyennes under Chief Roman Nose and the stock stolen.

The stage station and adjacent stable were of stone and wood connected by a four-foot deep covered trench. There was a stone wall corral behind these buildings and covered trenches that led 10 yards in three different directions to 10-foot square, covered pits that were raised sufficiently above the ground to permit firing ports to aim in all four directions.

There are cellar holes and remains of the dirt fortifications still left on privately owned farm land; the original stage station has been restored and moved to a park at the eastern edge of Wallace. Bullet holes are still visible in the siding of the building. The original site is 1 mile west of Wallace on the south side of I-70.

Fort Pyramid. *Fort Monument.*

El Quartelejo. c. 1700. This was an adobe fort of the Picurie Indians, believed to be the first solid walls erected in what is now modern Kansas. Built in the early part of the 18th century by Picurie Indian fugitives from the Spanish rule of Taos, the stronghold was abandoned when Spanish troops found the Indians and persuaded them to return to their homes. Later Comanches moved in until, as legend has it, the building was destroyed by lightning. The ruins are in the Scott County Park on the east side of US 83 about 35 miles south of Oakley.

Fort Riley. 1853- . *Camp Center.* From a cholera-plagued beginning that killed almost the entire construction detail, this post became one of the most important in the West. The 7th Cavalry was organized here with George A. Custer as its second-in-command. In 1890, troopers of the 7th Cavalry from Fort Riley participated in the Battle of Wounded Knee, said by some to be revenge for the regiment's losses at the 1876 Battle of the Little Big Horn. Many historic buildings, including Custer's quarters, are still in use. The post is on Kansas 18 about 4 miles from Junction City.

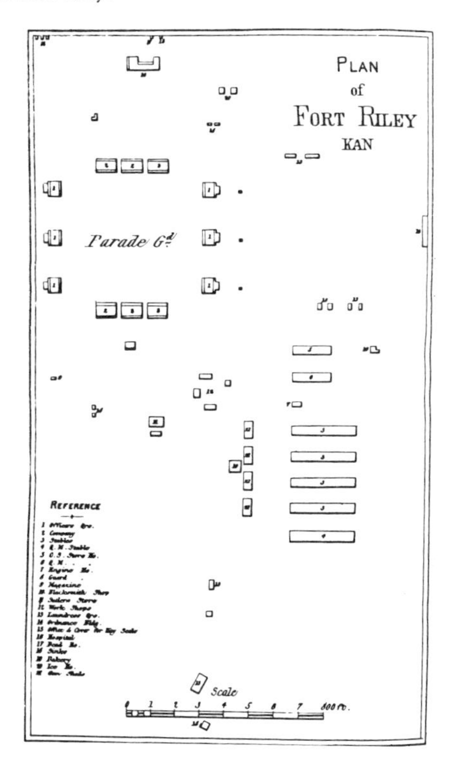

Detachment at Russell Springs Station. 1865-66. The significant difference between this station and the others on the Smoky Hills route was the large spring around which the buildings were clustered. Some cellar holes are still visible near the spring in privately owned pasture land. From Oakley, go west on US 40 about 18 miles to Kansas 25 to the south; turn left (south) and follow Kansas 25 for 12 miles to the hamlet of Russell Springs, site of the station.

Fort Scott. 1842-55; 62-65; 70-73. *Post of Southeastern Kansas.* This post participated in three phases of Kansas history – the Abolitionist period before the Civil War, the period of Confederate threat and the postwar recovery stage. The fort's quadrangle still is flanked by historic buildings. The city of Fort Scott is in eastern Kansas 85 miles south of Kansas City on US 69. To get to the post site, go north from the center of town to Wall street. The post is off of Wall street on historic Carroll Plaza, the former parade ground. The city of Fort Scott maintains several of the fort buildings and has a museum in one. The city jail occupies the former guardhouse.

Detachment at Smoky Hills Station. 1865-67. This circular, sodded dugout was hard for the Indians to capture unless they resorted to either starving or burning out the occupants, the tactic attempted in 1866. From the name it is obvious that this was on the Smoky Hill stage route. As late as 1875 troopers skirmished near here, a 5th Cavalry detachment killing two Indians against one trooper wounded in October of that year. Although the site is in a cultivated field, the cellar holes and circular trench have not been plowed. Take the route to Russell Springs station. From Russell Springs, go east on the improved road for 7 miles to a right (south) turn. Go south to the Smoky Hill river, about 3 miles. From this crossing, the station site is about 3 miles east on the north side of the river.

FORT RILEY *(1)*

FORT WALLACE, 1879 *(13)*

Post of Southeastern Kansas. *Fort Scott.*

Camp Sully. 1864. This was a redoubt of Fort Leavenworth.

Fort Titus. 1856. This was a privately built fort erected by Colonel H.T. Titus and a group of Southern sympathizers to oppose Free Staters. After the contingent participated in the sacking of Lawrence, they withdrew to Fort Titus where 600 Free Staters routed them with cannon fire that destroyed the stronghold. There are no remains at this unmarked site on privately owned farm land. From Lawrence go west on I-70 about 8 miles to where a dirt road to Lecompton ends at the expressway on the north (right) side. The farm is off of the highway at this point. Consult maps to see how the highway exits and crossovers can be navigated to get to this spot.

Fort Wallace. 1865-82. *Camp Pond Creek.* Three sites were occupied by Fort Wallace but only the final one, dating from 1866, has any traces. It was from this place that the relief column was sent to the Battle of Beecher Island. George Custer also spent much time here. Now only the cemetery and the outlines of fort buildings are left at the site. From Wallace, on US 40, go east 1/2 mile to a dirt road. Turn to the south (right). The fort cemetery is on the north side of this road, 2 miles. The fort site is directly across the road where sunken building sites fill the area to the Smoky Hill river. A museum and the restored Pond Creek Stage station are at the eastern edge of the town of Wallace.

Camp Witchita. *Camp Beecher.*

Camp Wynkoop. *Camp Aubrey.*

Fort Zarah. 1864-69. If the drawings are to be believed, Fort Zarah was a sandstone edifice the like of which was seldom seen in the West. It was a single building 120 foot by 52 with towers at two diagonally opposite corners and room inside for soldiers, horses, kitchen, storehouse and well. It afforded protection for the Old Walnut Crossing of Walnut Creek and stood in the middle of favorite Indian marauding grounds. From Great Bend, go east on US 56 for 3 miles to the Fort Zarah State Park on left (north) side of road. There are no traces of the fort amid the picnic tables and barbecue pits.

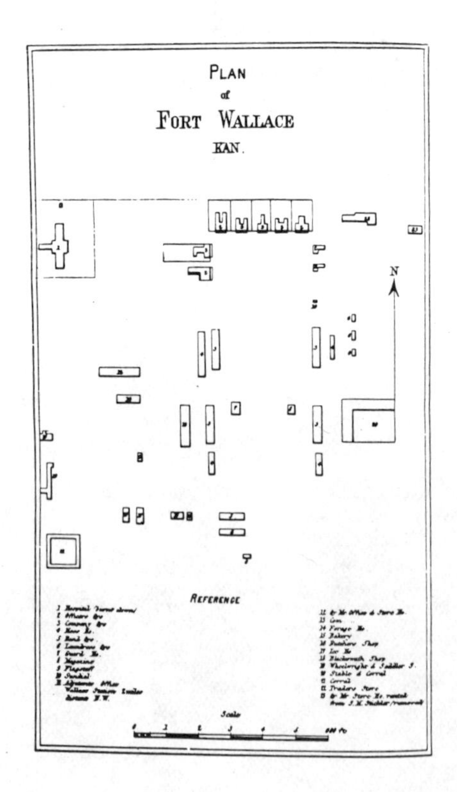

MONTANA

FORT CUSTER *(1)*

Fur trading brought the first forts to Montana and the banks of the Missouri and Yellowstone are dotted with so many that keeping them straight is an almost impossible task. Names and sites changed so frequently and were recorded by such a variety of travelers, traders and writers that this section must be viewed as a calculated guess in many cases.

Identifying the military posts is an easier matter, but this, too, is complicated by the many camps of the campaigns of the second half of the nineteenth century. This section presents most of the military and non-military forts of Montana with the request that local experts will come forth to correct any errors which have been committed in interpreting and evaluating the many conflicting sources.

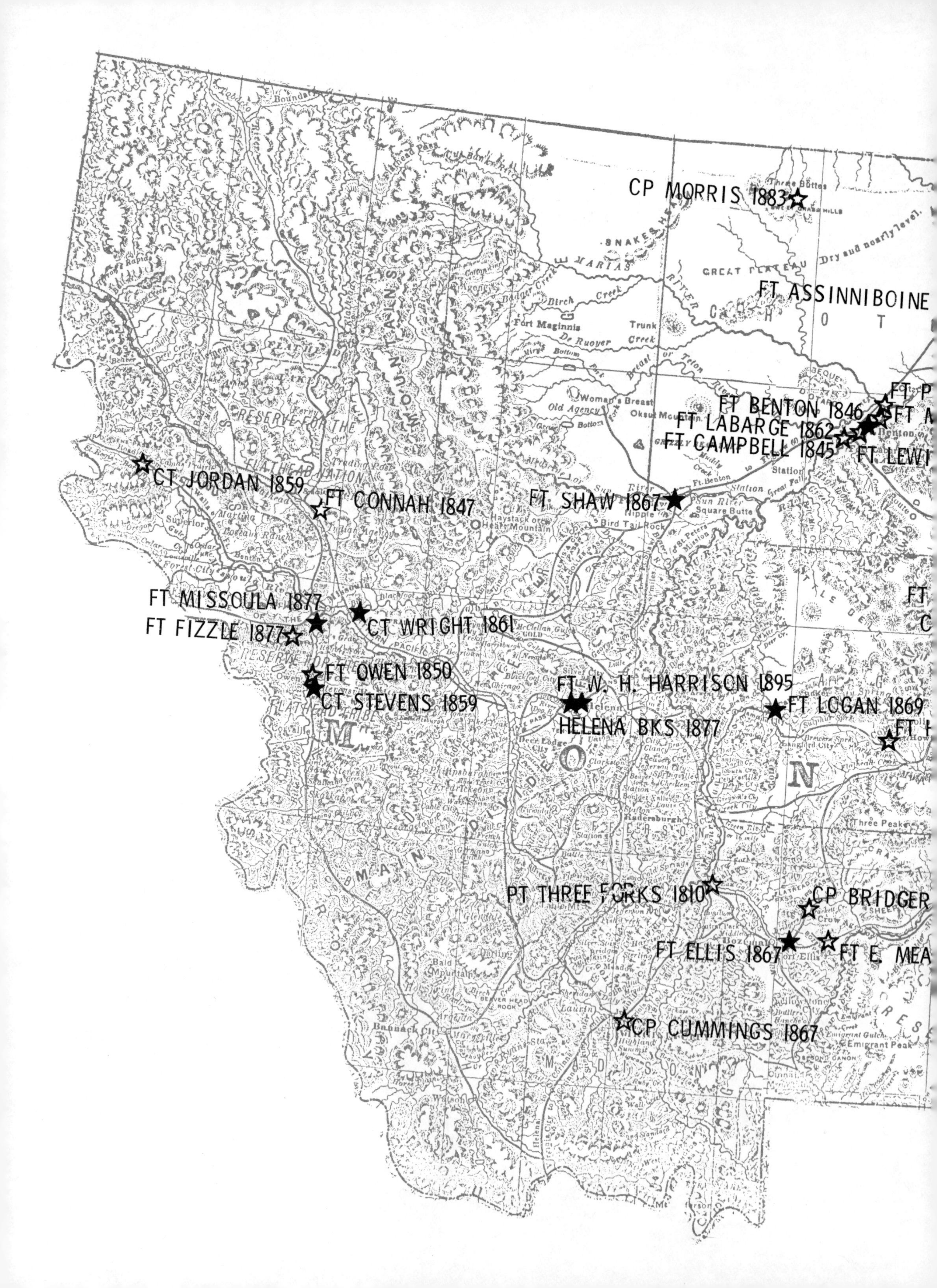
CP MORRIS 1883
FT ASSINNIBOINE
FT BENTON 1846
FT LABARGE 1862
FT CAMPBELL 1845
CT JORDAN 1859
FT CONNAH 1847
FT SHAW 1867
FT MISSOULA 1877
FT FIZZLE 1877
CT WRIGHT 1861
FT OWEN 1850
CT STEVENS 1859
FT W. H. HARRISON 1895
HELENA BKS 1877
FT LOGAN 1869
PT THREE FORKS 1810
CP BRIDGER
FT ELLIS 1867
CP CUMMINGS 1867
Fort Maginnis
Birch Creek
Trunk Creek
Woman's Breast
Old Agency
Square Butte
Bird Tail Rock
Three Peaks
Emigrant Peak

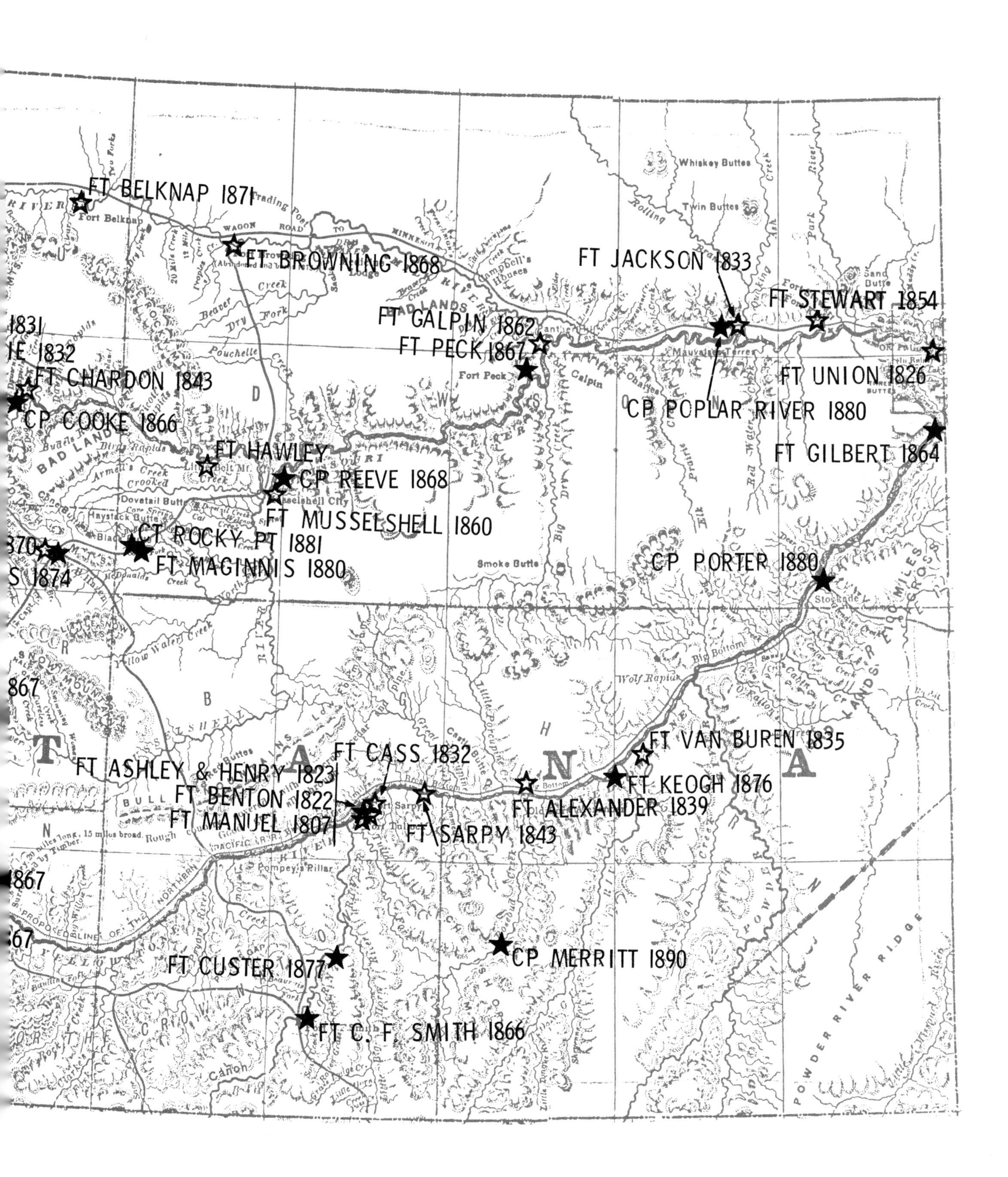

FT BELKNAP 1871
FT BROWNING 1868
FT JACKSON 1833
FT STEWART 1854
FT GALPIN 1862
FT PECK 1867
FT UNION 1826
FT CHARDON 1843
CP POPLAR RIVER 1880
CP COOKE 1866
FT GILBERT 1864
FT HAWLEY
CP REEVE 1868
FT MUSSELSHELL 1860
CT ROCKY PT 1881
FT MAGINNIS 1880
CP PORTER 1880
FT VAN BUREN 1835
FT CASS 1832
FT ASHLEY & HENRY 1823
FT KEOGH 1876
FT BENTON 1822
FT ALEXANDER 1839
FT MANUEL 1807
FT SARPY 1843
CP MERRITT 1890
FT CUSTER 1877
FT C. F. SMITH 1866

FORT BENTON *(1)*

Fort Alexander. 1839-50. A fur post built by Alexander McKenzie and Charles Larpenteur, this stockaded work was on the Yellowstone river opposite the mouth of the Rosebud. From Miles City, go west on I-94 for 33 miles. Turn right (north) and cross the Yellowstone river to the approximate site in the vicinity of Cartersville.

Fort Ashley and Henry. 1823-24. This trading post was near the site of Fort Manuel.

Fort Assinniboine. 1834-35. This 100-foot square temporary post was located on the Yellowstone river at the point where the steamboat *Assinniboine* went aground in the summer of 1834. Its site is unknown but its significance is that it marked the first advance of steamboats beyond the mouth of the Yellowstone.

Fort Assinniboine. 1879-1911. The largest military post constructed in Montana, this was a fort in the grand style. Long rows of brick buildings, castle-like towers at their corners, surrounded an immense parade ground. One of the major buildings and many other smaller ones are left at what is now a U.S. Agricultural Experiment station. From Havre, go south on US 87 for 7 miles to a gravel road. Turn left into station, 1 mile.

Camp Baker, *Fort Logan.*

Fort Belknap. 1871-86. This was a trading center that provided its name to the Indian agency 30 miles eastward. The site is in the vicinity of Chinook, on US 2 about 21 miles east of Havre.

Fort Benton. 1846-81. *Fort Lewis.* A fur post of the American Fur Company, Benton was taken over by the Army in 1869. The adobe trading post was inadequate for troop purposes. Several walls of the old post have been stabilized and an excellent museum tells the story of the post in the town park at the site. The town of Fort Benton is at the head of steamboat navigation of the Missouri river, 41 miles southeast of Great Falls off of US 87.

FORT ASSINNIBOINE *(1)*

FORT ASSINNIBOINE

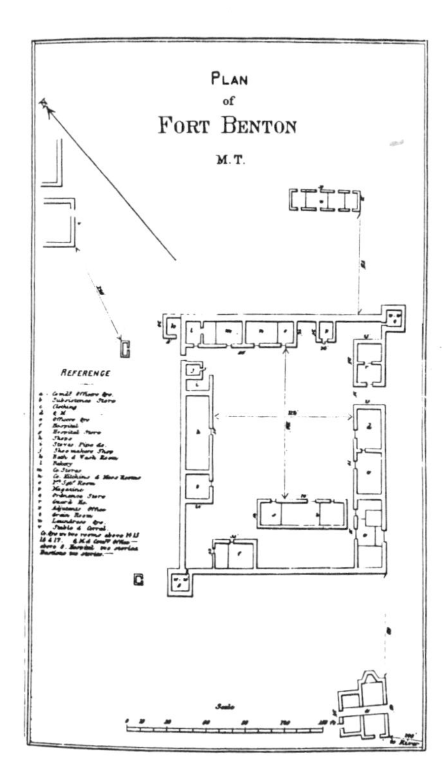

Fort Benton. 1822-23. This fur post was built by Joshua Pilcher at or near the earlier Fort Manuel.

Big Horn Post. *Fort Custer.*

Camp Bridger Pass. 1867. Montana militiamen put up this barricade to protect the Gallatin Valley from hostile Indians after the murder of John Bozeman in 1867. Two other temporary posts were Forts Howie and Elizabeth Meagher. The camp was at Bridger Pass which can be reached from Bozeman city on County route 293.

Fort Browning. 1868-72. This was a trading post. From Malta, go west on US 2 for 18 miles to Dodson. The site was 2 miles west of Dodson on the Milk river.

Fort Brule. *Fort McKenzie.*

Fort Campbell. 1845-60. Originally a wooden stockade, this trading post was first on the south bank of the Missouri near Fort Benton but in 1847 was moved across the stream and closer to Benton. It was built of adobe after the move, causing it to be the first adobe building in Montana. The approximate site is 1 mile west of Fort Benton on the river bank.

Fort Cass. 1832-35. *Tulloch's Fort.* Said to have been 130 feet square, of sapling cottonwood pickets with two bastions at extreme corners, this trading post was built by Samuel Tulloch. To reach the approximate site, go north from Bighorn, on I-94 about 44 miles west of Forsyth, for 2 miles to the south bank of the Yellowstone river.

Fort C.F. Smith. 1866-68. The Hay Field Fight, one of the highlights of Western military history when 31 soldiers held off an estimated 800 Cheyennes, took place eight miles from this isolated Bozeman Trail fort. Under siege almost continually, this 300-foot square stockade was unable to communicate with the outside world for six months in 1866-67. From Hardin, take county 313 to Xavier, 23 miles. From here the route is a fair weather road to Yellowtail Dam. Within sight of the fort site and about a mile short of it, dirt road turns off to the rectangle of low mounds marked by a Boy Scout-placed stone memorial. The property is on Crow Indian tribe land.

Fort Chardon. 1843-45. Trader Alexander Culbertson built this short-lived post and then moved it closer to Fort Benton, changing the name to Fort Lewis. This site can be reached by following the directions to Camp Cooke but continuing north on county 236 across the free ferry. The Fort Chardon site was in the vicinity of the ferry landing on the north bank of the Missouri river.

Fort Connah. 1847-72. This was the last Hudson Bay post established in the United States.

FORT C.F. SMITH *(1)*

The post remained an important trade center until 1872. State historical marker 45 stands on the site near an old stone house from trading days. From Missoula, go north on US 93 for 39 miles. At this point 6 miles north of St. Ignatius is the marker; the fort site is ¼ mile to the east (right side).

Camp Cooke. 1866-70. Indians were active against this stockaded post, scattering the horse herd at least once and later attacking the fort when the troops were away. Almost all traces have disappeared but there are evidences of excavations when the underbrush is not too heavy. From Lewistown, take Montana 19 north for 15 miles to Hilger. Turn left on gravel road, go 23 miles to Lohse Ferry, free ferry across Missouri. Half mile short of ferry landing is a building remaining from Power-Norris store, dating from last half of 19th century. Behind this building is the mouth of the Judith river. Cooke site can be reached by wading the Judith at this point and walking westward 1 mile.

CAMP COOK *(33)*

Camp Cummings. 1867. This was a militia protection against the Indian scare in conjunction with outposts at Bozeman and Bridger Passes. This site was in Virginia City, then the capital of Montana Territory but now a lively ghost town.

Fort Custer. 1877-98. *Big Horn Post.* Scattered cellars surrounding a DAR marker indicate where more than 1,000 soldiers were stationed to keep peace after and 15 miles away from the Custer Massacre of 1876. Most of the buildings served as the nucleus of nearby Hardin after the elaborate post was dismantled. From Hardin, go south on US 87 for 2 miles. After crossing Bighorn river, turn right (west) on dirt road that climbs to top of bluff and site of fort where the marker, cellars, and a golf clubhouse are the only evidences.

FORT CUSTER *(1)*

Fort Elizabeth Meagher. 1867. Named after the wife of the former acting governor of Montana Territory, this stockade was built by the militia during the Indian scares following the murder of John Bozeman. Take I-90 for 6 miles east from Bozeman to the approximate site near the mouth of Rock Creek.

Fort Ellis. 1867-86. Soldiers were dispatched from this key military fort throughout the post-Civil War period; its troops were part of the 1876 three pronged-pincer against the Sioux and Cheyenne that was blunted by the Custer Massacre. From Bozeman, go east on I-90 for 3.4 miles to marker on left (north) side of highway. The Fort Ellis Experiment Station now occupies the site.

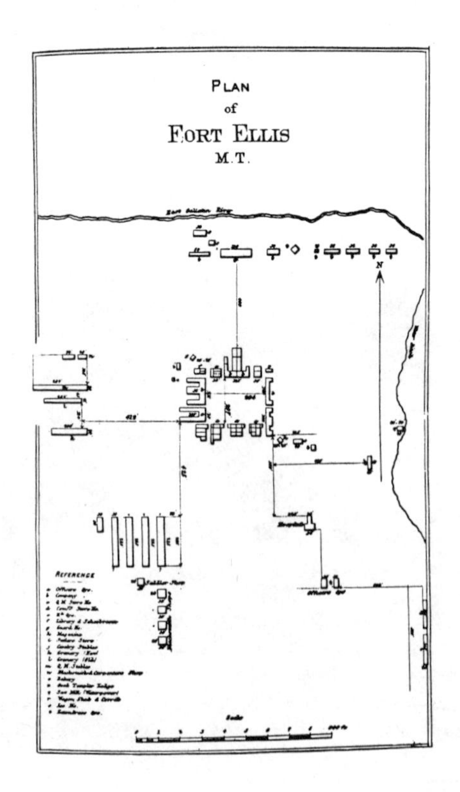

Fort Fizzle. 1877. This series of entrenchments and barricades were erected by men of the 7th U.S. Infantry and local volunteers when word reached Missoula that the Nez Perce Indians were fleeing in their direction. The Indians so outnumbered the defenders when they arrived on July 28, 1877, that the temporary fort's defenses fizzled— hence the uncomplimentary name. From Lolo (on US 93 about 13 miles south of Missoula), take US 12 for 5 miles west (right) of

FORT KEOGH *(1)*

Lolo to where the Lolo Trail enters the Bitterroot Valley.

Fort Galpin. 1862. This was a trading post near the mouth of the Milk river on the Missouri. The site is in the vicinity of modern Fort Peck.

Fort Gilbert. 1864-67. This was a trading post at the edge of the Fort Buford, N.D., reservation, suggesting that one of its economic interests may have been the extracurricular attractions unavailable on the military reservation. From Glendive, go north on Montana 16 for 52 miles to Sidney; 5 miles north of Sidney on Montana 200 is State Historical marker 104 indicating that the fort site is east of the road marker on the bank of the Yellowstone river.

Fort Harrison. *Fort William Henry Harrison.*

Fort Hawley. This fur fort site can be reached only via a considerable overland trek. Follow the directions to Fort Musselshell. From this site, Fort Hawley location can be reached by swimming across Musselshell river and following river to its mouth and intersection with the Missouri river. Follow the bank of the Missouri around to north and west to approximate fort site, approximately 25 miles directly east of US 191 crossing of the river.

Helena Barracks. 1877-78. This was the campsite of troops sent to maintain the peace in Helena. They were quartered at the Helena fairgrounds.

Fort Howie. 1867. This was another militia stockade erected for the Indian scare of 1867. The general site is on the bank of the Yellowstone near the mouth of Shields river. This would put this temporary post approximately 7 miles east of Bozeman.

Fort Jackson. 1833-34. This 50-foot square post was built by trader C.S. Chardon as a wintering-over camp. The approximate site is on the Missouri river at the mouth of the Poplar in the vicinity of the town of Poplar.

Cantonment Jordan. 1859-60. This was a winter camp for the construction crew of military road builder Captain John Mullan while he was pushing a wagon road into the Pacific Northwest. From DeBorgia (83 miles west of Missoula), go 2 miles east on I-90 to State Historical Marker 11 at the site.

FORT KEOGH, Company Quarters *(1)*

Fort Keogh. 1876-1908. *Cantonment on the Tongue River, New Post on the Yellowstone, Tongue River Barracks.* The first site of Fort Keogh was known as Tongue River Barracks and it was from this site next to the Tongue river that General Nelson A. Miles fielded troops in 1876. Later the elaborate new post was built a mile to the west.

Only a well marks the first site; two old officers quarters are at the second site, used by the U.S. Range Livestock Experimental Station.

From Miles City, take Main street west to the edge of town. On the right is the Range Riders Museum and, next to it, one of the officers quarters moved from Fort Keogh. Beyond, in the field next to the river, is the site of Tongue River Cantonment.

Further west 1 mile is the Livestock Experimental Station, site of Fort Keogh. Until destroyed by fire in 1973 the quarters occupied by General Miles were in use at the apex of officers' row.

Fort Kipp. *Fort Stewart.*

Fort LaBarge. 1862-63. The St. Louis firm of LaBarge, Harkness and Company intended this inclosure—300 feet long by 200 wide—to be their principal trading post and named it after one of their founders, the leading Missouri river steamboat captain. After a year of operation, the post was sold to nearby Fort Benton. Follow directions to Fort Benton; Fort LaBarge was west of Fort Benton in the town.

Camp Lewis. 1874. This short-term temporary post was once to the west of Lewistown, but now has been swallowed up by the city. The site is on the western edge of the city.

Fort Lewis. *Fort Benton.*

Fort Lewis. 1845-46. This trading post was on the right bank of the Missouri river opposite Pablois Island, 18 miles above the Fort Benton bridge. This fort was torn down in 1846 and moved to the site of Fort Benton. From Fort Benton go south on US 87 about 14 miles to Carter and the intersection with an improved road. Turn south (left) and cross river. The approximate site was on the south bank of the river.

Fort Lewis. 1846-50. Fort Benton's first name until this trading post was torn down in 1850, Fort Lewis was then built of adobe and rechristened Fort Benton on Christmas Day, 1850, Follow directions to Fort Benton.

Fort Lisa. *Fort Manuel.*

Fort McKenzie. 1832-43. *Fort Brule.* This 140-foot square trading post fell victim to alcohol rather than Indians, although both were involved. It was the reduction in the whiskey ration that increased Indian restlessness and forced abandonment of this prominent fort. Afterward, the Indians burned the deserted stockade; in later years, the remnants often were called Fort Brule. From Fort Benton, go north on US 87 for 11 miles to Loma. The approximate site of Fort McKenzie is on the north bank of the Missouri about 6 miles south of Loma.

Camp Merritt. 1890-98. Providing protection to the Tongue River Agency in the latter stages of Indian difficulties was the mission of this post on Lame Deer Creek in what is now the Northern Cheyenne Indian reservation. From Hardin, take I-90 south 15 miles to US 212 (not far from the Little Big Horn battlefield). Turn left (east) for 42 miles to Lame Deer, vicinity of the site of Camp Merritt.

Fort Missoula. 1877-1946. Troops from Missoula participated in the nearby Battle of the Big Hole in 1877 and in a second battle with the Nez Perce in 1878. From Missoula, take US 93 southwest to the edge of the city. Road to the fort branches off to the right at the city limits. Some period buildings are left amidst modern construc-

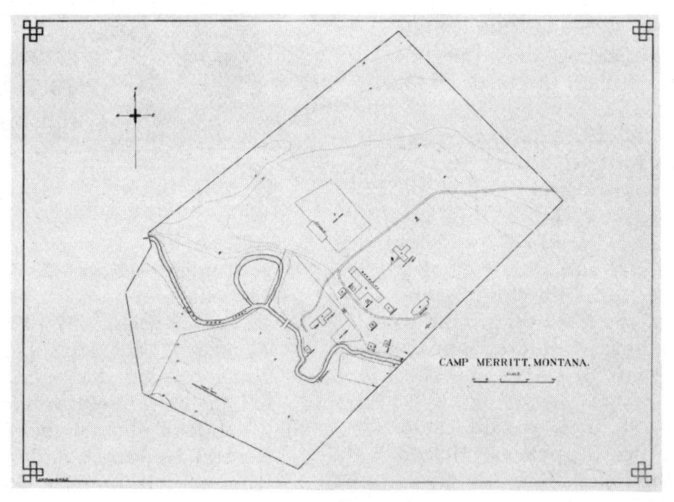

Plan of Camp Merritt *(1)*

FORT MISSOULA *(1)*

FORT LOGAN *(33)*

tion used by reserve units and government agencies. The former quartermaster building is a State Historical Society museum and a non-commissioned officer's quarters has been renovated by the Western Ghost Town Preservation Society.

Fort Logan. 1869-80. *Camp Baker.* This horseshoe-shaped post included a blockhouse that is still at the site. Known as Camp Baker for most of its active life at two sites, Fort Logan's second location has many buildings in modern use as farm residences or utility sheds. From White Sulphur Springs, take asphalt road past post office west of town. In about 1 mile, turn right on gravel road. Go 19 miles to Byrd Ranch, privately owned site of the fort from 1870 to 1880. First location, 1869-70, was ten miles north on the west bank of the Smith river. There are no traces here. Baker name was given to first temporary post, honoring commander, Brevet Colonel Eugene M. Baker; it was renamed to memorialize Captain William Logan, killed in the Battle of the Big Hole, in 1878.

Fort Maginnis. 1880-90. Both Indian and civilian rustlers were the main targets of this large post that was built after the real Indian wars were over. All of the buildings have been dismantled but the foundations still are prominent and, weather depending, marked. From Lewistown, take US 87 east 14 miles to gravel road leading to ghost town of Giltedge. About 1 mile short of Giltedge (buildings can be seen in distance), turn right and follow winding road about 9 miles to site of fort. Small markers appear at road junctions, but do not depend on this. Fort is across Forge Creek, left side of road. Do not attempt to reach site from the north; despite oil company map indications, this route is closed.

Fort Manuel. 1807-11. *Fort Lisa.* The first building in Montana, this fur post was erected on the site of Lewis and Clark's camp of July 26, 1806; seventy years later, the same site was the jumping off point for General Terry's column's unsuccessful attempt to contact Custer before the massacre. State marker 22 is 1 mile west of Bighorn off of I-95 on the south side of the Yellowstone river.

Camp Morris. 1883. This temporary post was officially listed as being on the "west side of Cottonwood Creek near the Sunset Grass Hills." From Shelby, go north on I-15 for 15 miles to Oilmont exit. Turn right (east) and follow gravel and dirt road for about 43 miles of miscellaneous turns to Whitlash, the approximate site of Camp Morris.

Fort Musselshell. 1860-70. This trading post catered to Indians and river workers during its active days; its vicinity was a hangout for rustlers until Vigilantes took over. From Lewistown, go east on US 87 for 30 miles to the point where Montana 200 branches off. Continue on Montana 200 for 55 miles to Mosby. At Mosby, take unimproved road north along the Musselshell river about 35 miles to the Missouri river and the approximate site of the post. State marker 66, 1.5 miles east of Mosby, tells about this fort.

Fort Owen. 1850-59. Father DeSmet built St. Mary's Mission at this site in 1841 but Indian troubles caused his missionaries to sell it to Major John Owen in 1850 for use as a trading post. One building is left. From Missoula go south on US 93 for 28.5 miles to a gravel road. Turn left (east) on gravel road across the Bitterroot river bridge .5 mile.

Fort Peck. 1867. This trading post was a 300-foot square stockade 12-feet high that boasted three bastions on the front and two along the rear. Both soldiers and Indian peace commissioners used it as a base camp. Montana marker 105 tells the story 1.5 miles west of the modern town of Fort Peck on Montana 24. The actual site of the fort has been inundated by Fort Peck reservoir; it was about 1 mile west of the Fort Peck dam.

Fort Piegan. 1831-32. James Kipp built this trading post for the winter. As soon as he left it, after a successful beaver trading season, the fort was burned by the Indians. From Fort Benton, go north on US 87 to Loma, 12 miles. Montana marker 43, ¾ miles south of Loma, tells the story of this fort and also of the Lewis and Clark camp of June 3, 1805. A dirt road, to the right (east), leads to the intersection of the Missouri and Marias river, site of Fort Piegan.

Camp Poplar River. 1880-93. This tiny post has disappeared except for the fact that the town of Poplar, on the site, bears the same name. The post was 2 miles north of the Missouri on the south bank of the Poplar river.

Camp Porter. 1880-81. This single-year camp provided protection to Northern Pacific railroad construction crews. The town of Glendive now occupies the site on I-94.

Fort Raymond. *Post Three Forks.*

Fort Reed. 1870. The decade of the 1870's saw this active trading post in operation amidst favorite Indian hunting grounds. Montana marker 93 tells the story on US 87 about 1 mile west of Lewistown.

Camp Reeve. 1868. This stockaded post was garrisoned by troops from Camp Cooke during the summer of 1868, providing protection for the settlers who tried to establish the town of Musselshell. The project was sponsored by the Montana Hide and Fur Company, had eight buildings and 50 inhabitants, but was abandoned when the Indians rustled the stock and killed two soldiers. The post consisted of tents surrounded by a stockade south of the town site. Follow directions to Fort Musselshell, the approximate site of the town.

Camp Reynolds. *Fort Shaw.*

Cantonment Rocky Point. 1881. This was the construction camp for nearby Fort Maginnis and was abandoned when the fort was completed.

Fort Sarpy. 1843-60. Fifteen-foot high pickets were set into a 100-foot square stockade to protect this final Crow Indian trading post of the American Fur Company. From Forsyth, go west on I-94 for 26 miles to Hysham turnoff. Go north to Yellowstone river; Fort Sarpy was on the south bank of the river at this approximate location.

CANTONMENT STEVENS, 1859
From Railroad Survey Report *(8)*

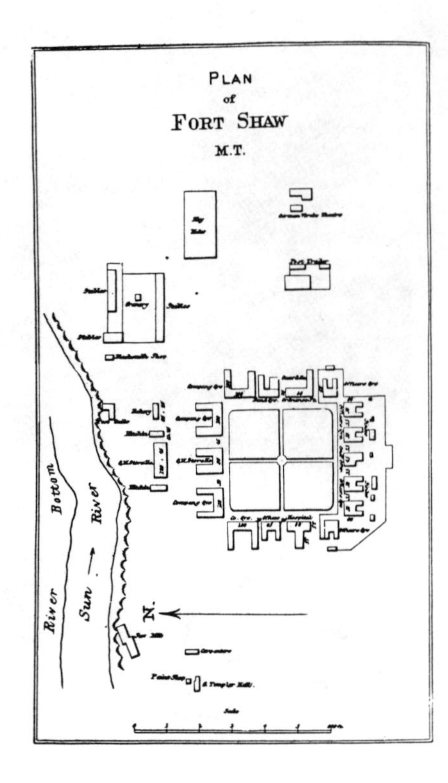

Fort Shaw. 1867-91. *Camp Reynolds.* General John Gibbons took his garrison to the Little Big Horn in 1876 but was too late to prevent the Custer massacre. Built around a 400-foot square, many of the adobe and shingled buildings continue to be used by the county school system. From Great Falls, go west on I-15 and US 89 about 19 miles to the intersection with Montana 200. Follow this for 5 miles to the town of Fort Shaw. The cluster of fort buildings is a half mile north of the town next to the Syn river.

Fort Sherman. 1873-74. This was a trading post at the site of what later became Lewistown. The buildings were dismantled when trade proved unprofitable.

Cantonment Stevens. 1853. This post was so-called after Governor Isaac I. Stevens of Washington, who stayed here in 1859 with Major Owen of Fort Owen and Lieutenant John Mullan, the road builder, during their railroad survey expedition. It included four log buildings, a corral and tents. Mullan's initiative in establishing and erecting the camp drew praise from Stevens who noted that now the government would save money by not having to rent quarters. The site is the location of the community of Stevensville, about 1 mile south of the turnoff to Fort Owens.

Fort Stewart. 1854-63. *Fort Kipp.* Actually two trading posts were established at the same site, the Kipp post coming first and followed by Stewart about 200 yards away. By 1860 both had been burned down and Stewart was rebuilt on the Kipp site because usable chimneys were still standing. From Poplar, go east on US 2 for about 23 miles; walk south across railroad tracks ¾ mile to open plain 1 mile north of Missouri river (where the river makes so-called Devil's Elbow).

Post Three Forks. 1810. *Fort Raymond.* This Lewis and Clark campsite was used by the St. Louis Missouri Fur Company as the location of a 300-foot square double stockade of logs but Indian trouble forced the abandonment of the post after a single summer of operation. From Bozeman, go west on I-90 for 28 miles to Three Forks turnoff. Montana marker 14 gives the history of the Three Forks of the Missouri, 1 mile east of the town of Three Forks. The fort site was on the bank of the Missouri, north of the town, and is believed to have been washed away.

Cantonment on the Tongue River. Tongue River Barracks. *Fort Keogh.*

Tulloch's Fort. *Fort Cass.*

Fort Union. 1826. This trading post was the first Fort Union and is one reason that the famous North Dakota fort is often erroneously said to be in Montana. From Glasgow, go east on US 2 for 28 miles to Frazer, the approximate site of the fort on the banks of the Missouri.

Fort Van Buren. 1835-43. The second American Fur Company trading post on the Yellowstone, Fort Van Buren was burned after its abandonment. The approximate site is probably the same as the first Cantonment on the Tongue River, the early version of Fort Keogh, next to Miles City on I-94.

Fort William Henry Harrison. 1895-1913. The Veterans Administration now occupies this last of many Montana forts, built originally as part of the scheme to consolidate troops into larger camps from which they could be rushed by railroad to the trouble spots. The fort is in Helena.

Cantonment Wright. 1861-62. This was the winter camp for Captain John Mullan's road builders. From Missoula, go east on I-90 for 17 miles to Milltown. The site is a quarter mile west of Milltown on the edge of the highway, marked by Montana marker 9.

New Post on the Yellowstone. *Fort Keogh.*

NEBRASKA

FORT MITCHELL *(31)*

The Platte River Road wound its way through Nebraska in company with the Oregon Trail and military and trading posts flanked both traces. Troops were stationed at many of the stage stops and for that reason many places are included here that otherwise would not qualify as forts.

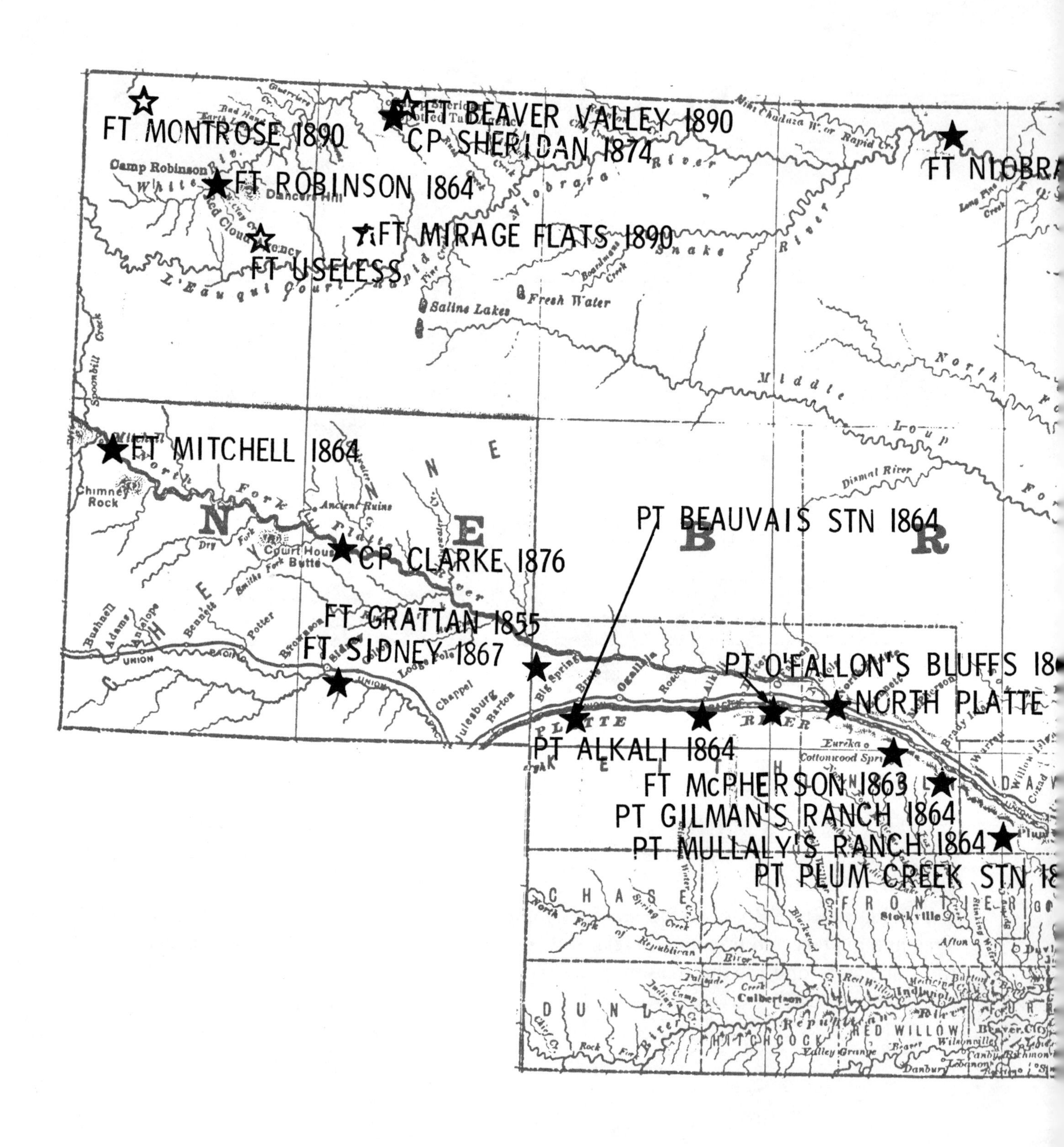
FT MONTROSE 1890
FT BEAVER VALLEY 1890
CP SHERIDAN 1874
FT NIOBRA
Camp Robinson
FT ROBINSON 1864
FT MIRAGE FLATS 1890
FT USELESS
Saline Lakes
Fresh Water
Snake River
Middle Loup
Dismal River
FT MITCHELL 1864
Chimney Rock
Ancient Ruins
Court House
CP CLARKE 1876
PT BEAUVAIS STN 1864
FT GRATTAN 1855
FT SIDNEY 1867
PT O'FALLON'S BLUFFS 18
NORTH PLATTE
PT ALKALI 1864
FT McPHERSON 1863
PT GILMAN'S RANCH 1864
PT MULLALY'S RANCH 1864
PT PLUM CREEK STN 18
Cottonwood Springs
CHASE
FRONTIER
DUNDY
HITCHCOCK
RED WILLOW
Culbertson

CP KEYA PAHA 1879
FT MITCHELL 1833
FT HARTSUFF 1874
FT ATKINSON 1819
LONG'S CAMP 1819
PT COLUMBUS 1864
FT LISA 1812
CABANNE'S POST 1825
FT OMAHA 1863
FT CROOK 1891
NDEPENDENCE 1864
PT JUNCTION STN 1864
FT KEARNY 1846
ARNY 1847
PT PAWNEE RANCH 1864
PT LITTLE BLUE STN 1864

Post Alkali. 1864-66. Troops watched over the Oregon Trail from this stockade-style sod station; earlier, the Pony Express maintained a stop here. Vague outlines of the post can still be seen in a hay meadow south of the South Fork of the Platte river. From Paxton, go south on a gravel road to a ditch bank road after crossing the river. Turn west (left). Site is on private property of B.J. Guynan and permission to visit it should be requested of him in Paxton.

Fort Atkinson. 1819-27. *Cantonment Missouri, Camp on the Missouri.* The first permanent fort in the West – it was so close to the Missouri river that it was inundated in 1821 and had to be moved two miles further west – Atkinson fielded one major Indian campaign. The expedition was in 1823 when 220 men went 640 miles upriver to chastise the Arikaree.

Both versions of Fort Atkinson were built along the same general lines of a long palisade 16 feet high that formed a square 520 feet on each side.

From Omaha, go north on US 73 for 15 miles to the town of Fort Calhoun. The local historical museum is in the center of the town on the highway (left side).

To go to Fort Atkinson site, turn east (right) from US 73 on Madison street for 1/2 mile to 7th street. Turn south (right) for 1/2 mile to a side road on the left (east); take this road for 1/10 of a mile to the fort reconstruction.

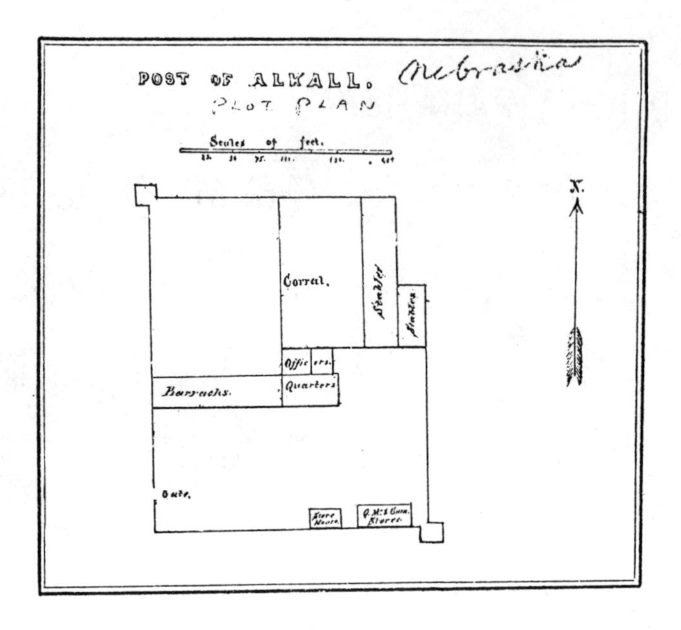

Post Beauvais Station. 1864-66. A company of Nebraska Cavalry was located at this site between the Overland road and the South Platte river. Inside the 325- by 125-foot stockade were the corral, stables, barracks, officers' quarters and storehouse. Remnants at the site suggest the locations of the blacksmith shop and telegraph office. From Brule, go south to the South Platte river bridge. Just south of the bridge on the west (right) side is the ranch headquarters of Herbert Beal who can provide directions to the Beauvais post's site on his private property.

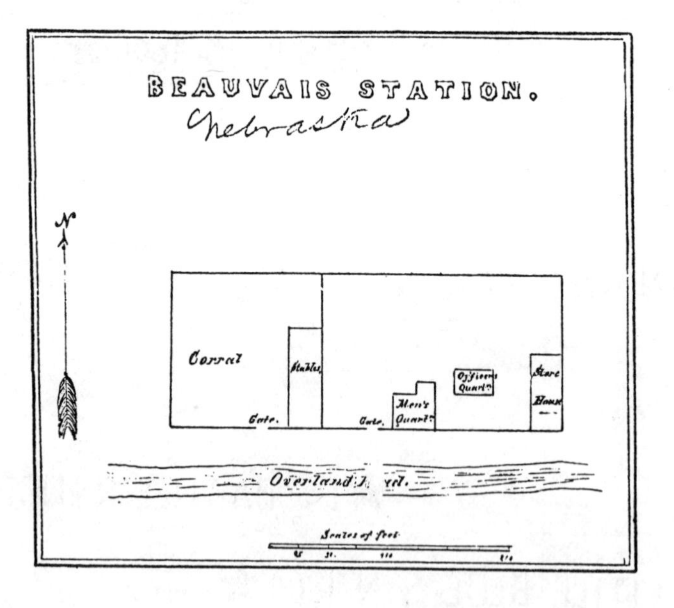

Fort Beaver Valley. 1890-91. Built by settlers at the same time as Fort Montrose, the site was near Camp Sheridan, 15 miles northwest of Chadron. The unmarked site is in Beaver Valley; directions should be requested locally in Wayside, on US 285 a mile south of the South Dakota border.

Cabanne's Post. See entry for *Fort Lisa,* a nearby fur fort.

Fort Calhoun. This is the name by which the site of Fort Atkinson and the nearby town came to be known after Atkinson was abandoned. The name change was in honor of Secretary of War John Calhoun.

Fort Childs. *Fort Kearny.*

Camp Clarke. 1876. Next to the North Platte river bridge built by Henry T. Clarke, this camp housed troops who were assigned to guard both ends of the bridge. All traces of the camp and other buildings were destroyed by a prairie fire in 1910. From Scottsbluff, go east on US 26 for

37.9 miles (this is 13 1/2 miles past Bayard) to the site of Camp Clarke.

Post Columbus. 1864-66. A stockade in the center of Columbus gave protection to the settlers in 1863 then a year later Iowa Cavalry were stationed in the town. Galvanized Yankees were stationed here at the end of the Civil War to protect a pontoon bridge over the Loup river. Columbus is at the intersection of US 81 and US 30. From the center of the city go east on 14th street to 18th avenue; turn south (right) to 6th street. Turn east (left) to the Buffalo Square at 18th avenue, site of the post in a historic park.

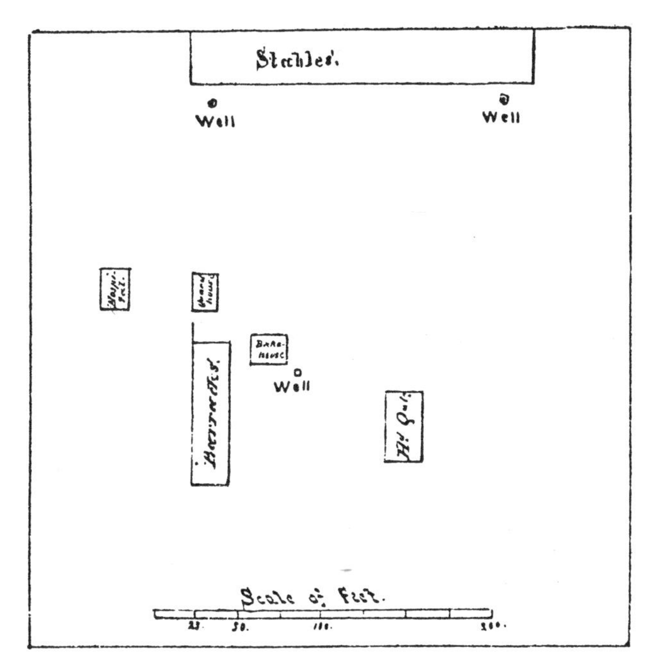

Plan of Post Columbus

Fort Cottonwood and **Post at Cottonwood Springs.** *Fort McPherson.*

Fort Crook. 1891-1948. The "old Army" evidences at this post have been modernized into Offutt Air Force Base, the headquarters of the Strategic Air Command. Officers row, barracks, and other historic buildings remain. Go south on US 73-75 about 8 miles from downtown Omaha to Bellevue; the entrance to Offutt is here.

Post Gilman's Ranch. 1864-66. Mark Twain tells in *Roughing It* of his visit to this ranch; across the Platte Valley road were the Army's stables and seven-room barracks occupied by a company of Nebraska Cavalry. There is a pump-and-wagon-wheel marker at the site. From Brady on I-80 go south about 5 miles to a dirt road. Turn east (left) for 4.2 miles to the end of the road (where it curves to the right). At this point is the station marker on privately owned property.

Fort Gillette. This was an earthwork fortification at the second Fort Kearny.

Government Corral. *Omaha Quartermaster Depot.*

Fort Grattan. 1855. A small field work built after the Battle of Blue Water, this fort was occupied for only about three weeks in September, 1855. The abandoned earthwork, usually called the "old sod fort," was a landmark near Ash Hollow on the Oregon Trail for many years. From Scottsbluff, go east on US 26 about 90 miles to where it crosses the North Platte river below Lewellen. About 1 mile beyond the crossing is the Ash Hollow cemetery, on the right (west) side of the highway. Across from the cemetery is a left turn onto a county road. Follow this road about 4 miles across a sand draw, angle to the northeast across a hay meadow to the south bank of the old river channel. The Grattan site is a large mound covered with brush alongside the bank. Fair weather road only.

Fort Hartsuff. 1874-81. *Post on the North Fork of the Loup River.* This post brought salvation to the Loup river valley, but not so much for the protection that it afforded as the employment it provided the settlers during the grasshopper scourge days when it was built. Many buildings are left as testimony to the efforts of Ord optometrist Dr. Glen Auble who owned and protected the site until he could convince the state to accept it as a gift. The restored post is now a state park. From Grand Island, go 23 miles north on US 281 to St. Paul. Turn left on Nebraska 11 to Ord, 41 miles and continue onward to Elyria, 7 miles. Follow signs from Elyria for 3 miles to Fort Hartsuff State Historical Park.

Fort Independence. 1864. A settler fort built by farmer William Stolley during the Indian War of 1864, this was a 24-foot square stockade heavily banked with sod for protection against flaming arrows. The stockade had 25 loopholes and also a

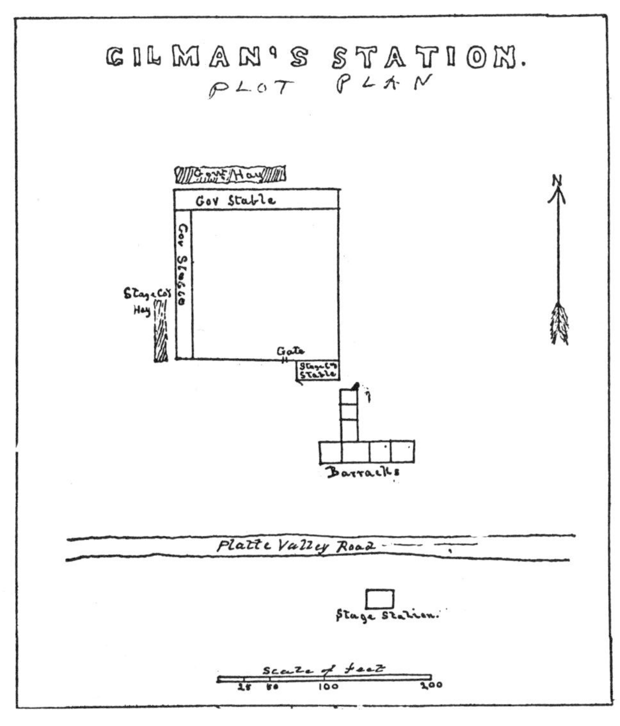

FORT KEARNY *(7)*

88-foot long underground stable. From Grand Island, go south on US 34 for 1.6 miles to signs to Stolley State Park (right side). Within the park is the site of Fort Independence; some of the buildings in this 43-acre park used timbers from the fort.

Post Junction Station. 1864-66. Not to be confused with a post of similar name and period in Colorado, this station was at the intersection of the Nebraska City road with the road between Fort Kearney and Plattsmouth south of the South Channel of the Platte river. Its stables and corral were 1/4 mile from the huts occupied by the troops. The approximate site is southeast of the Grand Island exit on I-80, where it intersects with US 3.

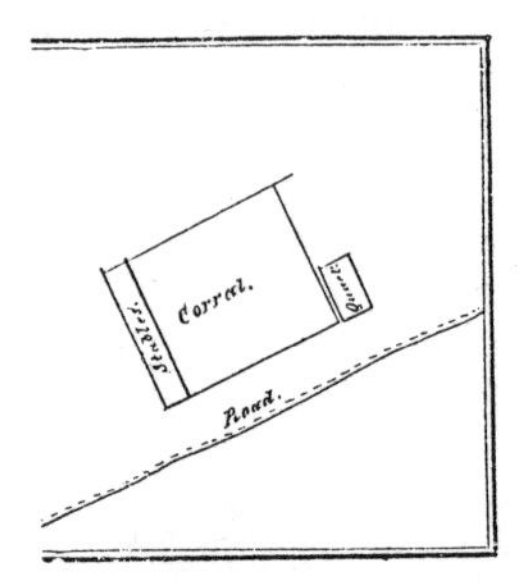

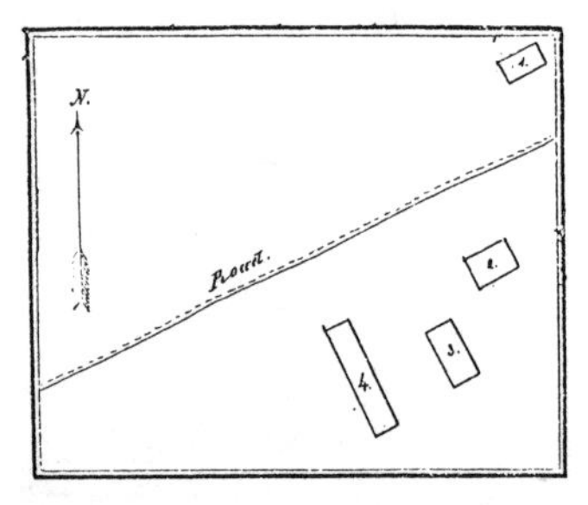

Plan of Junction Station

Fort Kearny. 1846-71. *Fort Childs.* After a year as a blockhouse-style post overlooking the Missouri river at Nebraska City, Fort Kearny was moved to its permanent site where it was a key to the Oregon Trail. Its frame buildings were scattered over four acres cornerstoned by two earthwork fortifications, Forts Mitchell and Gillette. This is a state park in which the building sites have been marked and a stockade reconstructed. The first post is on the Main street of Nebraska City. To visit the second site, go south from the city of Kearny on Nebraska 44 for 3.8 miles; turn left (east) for 4.4 miles to the state park, left (north) side of road.

Camp Keya Paha. 1879. One of many camps established to watch over the Indians during a single season, this camp was outposted from Fort Randall, 28 miles to east. This location would place it south of Naper (on Nebraska 12) and on the Keya Paha river, but the exact site is uncertain (and often placed in South Dakota).

Fort Lisa. 1812-20. The principal trading post of the plains region during its active years, this fur fort was built by Manuel Lisa. The fort was succeeded in 1825 by Cabanne's Trading Post nearby. This, in turn, was moved in 1840 to the vicinity of Bellevue. There is nothing at the site. From Omaha, go north on US 73 for 8.7 miles to Ponca road. Turn right (east) 1.9 miles to a junction; turn left (north) up a steep hill to a point, 4 miles, from which the probable site of Fort Lisa can be seen along the Missouri river. Hummel Park on River drive in suburban Omaha once claimed to be the location of Lisa's and Cabanne's posts, but research has shown this location to be too far south.

Post Little Blue Station. 1864-66. One company of Nebraska Militia manned this rectangular guard station that tried to keep peace in this massacre-prone area. The 1864 Eubank Massacre-

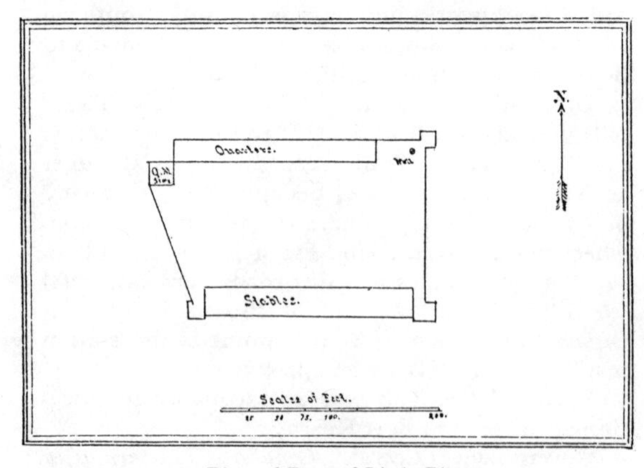

Plan of Post of Little Blue

kidnapping took place nearby. The site is reached by a series of farm roads to the crossing of the Little Blue river 2 3/4 miles northwest of Oak; directions should be asked in Oak to the marker at Little Blue Crossing.

Long's Camp. 1819-20. The Missouri river expedition under Major Stephen S. Long spent the winter of 1819-20 at this temporary camp. There are no traces. Follow the directions to Fort Lisa from Omaha. From the observation point for Fort Lisa, continue for 4.8 miles further on this dirt road running between the bluff and the river to the approximate site of the camp.

Cantonment McKean. *Fort McPherson.*

Camp McKean. *Post at Omaha.*

Fort McPherson. 1863-80. *Cantonment McKean, Post at Cottonwood Springs, Fort Cottonwood.* A five-company post under the McKean name in 1863, this fort took the Cottonwood title until changed in 1866 to honor a Union general. Its main function was to inspect all trains passing on the Oregon Trail, and to insure that they were properly armed. The post cemetery is the only remnant of the fort; it is now a National Cemetery where the dead of many Western fort cemeteries have been re-buried. From North Platte, go east on I-80 for 13 miles to the Maxwell exit. Go south about 2 miles to the cemetery, right side of road. Continue further south on this road, bearing left, 1 mile to a soldier statue which marks the site of the fort.

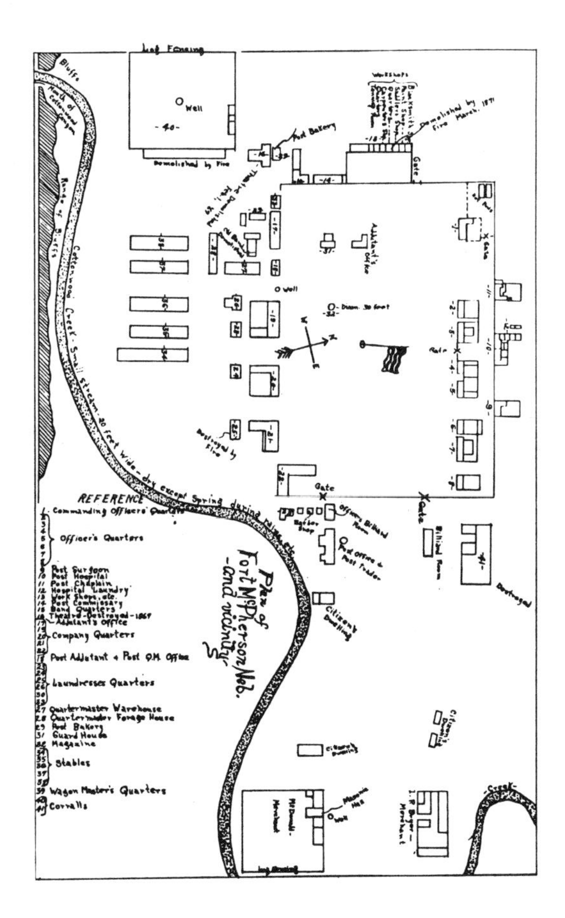

Camp at the Military Bridge, N.T. *Post of Omaha.*

Fort Mirage Flats. 1890-91. A settler fort built for the same reason as Fort Montrose, this was a sod imitation of the old frontier blockhouse, including a plank door and loopholes for rifles. The site is southeast of Hay Springs, in northwestern Nebraska on US 20; directions should be requested locally to Mirage Flats.

Cantonment Missouri. *Fort Atkinson.*

Camp Mitchell. *Post at Omaha.*

Fort Mitchell. 1833-37. Narcisse Le Clerc established this trading post but it appears that its major contribution to the area was the fuel its timbers supplied to passing steamboats after the post was abandoned. The site is in the vicinity of the ferry landing 3 miles east of Niobrara (at the junction of Nebraska 12 and 14).

FORT MITCHELL *(31)*

Fort Mitchell. 1864-67. *Camp Shuman.* A fort in the traditional style of stockade, blockhouse, rifle ports and all, this one company post guarded the Oregon Trail as it dropped down from Mitchell Pass in the shadow of 600-foot high Scott's Bluff. From Scottsbluff (a one-worded city named after a two-worded natural wonder), go west on Nebraska 92 across the North Platte river. Take the first left, head south about 1 mile. On the west side (right side of road) at the top of the rise are markers for the fort and the Oregon Trail; the fort site is across the road on the left (east) side.

Fort Mitchell. This was an earthwork fortification at the second Fort Kearny.

Fort Montrose. 1890-91. The settlers dug this fort at the time of the so-called Wounded Knee Massacre in nearby South Dakota. Atop a pinnacle on the Konrath farm at Montrose, the fort consisted of a circular trench reinforced with a breastwork; underneath was an underground room, 20 by 30 feet and seven feet high, for the protection of the families. From Crawford, go north on Nebraska 2 for about 30 miles to a turnoff to the left about 2 miles south of the South Dakota line. Take this turnoff to the west about 12 miles to Montrose, site of the "fort" where a marker is at the location.

Post Mullaly's Ranch. 1864-66. Variously spelled as "Mullala's" and "Millillas," the ranch was owned by Patrick Mullaly and served earlier as a Pony Express station under the designation of "Midway Station." There was a company of Nebraska Cavalry stationed here in a small enclosure to watch the Platte Valley road south of the Platte river. The original station has been carefully preserved by the Williams family, the modern owners, at its site on the Lower 96 ranch. From Gothenburg, go south on Kansas 47 for 3 miles to turnoff (left) to Lower 96 ranch, privately owned. The station is incorporated into the modern ranch-house and has a protective roof.

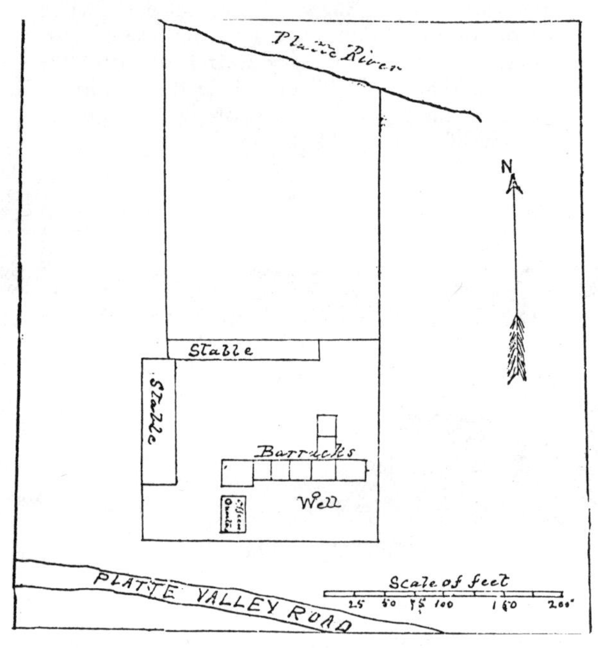

Plan of Post Millillas

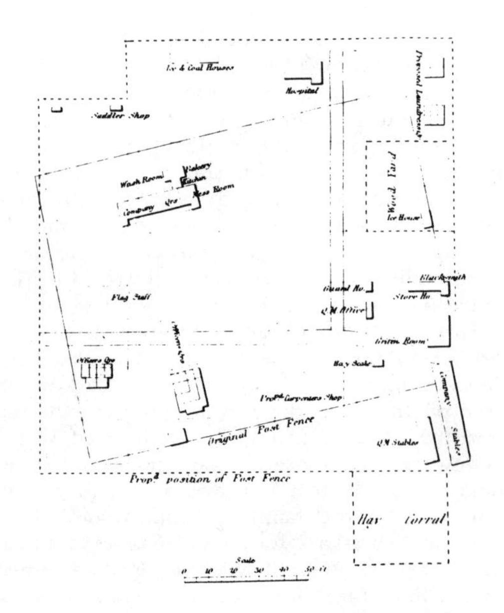

Plan of North Platte Station

Fort Niobrara. 1880-1906. The latter days of the Indian Wars depended heavily upon this large permanent post. Although all of the Army buildings have been dismantled, their locations can still be identified by the foundation outlines of almost every building. A museum at the nearby Fish and Wildlife Service headquarters includes photographs and information on the fort. From Valentine, at the intersection of US 20 and 83, go east on Nebraska 12 for 5 miles to the Fort Niobrara National Wildlife Refuge, the post's site is presently under the jurisdiction of the Department of the Interior.

Post on the North Fork of the Loup River. *Fort Hartsuff.*

North Platte Station. 1867-81. *Camp Sergeant, Camp Sargent.* Protecting the railroad and serving as a supply depot were the two major missions of this town post. Most of the buildings were of pine and the 127- by 30-foot barracks survived until well into the 20th century. The site of the post is in the 400 block of West Front street, across from the Hickman Lumber company, in North Platte.

Post O'Fallon's Bluffs. 1864-66. One company of Iowa Cavalry protected the Platte Valley road at this point, using as their headquarters a 125-foot square stockaded stables-corral, a six-room barracks and a blacksmith shop. Although O'Fallon's Bluffs are still prominent, the site of the post is indefinite, possibly bisected by I-80. From Sutherland, go south on Kansas 25 to the left turn to Sutherland Reservoir. Do not turn but

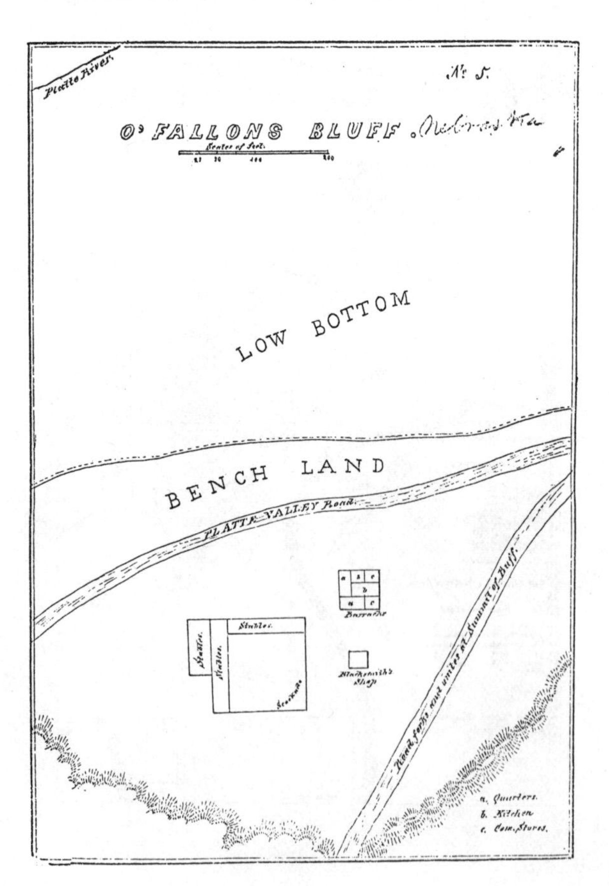

continue westward for 3.3 miles. Then turn south (left) for 1 mile. Post site was in field at right (west) side of road.

Post at Omaha. 1862-66. *Camp Mitchell. Camp McKean. Camp at the Military Bridge, N.T.* Rented quarters and the territorial capitol were used by the Army to man the headquarters of the Military District of Nebraska. The Herndon House, at the northwest corner of 9th and Farnam streets was headquarters and troops were billeted in the capitol — also later used as headquarters. The 7th Iowa and other troops who were encamped on the west edge of Omaha informally termed their tent clusters Camp McKean and Camp Mitchell after various commanders of the District of Nebraska. A company-sized post was set up at North Omaha Creek after an 1864 Indian raid; this was designated Camp at the Military Bridge, N.T. There are no modern-day evidences of this five year Army tenancy in Omaha city.

Omaha Quartermaster Depot. 1866-1964. *Government Corral.* The railroad importance of Omaha dictated that the Army establish a supply distribution point there for the western frontier. Initially a rectangularly shaped depot with two temporary storehouses, the depot was built along the Union Pacific siding from Thirteenth and Webster streets. In 1879 the Army tried to move depot activities to a new storehouse at Fort Omaha but Omaha businessmen counteracted by donating a new city site for another depot. Started in 1880, the depot was a seven acre triangle formed by modern Twenty-second street on the west and Woolworth avenue on the north with the mainline Union Pacific tracks closing the triangle. Two of the original buildings still stand, a long brick storehouse and the brick oil house. An ordnance storehouse and a quartermaster and commissary storehouse are left from 1889 and 1894 construction. The depot went through various missions including supply point for 34 Civilian Conservation Camps in the 1930s, a POW camp and World War II supply point, and, in 1958, Headquarters for the XVI Army Corps.

Fort Omaha. 1863-1947. *Omaha Barracks.* General W. T. Sherman said that this headquarters post was so far to the rear that it should be called "hind quarters" during the period when General George Crook commanded operations of the Department of the Platte from here. Most of the brick buildings dating from the late 19th century are left at what is now a city park with Crook's former quarters a museum. From downtown Omaha, go north on 30th street (US 73) to Fort street where the main entrance is on the left. A former field grade officers' quarters has been moved and now is a private residence at 4758 N. 24th street. It was built in 1881 and moved to this site in 1896.

Post Pawnee Ranch. 1864-66. At the intersection of Pawnee creek and the Little Blue river, this was a palisaded station that included bastions at all four corners. The general site includes the remnants of the town of Spring Ranch and a

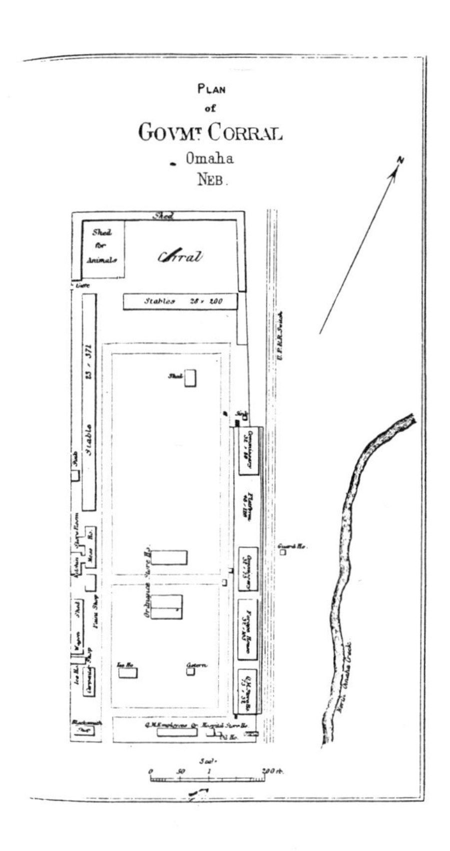

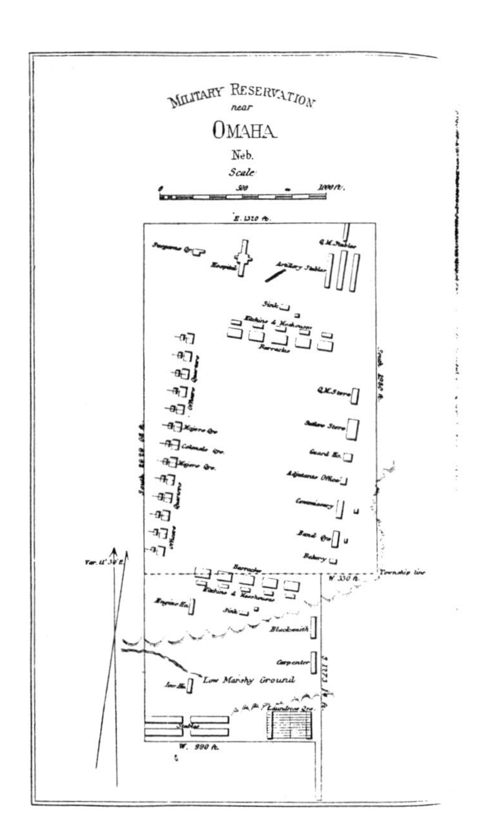

OLD FORT ROBINSON *(1)*

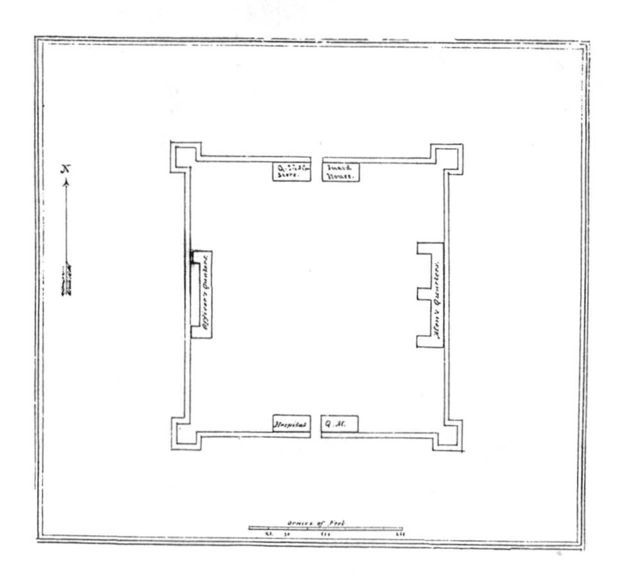

fenced-in grave dating from 1860. From Fairfield, go west for 6 miles on Nebraska 74. Turn south (left) for 2 miles to the Little Blue river and the site.

Post Plum Creek Station. 1864-66. Midway in the mile distance between the stage station and Plum Creek ranch, this was a 325-foot square that included six rough buildings. An important location, the post was manned by three companies of Nebraska Cavalry in 1864 and two companies of Galvanized Yankees after the war. The modern site includes the fenced-in graveyard of fourteen victims of the 1865 Plum Creek Massacre. From the Overton exit on I-80 about 11 miles east of Lexington, go south 1.5 miles to a dead end. Turn west (right) for 3.5 miles to the cemetery on the right (north) side of the gravel road.

Camp Recovery. 1820. This was a temporary camp three miles south of Fort Atkinson where sick men were treated for scurvy and other diseases after the winter of 1819-20. Follow directions to Fort Atkinson.

Post at Red Cloud Agency. *Fort Robinson.*

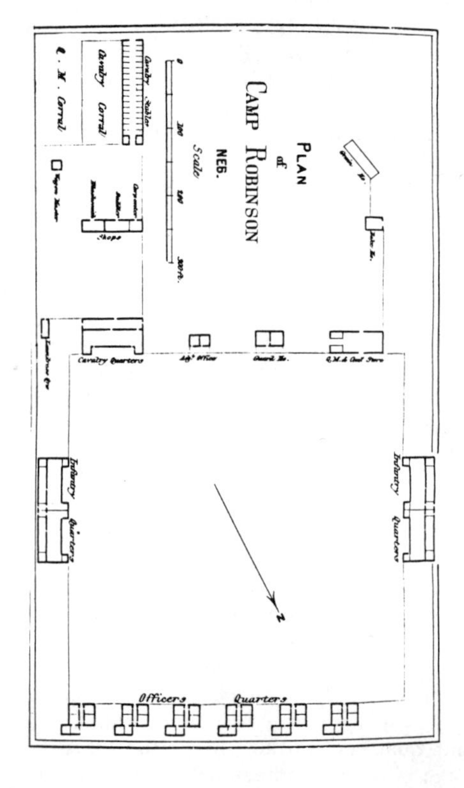

Fort Robinson. 1864-1948. *Post at Red Cloud Agency.* Dull Knife's warriors died against the bluffs to the rear of the 1879 Fort Robinson and Crazy Horse was shot dead near the original guardhouse here. This historic post was active in the Army until after World War II. Most of the buildings from the Army days are still maintained by various state and federal agencies as offices. The state sponsors an outstanding museum, has signs at the locations of the early Army buildings, and provides hotel-type accommodations for visitors in former Army quarters. From Scottsbluff, go north on Nebraska 87 for 48 miles to Nebraska 2. Turn left (west) for 26 miles to Crawford. The Fort Robinson State Historical Park flanks US 20 one mile west of Crawford.

Camp Sargent and **Camp Sergeant.** *North Platte Station.*

Camp Sheridan. 1874-81. *Camp near Spotted Tail Agency.* This cluster of frame buildings served variously as an outpost of Fort Robinson and as an independent command. Tradition has it that the body of Crazy Horse was kept on a scaffold on a bluff overlooking the fort. There is nothing at the site in a farm pasture on the Cilek ranch, privately owned 14 miles north of Hay Springs on Beaver road.

Camp Shuman. *Fort Mitchell.*

Fort Sidney. 1867-94. *Sidney Barracks.* The troopers of this lively railroad town spent more time keeping and breaking the peace of the entrance to the Black Hills than in Indian fighting. Tradition has it that Sidney's forces arrived at the Battles of the Little Big Horn and Wounded Knee after the shots had been fired, but in time to clean up the field. Several fort buildings, including a restored duplex officers' quarters and the magazine, are left. The city of Sidney is on US 30 in western Nebraska; the fort site is 1 block south of US 30 at the eastern edge of the city.

Camp near Spotted Tail Agency. *Camp Sheridan.*

Fort Useless. A typical settler protection from the Indians, this fort's value was hinted by its name, although this disregards the deterrent value of the sod enclosure. The fort site is now a ranch. From Chadron, go west on US 20 for 11 miles to Whitney; turn left (south) for 9 miles to the privately owned ranch, the site of the fort.

PLAN
of
CAMP SHERIDAN
NEB.

Scale

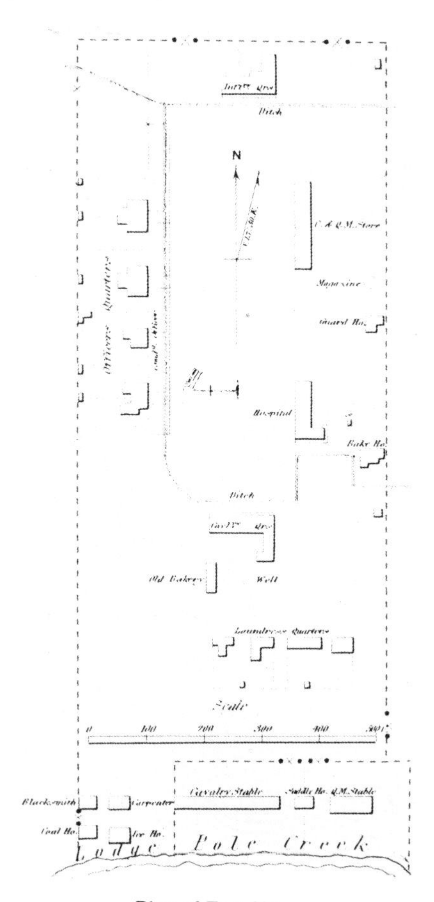

Plan of Fort Sidney

FORT SIDNEY *(7)*

NEVADA

FORT CHURCHILL *(1)*

Few military posts were maintained permanently in Nevada, but there were many camps and temporary forts during the Pyramid Lake War before the Civil War and volunteer or settler forts during the Civil War. Although difficult to reach, there are remnants at many of these sites that make a visit interesting.

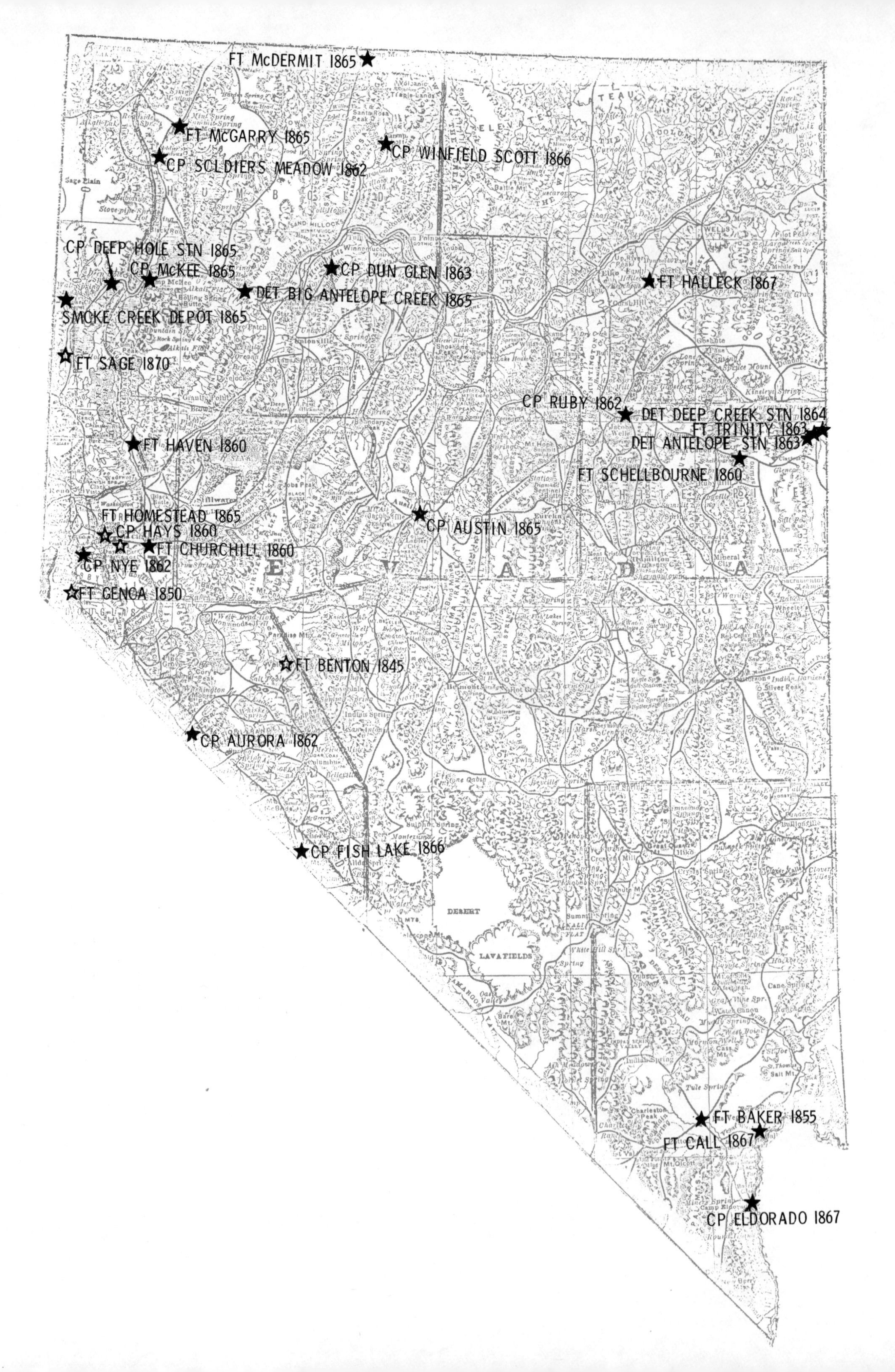

FT McDERMIT 1865
FT McGARRY 1865
CP WINFIELD SCOTT 1866
CP SOLDIERS MEADOW 1862
CP DEEP HOLE STN 1865
CP McKEE 1865
CP DUN GLEN 1863
DET BIG ANTELOPE CREEK 1865
FT HALLECK 1867
SMOKE CREEK DEPOT 1865
FT SAGE 1870
CP RUBY 1862
DET DEEP CREEK STN 1864
FT TRINITY 1863
DET ANTELOPE STN 1863
FT HAVEN 1860
FT SCHELLBOURNE 1860
FT HOMESTEAD 1865
CP HAYS 1860
CP AUSTIN 1865
FT CHURCHILL 1860
CP NYE 1862
FT GENOA 1850
FT BENTON 1845
CP AURORA 1862
CP FISH LAKE 1866
DESERT
LAVA FIELDS
FT BAKER 1855
FT CALL 1867
CP ELDORADO 1867

Las Vegas, Nevada in 1876 *(12)*

Detachment at Antelope Station. 1863-64. California Infantry Volunteers frequently manned this stage station during Indian scares. The station had been burned by Indians in 1859. From Fort Schellbourne, continue eastward on the improved road for about 30 miles; the site is within the Goshute Indian Reservation and permission to visit should be obtained.

Camp Aurora. 1862. This was a short-term camp at which Fort Churchill troops were stationed to arbitrate differences between the settlers and Indians in the Mono Lake and Adobe Meadows areas – and to keep an eye on a secessionist minority in the fledgling town of Aurora, a mile away. There are no remains of the Army site but the town is one of Nevada's well-vandalized ghost towns. From Hawthorne, go south on Nevada 31 for 14 miles to right turn (north) on gravel road marked toward Bodie. In 13 miles this rough road meets a junction; take left turn on to rougher gravel road which in 8 miles will arrive at the remnants of Aurora. The Army site was a mile from here at an uncertain location.

Camp at Austin. 1865. This mining town was in its boom days when a detachment of soldiers was stationed here for a short period. The modern town is half ghost, as suggested by the shells of buildings that dot the area, but the new buildings outnumber any construction that may date from the Army's occupation. Austin is on US 50 in almost the center of the state.

Fort Baker. 1855-58. *Mormon Fort, Detachment at Las Vegas.* This 150-foot square adobe fortification was built by the Mormons who founded Las Vegas. It served as a stage station and patrol base after the Mormons were summoned back to Salt Lake. In 1861, the Union announced plans to "re-establish" Fort Baker at Las Vegas although no federal post by this or any other name actually had existed at the town. It appears that the "Fort Baker" tag was applied to the Mormon Fort to mislead the Confederates. Meanwhile, goods prominently marked for Fort Baker shipment actually were shipped to Fort Yuma where they supported the California Column's eastward march. The Mormon Fort is an adobe building at 908 Las Vegas boulevard, next to the Elks Club.

Fort Benton. 1845. Legend has it that in November, 1845, John Charles Fremont passed this way with Kit Carson while on the third Fremont western expedition. He named Walker Lake after his guide and his campsite after his father-in-law, Missouri Senator Thomas Hart Benton. The half-dozen rock ruins at this site are hard to reconcile with this short-term occupancy but don't tell that to any local history buffs! From Luning, 29 miles east of Hawthorne on US 95, go north on Nevada 23 for 3 miles to dirt road on left (west). Follow this rough track, once the main supply route for the area, for 5 miles to where it runs past the ruins.

Detachment at Big Antelope Creek. 1865. Not to be confused with the troops at Antelope Station on the opposite border of Nevada, the Big Antelope Creek Station was guarded by California Cavalry. From Winnemuca, go southwest about 33 miles on I-80 to the Imlay interchange (beyond Mill City). Turn right (west) on this improved road about 15 miles to the Antelope Range crossing, the approximate site of the station.

Fort Call. 1867. *Detachment at Callville, Fort Callville.* Troops occasionally outposted this Colorado river port, now inundated by Lake Mead. The approximate site can be reached by heading east from Henderson on Nevada 41 for about 30 miles; the town and Army location was on the right (east) of the road, now under the lake.

Camp near Carson City. *Camp Nye.*

Post on Carson River, Utah Territory. *Fort Churchill.*

Fort Churchill. 1860-69. *Churchill Barracks, Post on Carson River, Utah Territory.* Started as an elaborate and expensive post, Fort Churchill still had an expansive layout despite economy cuts. It was Nevada's Civil War military headquarters, both for recruit training and patrols against the Indians and secessionists. The adobe remnants of today actually are from the 1935 CCC reconstructions. From Reno, take I-80 east for 32 miles to Fernley turnoff, the intersection with US Alternate 95. Go south on US Alternate 95 about 23 miles to Nevada 2B; turn right (west) on this gravel road which leads into Fort Churchill State Park where numerous ruins and the cemetery from Fort Churchill are in varying stages of repair, depending upon whether the Legislature has appropriated money for the park recently.

Camp Clark. This was a mustering-in post at Carson City during the Spanish-American War.

Detachment at Deep Creek Station. 1864. This was a temporary stopover for troops protecting the stage route of eastern Nevada. A detachment manned the station fulltime for a short period in the spring of 1864. From Fort Schellbourne, go eastward on the improved road to just beyond Fort Trinity site. The approximate location of Deep Creek Station was about 3 miles northeast of Fort Trinity.

Camp Deep Hole Station. 1865. A detachment of Nevada Cavalry outposted this stage station after it was abandoned in April, 1865. From Gerlach, the approximate site of Camp McKee, continue north on Nevada 34 for about 9 miles to an improved road on the left (west). Follow this road about 7 miles in a southwesterly direction skirting the Smoke Creek Desert on the left to the approximate site of Deep Hole Station.

Camp Dun Glen. 1863; 1865-66. California Volunteers manned this town post twice even though they were outnumbered and out-gunned by settlers. Several bloody Indian fights were fielded from here before the soldiers left. Excavations at the site may be from the town and camp of Dun Glen or from the later town of Chafey on the same site. From Winnemucca, take I-30 west for 28 miles to the Mill City interchange. Go east from the interchange onto a dirt road at the south edge of the "town" of Mill City. Follow this sand-drifted road for 6 miles into cluster of ranch buildings in Dun Glen canyon; at the one intersection, 1/2 mile from the start, go left. This is a fair-weather, heavy-duty route; the property is privately owned.

Detachment Eight Mile Station. *Fort Trinity.*

Camp Eldorado. 1867. *Camp in El Dorado Canyon.* This temporary post was manned by a detachment that watched over mining and settler activity north of Fort Mojave. Take US 95 from Las Vegas to Nevada 60 (which is 10 miles south of Alunite intersection). Turn left (east) on Nevada 60 to Nelson, 12 miles. Turn left (east) at Nelson across the Eldorado mountains and go east 7 miles to the Colorado river and approximate site of Camp Eldorado.

Camp Fish Lake. 1866-67. *Fish Lake Valley Military Station.* Troop detachments frequently outposted this camp in order to protect the mining settlements. The site was so temporary that nothing associated with it can be identified in the general area of the scattering of houses of "modern" Fish Lake. From Hawthorne, go east on US 95 for 67 miles to Coaldale; turn right (west) on US 6 for 7 miles to Nevada 3A. Take 3A south (left turn) for 28 miles to unimproved road on left (east); follow this road for about 4 miles to what is left of Fish Lake.

Fort Genoa. 1850-57. *Mormon Station.* This stockade was built by the Mormon founders of Genoa but never was an official Army post. It was a rest and re-stocking place for travellers before they entered the Sierra Nevada mountains on California's border. The original log stockade

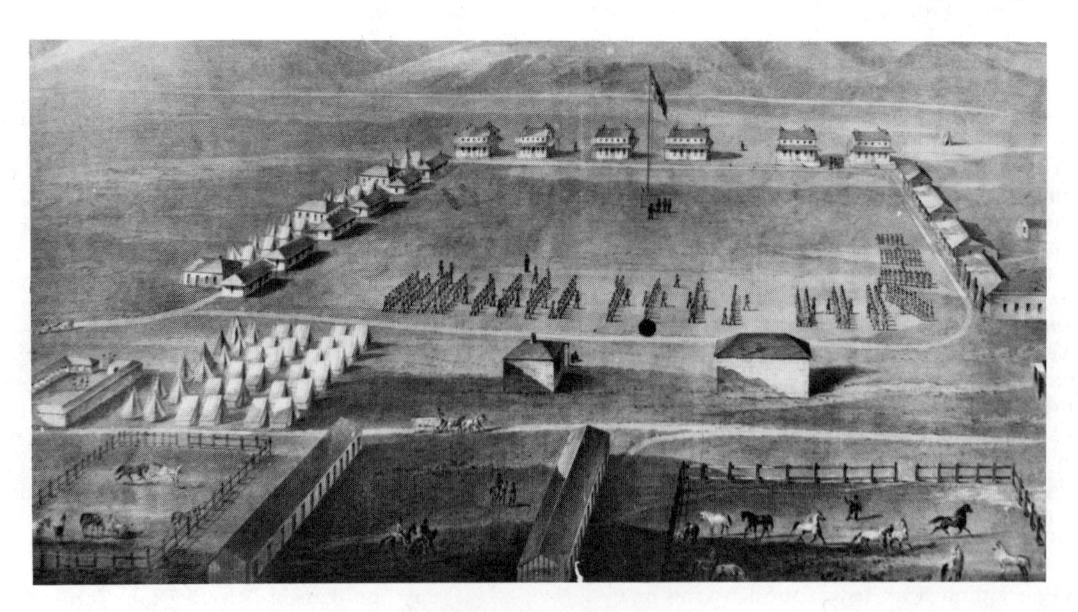

FORT CHURCHILL *(1)*

station burned in 1910 but was reconstructed as a park in 1947. From Carson City, take US 395 south 11 miles to Nevada 57. Turn right (west) 4 miles where the route ends at Genoa. The stockade can be seen from the town intersection.

Granite Creek Station. Detachment at Granite Creek. *Fort McKee.*

Fort Halleck. 1867-86. When this post was founded, the impression was that the climate was warm — the fact that oftentimes the temperature hit minus 50 degrees was not considered. This was not the biggest problem of the garrison; disease, barroom fights and Indians took their toll. Now only the building excavations and stone outlines are left. From Elko, go east on I-80 for 20 miles to Halleck interchange at Nevada 11. Turn right to Halleck townsite, 1 mile, and continue south through Halleck for 17 miles on a dirt road to a stone marker, left side of the road. The fort site was at the far end of the pasture behind the sign.

CAMP HALLECK, Officers' Quarters *(11)*

Fort Haven. 1860. This was an earthwork occupied for about 40 days by the "Carson River Expedition" that fought the Piutes in June, 1860. The camp was abandoned when the troops were moved further south to establish Fort Churchill. From Reno go east on I-80 for 32 miles to the Wadsworth interchange. Turn north onto Nevada 34, go through Nixon in 13 miles. In about 4 more miles, road will skirt Truckee river about 1 mile from Pyramid Lake; this is the approximate site of Fort Haven.

Camp Hays. 1860. Nevada militiamen rendezvoused here at Reed's Station to fight under Colonel Jack C. Hays against the Indians in the Pyramid Lake War. The camp lasted less than a month and there is nothing left to show military use of what was also a Pony Express station. From Carson City go northeast on US 50 for 19 miles to Nevada 2B. Turn right (east) on this unimproved road; the approximate site of Camp Hays is 1 mile east of the intersection on the Carson river.

Fort Homestead. 1865. Not really a fort, this earthwork was on the heights overlooking Gold Hill, 2 miles south of Virginia City on Nevada 80. A 24-pounder gun mounted here was used to

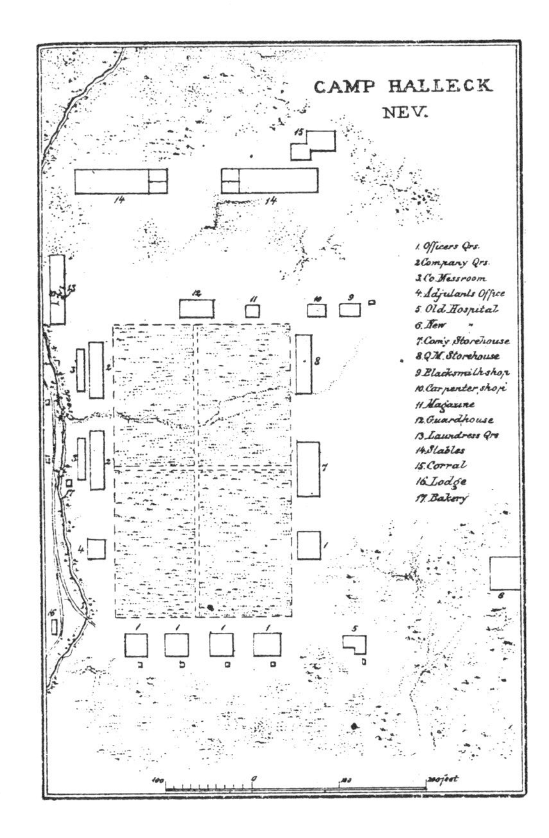

herald special events until 1874 when the cannon was moved in deference to the window panes of nearby houses.

Detachment at Las Vegas. *Fort Baker.*

Fort McDermit. 1865-89. *Quinn River Camp Number 33, Quinn's River Station.* Troops from here participated in the Bannock Indian wars, in which they played a major role, and in numerous minor "keep the peace" engagements. Established in order to protect the 2,000 Paiute Indians living in the area and to watch over the road northward to Oregon, many of the post's buildings remain as offices or residences of the Indian Agency. From Winnemucca, go north on US 95 for 96 miles. One mile south of the Oregon border, turn right at the Indian Agency sign. The fort site is still occupied by ex-Army buildings surrounding the former parade ground at the end of the road, 2 miles.

Fort McGarry. 1865-68. *Camp Summit Lake.* This is one of the most isolated sites in the West — almost 200 miles round trip from the nearest gas station — but the trip is worth it to see the remnants of several stone buildings scattered around an overgrown parade ground. This was an active patrol post in its heydey and for a short time was headquarters of the District of Summit Lake.

The trip to the site is for fair weather only and not for the family car. From Gerlach, go north on Nevada 34 for 10 miles. When it crosses rise of Granite Peak-Division Peak range at sharp left, take the dirt road to the right across an alkali flat. Continue along this vague dirt road through many gates to Soldiers Meadows, 61 miles from Gerlach, once an Army outpost.

Continue north through the corral and up into the hills until the road levels off and Summit Lake can be seen to the right front. At the first intersection to the right after skirting the lake, turn right (east). After a mile, rock ruins can be seen on private grazing property to the south (right) side of road across Sagebrush Creek.

Camp McKee. 1865-66. *Granite Creek Station, Detachment at Granite Creek.* Troops were temporarily at the Granite Creek Station after it was burned and the three employees massacred in 1865. For four months in summer, 1866, the site was occupied under the official name of Camp McKee until October when the troops and stores were moved to Camp McCarry. The approximate location of the post is the hamlet of Gerlach on Nevada 34 about 74 miles north of the Fernley or Wadsworth interchanges on I-80.

Mormon Fort. *Fort Baker.*

Mormon Station. *Fort Genoa.*

Camp Nye. 1862-65. California and Nevada Volunteer troops manned this Civil War field camp. From Carson City, go north on US 395 for 5 miles to the south shore of Washoe lake, approximate site of this post.

Quinn River Station, Quinn River Camp No. 33. *Fort McDermit.*

Camp Ruby. 1862-69. Regulars of the 9th Infantry took over this isolated post from California and Nevada Volunteers after the Civil War, protecting the mail and emigrant routes. Most of the buildings were merely low walls and roofs over four-foot deep holes. Three buildings still are left, used for ranching purposes. From Wells, go south on US 93 for 22 miles to Nevada 11. Turn right, stay on this route 17 miles until it turns sharply right (north). Turn left onto dirt road and head south along Ruby Valley for 30 miles to Fort Ruby Ranch, privately owned set away from the left (east) side of the road. Stock up on gas before leaving Wells; there are no facilities on this desolate, dusty road.

Camp Sadler. Not to be confused with a Civil War temporary Camp Sadler near Carson City at the mouth of Kings Canyon, this was a mustering-in post during the Spanish-American War – also at Carson City.

Fort Sage. 1870. Apparently a field camp along the emigrant route west of Pyramid Lake, the only modern evidence of this site is Fort Sage Mountain, altitude 8102, near the California-Nevada border, 10 miles southwest of Flanagan (46 miles north of Reno).

Fort Schellbourne. 1860-65. *Schell Creek Station, Fort Schell.* This was a stop on the many roads west, not the least of which was the Pony Express. The old stage station and the iron doors of the Wells Fargo buildings still remain on private property. From Ely, head north on US 93 for 40 miles to County 2. Turn right (east) on gravel road. In about 4 miles, at the western approach to Schellbourne Pass, are the remains of the town where Army garrisons frequently were posted.

Smoke Creek Depot. 1865-66. *Camp Smoke Creek.* Convenient and comfortable was how Smoke Creek Station was described by citizens who wanted troops rushed in to protect the Honey Lake Stage Route. When troops did arrive to permanently outpost the station, it was found that there were quarters for only half of the company of California Cavalry. Previously, the detachments frequently stationed there after Indian trouble in the Honey Lake area had lived in tents. The same solution was reached by the permanent detachment. From Gerlach, the site of Camp McKee, follow the directions to Camp Deep Hole Station and then continue in a southwesterly direction about 23 miles to an unimproved road to the west (right turn). About 6 miles west, and at a point 5 miles short of the California border, is the site of Smoke Creek Depot.

Camp Soldiers Meadow. 1862. Military detachments outposted this site, supposedly using the stone buildings now incorporated in a ranch-house. Follow the directions to Fort McGarry; Soldiers Meadows is 20 miles southwest of McGarry.

Camp Summit Lake. *Fort McGarry.*

Fort Trinity. 1863-64. *Eight Mile Station.* Troop detachments frequently watched over emigrant trains from this desolate, desert field camp. Follow the directions to Fort Schellbourne, continue on County 2 through Schellbourne Pass. The site is 2 miles from the Utah border, about 50 miles from the turnoff from US 93.

Camp Winfield Scott. 1866-71. At the foot of the Santa Rosa mountains, the remaining buildings of this post still are used for ranching purposes, a far cry from their first role of fielding patrols to protect property. From Winnemucca, go north on US 95 for 22 miles; bear right on Nevada 8B for 18 miles to Paradise Valley, a near-ghost town. At eastern end of main street, turn right (south) then take next left to west for 4 miles to private ranch, site of fort.

NEW MEXICO

FORT BAYARD, 1885 *(1)*

Explorations, Navajos, the Rio Grande, Confederates and the California Column, and the Apache Wars all contributed to the location of many permanent and semi-permanent forts and fort-type places in New Mexico. The Rio Grande Valley and the southwestern corner of the state are especially crowded with the sites and supposed sites of these camps.

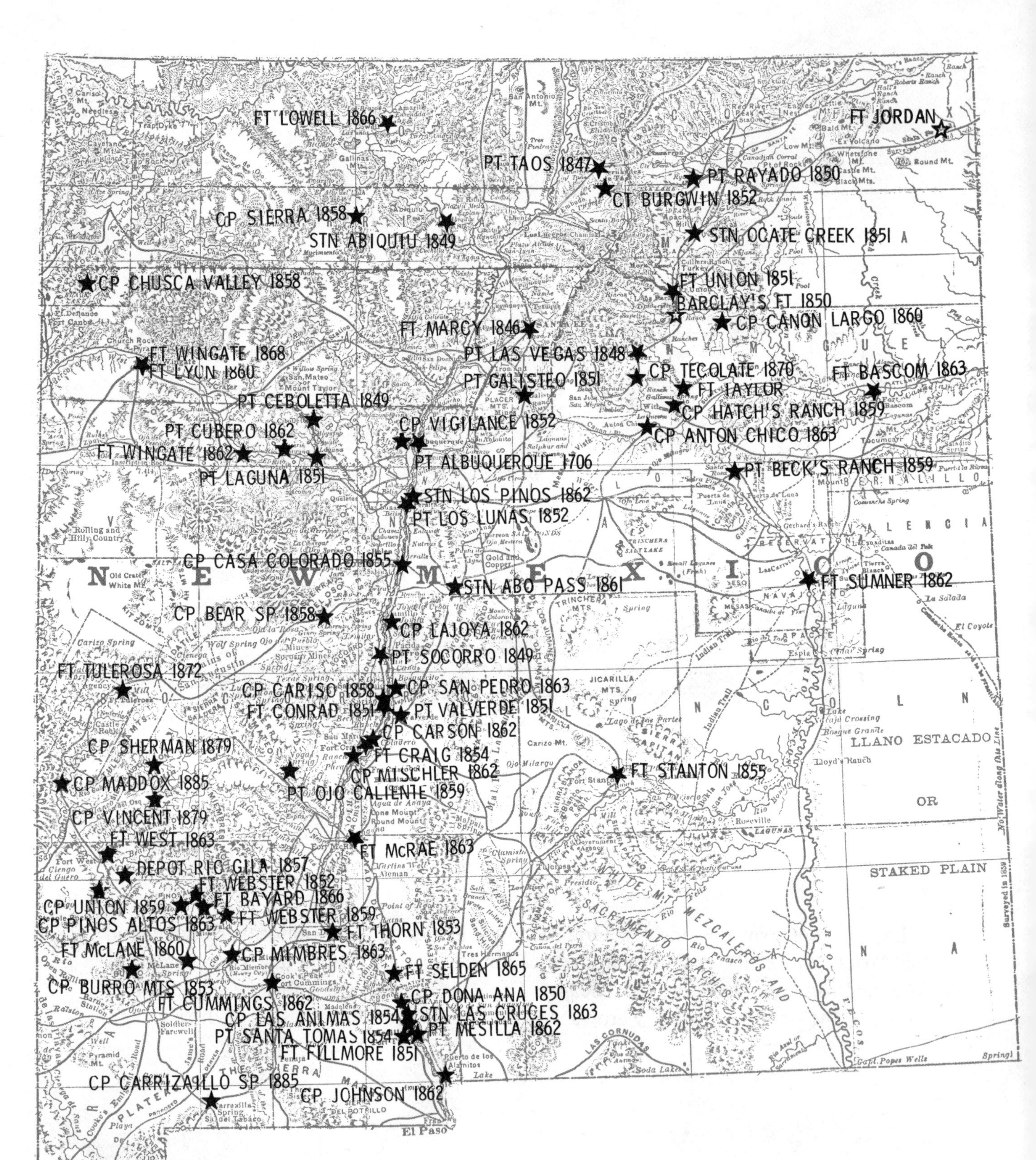
FT LOWELL 1866
FT JORDAN
PT TAOS 1847
PT RAYADO 1850
CT BURGWIN 1852
CP SIERRA 1858
STN ABIQUIU 1849
STN OCATE CREEK 1851
CP CHUSCA VALLEY 1858
FT UNION 1851
BARCLAY'S FT 1850
CP CANON LARGO 1860
FT MARCY 1846
PT LAS VEGAS 1848
FT WINGATE 1868
FT LYON 1860
CP TECOLATE 1870
FT BASCOM 1863
PT GALISTEO 1851
FT TAYLOR
PT CEBOLETTA 1849
CP HATCH'S RANCH 1859
CP VIGILANCE 1852
PT CUBERO 1862
CP ANTON CHICO 1863
FT WINGATE 1862
PT ALBUQUERQUE 1706
PT BECK'S RANCH 1859
PT LAGUNA 1851
STN LOS PINOS 1862
PT LOS LUNAS 1852
CP CASA COLORADO 1855
N E W M E X I C O
STN ABO PASS 1861
FT SUMNER 1862
CP BEAR SP 1858
CP LAJOYA 1862
PT SOCORRO 1849
FT TULEROSA 1872
CP CARISO 1858
CP SAN PEDRO 1863
FT CONRAD 1851
PT VALVERDE 1851
CP CARSON 1862
CP SHERMAN 1879
FT CRAIG 1854
LLANO ESTACADO
CP MISCHLER 1862
FT STANTON 1855
CP MADDOX 1885
PT OJO CALIENTE 1859
OR
CP VINCENT 1879
FT WEST 1863
FT McRAE 1863
DEPOT RIO GILA 1857
STAKED PLAIN
FT WEBSTER 1852
FT BAYARD 1866
CP UNION 1859
FT WEBSTER 1859
CP PINOS ALTOS 1863
FT THORN 1853
FT McLANE 1860
CP MIMBRES 1863
FT SELDEN 1865
CP BURRO MTS 1853
CP DONA ANA 1850
FT CUMMINGS 1862
STN LAS CRUCES 1863
CP LAS ANIMAS 1854
PT MESILLA 1862
PT SANTA TOMAS 1854
FT FILLMORE 1851
CP CARRIZAILLO SP 1885
CP JOHNSON 1862
El Paso
CP CLOVERDALE 1882

PLAZA OF ALBUQUERQUE *(32)*

Station Abiquiu. 1849-51. Rented adobe buildings provided quarters for both trooper and mount at this town post. The Army did not own any property at this location but the modern town could easily pass for construction of the mid-nineteenth century. Take US 84 from Santa Fe, remaining on it even though its other designations turn off, Abiquiu turnoff is 42 miles north of Santa Fe; turn left (west) up the hill onto plaza.

Station at Abo Pass. 1861. Protection of this pass through the Los Pinos mountains was the mission of this short-term tent camp. From Socorro, go north on I-25 for 26 miles to Bernardo. Turn right (east) on US 60 to Abo Pass, about 20 miles.

Post at Albuquerque. 1706-1867. *Presidio of Albuquerque.* The Spanish founded a presidio with the Church of San Felipe de Neri, today the second oldest active church in the U.S. Army moved to rented buildings in Albuquerque in 1847; in 1862, the Confederates were the temporary occupants. From downtown Albuquerque, take US 66 west to Romero street. Turn right (north) to the Old Town Plaza, site of the Post of Albuquerque and location of the Church of San Felipe de Neri. Cannon buried by the retreating Confederates in 1862 are in this plaza.

Algodones Quartermaster Depot. 1851. A small supply center that occupied rented buildings at Algodones, about 45 miles south of Santa Fe east of I-25.

Camp at Anton Chico. 1863-64. Troops of Company E, 2d California Cavalry Volunteers, outposted this town during part of the Civil War. From Albuquerque, go east on I-40 for 97 miles to US 84 exit. Head north on US 84 for 15 miles to Dilia; turn left to Anton Chico, 5 miles.

Fort Baker. At one time plans were made to set up a post at Manzano, south of Albuquerque, to replace Fort Stanton. When Stanton was re-established, the plans for Baker were dropped.

Barclay's Fort. 1849-53. This was a trading post at which the military frequently stopped, rested, sampled Alexander Barclay's wares and wines, and let off steam. There were circular bastions at two opposite corners on a 64-foot square, double-storied adobe post. The foundation line still can be seen next to the Mora river and barely free from construction of I-25. Take this route north-east from Las Vegas for 20 miles to Watrous. Turn onto County 160 at Watrous. About 1 mile north, just before road turns sharply to left, is site of Barclay's Fort on right side between road and river. The rock foundation is in the pasture.

Fort Bascom. 1863-70. *Camp Easton.* The Comancheros – the traders in illegal goods with the Indians – were the main objectives for many of Bascom's operations but nearby Indian raids contributed to the garrison's alertness. Kit Carson and Ranald Mackenzie led expeditions from here. There are many traces of the once extensive adobe buildings, but mainly as depressions or basement remnants. An unusual sidewalk made of bottles was uncovered in 1971 next to Sutler's store site. This is on a working ranch 9 miles north of Tucumcari and the new owner planned to construct an access road convenient to Tucumcari. Advance permission should be requested to visit this privately owned site.

Fort Bayard. 1866-1900. Bayard's strategic location in the Pinos Altos area of southwestern New Mexico meant that it was active in the many expeditions after the Civil War. It remained active long after the Army left as a Veterans Administra-

FORT BAYARD, guardhouse

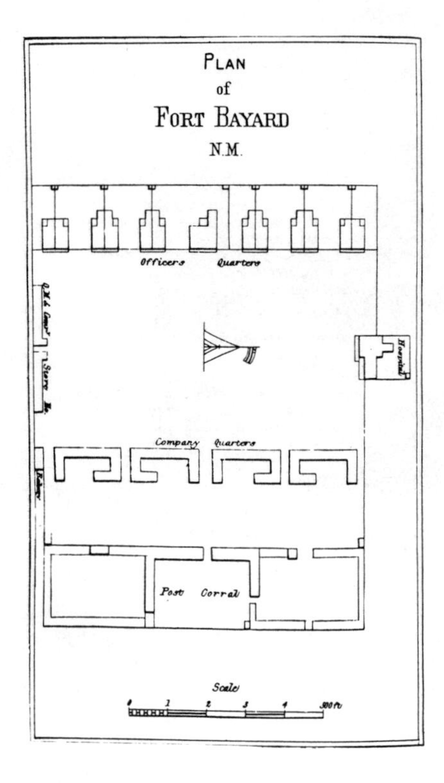

tion hospital until 1965. From Silver City, go east on US 180 for 9 miles to Central. Turn left (north) 1 mile to Fort Bayard Hospital, now operated by the state.

Camp Bear Spring. 1858. This was a temporary camp of which there are no remains. From Socorro go west on US 60 for 27 miles to Magdalena. Turn right (north) on unimproved road toward Riley; Bear Springs is about 10 miles north of Magdalena on this road.

Post at Beck's Ranch. 1859-60. This outpost camp was 2 miles northeast of Santa Rosa. From Santa Rosa, on I-40, cross the Pecos river to approximate site of the camp.

Cantonment Burgwin. 1852-60. This Army post consisted of single-storied, flat-roofed buildings facing inward with no windows on the outside walls, necessary protection in view of the occasional Indian attacks on this early fort. From Taos, go south on US 64 to New Mexico 3. Turn left (south) and go 7 miles to Fort Burgwin Research Center, the reconstructed version of the fort on the original site. Prior arrangements should be made in order to visit.

Camp at Burro Mountains. 1853, 1859. *Fort Hook.* This was a temporary camp along a creek in the Burro Mountain area of southwestern New Mexico. Bartlett camped in the vicinity during his 1850 boundary survey. During its later years as a patrol base, it was proposed that a permanent post, using the Fort Hook name, be established here but this was disapproved. A rock corral and several building dugouts are on the site. From Silver City, go south on New Mexico 90 for 18 miles. One mile short of the White Signal town cluster, turn left (east) on dirt road. About 10 miles along this road, the rock corral can be seen in a pasture on the low land to the right (south).

Fort Butler. This post appears on many old maps as being west of Tucumcari. It was to be built after the Civil War. The land was reserved but the post never was built.

Camp in Canon Largo. 1860+. This outpost and patrol base was located in the so-called "long canyon" that opens into the Canadian River in northeast New Mexico. There is no road net direct to the approximate site; maps should be consulted, using New Mexico 104 between Las Vegas and Tucumcari as a basing point.

Camp near Cariso. 1858. This outpost was at Cariso Spring north of Fort Conrad. Follow directions to Fort Conrad to reach the approximate site.

Camp Carrizaillo Spring. 1885. An outpost for the latter stages of the Apache War, this detachment also kept watch on the Mexican border 5 miles to the south. From Columbus, go west on New Mexico 9 for about 20 miles to Hermanas, the approximate site of the camp.

Camp Carson. 1862. This was the tent camp occupied by militia helping defend Fort Craig during the Confederate actions around it. The camp was between Craig and the Rio Grande.

Camp near Casa Colorado. 1855. This campsite was temporary, 5 miles southeast of Belen. Take I-25 south from Belen (31 miles south of Albuquerque) for 5 miles; camp site was on left (east) side near river.

Post at Ceboletta. 1849-51. This town post of the 2d Dragoons used rented, bedbug-infested, adobe buildings. No remnants appear to exist although local tradition tells of the approximate site of towers that supposedly were occupied by the Army. From Albuquerque, take I-40 west for 44 miles to Laguna. Take New Mexico 279 north for 12 miles to Ceboletta, now called Seboyeta.

Camp in Chusco Valley. 1858. This field camp was in the vicinity of Chuska Peak, northwest of Tohatchi (25 miles north of Gallup west of US 666).

Camp near Cloverdale. 1882-86. This was an important base camp and depot for the final Apache Campaign, less than 10 miles from the Mexican border and so close to Arizona that it frequently appears in records as being in that state. From Lordsburg, go west on I-10 for 10 miles to New Mexico 338. Go south on 338 for 63 miles to a deadend with New Mexico 79. Turn right (west) for 3 miles to the abandoned two-house hamlet of Cloverdale, site of the camp.

Post at Columbus. *Camp Furlong.*

Camp Connelly. 1862. A New Mexico Volunteers camp at Polvadera, 12 miles north of Socorro.

Fort Conrad. 1851-54. The result of the 1850 decision to move the troops out of the "vice ridden" towns, Conrad also was intended to watch over the Indians and feed itself with a post farm. Neither objective was accomplished and the post was abandoned when Fort Craig was built.

FORT CRAIG *(1)*

There are no remains at the approximate site but vandals continue to dig up the area. From San Antonio, go south on I-25 for 15.5 miles. The approximate site was to the east of the road at this point, near the Rio Grande.

Station at the Copper Mines. *Fort Webster.*

Detachment at Cottonwoods. *Camp Johnson.*

Fort Craig. 1854-85. This is the historic fort which at one time in the early days of the Civil War had 3,810 Union regular, volunteer and militia troops in and around it to oppose an estimated 2,600 Confederates. The Battle of Valverde that followed was the bloodiest of the Civil War in 1862. Many imposing adobe ruins remain. Take I-25 south from Socorro for 31 miles. State marker on the left (east) side of the highway indicates the gravel road which terminates in 5 miles at the ruins of Fort Craig.

Post at Cubero. 1862. A temporary field camp with no modern reminders of Army use. From Albuquerque, go west on I-40 for 56 miles to the exit after Casa Blanca. Turn north 1 mile to New Mexico 279, then back to the east (right turn) for 2 miles, then left turn (north) for 1 mile to the hamlet of Cubero.

Fort Cummings. 1862-70; 1882-85. This adobe post was founded and abandoned four times while it kept watch on the stage routes and served as the base of numerous patrols and expeditions. Its "permanent" garrison began in the Civil War but it was used as the site of a tent camp for the Apache campaign in the 1880's. Take US 180 north from Deming for 1 mile and turn right (east) at New Mexico 26. In 15 miles, turn left on dirt road at historical marker and black tanks marked "Florida." Continue for 5 miles then turn left at Hyatt ranch. After obtaining permission here to visit, take right fork in road along fence line, open and close gate, until road terminates at fort site, 1 mile. There are numerous adobe ruins.

Camp Datil. 1885-86. Troops scouted the surrounding area during this period but with no con-

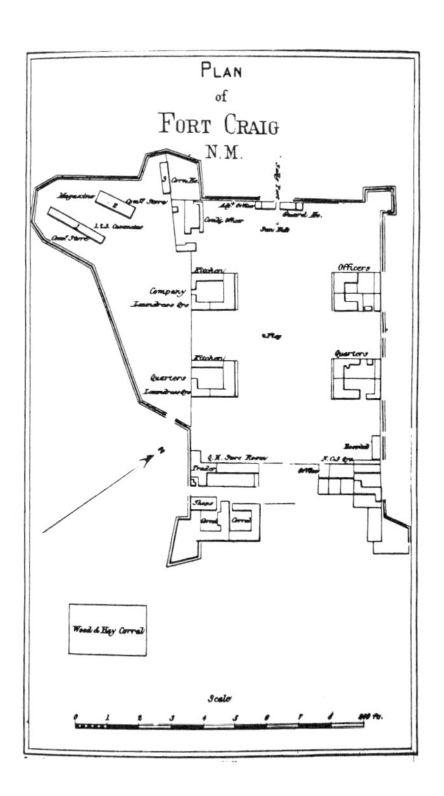

tacts as they guarded the perimeter against Apaches returning from Mexico. From Socorro, go west on US 60 to New Mexico 12 where Datil remnants are left, but no reminders of Army canvas life can be seen.

Cantonment Dawson. *Fort Webster.*

Camp Dona Ana. 1850-51; 1855-56; 1862. Dragoons were located here to watch a favorite Apache river crossing; Union troops occupied it for a short period in the Civil War. The Confederates had a hospital here in 1861. Rented quarters were used. Dona Ana is 5 miles north of Las Cruces west of I-25.

FORT CUMMINGS *(1)*

FORT CUMMINGS *(1)*

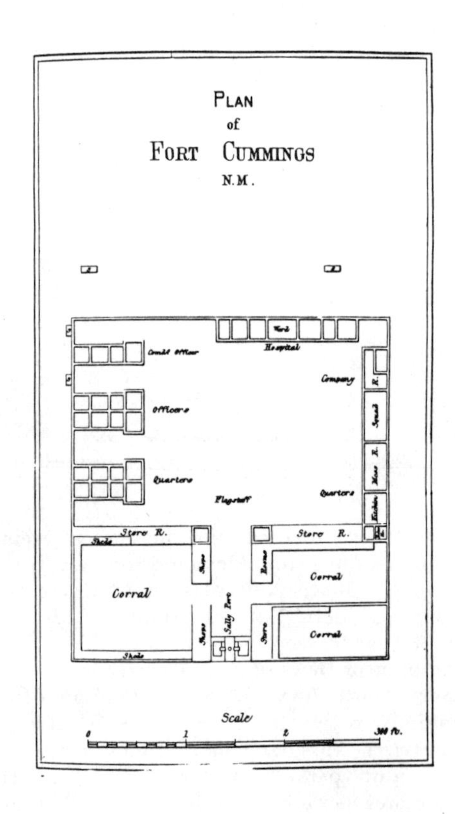

Camp Easton. *Fort Bascom.*

Fort Faunterloy. *Fort Wingate.*

Camp at Fernanda de Taos. *Post of Taos.*

Fort Fillmore. 1851-61. This was the only Western fort to be surrendered completely without a fight to an opponent – the sorry tale of its early days in the Civil War when it was taken by the Confederates. Although later evidence indicated that the surrender was according to orders, the blot was hard to erase. Go south from Las Cruces through Mesilla on New Mexico 478. Site is about 5 miles south of Mesilla on the left side of New Mexico 478, between it and I-10. Only adobe mounds are left, covered by wind swept sand, at the private site.

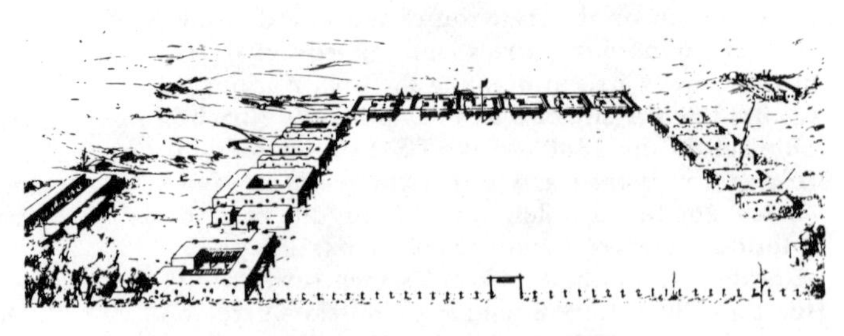

Fort Fillmore, 1861

Fort Floyd. *Fort McLane.*

Camp Furlong. 1916-18. *Post at Columbus.* This was the tent and frame post that was attacked by Pancho Villa on March 13, 1916, and was important during the Border period. The remains of the camp, including the adobe headquarters, officer of the day, and legal office buildings, frame recreation structures, and the airfield (the Army's first used in combat) are in or near Pancho Villa State Park, an ironic name for the location next to the center of Columbus. The station also attacked by Villa is prominent, now a museum. Columbus is a sleepy retirement village 3 miles north of the Mexican border and 32 miles south of Deming on New Meixco 11.

Post at Galisteo. 1851-58. Troopers periodically outposted this historic site of ancient pueblos, but occupied tents and rented quarters. From Santa Fe, go east on I-25 for 10 miles to US 285. Follow US 285 south for 7 miles to New Mexico 41. Turn right (west); the hamlet of Galisteo is 6 miles from the intersection.

Camp Gallina. *Camp Sierra.*

Camp Garland. *Fort Stanton.*

Cantonment Garland. *Fort Thorn.*

Post at Gila Copper Mines. *Fort Webster.*

Gila Depot. *Depot on the Rio Gila.*

Field Camp in Guadalupe Canyon. See this entry under Arizona; doubt exists in which state the exact site is located.

Camp at Hatch's Ranch. 1859-64. Various spellings of this frequent outpost also term it "Hatche's Ranche," a moot point from the soldiers' viewpoint – troopers of the Mounted Rifles and 8th Infantry in 1859 and New Mexico Volunteers in the Civil War. About 20 remnants of buildings remain at the site, including a large main building 115 by 288 feet and 10 feet high. Take I-25 east from Santa Fe for 58 miles to US 84. Go south on 84 to 1 mile past Dilla (which is 26 miles from the intersection). Turn left (east) onto ranch road to privately owned Park Springs ranch. If permission to visit is granted, Hatch's Ranch site can be reached 4.5 miles north.

Camp Henley. 1886. This was a heliograph station outposted during the final campaigns against the Apaches. The site is at Soldiers Farewell, 20 miles east of Lordsburg.

Fort Hook. *Camp Burro Mountains.*

Camp Horse Springs. A post was proposed for this site and construction started in lieu of the Warm Springs Reservation at Tulerosa, but the decision was made to move to the location of Camp Ojo Caliente. Old Horse Springs is on New Mexico 12 southwest of Datil 30 miles.

Camp Johnson. 1862. *Detachment at Cottonwoods.* A company of California Cavalry Volunteers under Captain William McCleave and a light artillery battery were quartered in tents at this picket post as they watched for Confederate movements along the Rio Grande. Officially, the site was 17.5 miles south of Fort Fillmore on the "Arizona side of the Rio Grande." Taking into account the river's shift in course and the organization of the eastern half of Arizona Territory into New Mexico, this would put Camp Johnson's site in the vicinity of Anthony, on N.M. 478 at the state line.

Fort Jordan. Not really a fort, this is a reproduction of a frontier stockade that includes displays of early automobiles, horsedrawn vehicles and a museum. The usual tourist facilities also are available. From Clayton, in the northeast corner of the state, go northwest on US 64-87 for .5 mile; the fort is next to the highway.

Camp La Joya. 1846-64. California Infantry Volunteers outposted this field camp on the "Journey of Death" route through sand swept wastelands east of the Rio Grande. Dragoons camped there in 1846. Take I-25 north from Socorro for 25 miles to US 60 at Bernardo. Turn right (east) onto US 60 and cross Rio Grande. Four miles from I-25, turn right (south) on New Mexico 47. Lajoya hamlet is 6 miles from this turn.

Post at Laguna. 1851-52. This field camp was near the Laguna Pueblo and provided mutual protection for the Indians and California-bound emigrants. Take I-40 west from Albuquerque to Laguna.

Post of La Mesilla. *Post of Mesilla.*

Camp at Las Animas. 1854. This summer-season camp outposted the emigrant route along the Rio Grande in the vicinity of Dona Ana during one of the periods in which troops were not stationed at Dona Ana. Follow directions to Camp Dona Ana to reach the approximate site.

Station at Las Cruces. 1863-65. This was a troop center and supply depot out of which pickets were posted to temporary camps along the Rio Grande. Only rented quarters were used. Las Cruces is a modern city at the intersection of I-10 and I-25.

Post of Las Vegas. 1848-51. Illinois Volunteers founded this post not long after the United States had proclaimed itself the authority in New Mexico. Until 1851, this was the headquarters for military operations in northern New Mexico. Rented quarters were used and there are no traces of Army use. The city of Las Vegas is on I-25 about 65 miles east of Santa Fe.

Camp Lewis. 1862. This was the camp at Martin Kozlowski's station and tavern where the First Colorado Volunteers readied for the Battle of Glorietta Pass, the Gettysburg for the Confederates in the West. It is 6 miles south of Pecos.

Post of Los Lunas. 1852; 1859-60; 1862. Captain Richard S. Ewell, later a Confederate general, commanded the dragoons who founded this post and operated from its rented quarters. The town of Los Lunas is on I-25 about 20 miles south of Albuquerque.

Station Los Pinos. 1862-66. *Camp at Peralta, U.S. Depot, Los Pinos, near Peralta, N.M.* This was mainly a remount and quartermaster station using houses rented at the rate of $5,000 a year from the governor of New Mexico. There are no remains of Army use at the site. From Albuquerque, go south on I-25 for 23 miles to

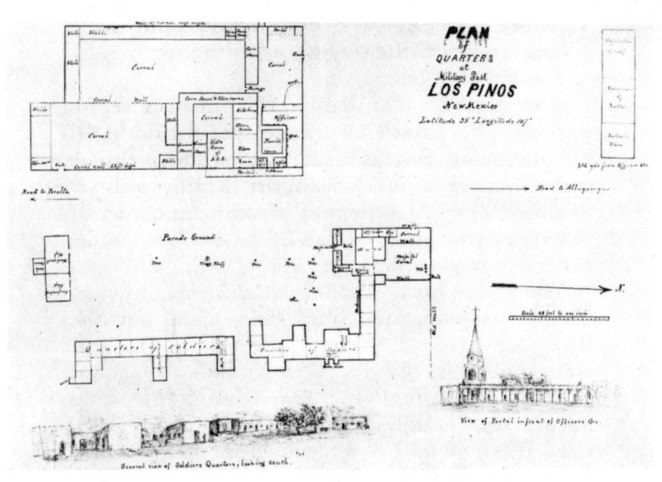

Plan of Los Pinos *(1)*

Belen. Turn left (east) on New Mexico 6 for 2 miles then turn left (north) again for another 2 miles to the hamlet of Peralta.

Fort Lowell. 1866-69. *Camp Plummer.* This was a cluster of log buildings overlooking the Chama river at which the two main occupations of the garrison seem to have been preventing settlers from making slaves out of the Indians, and preventing the post sutler from over-charging for his wares.

Known locally as "El Campo," the site can be reached from Tierra Amarilla in Northern New Mexico. From the intersection of US 84 and New Mexico 112, 1 1/2 miles northwest of the center of Tierra Amarilla, go south on New Mexico 112 for 1.7 miles to the intersection with a gravel road. Turn right (west) and follow this gravel road for about 3 miles to the hamlet of La Puente.

At the far end of the community's single street, turn right at the church on a dirt road and go north on this road for about 1 1/2 miles until the road tops a rise, placing the Chama river on the left and a broad meadow on the right. Fort site was in this meadow, privately owned property.

Fort Lyon. *Fort Wingate.*

Camp Maddox. 1885-86. A tent and ranch-house post occupied for the Geronimo uprising, this location remembers the 8th Cavalry's occupation by the two soldier graves in a hillside cemetery near the ranch headquarters. The ranch, and the old cemetery, are on the west side of US 180, seven miles north of Glenwood. The camp site is five miles north of the headquarters on privately owned property.

Fort Marcy. 1846-94. *Post at Santa Fe.* This was a fort that never was finished and from which no battle ever was fought. As with many Western forts, the very presence of Marcy won its battles without any need for bloodshed. It overlooked Santa Fe and was planned to be a fortress housing the 280 troops.

The nature of Santa Fe as a headquarters post soon made a fortification unnecessary and the Army moved into buildings around the Plaza,

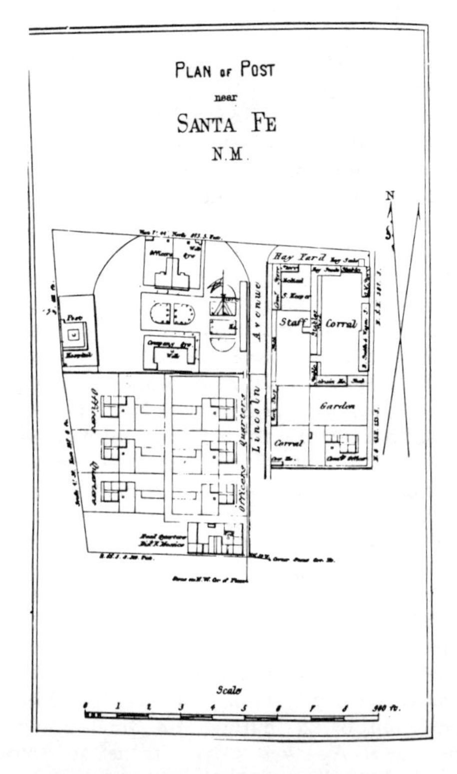

POST OF SANTA FE, FORT MARCY *(1)*

FORT MCRAE *(1)*

including the Governor's Palace, the oldest government building still in use in the United States.

The original Fort Marcy is on a bluff directly north of downtown Santa Fe – only adobe foundations are left, covered by undergrowth and dirt. The remainder of the post is north of the Plaza, bounded by Federal, Washington, Palace and Grant streets.

Fort McLane. 1860-63. *Fort McLean, Camp Webster, Fort Floyd, Camp Wheeler.* It is difficult to unravel the chronology of this oft-christened post from that of Fort Webster to the north. Most of the activities of this post took place after the arrival of the California Column. Now only a few adobe foundations remain in a corral. From Deming, go north on US 180 for about 38 miles to the Kennecott Copper Corporation's Apache Tejo pumping station, right side (east). Approximately 1 mile south of this station and on the opposite side of the highway (west side) is the 2-C Cattle Company. The ranch buildings are believed to be on the site of Fort McLane.

Fort McRae. 1863-82. Despite rumors, this post has not been inundated by Elephant Butte Reservoir but the presence of the lake has prevented easy access, and destruction, of the remains. The stone foundations of its adobe buildings show precisely how the post was laid out.

The site is the private property of the Victorio Land and Cattle Company, Bakersfield, Calif., which leases it to a tenant. Permission to visit should be obtained from both.

Site may be reached by boat across the Elephant Butte Reservoir, going to Fort McRae Canyon and walking up the canyon 3 miles. A rough duty vehicle can reach it overland from Truth or Consequences via New Mexico 51 for 5.4 miles past Elephant Butte Dam to a road intersection. Take the right fork (toward Engle) 7.4 miles to dirt track on the left. With permission in hand, turn left onto this track for about 4 miles overland past the 7TX Ranch. When the track disappears completely, continue on foot westward 1 mile down a dry arroyo to the site.

Post at Mesilla. 1863-64. *Post at La Mesilla.* Troops of the 5th Infantry, California Volunteers, manned this camp along with New Mexico Infantry Volunteers, using rented quarters after Fort Fillmore, to the south, was abandoned. There are no remains that can positively be linked with the Army's use although the Plaza in Old Town Mesilla is reminiscent of the period, and earlier. Mesilla is 3 miles southwest of Las Cruces on New Mexico 28.

Camp Mimbres. 1863-66. *Camp Miembres, Camp on Rio Mimbres.* This was an important short-term tent post of the California Volunteers, providing protection for the crossing of the Mimbres river and serving as a base of operations against the Indians in the nearby Florida mountains. The approximate site can be reached from Deming by going north on US 180 for 27 miles to New Mexico 61. Turn right (east) for 10 miles to county line. This is the approximate site on the right side, south of the village of Dwyer.

Camp Mischler. 1862. This was a volunteer camp occupied by some of the many Union troops protecting Fort Craig from the Confederates in the early days of the Civil War. The site is 8 miles south of Fort Craig along the Rio Grande.

Camp Monument Springs. 1875. Location of a large stone monument erected by nine companies of troops under Lieutenant Colonel William Shafter, 24th Infantry, at a fresh water spring to aid future travelers. This is at Monument, southwest of Hobbs.

Station at Ocate Creek. 1851-54. This was the military farm for Fort Union but proved unsuccessful after a couple of seasons. The approximate site is now the town of Ocate at the intersection of New Mexico 21 and 120 about 24 miles west of I-25's Wagon Mound exit.

Post of Ojo Caliente. 1859; 1874-82. The Army was here periodically, keeping an eye on the wards of Indian Agent John Clum – and on occasion such Indians as Geronimo were captured here. A series of adobe buildings lie in ruins but this is private property on which souvenir hunter ravages have convinced the owners that visitors usually are unwelcome. From Socorro, go west on US 66 through Magdalena to New Mexico 52 for about 40 miles. Turn left (south) for about 40 miles. The post ruins are on the privately owned and posted property to the left (east) as the road crosses the Alamosa river.

Camp at Peralta. *Station Los Pinos.*

Camp near Pinos Altos. 1863. A company of California cavalry protected settlers and miners from the dual threats of Indian and bandit raiders at this prosperous yet rowdy mining center. Go north for 6 miles on New Mexico 25 from Silver City to the town of Pinos Altos, location of the Army camp.

Camp Plummer. *Fort Lowell.*

Camp Pope's Wells. The location of this site is variously described in Texas and New Mexico. See the entry in the Texas chapter of this book.

Post Rayado. 1850-51; 1854. Two under strength companies of Dragoons occupied quarters rented from New Mexico land baron Lucien B. Maxwell in performing their mission here of commanding the Indian and emigrant routes in the area. Maxwell leased his newly built mansion, described by various sources as having from 20 to 40 rooms, to the Army for $2,400 a year at first, then increased it to $3,400.

When the troops were withdrawn in mid-1851, Maxwell was anxious to retain the Army's protection and provided quarters and stables at no cost to the 15-man detachment left behind.

From Las Vegas, go north on I-25 for 68 miles to Springer. Just before arriving at Springer turn left (west) on New Mexico 199. Follow this secondary road for 20 miles to a deadend intersection with New Mexico 21; turn right (north) for 2 miles to the hamlet of Rayado.

Depot on the Rio Gila. 1857. *Gila Depot, Camp on Rio Gila, Rio Gila Depot.* This was the base camp for Colonel Benjamin L.E. Bonneville's Gila Expedition of 1857. The site was occupied temporarily in 1863 by the California Column before they established Fort West five miles to the northwest. From Silver City, go northwest on US 180 for 25 miles to a point about 5 miles south of the intersection of the highway with the Gila river. Depot on the Rio Gila site was on the hillside on the right (north) side of the highway.

Camp on the Rio Mimbres. *Camp Mimbres.*

Camp at Roswell. 1878-79. This was a temporary camp during the Lincoln County War. It was at Roswell with no traces.

Camp San Pedro. 1863-64. California Infantrymen were stationed at this temporary "Journey of Death" camp. From Socorro, go south on I-25 for 11 miles to San Antonio. Turn left (east) on US 380 for 3 miles to the hamlet of San Pedro.

Post of Santa Fe. *Fort Marcy.*

Post Santa Tomas. 1854-55. *Post Santa Tomas de Iturbide.* One company of the 3d US Infantry outposted this temporary camp, most likely a sub-post of Fort Fillmore despite contradictions in the official record. From Mesilla, go 6 miles south to the town of Santo Tomas, the camp site, now across the Rio Grande and with an alteration of its spelling.

Fort Selden. 1865-92. This imposing adobe restoration marks a fort that began at the end of the Civil War and included service in the Apache wars. Vacated when the railroad arrived in 1879, the post was re-garrisoned for the Mexican border patrols in 1881. The site is now the property of the State of New Mexico, culminating many years of work on the owner's part to donate it to the state. From Las Cruces, go north for 17 miles on I-25 to the intersection with US 85. The reconstructed fort is at this point.

Camp Sherman. 1879. This one-company outpost is of the era and had the same mission as Camp Vincent. Directions to it are similar as to Camp Vincent, except that from the Mimbres Post Office on New Mexico 61, continue north a total of 55 miles to Beaverhead. The approximate site of Camp Sherman was in this area at Adobe Ranch at the headwaters of Corduroy Canyon.

Camp Sierra. 1858. *Camp Gallina.* This was a temporary outpost with no remaining trace of Army use. Take I-25 north from Santa Fe to US 84 at Espanola, 21 miles. Follow US 84 for 41 miles to New Mexico 96, left turn. From this intersection the village of Gallina is 33 miles west.

Post of Socorro. 1849-51; 1863; 1877-81. As with the other town posts of the mid-century Army in New Mexico, the garrison at Socorro occupied rented quarters and there is no evidence of Army occupation in modern Socorro on I-25 almost in the center of the state.

Fort Stanton. 1855-96. *Camp Garland.* The Indians kept this post busy until it was abandoned at the start of the Civil War. Kit Carson commanded it for awhile during the war. Several Army buildings – including one in which Billy the Kid was imprisoned overnight – are used by the state as a tuberculosis hospital. From Roswell, go west on US 380 for about 66 miles to a turnoff at the left (south) marked for Fort Stanton State Tuberculosis Hospital. Fort site, and location of hospital, is about 5 miles south.

Star Fort. This was the earthwork fortification built at Fort Union at the start of the Civil War. Soon it was deemed inadequate because of weather and collapsing walls.

Fort Sumner. 1862-69. The unsuccessful Navajo farming experiment took place at this post which was also where Billy the Kid was killed. Although there were no visible surface traces of the fort in recent years, the post has been interpreted by the New Mexico State Museum and is now open for visitors. From town of Fort Sumner at the junction of US 60 and New Mexico 20, go east on US 60 for 3 miles to New Mexico 212. Three miles south on New Mexico 212 is the site of Fort Sumner, the Billy the Kid graveyard, and the fort.

Post Taos. 1847-52. *Camp at Fernanda de Taos.* After Governor Bent was murdered in the Taos Uprising of 1847, soldiers moved in to keep the peace, occupying the usual rented adobe quarters. The town of Taos is now an artist's

FORT THORN *(32)*

center on US 64 about 80 miles north of Santa Fe.

"Fort" Taylor. This is the local name attached to an extensive group of ruins about 3 miles northeast of and across the Gallinas river from the Camp at Hatch's Ranch. Follow directions to Hatch's ranch then walk northeast from site to Gallinas river. Cross river to group of ruins. So-called "Fort Taylor" site is 1.5 miles north of this second group of ruins.

Camp Tecolate. c. 1870. This was a forage camp for Fort Union and for the troops operating in the expeditions of the 1870's. Remnants of several buildings are left at the site in the hamlet of Tecolate on I-25 about 11 miles south of Las Vegas.

Fort Thorn. 1853-59; 1862-63. *Cantonment Garland.* A walled fort 600 feet along two sides and 520 on the others, Thorn had its share of problems – ranging from Indians and Confederates to alcohol. To reach the approximate site of the post go north on US 85 from Hatch (30 miles north of Las Cruces) 1.2 miles. Turn left on improved road. Follow this about 2 miles to Oak road, an angle to the right. Almost immediately, go left at the next fork. At next intersection, about .5 mile, turn left. Road tapers out in about a mile which is the approximate site of the post, all traces having been washed away by floods of the Rio Grande.

Camp Tome. 1848. This was a temporary tent camp post to protect settlers from Indian raids. From Socorro go 40 miles north on I-25 to Belen. Turn east, then north for 6 miles to hamlet of Tome alongside the Rio Grande.

Fort Tulerosa. 1872-74. Log huts with earthen roofs made up most of this post, although frame construction was used for the barracks, granary and hospital, and adobe for the officers' quarters. The camp was established to watch over the Indian Agency nearby and was abandoned when the Indians were moved.

At one time it was planned to shift the post to Old Horse Springs, 18 miles away, but this was cancelled with the departure of the Indians. During one spirited engagement with the Indians the heroism of Sergeant George Jordan won him one of the Army's early Medals of Honor.

From Silver City, go north on US 180 for 96 miles to New Mexico 12. Turn right (north) on New Mexico 12 and follow it for 26 miles to Aragon. A half mile north of the center of Aragon is the site of Fort Tulerosa, at the base of the hillside to the right (east) of the road. This is private property.

Camp Union. 1859. This was the troop camp across the Gila and a mile downstream from the Depot on the Rio Gila. For directions to the approximate site, see the latter's entry.

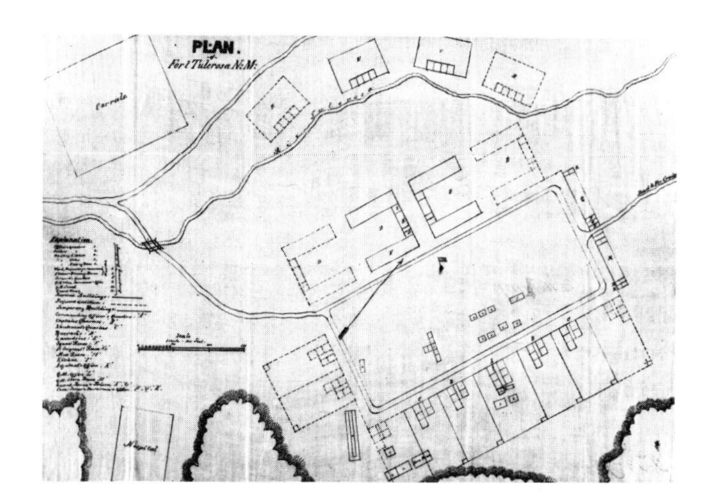

Plan of Fort Tulerosa *(1)*

Fort Union. 1851-91. This was the most important headquarters and supply depot of the southwest and, according to some disenchanted inspectors, the most extravagant. The adobe ruins have been stabilized by the National Park Service which now maintains the site as a National Monument. Take I-25 north from Las Vegas to the Watrous exit, 20 miles. From Watrous, take New Mexico 477, a hard surface road that ends in 7 miles at the post.

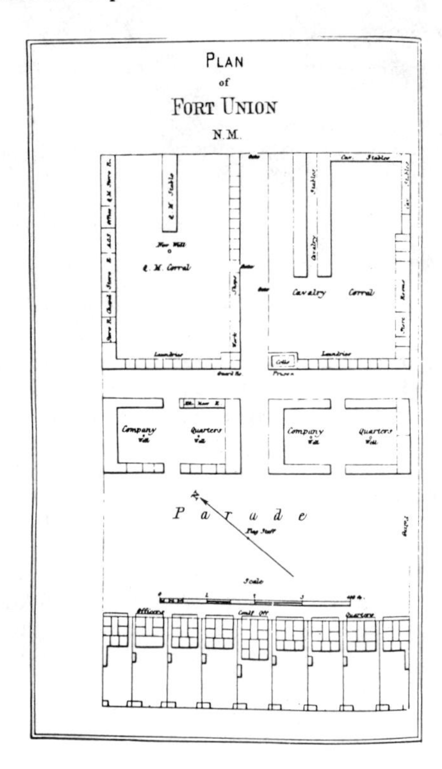

Camp Valverde. 1864. Company K of the 1st California Cavalry Volunteers occupied this field camp near Fort Craig and the site of the Battle of Valverde. From Socorro, go south on I-25 for 11 miles to US 380. Turn left (east) 2 miles to San Pedro. Turn right at San Pedro onto primitive road which ends in 17 miles at Valverde.

Camp Vigilance. 1852-53. This was the troop encampment near Albuquerque.

Camp Vincent. 1879. Located on a bench of comparatively level ground 100 yards southwest of the mouth of Taylor and Beaver creeks, this one-company post was established to defend against raids by Victorio's Apaches. Except for the remnants of two rock-topped graves, there are no traces of Army use at the site.

This is an excursion into primitive back country that should not be attempted without a heavy duty vehicle, survival gear, good maps and local directions. From Silver City, go east on US 180 about 9 miles to Central. Turn left on New Mexico 90 for 16 miles to New Mexico 61. Turn left (north) on 61 for 5 miles to Mimbres Post Office. Inquire here for directions to North Star Mesa road turnoff (about 20 miles north and west on New Mexico routes 61 and 11).

Turn right on North Star Mesa road, going north to cross Black Canyon, then down South Diamond Mesa to Main Diamond Creek; turn west down Main Diamond, out of Main Diamond on to ridge on north side of Main Diamond. Take first right hand road northwest to Fowler ranch (total distance to ranch from turn onto North Star Mesa road is about 50 miles). From Fowler ranch go about 3 miles up (north) East Fork of the Gila river to mouth of Beaver and Taylor creeks. Vincent was at the junction on the south bank of the Beaver.

Camp Webster. *Fort McLane.*

Fort Webster. 1852-53; 1857-60. *Post at Gila Copper Mines, Station at Copper Mines.* This was the site of a Spanish Presidio that dated from the early 19th century. The Bartlett Boundary Survey of 1851 stayed here and the Army outposted the two sites irregularly until the Civil War. Another site connected with Webster is that of Fort McLane, occasionally carried as Fort Webster in records.

The first site is at the Kennecott Copper Mines. From Bayard, take New Mexico 316 north for 1.7 miles to Hanover Junction. Turn right, go 1.5 miles east where the road overlooks the deep mine excavation – the approximate site of the first Fort Webster.

The second site was on the Mimbres river and can be reached by returning to New Mexico 316, then heading north for 2.7 miles to New Mexico 90. Follow this former wagon route through "Copper Mine Pass," bearing left at both forks (at 10.5 and 10.7). The road is adjacent to the privately owned site at mileage 11.3, between the road and the river bluff (right side).

Fort West. 1863-64. The California Column settled here for a short time and was kept busy by the Indians throughout their stay. The site is indefinite, but a probable location has been accepted by most researchers.

From Silver City, go west on US 180 about 25 miles to right fork onto County 211. Continue on 211 for 4 miles to crossing of the Gila river. At dirt road that runs beside airstrip, turn left and follow this road to base of hill, then as it winds up to private residence of Harsh family.

Fort West is believed to have been on hill immediately behind this house; permission to visit must be obtained. (It should be noted that from this location the site of Depot on the Rio Gila can be seen about 1 mile to the east).

Camp Wheeler. *Fort McLane.*

Fort Wingate. 1861-1911; 1914. *Fort Faunterloy, Fort Lyon.* There are two vastly separated sites of the fort. Technically there were three sites, except that the first and third are the same. To further confuse matters, the first site did not use the Wingate name at first but was called Fort Faunterloy, 1860-61, and then Fort Lyon, 1861-62. The New Mexican Volunteers manning the post left it in the hands of mail handlers in mid-1862 and moved southeastward 50 miles.

This new stockaded post was named Wingate as soon as the site was selected. In 1868 the troops moved back to the original Faunterloy-Lyon site, carrying the Wingate name with them. This permanent post kept the peace in Navajoland until shortly before World War I and now is the site of an Indian School (where a few Army buildings and the cemetery remain).

This site can be reached from Gallup via I-40, heading east to the Fort Wingate turnoff, 12 miles. Three miles south on New Mexico 400 is the Indian School, the Faunterloy-Lyon-Wingate II site.

The Wingate I site can be reached by continuing on I-40 eastward 48 miles to Grants. Turn right (south) on New Mexico 53 for 3 miles to San Rafael. The fort site was 1/2 mile east of the village on privately owned land between New Mexico 53 and the western edge of the lava flow.

—NORTH DAKOTA—

FORT TOTTEN *(5)*

Once the life blood of the river trade and the trading and military forts on its banks, the Missouri River has become the executioner of many because of reclamation projects. For this reason it is easy to give directions to the approximate sites; the exact sites no longer matter because they are under many feet of reservoir water.

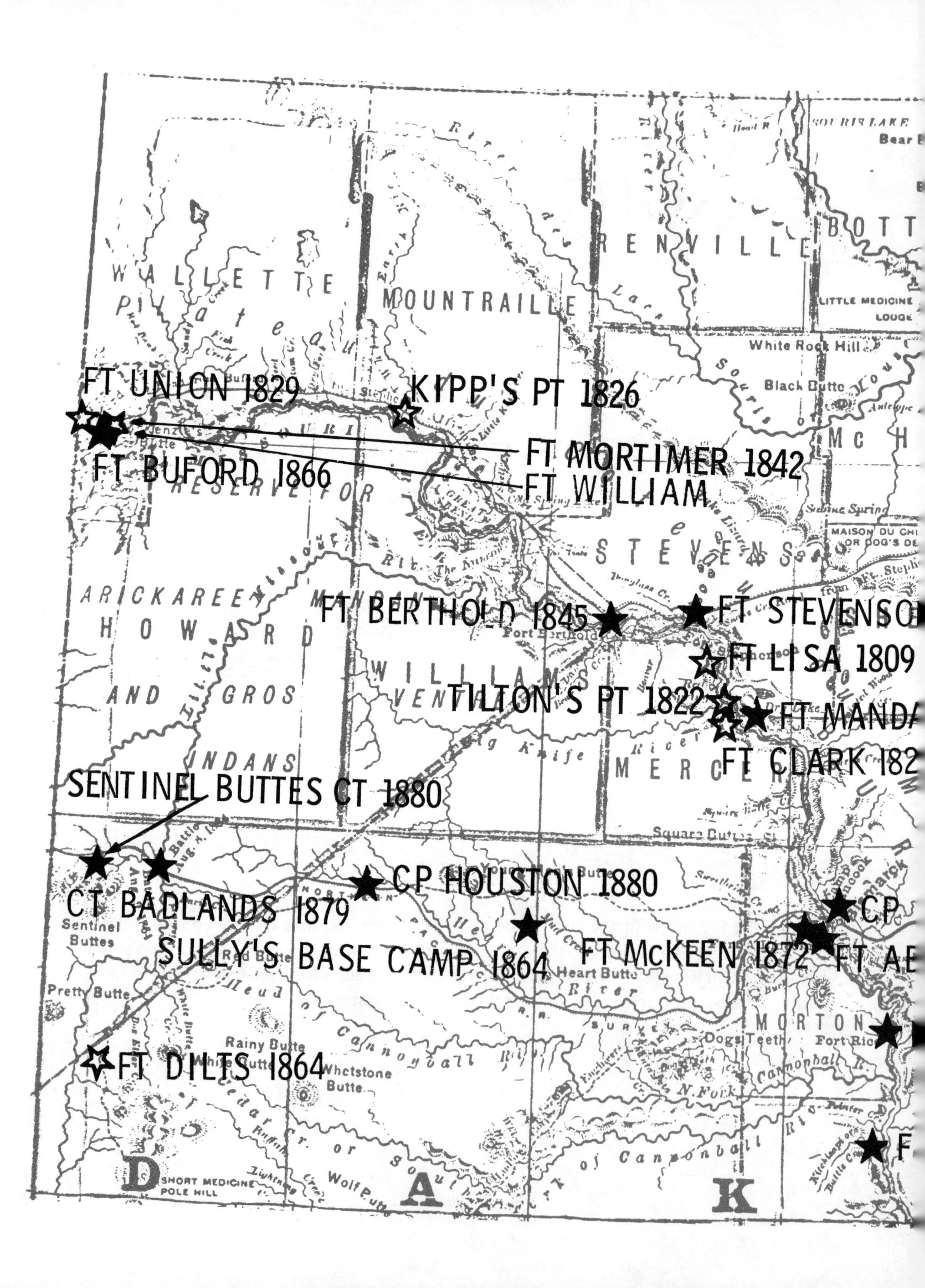

FT UNION 1829
KIPP'S PT 1826
FT MORTIMER 1842
FT BUFORD 1866
FT WILLIAM
FT BERTHOLD 1845
FT STEVENSO
FT LISA 1809
TILTON'S PT 1822
FT MANDA
FT CLARK 182
SENTINEL BUTTES CT 1880
CT BADLANDS 1879
CP HOUSTON 1880
SULLY'S BASE CAMP 1864
FT McKEEN 1872
CP
FT AB
FT DILTS 1864
WALLETTE
MOUNTRAILLE
RENVILLE
STEVENS
ARICKAREE
HOWARD
AND GROS
INDANS
MERCER
MORTON
SOURIS LAKE
LITTLE MEDICINE LODGE
White Rock Hill
Black Butte
Fort Berthold
Square Buttes
Sentinel Buttes
Pretty Butte
Rainy Butte
Whetstone Butte
Heart Butte
Dogs Teeth
SHORT MEDICINE POLE HILL
D
A
K

FT PAMBIAN 1797
FT DAER 1812
FT HENRY 1801
DET PEMBINA 1863
PEMBINA HOUSE 1803
FT PEMBINA 1870
FT TOTTEN 1867
CP ATCHESON 1863
CP KIMBALL 1863
CP CORNING 1863
CP GRANT 1863
CP ARNOLD 1863
FT SEWARD 1872
CP SHEARDOWN 1863
CP WEISER 1863
FT RANSOM 1867
CP HAYES 1863
CP BEUEL 1863
FT ABERCROMBIE 1857
OCK 1872
AM LINCOLN 1872
CE 1864
ES 1874
DEVILS LAKE
Butte Morale
James River
GINGRAS
FOSTER
KIDDER
LOGAN
GRAND FORKS
Grand Forks
Mail Station
Lake Jessie
Storm Sta.
Red Lake
White Stone Hill
Battle Field
FOUR HILLS

Fort Abercrombie. 1857-77. This post's most critical period was an 1861 siege when an estimated 300 Sioux attacked the post. The fort was saved in a defense that called upon all occupants, military and civilian alike. The post is now a state park with restored blockhouses, guardhouse and stockade at the eastern end of the main street of Abercrombie, a town in southeastern North Dakota, 45 miles south of Fargo on US 81.

Fort Abraham Lincoln. 1872-91. One of the most significant forts of the west, this was the post from which Custer left in 1876 for his ill-fated Battle of the Little Big Horn. Locations of buildings are outlined by stones and identified by markers in what is now a state park and near which a Custer pageant, "Trails West," is presented nightly during the summer season. From Bismarck, take Main avenue (US 10) across Missouri river to Mandan, 4 miles. Turn south at Sixth avenue, go 5 miles to Fort Abraham Lincoln State Park. Museum is on left (east) side of road, main fort site on right.

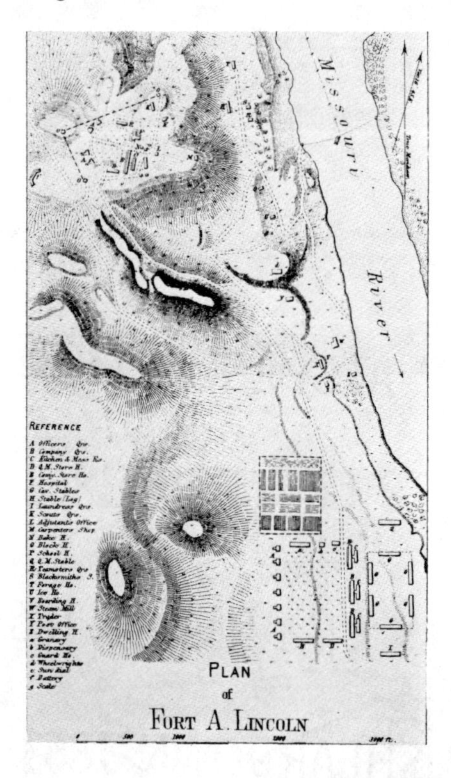

Camp Arnold. 1863. This was a field camp on the return march of General H.H. Sibley's 1863 expedition. It was one of many overnight or short-term camps. Some of the sites have been acquired by the state; only the campsites so identified as Historic Sites will be listed in this *Guide*. Take I-94 west for 49 miles from Fargo to the Oriska exit at North Dakota 32. Go north on 32 for 5 miles to the site, left (west) side of road.

Camp Atcheson. 1863. Sibley's troops were at this camp longer than many because two infantry companies were left here with slower elements of the expedition while the main column rushed ahead after the fleeing Sioux. Trenches and breastworks were prepared for the month-long encampment on the northeastern shore of Lake Sibley; the site of the grave of a private who died here is on a hill to the northeast. Take I-94 east from Jamestown 24 miles to North Dakota 1 exit. Go north on 1 for 53.5 miles to a left turn to Lake Sibley, ½ mile; the campsite was on the northeastern shore.

Fort Atkinson. *Fort Berthold.*

Cantonment Badlands. 1879-83. *Cantonment at Little Missouri Crossing.* Troops were stationed here on the west bank of the Little Missouri river to protect workmen of the Northern Pacific Railroad. From Dickinson, go west on I-94 to Medora exit, 34 miles. Specific directions to the cantonment's site should be requested from National Park Service headquarters 1 mile south of the exit.

Camp Banks. 1863. Sibley's Expedition camped here at what is now called Chaska Historic Site after Indian scout who died during expedition and is buried here. The state-owned park, with marker, is north of Driscoll.

Fort Berthold. 1845-66. *Fort Atkinson.* Fort Berthold was originally a trading post that was joined in 1859 by a fur trading competitor, Fort Atkinson. The American Fur Company, owners of Berthold, bought out the Atkinson venture and moved their operation to the newer post, designating it New Fort Berthold.

The Army arrived in 1864 and, in 1866, moved to the site of Fort Stevenson 17 miles away and for a short time called it "New Fort Berthold," too. All of the sites have been inundated by the Garrison Dam reclamation project and are under Lake Sakakawea.

An overlook of the sites can be reached by going from Bismarck on I-94 for 48 miles to North Dakota 49; head north about 46 miles on this road until it deadends at Lake Sakakawea.

Camp Beuel. 1863. This was one of the first campsites for Sibley's troops after they entered the present boundaries of North Dakota. From Fargo, go south on I-29 about 50 miles to North Dakota 13. Turn westward on 13 about 25 miles to a turnoff to Milnor, right (north). Camp Beuel site is at Milnor.

Fort Buford. 1866-85. This post was one of the most be-deviled forts in the west. It was even the victim of a country-wide rumor that the garrison had been massacred, but there was more imagination than fact to this. The state now manages the site and the remaining buildings. From Williston, go west on US 2 for 7 miles to the town of Buford. The Fort Buford Historic Site is 1 mile south of the town.

Chaboillez Post. *Fort Pambian.*

Fort Clark. 1829-37. Trader James Kipp built this 132-by 147-foot stockade for the American Fur Company. Until closed by a smallpox epidemic in 1837, Clark was one of the most important fur posts of the Missouri. It is now a State Historic Park; no traces of the stockade remain.

FORT BERTHOLD, outside *(1)*

FORT BERTHOLD, inside *(1)*

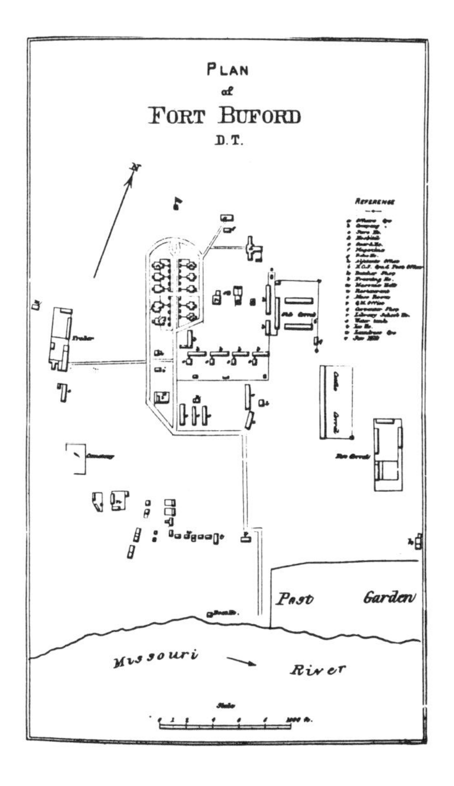

From Bismarck go west on I-94 for 31 miles to New Salem exit at North Dakota 31. Go north on North Dakota 31 for 31 miles to North Dakota 7; turn right (east) for 3 miles, then right again on gravel road (directly east across the river is the site of Fort Mandan, Lewis and Clark wintering-over post).

Fort Clark park is on left (east) side of the road about 6 miles south of the intersection.

Camp Corning. 1863. Sibley's expedition overnighted here on July 16, 1863. From Jamestown, take I-94 east 24 miles to North Dakota 1. Go north on North Dakota 1 for 19 miles to a gravel road south of Dazey. Turn right (east) for 6 miles to an intersection with another gravel road; turn left (north) for about 2 miles to Camp Corning Historic Site.

Fort Cross. *Fort Seward.*

Fort Daer. 1812. This was protection for a group of Scottish and Irish settlers, the first permanent settlement at the mouth of the Pembina river. The site was the same as for Fort Pambian.

Fort Dilts. 1864. This was a sod breastwork in which an immigrant train withstood Indian attacks for 14 days. The lonely site is marked and grave stones memorialize the soldiers killed in the defense. From Bowman, in southwestern North Dakota, go west on US 12 for 18 miles to a hard right turn (north) onto a gravel road. After 2.5 miles, turn left (west) onto single track dirt road. Site is on left (south) side of road, 2 miles further.

Fort George H. Thomas. *Fort Pembina.*

Camp Grant. 1863. Another one of the Sibley expedition campsites, now a State Historic Site. From Jamestown, go northwest on US 52-281 for 35 miles to gravel road (2 miles north of Melville). Turn left (west) for 8 miles—where another Sibley site, Camp Kimball, is north of the road—and then another 8 to a road intersection; Camp Grant site is southwest of this intersection.

Camp Greeley. *Camp Hancock.*

Camp Hancock. 1872-77. *Camp Greeley.* Under the Greeley name this post was intended to protect the railroad construction crews but its mission expanded to supply depot status when the railroad arrived at Bismarck. A single log barracks, 100 by 20 feet, and six other buildings made up this supply point for the Dakota posts, especially Custer's Fort Abraham Lincoln to the south. The site includes a remodeled building, now used as a museum to Dakota pioneers and Indian tribes, at 117 Main avenue in downtown Bismarck.

Camp Hayes. 1863. This was a week-long camp for Sibley's column, giving them time to dig trenches and breastworks—some still in slight evidence—while awaiting supplies and mail. From Valley City, go south on North Dakota 1 for 37 miles south to North Dakota 27. Turn left (east) for 23 miles to a gravel road. Turn right (south) for 2 miles. Turn left (east) for 3 miles to another junction; turn right (south)

FORT MORTIMER
From a drawing by Alexander H. Murray *(1)*

4.8 miles to the site of Camp Hayes on the first level above the Cheyenne river flood plain.

Heart River Corral. *Sully's Base Camp.*

Fort Henry. 1801-09. Alexander Henry maintained this North West Company trading post at Pembina, immediately north of the mouth of the Pembina river. The site is across Rolette street from the site of Pembina House.

Camp Houston. 1880. This was a temporary camp for the protection of railroad construction crews at Dickinson, south of I-94 on North Dakota 22 in southwestern North Dakota.

Camp Kimball. 1863. Sibley's troops camped here July 22 and 23, 1863, before moving southwest for the Battle of Big Mound. Now a State Historic Site. Directions to the site are at the Camp Grant entry.

Kipp's Post. 1826-30. Fur trader James Kipp built this 96-foot square stockade in order to capitalize on the Indian business until the establishment of Fort Union.

Only slight surface traces indicated the site until the State Historical Society conducted archeological excavations in 1954. These showed that the buildings had been destroyed by fire and, from metal fragments unearthed, had at least one 1-pounder cannon for protection. The latter does not seem to have been much protection: the remnants indicated the cannon had exploded.

Smithsonian Institution River Basin Survey Paper Number 20, publihsed in 1958, gives detailed data on the excavation project. From New Town, go north along Spanish Bay and cross the Little Knife river. Continue bearing left on gravel roads for a total of about 40 miles to a point 1 mile southeast of the mouth of the White Earth river. To the left and probably inundated by the Garrison Dam project is the site of Kipp's Post.

Fort Lewis. *Fort Lisa.*

Fort Lisa. 1809-12; 1823. *Fort Manuel Lisa, Fort Lewis, Fort Vanderburgh.* The Missouri Fur Company built this trading post under the direction of Manuel Lisa and Reuben Lewis, brother of Meriwether Lewis of Lewis and Clark fame, managed the post until it was abandoned in 1812. Under the Vanderburgh name, the post was occupied for a short time by Joshua Pilcher in 1822 or 1823. The site has been inundated by the Garrsion Dam project but the general area can be seen from Pick City near the western edge of the dam.

Cantonment at Little Missouri Crossing. *Cantonment Badlands.*

Fort Mandan. 1804-05. Lewis and Clark built this triangular shaped stockade for the winter of 1804-05; houses made up two sides, pickets the third. It was here that Sakakawea, the Indian girl, joined this expedition. A year later, on the way back from the Pacific coast, the duo noted that all but one house and some pickets had been burned. From Bismarck, take US 85 north for 40 miles to Washburn. From Washburn take a gravel road to the west 14 miles to Fort Mandan State Park, the approximate site of the post, where a replica has been built by the McLean County Historical Society.

Fort Manuel Lisa. *Fort Lisa.*

Fort McKeen. 1872-91. On a bluff 270 feet above Fort Abraham Lincoln, this stockaded post preceded the larger camp and, after completion of Abraham Lincoln, became a sub-post of it. There are reconstructed blockhouses and marked building sites at the location, now part of the Fort Abraham Lincoln State Park. Directions to the site are in the entry for Fort Abraham Lincoln.

Fort Mortimer. 1842-46. Fox, Livingston and Company built this trading post near the remnants of Fort William as competition for the American Fur Campany's Fort Union, three miles to the west. In three years it sold out to the competition. An adobe trading post was on the same spot in 1858; the Army built Fort Buford here in 1866. Follow directions to Fort Buford; the sites are almost the same.

Fort Pambian. 1797-98. *Chaboillez Post.* The first trading post in North Dakota, this was a rough camp built by Charles Chaboillez of the North West Company. Four canoes full of furs were the season's total of trade from the Indians, usually received in barter for rum. The buildings were burned in 1815. The site is on the south side of the mouth of the Pembina river, now Selkirk Park on Stutsman street in Pembina (on I-29 about 3 miles south of the Canadian border).

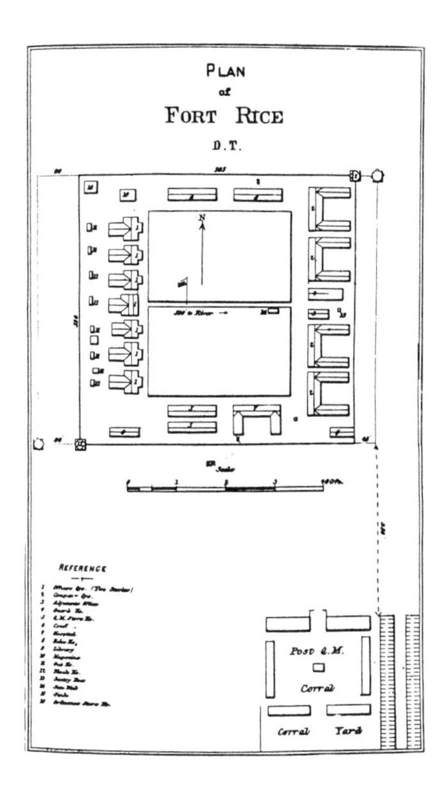

Although the stockade and all buildings have disappeared, mounds and impressions on the surface indicate the layout of the post.

Take I-94 west for 48 miles to North Dakota 32. Turn left, going south on 32 for 20 miles to North Dakota 46. Turn right (west) for 2 miles to a gravel road on the left. Turn left (south) and follow this curving road for about 15 miles to the village of Fort Ransom. The fort site is in a valley south of the Sheyenne river on the left side of the road 1 mile south of the town.

Fort Rice. 1864-78. Most of the major expeditions between 1864 to 1873 started from Fort Rice, a stockaded post that commanded most of the Missouri river in the Dakotas during its early days. Several blockhouses have been reconstructed and building sites are marked in a state park, though one burned in 1977. From Bismarck, proceed to Fort Abraham Lincoln and then continue south for 30 miles to the town of Fort Rice. Turn left (west), cross railroad tracks, bear right one mile to the fort site overlooking the Missouri river.

Cantonment at Sentinel Butte Station. 1880-82. Troops protected the Northern Pacific construction crews in the shadows of the strategic Sentinel Buttes beginning in late 1880 and periodically for a couple of years. From Cantonment Badlands continue west on I-94 to Sentinel Butte exit; turn south to the railroad, approximate site of the cantonment.

Fort Pembina. 1870-95. *Fort George H. Thomas.* Last of the several fort-type places in the Pembina area, this Army post had facilities for more than 1,000 soldiers. It was auctioned off in 1902, providing the area with several evidences of Army presence: a renovated officers quarters in the town of Pembina and water hydrants and mains in the town water system. The site of the post cemetery still is used. From Pembina, go south on I-29 for 3 miles to fort site adjacent to Pembina airport.

Fort Pembina. *Pembina House.*

Pembina House. 1803-23. *Fort Pembina.* This Hudson Bay Post operated on the north bank of the mouth of the Pembina river until it was determined that the site was in the United States rather than Canada. The site is on Rolette street where Minnesota Volunteers were stationed in 1863 (Pembina Detachment), in Pembina on I-29 south of the Canadian border.

Detachment at Pembina. 1863-64. Minnesota Volunteers set up a temporary cantonment at the site of Pembina House to protect the settlers during the so-called Sioux Uprising. A marker on the site records the fact that members of the garrison organized North Dakota's first Masonic lodge during their duty here.

Fort Ransom. 1867-72. Protecting the railroad was a major concern at this post and frequently only a skeleton guard was left behind to protect the families and government property. This stockaded fort is now a state park.

FORT RICE, 1865 *(6)*

FORT YATES *(l)*

Fort Seward. 1872-77. *Fort Cross, Fort Sykes.* A detachment of infantrymen arrived at this site in 1871, built a small building for shelter, and began to guard the railroad construction crews. The permanent post included the area of this shelter and, 100 yards north and atop a bluff, the rectangular main post, including a two-company barracks 230-feet long. The modern site is marked by a cannon on the bluff northwest of Jamestown about 2 miles on US 52-281.

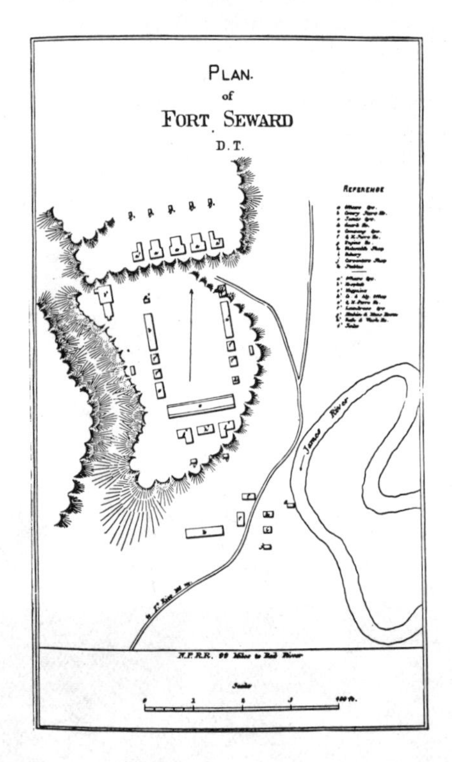

Camp Sheardown. 1863. Rifle pits at this Historic Site are the only traces of Sibley expedition use on their way to engage the Sioux. From Valley City, on I-94, go south about 3 miles on a gravel road to the marked site, left (east) side of road.

Fort at Standing Rock Agency. *Fort Yates.*

Fort Stevenson. 1867-83. *New Fort Berthold.* Although given the latter name when it was first occupied by troopers from Fort Berthold, the Stevenson name soon was adopted. It was an important post because of its strategic location, both along the Missouri river and on the trans-Dakota east-west trail.

The post was quadrangular in shape, buildings or fences surrounding a parade ground that was flanked by 10 buildings. The post was inundated by the Garrison Dam project.

To reach an overlook of the general area, take US 83 from Bismarck for 73 miles north to North Dakota 37. Turn left (west) on 37 for 6 miles to Garrison. Three miles south of Garrsion is the Fort Stevenson Recreation Area, overlooking the approximate site of Fort Stevenson.

Sully Base Camp. 1864. *Heart River Corral.* The forwardmost base of Sully's 4,000-man expedition in 1864 was this camp on the Heart River, a 10-day post manned by 125 soldiers, 250 emigrants and a decoy cannon. A stone marker in the center of a pasture memorializes the Army use for the Battle of Killdeer Mountain. From Dickinson, go east on I-94 for 27 miles to Antelope exit. Go south on gravel road for 14.3 miles. Marker can be seen in field to the left (east) of the road just before crossing the Heart river bridge.

Fort Sykes. *Fort Seward.*

Tilton's Post. 1822-23. This was another post built by James Kipp. It was just about the Fort Clark site and was soon abandoned because of

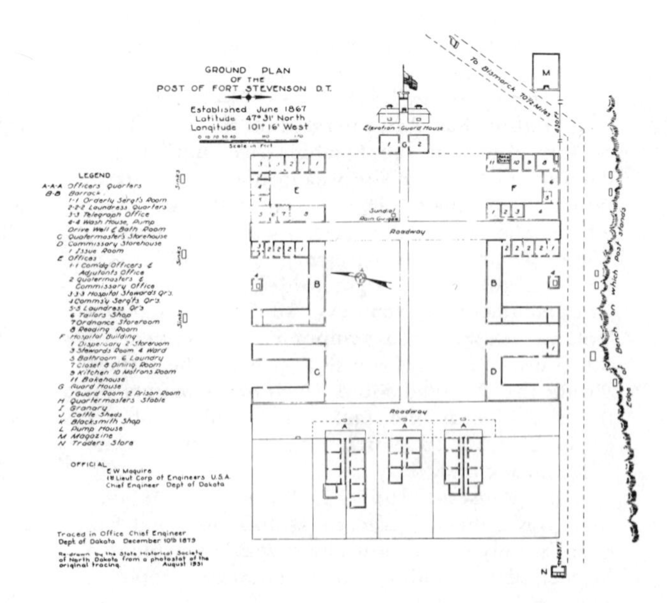

Indian hostility – one of the employees was killed at the fort's entrance, in fact. The approximate site can be reached by following the directions to Fort Clark; Tilton's Post was a mile or so north of Fort Clark but there is no trace. Kipp contributed to the deterioration of the site by tearing down many of the pickets and using them in a trading post he operated across the river at the Mandan Villages during the winter of 1825-26.

Fort Totten. 1867-90. One of the best preserved of the forts of the old west, Fort Totten's period photographs are hard to distinguish from modern photography. Almost all of the Army's brick buildings are left around the parade ground; the only difference is that the saplings planted 100 years ago are now substantial trees. The state has made a park of the parade ground and its flanking 15-plus buildings. From Devil's Lake, take North Dakota 20 south for 5 miles to North Dakota 57. Turn right (west) on 57, following it around to Fort Totten Indian Agency and State Park. The town of Fort Totten is immediately north of the park and fort site.

PLAN
of
FORT TOTTEN
D.T.

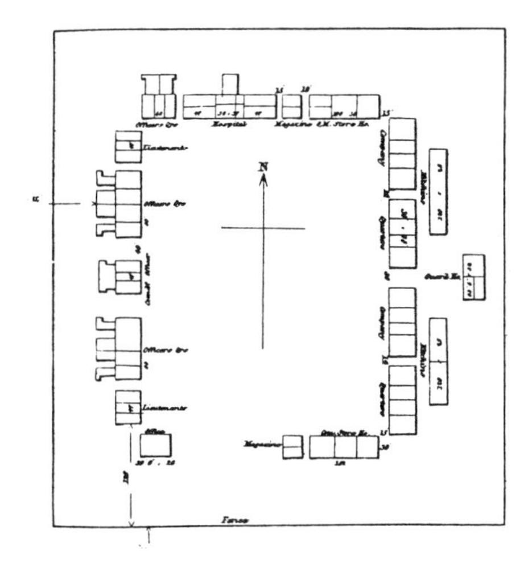

Fort Union. 1829-1865. Kenneth McKenzie built this 220- by 240-foot stockaded trading post to be the model fur post of the Missouri. It overcame all opposition during its heyday until the Army clamped down on illicit liquor bartering. Troops were stationed at the fort in 1864 until it was closed in mid-1865. The National Park Service is developing the site at the Fort Union Trading Post Historic Site. Follow directions to Fort Buford; take the gravel road west from the town west to the Montana border. Fort Union is on the Dakota side, 50 yards south of the road.

Fort Vanderburgh. *Fort Lisa.*

Camp Weiser. 1863. The Sibley column overnighted here July 13-14, 1863, naming the site in honor of the surgeon of the First Minnesota Mounted Rangers who was later killed at the Battle of Big Mound. From Valley City, go south on North Dakota 1 for 24 miles to North Dakota 46. Turn left (east) for 9 miles to a dirt road. Turn left (north) on dirt road 1 mile to the Historic Site.

Fort Yates. 1874-1903. *Post at Standing Rock Agency.* Although this post was established in order to watch over the Indian agency, it was here that the Messiah Craze and ultimately the Messiah War began. Some Army buildings and the cemetery remain, mixed with buildings of the agency; the Standing Rock is mounted on a bluff at the north end of the town. From Mobridge, S.D., take US 12 cross Missouri river for 34 miles northwest to McLaughlin. Turn right on South Dakota 63 for 9 miles to the state line where the route becomes North Dakota 6. Six miles north of the line, turn right (east) on North Dakota 24. Follow this gravel road to its end at the Standing Rock Agency and town of Fort Yates.

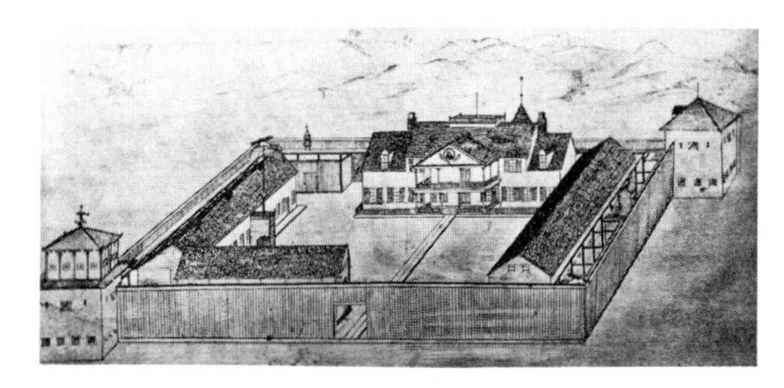

FORT UNION *(1)*

OKLAHOMA

FORT COFFEE, 1853 *(28)*

Choctaw Nation, Indian Territory, Oklahoma — regardless of the name this state had its full share of both military and trading posts. Markers and state or local efforts have recorded and preserved the sites of many posts as this section indicates.

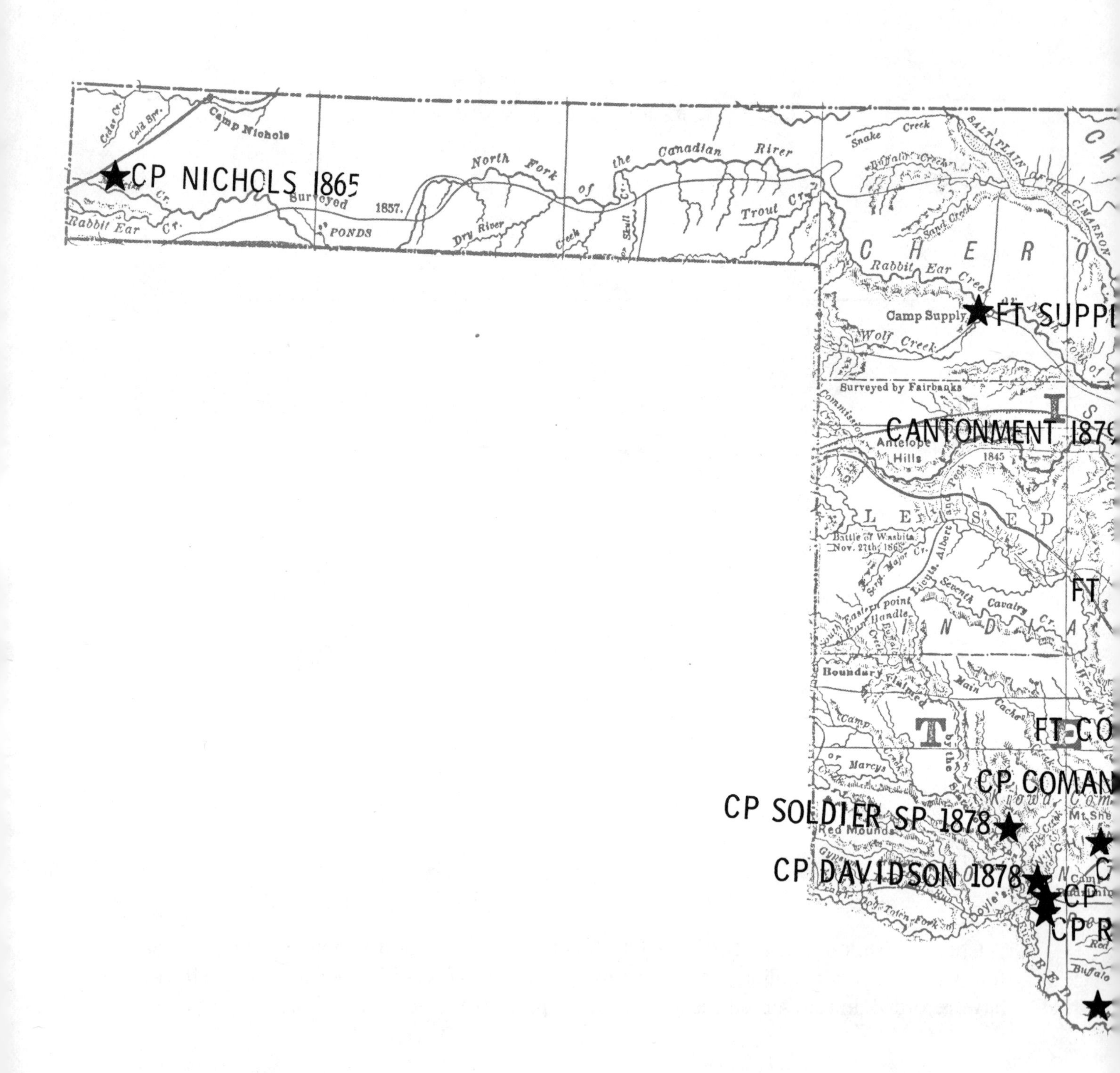

CP NICHOLS 1865
Camp Nichols
Cedar Cr.
Cold Spr.
Rabbit Ear Cr.
North Fork of the Canadian River
Surveyed 1857.
PONDS
Dry River
Trout Cr.
Snake Creek
Sand Creek
Rabbit Ear Creek
Camp Supply
Wolf Creek
Surveyed by Fairbanks
Antelope Hills
1845
Seventh Cavalry
Boundary
Main
Cache
Marcys
Red Mounds
CP SOLDIER SP 1878
CP DAVIDSON 1878

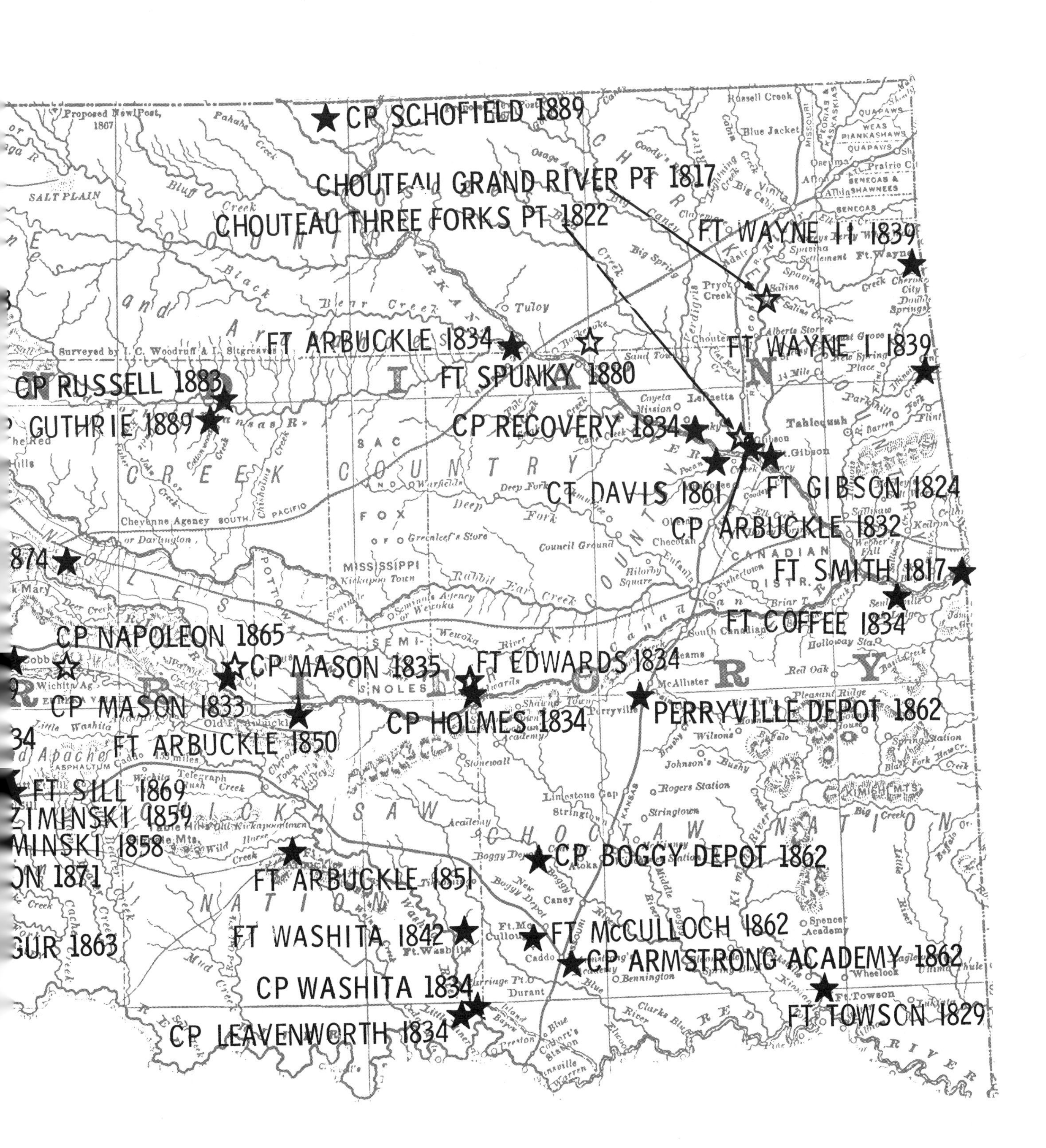

CP SCHOFIELD 1889
CHOUTEAU GRAND RIVER PT 1817
CHOUTEAU THREE FORKS PT 1822
FT WAYNE II 1839
FT ARBUCKLE 1834
FT SPUNKY 1880
FT WAYNE I 1839
CP RUSSELL 1883
GUTHRIE 1889
CP RECOVERY 1834
CT DAVIS 1861
FT GIBSON 1824
CP ARBUCKLE 1832
FT SMITH 1817
FT COFFEE 1834
CP NAPOLEON 1865
CP MASON 1835
FT EDWARDS 1834
CP MASON 1833
CP HOLMES 1834
PERRYVILLE DEPOT 1862
FT ARBUCKLE 1850
FT SILL 1869
CP BOGGY DEPOT 1862
FT ARBUCKLE 1851
FT WASHITA 1842
FT McCULLOCH 1862
CP ARMSTRONG ACADEMY 1862
CP WASHITA 1834
FT TOWSON 1829
CP LEAVENWORTH 1834
CREEK COUNTRY
CHOCTAW NATION

Fort Arbuckle. 1832-70. *Cedar Camp, Fort near the Crossing of the Washita.* There were four posts called Arbuckle and these dates show the age span of the entire group. The first (1832-33), usually called Camp Arbuckle, was a temporary camp of the Rangers a mile and a half from Fort Gibson. The approximate site is near the northern bank of the Arkansas river about where the Muskogee Turnpike crosses the river.

OLD FORT ARBUCKLE
From an oil painting by Vinson Lackey *(2)*

NEW FORT ARBUCKLE
From an oil painting by Vinson Lackey *(2)*

The second Arbuckle, usually called Old Fort Arbuckle (1834) consisted primarily of a picket stockade with a 25-foot square blockhouse at one corner. The post was intended to be permanent, but the movement of the Indians eliminated its mission and it was closed after a single season. Also called Cedar Camp on occasion, the site was flooded by the Keystone reservoir about 17 miles northwest of Tulsa.

The third Arbuckle was a temporary shanty-type post for wintering over the 1850-51 season when the site, originally intended to be permanent, was disapproved after the soldiers started to build. It was too late to move before winter, so the troops hutted up against the cold. The site can be reached from Oklahoma City via I-35 south to Wayne exit then turn east on Oklahoma 59 for 17 miles to Byars. The approximate site is 1 mile west and 1.5 miles north of Byars at a location about 1 mile south of the Canadian river. Local roads and directions are necessary.

The final Fort Arbuckle, and the most important, was at the site to which the troops moved after the winter of 1850-51. Several dozen sturdy log buildings comprised the fort, termed Fort near the Crossing of the Washita for a short period, during its pre- and post-war use by the Union and Civil War use by the Confederates. Several fireplaces are left at the site on a private ranch; from Davis, take Oklahoma 7 west for 7 miles and turn left 1/2 mile on a gravel road to the site on the left (west) side of the road.

Camp and **Hospital at Armstrong Academy.** 1862-65. Armstrong Academy was founded in 1844 as an educational institution, later was the site of the Choctaw Nation capital, and during the Civil War was used by the Confederates as a camp and hospital. Go west from Durant on US 70 for 14 miles to Bokchito. Turn left (north) 2.3 miles to the ruins of the Armstrong Academy, remnants of a fire in 1921.

Camp Augur. 1873-74. This was a field camp sub-post of Fort Sill, manned by troops from Sill. Its sketchy history included an incident in April, 1874, when Indians fired on it from a range of 85 paces. The approximate site is 5 miles southwest of Grandfield (on US 70 about 12 miles west of the Bailey Turnpike).

Fort Beach. 1874. *Fort Otter.* The same site as the first Camp Radziminski, this was a redoubt that was a relay point for supply trains.

Fort Blunt. 1863-65. This was a temporary Civil War earthwork 1 1/4 miles long manned by 6,000 troops and 18 cannon on the hill above Fort Gibson.

Camp at Boggy Depot. 1862-65. Confederates occupied this Indian center throughout the Civil War, the Stars and Bars floating from the town flagpole the entire time. The cemetery still has markers for Confederates who died here. The original town was abandoned when the railroad missed it and now the only remnants are overgrown foundations and cisterns. Take US 75 south from Atoka 1.2 miles to Oklahoma 7. Turn right (west) for 11.3 miles to a gravel road; turn left (south) 15.1 miles to the site of Old Boggy Depot (the present town is 2.5 miles to the south).

Camp Canadian. *Fort Holmes.*

Cantonment. 1879-82. *Cantonment on North Fork of the Canadian River.* Despite its mission to support Ranald Mackenzie and its three-year tenure, this post never acquired a more formal name than this single word title. Several buildings are left. From Canton (at the intersection of Oklahoma 51 and 58), go west on Oklahoma 51 for 2 miles, turning right (north) at gravel road near historical marker. Go north 2.8 miles to dirt road (right turn to east) up slight rise overlooking Canton Reservoir. Cantonment's site and remaining buildings are on the slope above the reservoir.

Cedar Camp. *Fort Arbuckle.*

Camp near Cheyenne Agency. *Fort Reno.*

Chouteau's Grand River Post. 1817-22. The Chouteau family established this trading post early in the 19th century but it was not really active until 1817. Five years later the post was moved to the Three Forks area, across from Fort Gibson and north of modern Muskogee. The post is memorialized by a marker on the Main street in Salina, on Oklahoma 20 about 10 miles east of Pryor. The site of the post is occupied by the Salina High School where a spring once used by the post is inclosed by a blockhouse built in post-Choteau days by Cherokee Chief John Ross.

Chouteau's Three Forks Post. 1822-28. This was the site to which Auguste Pierre Choteau moved his Salina trading post, occupying a post operated earlier in the 19th century by the firm of Brand and Barbour. In 1828 the government bought the property from Chouteau for use as a Creek Indian Agency. The site is approximately 1/2 mile south of the resort town of Okay, north of the Okay exit of the Muskogee Turnpike (3 miles north of Muskogee).

Fort Cobb. 1859-60. Established to protect the Indians, Cobb was evacuated in 1861 by Union troops and then occupied by Confederates until it was sacked by Indians. It was used occasionally by Confederates during the war and regarrisoned by Federals. Its largest garrison was the temporary encampment of Sheridan and Custer after the Battle of the Washita. There are no remains on the slope east of the town of Fort Cobb, on Oklahoma 9 about 35 miles west of the Chickasha exit on the Bailey Turnpike.

FORT COBB
From an oil painting by Vinson Lackey *(2)*

Cantonment N.W. of Canton, 1892
From an oil painting by Vinson Lackey *(2)*

Fort Coffee. 1834-38; 1862-63. The Army's main mission at Fort Coffee was to curtail whiskey smuggling but in the Civil War the post was a base for Confederate operations. Only the site is left. From Fort Smith, Arkansas, go southwest on US 271 to the state line. After entering Oklahoma, continue on US 271 for 9.4 miles to a right (north) turn onto a gravel road; historical markers are at the intersection. After 5 miles, turn right again. Fort Coffee site is about 1 mile down this road on a bluff overlooking the Arkansas river.

Fort near the Crossing of the Washita. *Fort Arbuckle.*

Camp Comanche. 1834. When Colonel Henry Dodge and his Dragoons met the Comanches to parlay over what was to become the Treaty of 1835, Dodge encamped his troops north of Cache creek. The tents were arranged in the form of a hollow rectangle with sentinels all around and creeks protecting three sides. The site is on the Fort Sill reservation near magazine 19.

Camp Davidson. 1878-82. This was a temporary camp from Fort Sill for Indian Police and Sill troopers to watch over the cattle trails. The approximate site is on Otter Creek about 4 miles east of Humphreys (which is about 8 miles southeast of Altus).

Cantonment Davis. 1861-62. Confederate General Albert Pike spent one million Confederate dollars in building this log and plank headquarters post from which troops were provided for the Battle of Pea Ridge. The fort was taken and burned by Federals two days after Christmas, 1862. Go north from Muskogee to the Bacone Indian College near which is the memorial and site of Fort Davis.

Fort Edwards. *Fort Holmes.*

Fort Elliott. *Fort Sill.*

Fort Gibson. 1824-90. The dates for Fort Gibson were not exactly continuous but even in its inactive days this post was an influence in the area. It was the farthest west for awhile after its completion in 1826. In 1831, the entire 7th Infantry was stationed at this stockaded post. More than 6,000 troops occupied earthworks nicknamed Fort Blunt on the hill above the original fort. There are elaborate remains of both the original fort – mostly reconstructions – and its Civil War successor. Confederates occupied the post from 1861 to 1863. The town of Fort Gibson is on Oklahoma 10 about 4 miles east of the Muskogee exit of the Muskogee Turnpike. The town's Main street runs north directly into the stockade reconstruction of the first site of the post. The second site is on the hill to the east, up the winding road to the right of the stockade.

Camp Guthrie. 1889-91. Keeping watch over the founding days of an early capital of Oklahoma – 1890 to 1910 – was the mission of this camp. The site is in the city of Guthrie north of Oklahoma City on I-35.

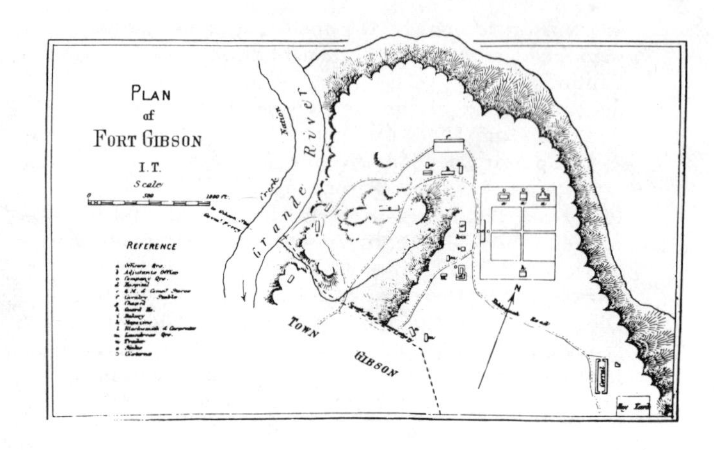

FORT GIBSON
Officers' Quarters, 1885 *(1)*

FORT GIBSON
From an oil painting by Vinson Lackey *(2)*

Camp Holmes. 1834-35. *Camp Canadian, Fort Edwards.* Located near the site of the Edwards Trading Post – hence the misnomer Fort Edwards occasionally attached to the post – Holmes was at the crossing of the Canadian on the Osage Trail. It proved unhealthful, however, and was abandoned after a year of operation. The trading post, located across the Little river, operated for a number of years after Camp Holmes was given up. From Oklahoma City, go east on I-40 for 61 miles to Oklahoma 56. Go south on Oklahoma 56 for 19 miles to US 270. Turn left (east) on US 270 for 7 miles to Oklahoma 48-68. Turn right (south) on 48-68 for 6 miles to the Little river. Fort Edwards was on the north bank at this point, Camp Holmes on the south bank.

Camp Leavenworth. 1834. General Henry Leavenworth died here while leading an expedition of Dragoons to a peace conference with the Plains Indians. The expedition continued to the parlay site, establishing Camp Comanche there. Go east on US 70 for 20 miles to Kingston where a marker commemorates the site of Camp Leavenworth, 2 miles south of town.

Camp Mason. 1835. This was a very short-term post established by Major Richard B. Mason, 1st U.S. Dragoons, for the Indian Council of 1835. After it ended, the site was taken over by Auguste Chouteau, founder of many trading posts, as another commercial center. The name Fort Mason was used by the trading post between 1835 and 1837 when it was closed. From Oklahoma City, go south on I-35 to Purcell, then across the Canadian river east on US 77 toward Lexington. At the "Y" upon leaving the bridge is the approximate site of Camp Mason and the Chouteau post.

Fort McCulloch. 1862-65. After leaving Fort Davis, Confederate General Albert Pike built this extensive Civil War encampment. In addition to a canvas-roofed headquarters log hut, there were a few more log cabins, many tents and huts, and three earthen breastworks designed in the classic 5-pointed star ground plan. Eighteen cannon defended the place but no Federals appeared to chal-

FORT RENO *(1)*

lenge it before it was abandoned at the end of the war. From Durant, go north on US 69-75 for 3 miles to Oklahoma 48-78. Follow the Oklahoma route, remaining on 48 after 78 branches to the left in 2 more miles, north to the Blue river (total of 4 miles from US 69-75). Some traces of Fort McCulloch's earthworks can be seen on the south bank of the Blue river.

Camp at Medicine Bluff Creek. *Fort Sill.*

Camp Napoleon. 1865. Representatives of the Five Civilized Tribes met here with other tribes which had sympathized with the Confederates in a Confederate-sponsored compact to unify their efforts against encroachment by the Federal government and the warlike hostile Indians. Rather than a military alliance, it was a peace agreement that is now commemorated by a marker in Verden, the site of the cottonwood grove that sheltered the historic parlay. Verden is on US 62 about 10 miles west of the Chickasha exit on the Bailey Turnpike.

Camp Nichols. 1865. Kit Carson was both founder and sole commander of this short lived stone fort that protected the Santa Fe Trail through what later became Oklahoma's Panhandle. Picturesque stone ruins are left at the site near deep ruts of the Santa Fe Trail. From Boise City, go west on the blacktop road for 15 miles. It turns left, then 1/2 mile later, right, to Wheelus, 7 more miles. One mile past Wheelus turn right (north) on dirt road marked, possibly, by a Boy Scout temporary sign. A mile north on this dirt road go through a gate (closing it after!), and follow tracks bearing left. They will cross the Santa Fe Trail ruts. In 3/4 of a mile track dips into a ravine, then out. Bear right to the stone remnants of Camp Nichols. This is a fair weather route only.

Depot on the North Canadian. *Fort Supply.*

Cantonment on the North Fork of the Canadian River. *Cantonment.*

Fort Otter. *Fort Beach.*

Camp and **Station Otter Creek.** *Camp Radziminski.*

Perryville Depot. 1862-63. This was a Confederate military post and supply camp until the Federals defeated the South in the Battle of Perryville in 1863. Before abandoning the town, the rebels dumped salt into the wells; the Federals burned the buildings when they entered the area. From McAlester, go south on US 69 for 5.4 miles to a marker on the right (west) side of the highway which tells the story of Perryville, .3 mile to the west.

Camp Phoenix. *Fort Towson.*

Camp Radziminski. 1858-59. *Camp Otter Creek, Otter Creek Station.* Not only did Radziminski field troops for two major Indian battles, but in its short career it also occupied three sites and thereby generated considerable confusion among future historians.

The first site, September to November, 1858, was a picket stockade on the southeast bank of Otter Creek (near Tipton on Oklahoma 5, later occupied by Fort Beach).

When grazing gave out, the troops occupied a second site from November, 1858 to March, 1859, higher up Otter Creek. This location is vague due to the equally vague description of the site.

Site number 3, March to December, 1859, and for a year after used by Texas Rangers, provided better protection from the weather. It was the most noted of the three locations and, in 1869, the troops of the Sheridan-Custer "Winter Campaign" camped in the old ruins. From Snyder, go north on US 183 for 3 miles to Mountain Park. Turn left (west) for 4.2 miles; right (north) 1.1 mile to where the road becomes dirt. Continue 1.1 miles more to another dirt road to right (east). General site is .5 mile down this track.

Camp Recovery. 1834. After the Expedition of 1834, three companies of Dragoons were sent to this site to recover their strength – after they built the log cabins in which they were to recover. The site is 20 miles up the Arkansas river from Fort Gibson, on the Arkansas about 5 miles south of Porter.

Fort Reno. 1874-1948. *Post at Cheyenne Agency, Camp near Cheyenne Agency.* The troopers of Fort Reno handled the arrangements for the opening of the Oklahoma Land Rush, from arresting "sooners," who tried to enter the area early, to giving the signal for the start of the rush. This was also an important base for Indian operations. Many Army buildings are left and still in use at the Fort Reno Livestock Research Station 4 miles west of El Reno on US 66. Also on US 66 is a two-room log building, said to have been Sheridan's quarters in 1874, moved to this location on the north side of the highway at the edge of El Reno.

Camp Robinson. 1871. This was a sub-post of Fort Sill on Otter Creek in the vicinity of the first site of Camp Radziminski.

Camp Russell. 1883-86. This was a sub-post of Fort Reno occupied by four cavalry troops and one infantry company while enforcing the laws against Boomers (or Sooners) before the Oklahoma Land Rush started officially. From Guthrie go north on I-35 to the Cimarron river. The approximate site of Camp Russell is on the north bank of the Cimarron near the highway.

Camp Schofield. 1889. Used as a temporary field camp for maneuvers, this site was 3 miles east of Chilocco, 25 miles north of Ponca City off of US 77.

Fort Sill. 1869- . *Camp at Medicine Bluff Creek, Fort Elliott, Camp Starvation, Camp Wichita.* One of the most historic of western forts, Sill retains many of the old buildings, including the quarters in front of which the Indians planned to murder General William T. Sherman. Geronimo's grave is in the Apache cemetery here. An excellent museum is maintained by the Army in the "old post" portion of Fort Sill. The still active fort is 3 miles north of Lawton on US 277. Visitors are welcome.

Fort Smith. 1817-71. Although Smith usually is considered as being in Arkansas, the first post (1817-24 and 1833) was a stockade across the boundary in Indian Territory, modern Oklahoma before slight adjustments in the stateline were made to eliminate a "no man's land" east of the Arkansas river. Foundation excavations mark this site while reconstructed or stabilized buildings are at the 1838-71 site which includes Judge "Hanging" Parker's courtroom – all under National Park Service jurisdiction. In Fort Smith, Arkansas, take 2d street 1 block southwest of Garrison to Roger avenue; the second fort is at this intersection. Park Service guides and markers locate and identify the historic structures.

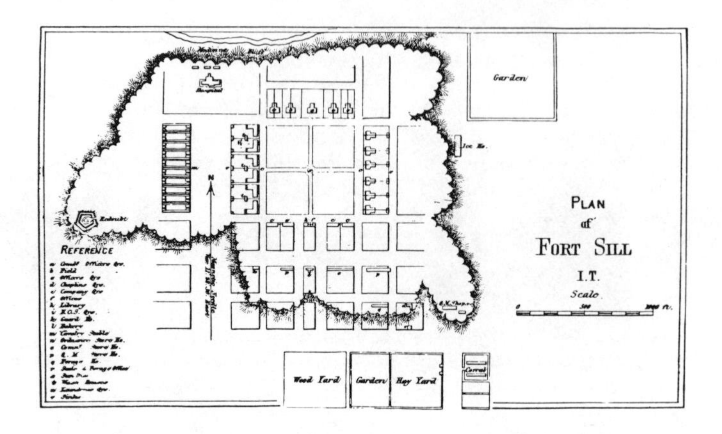

Camp at Soldier Spring. 1878-82. Located in the vicinity of the 1868 Battle of Soldier Spring, this field camp had the same mission as Camp Davidson. The site is on the North Fork of the Red River. From Altus, go north on Oklahoma 44 for about 17 miles to the river; from this point, the site was about 2 miles downriver.

Fort Spunky. 1880-83. A stop on the stage line, this never was a fort but took its energetic name from nearby Spunky creek. The site is near Catoosa (4 miles from the US 66 exit from I-44 about 7 miles northeast of Tulsa).

Camp Starvation. This was the sarcastic name that Kansas Volunteers suggested would be appropriate for Fort Sill, obviously based on their experiences there when it was being established.

Fort Supply. 1868-93. *Depot on the North Canadian.* The utilitarian name was attached to this base camp from which the Battle of Washita was fielded by Generals Sheridan and Custer. As its mission and size increased with age, the name remained the same, only exchanging "fort" for

FORT SMITH *(29)*

the original "camp." Many buildings left here include the quarters supposedly used by Sheridan, Custer and Nelson A. Miles. The town of Supply is at the entrance to the Panhandle where US 183 intersects with US 270. The site of Fort Supply is now Western State Hospital about 1 mile east of Supply on the north side of US 270.

FORT SUPPLY
From an oil painting by Vinson Lackey *(2)*

FORT SUPPLY, Opera House *(28)*

Fort Towson. 1824-29; 1831-54; 1863-65. *Camp Phoenix.* The 7th Infantry founded this stone fort although wooden shanties and tents comprised it until 1830. Confederate operations in Indian Territory were directed from here and this is where Confederate General Stand Watie surrendered his troops, the last organized Confederate force to give up. Many rock walls are being stabilized and preserved. From Hugo, in southeastern Oklahoma, go east on US 70 about 20 miles to Towson and continue through town to the first left after crossing the bridge. About 1 mile north, beyond a farmhouse on the left and about 500 yards west of the road, is the site of the fort on Oklahoma Historical Society owned property.

Camp Washita. 1834. A blockhouse and barracks were built here for the Leavenworth 1834 Expedition, but the site is uncertain. This temporary camp had no connection to the later

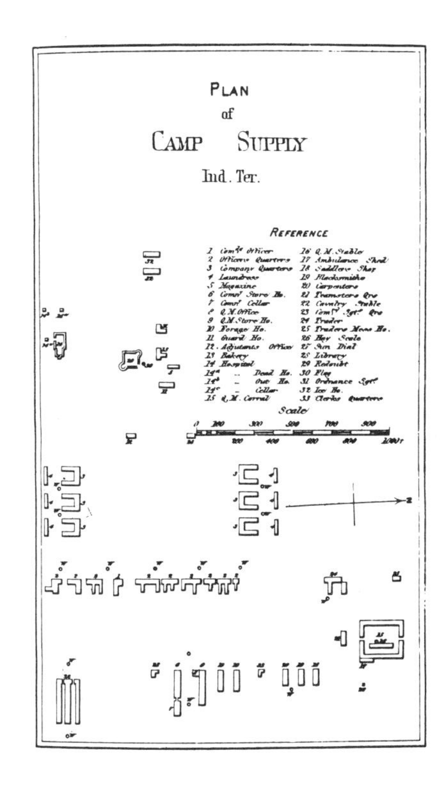

Fort Washita. The approximate site of Camp Washita is 3 miles north of the Red river and "a short distance" from the Washita, undoubtedly placing it under Lake Texoma.

Fort Washita. 1842-65. The ghostly double-storied brick walls of the barracks overlook the site of this post, a part of the Oklahoma state park system. This was an important fort throughout its career, serving the Federals before the Civil War and, as a supply depot and troop camp, the Confederates from 1861 to 1865. From Durant go north on US 69-75 for 3 miles to Oklahoma 78. Follow 78 to where it becomes Oklahoma 199 and takes a sharp turn to the southwest. The fort site is north of the road and within view.

FORT WASHITA
From an oil painting by Vinson Lackey *(2)*

Fort Wayne. 1838-52; 1861. The first site of this post was a wintering-over collection of huts that proved so unhealthful that it was abandoned in spring, 1839.

The permanent site was more healthy and work began on a four-company dragoon post which was to include large frame barracks and other buildings within a picket stockade. The location was abandoned before construction was complete after the Army decided that the post was too out of the way from the usual trails.

To reach the first site from Fort Smith, Arkansas, go west on I-40 for 26 miles to the Salisaw exit. Head north from Salisaw on US 59 for 53 miles to Watts; 2 miles north of Watts the road crosses the Illinois river, approximate site of the first Fort Wayne.

To get to the second site, continue north and west on US 59 to its junction with Oklahoma 10. Continue north on US 59-Oklahoma 10 for 5 miles to Oklahoma 116. Turn right (east) to Colcord, 4 miles. Turn left (north) for 6 miles to Spavinaw creek. From the point of crossing, Fort Wayne's second site is to the right (east) a couple of miles in privately owned pasture almost on the state line.

Camp Wichita. *Fort Sill.*

FORT WAYNE
From an oil painting by Vinson Lackey *(2)*

OREGON

FORT DALLES *(4)*

Campaigns before and during the Civil War contributed to the history of Oregon and to the number of settler and military forts in the state. The transitory nature of these campaigns, and the camps and posts developed by them, added to the difficulty in locating the sites, a problem not eased in the least by the rough terrain of Western Oregon and the high desert country of the east.

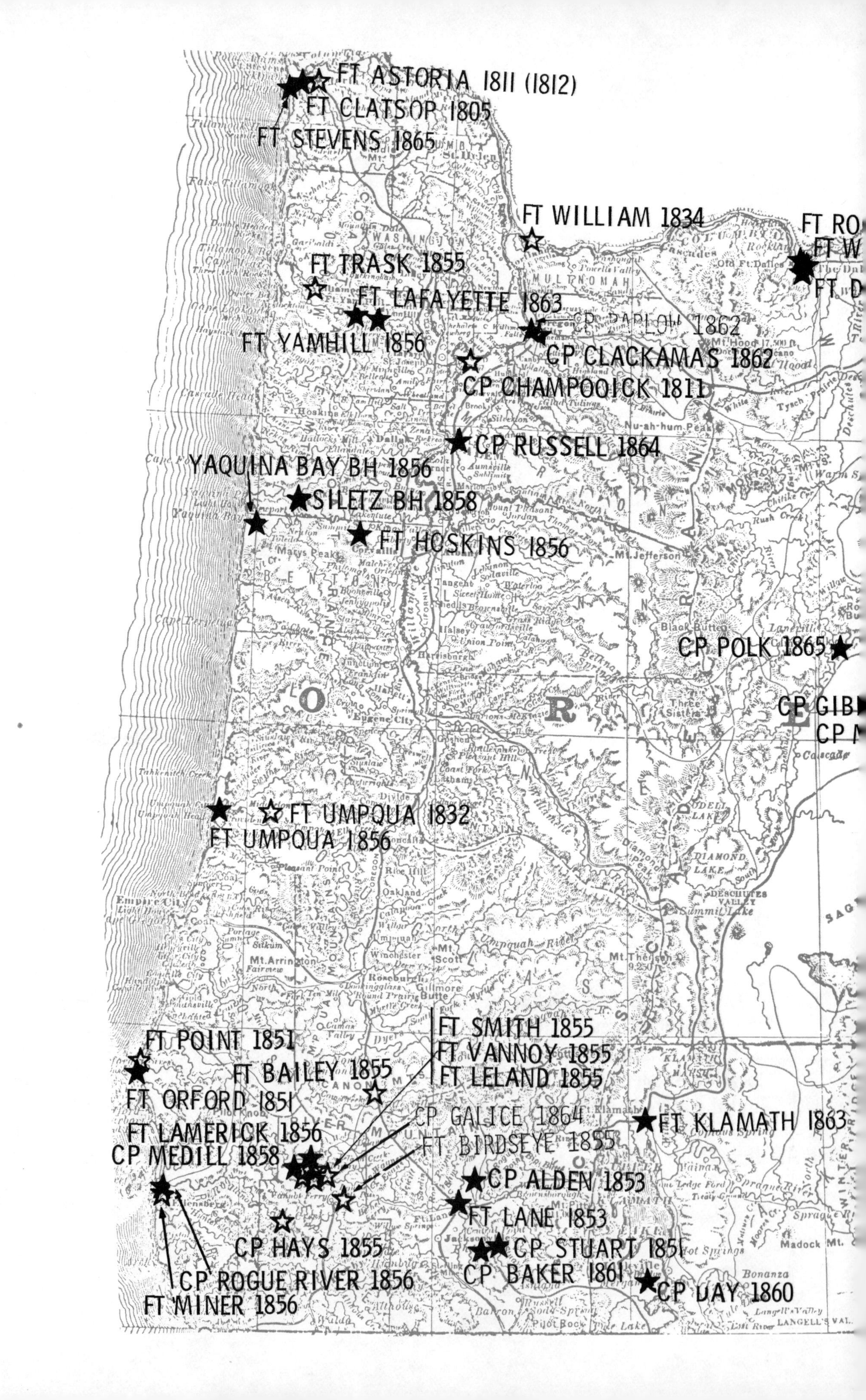

FT ASTORIA 1811 (1812)
FT CLATSOP 1805
FT STEVENS 1865
FT WILLIAM 1834
FT TRASK 1855
FT LAFAYETTE 1863
CP BARLOW 1862
FT YAMHILL 1856
CP CLACKAMAS 1862
CP CHAMPOOICK 1811
CP RUSSELL 1864
YAQUINA BAY BH 1856
SILETZ BH 1858
FT HOSKINS 1856
CP POLK 1865
FT UMPQUA 1832
FT UMPQUA 1856
FT SMITH 1855
FT VANNOY 1855
FT LELAND 1855
FT POINT 1851
FT BAILEY 1855
FT ORFORD 1851
CP GALICE 1864
FT KLAMATH 1863
FT LAMERICK 1856
FT BIRDSEYE 1855
CP MEDILL 1858
CP ALDEN 1853
FT LANE 1853
CP HAYS 1855
CP STUART 1851
CP BAKER 1861
CP ROGUE RIVER 1856
CP DAY 1860
FT MINER 1856

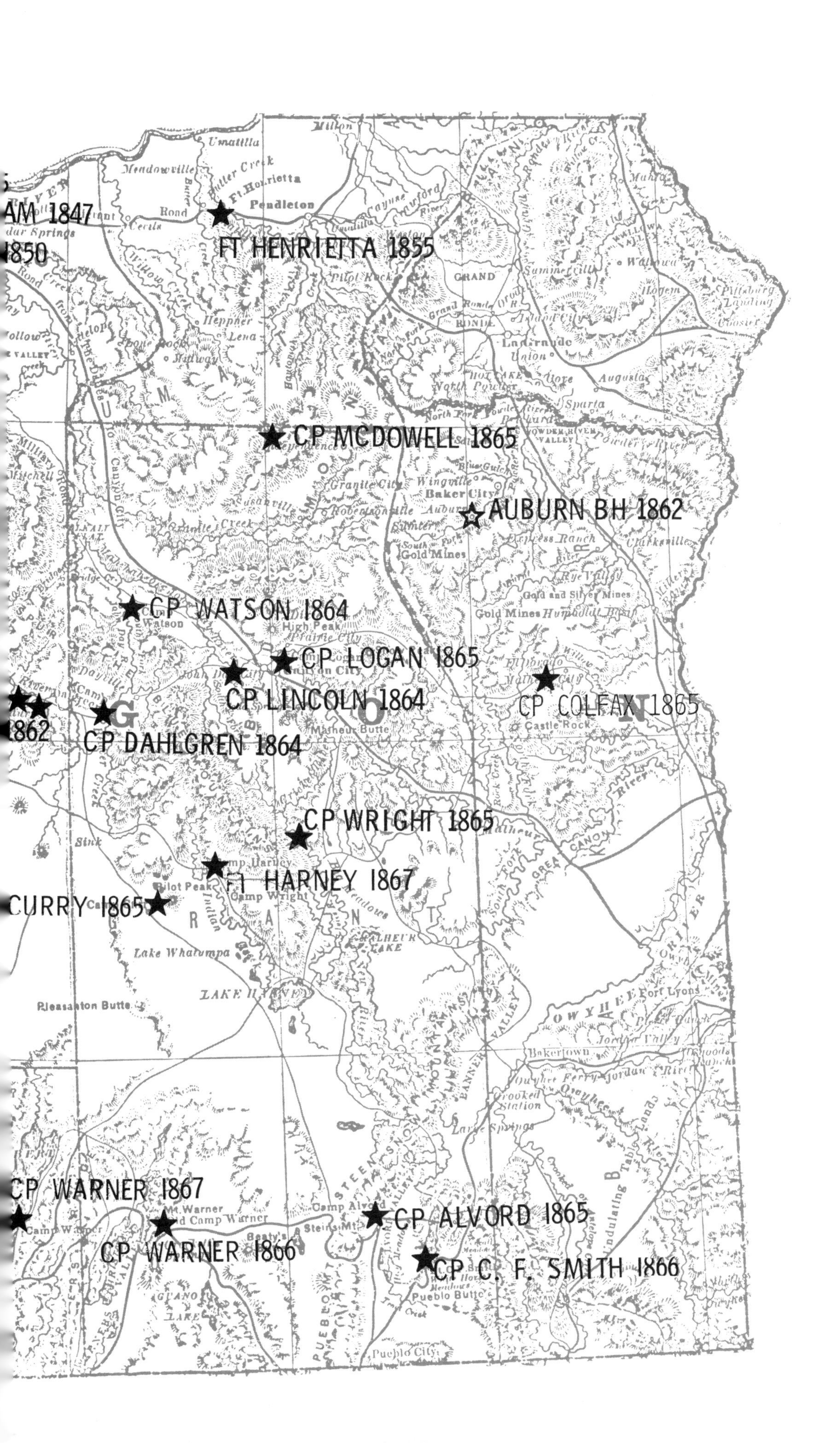

FT HENRIETTA 1855
CP MCDOWELL 1865
AUBURN BH 1862
CP WATSON 1864
CP LOGAN 1865
CP LINCOLN 1864
CP COLFAX 1865
CP DAHLGREN 1864
CP WRIGHT 1865
FT HARNEY 1867
CURRY 1865
CP WARNER 1867
CP WARNER 1866
CP ALVORD 1865
CP C. F. SMITH 1866
Umatilla
Pendleton
Ft. Henrietta
Pilot Rock
GRAND
RONDE
Heppner
Lena
Summerville
Wallowa
Union
Augusta
Sparta
North Powder
Granite City
Wingville
Baker City
Auburn
Gold Mines
Express Ranch
Clarksville
Rye Valley
Gold and Silver Mines
High Peak
Prairie City
Canyon City
Watson
Castle Rock
Malheur Butte
Camp Harney
Pilot Peak
Camp Wright
Lake Whatumpa
MALHEUR LAKE
LAKE HARNEY
Pleasanton Butte
OWYHEE
Fort Lyons
Jordan Valley
Bakertown
Crooked Station
Large Springs
Camp Alvord
Camp Warner
Pueblo Butte
Pueblo City
GUANO LAKE

Camp Alden. 1853. Established in early 1853, this was a temporary camp that preceded Fort Lane, both with the mission of watching over the Rogue River Indian Reservation. It was at Upper Table Rock which can be reached from Medford. Go north on I-5 to the next exit, Central Point. Go north on a secondary road from the Central Point exit for about 10 miles; Upper Table Rock is to the right of the road about 2 miles.

Camp Alvord. 1864-66. Lieutenant Colonel George B. Currey selected this as a headquarters and depot for the 1st Oregon Cavalry's winter campaign against the Indians in southeastern Oregon. Apparently it was chosen not only because of its proximity to an Indian winter camp but because it was the only patch of greenery in the desert country. There are no traces although it is claimed that the Alvord Ranch headquarters is built on the site of the camp. From Burns, go southeast on Oregon 78 for 66 miles to an improved road about 3 miles after passing Indian Creek Butte (right side). Turn right (southwest) on the improved road for 35 miles to the Alvord Ranch, left side.

Fort Astoria. 1811-1841. *Fort George.* This stockaded fur post was part of the U.S. and British race to establish supremacy in the Pacific Northwest. Built by the Pacific Fur Company, it was purchased by the British Northwest Company in 1813; U.S. interests had it 1818-23 until the Hudson Bay Company bought it and Dr. John McLoughlin used it as his headquarters for a year. The site is marked by a tiny park, painted backdrop and blockhouse replica at 15th and Exchange streets near downtown Astoria. The fort is outlined in paint on the streets and sidewalks at this intersection.

Auburn Blockhouse. 1862. Now a ghost town, Auburn had a Civil War population of more than 5,000 and a blockhouse to provide protection from the Indians. As the population increased, the need for the blockhouse lessened; by 1868 the town had declined to the point that there was no need for the blockhouse anyway because there was nothing left to protect. The various Army expeditions of the Civil War camped nearby and used Auburn as a supply and recreational center. From Baker, go south on Oregon 7 for 7 miles to a road to the left (west). Turn onto this road for 3.3 miles to sign memorializing Auburn at a fork; walk 1/2 mile along the right fork to the site of Auburn.

Fort Bailey. 1855. Oregon militia commanded by Captain Joseph Bailey operated from this tavern during the Rogue River Indian War. The site is 25 miles south of Roseburg above Cow Creek. From Roseburg go south on I-5 to the Azalea exit, the approximate site of Fort Bailey.

Camp Baker. 1861-65. Established to watch over the Confederate sympathizers in nearby Jacksonville, Baker became the recruiting center for southwestern Oregon. It was a primitive, log cabin type garrison. Volunteers used the site previously during the Rogue River War in 1835. From Medford, go south on I-5 to exit 5. Take Colemon Creek road to Camp Baker road. Turn right; a marker at the site is .9 mile west of the intersection on the left (south) side.

Camp Barlow. 1862. Four companies of Oregon Volunteers were recruited and then stationed at this temporary camp until June, 1862, when they were moved to Camp Clackamas. Barlow's site is indefinite about 2 miles north of Oregon City in the vicinity of Gladstone.

Fort Birdseye. 1855. This square hewn timber house was built by David Birdseye as a home but its solid construction provided protection and the nickname during the Rogue River war. A marker is on the site in the hamlet of Rogue River, 7 miles east of Grants Pass off of I-5.

Camp Burbank. *Camp Warner I.*

Camp C.F. Smith. 1866-69. Not to be confused with the more famous Montana fort, this post was almost as isolated but not as beset by Indians. It was a troop center in the Oregon desert immediately after the Civil War. Foundation stones and the general outline of the camp can be seen on a low plateau ½ mile north of the Whitehorse ranch, cattle center in southeastern Oregon. From Burns, go southeast on Oregon 78 for 82 miles to US 95. Turn right (south) on US 95 for 21 miles to a dirt road intersecting from the right (west). Turn onto this road for 22 miles to the Whitehorse ranch. The site of the camp is on private ranch property ½ mile north of the ranch headquarters; a dirt road leads up the mesa to it.

Fort Champooick. 1811-1852. *Fort Wallace, Fort Champoeg, Willamette Post.* It was by the Willamette Post name that this Pacific Fur Company trading post was first known but during later ownership by the Hudson Bay Company it was rechristened Champooick, after a nearby Indian village (named, in turn, for an edible plant). The more sophisticated spelling came later when the town of Champoeg grew up and then became instrumental in the political future of the area. The town and fort site were inundated by floods in 1861 and the area is now the Champoeg Memorial State Park. From Portland, go south on US 99W to Newberg. Take Oregon 219 east, just before arriving at Newberg, and in 4 miles turn off of 219 onto a paved road toward Champoeg State Park, 2 miles.

Camp Clackamas. 1862. This was a very temporary camp of less than a month's duration at the mouth of the Clackamas river north of Oregon City. It replaced nearby Camp Barlow and for the last two weeks in June, 1862, included the four companies from Barlow. After these left, it was occupied by a single company until mid-July, 1862, when it was moved to Jacksonville. The indefinite site is a mile north of Oregon City in the vicinity of the crossing of Clackamas river by US 99E.

Battery Clark. This was an Endicott period 12-inch position at Fort Stevens.

Fort Clatsop. 1805-06. The first U.S. fort on the Pacific, Clatsop was military only because of the military connection of the members of the Lewis and Clark Expedition who wintered over

FORT DALLES *(4)*

in this stockade in 1805-06. The National Park Service has erected a replica at the site of this log fort. From Astoria, go south on US 101 across the Youngs Bay Bridge. At .7 mile after crossing the bridge, turn left at the Airport-Fort Clatsop sign. Go 2.4 miles to the Park Service replica, staffed daily.

Camp Colfax. 1863; 1867. Oregon Volunteers who thought they were to be mustered out found, instead, that they were to be stationed at this field camp on the south fork of Willow Creek at the foot of Mount Ironsides. Their assignment was to protect the Dalles-Fort Boise Military Road. It was a tent camp until, the weather turning colder, the troopers made dugouts along Willow Creek. The camp was abandoned shortly after Christmas and reportedly burned but the site was used again during the summer of 1867. From John Day, at the junction of US 395 and 26, go east on US 26 for 67 miles to a gravel road 1 mile west of Ironside. Turn right (south) 5 miles to approximate site along Willow Creek which this road parallels.

Camp Crook. *Fort Harney.*

Camp Curry. 1865-66. Detachments of California, Oregon and Washington Volunteers shared this post with a company of the 14th U.S. Infantry during operations in southeastern Oregon. About 40 cabins, 10 by 12 feet, of hewn logs apparently made up the camp, plus a storage room dug into a hillside and a three-grave cemetery. The site is a privately owned ranch on Silver Creek to the north of Suntex. From Burns, go west on US 20 for 27 miles to Riley; turn right (north) on gravel road to Suntex, 8 miles.

Camp Dahlgren. 1864. After the grass gave out at Camp Gibbs, the 1864 Expedition to Southeast Oregon moved its depot to this field camp, 20 miles east of Gibbs and 15 east of Camp Maury. The indefinite sites of all three temporary camps are on the same route from Prineville in the Ochoco National Forest area. From Prineville, go east on US 26 1 mile to a paved road entering from the right (south). Take this road for 27 miles (to 2 miles past Post); this is the approximate site of Camp Gibbs. Continue 5 miles east to the approximate site of Camp Maury. Continue 15 more miles, in the vicinity of Paulina, the approximate site of Dahlgren.

Fort Dalles. 1850-67. *Camp Drum, Fort Lee, Fort Wascopam.* The military headquarters before the Civil War for central and eastern Oregon, this elaborate post was a cluster of frame buildings laid out in a semi-circular pattern. After the Civil War it was the headquarters for Crook's expedition the first half of 1867. A single structure, of the same classical architecture as Fort Simcoe and by the same architect, is now a museum. From downtown The Dalles, take 15th street uphill (south) to Garrison street. The fort site is on the southwest corner. A block away, at 14th and Trevitt streets, is Colonel George Wright school on the site of the parade ground.

Camp Day. 1860. Company L, 3d U.S. Artillery, occupied this camp for three months to provide security for the Upper Klamath road at the time of the Piute war to the southeast in Nevada. This was a tent camp amidst the pine trees southwest of Upper Klamath Lake. From Klamath Falls, go west on Oregon 66 for 9 miles to Keno. At Keno, go right (north) to Oatman Junction on a dirt road. Turn left onto another dirt road to Camp Sa-wa-li-na-is, Seventh Day Adventist youth camp, site of Camp Day.

Camp Drum. *Fort Dalles.*

Battery Freeman. This was an Endicott period position mounting 6- and 3-inch guns at Fort Stevens.

Camp Galice. 1854. According to the American Guide book on Oregon, this was a powder house and arsenal constructed for the Rogue River Indian Wars. From Grants Pass, go north on I-5 to the Merlin exit. Twelve miles past Merlin is the site of Galice.

Fort George. *Fort Astoria.*

Camp Gibbs. 1864. This was a supply and grazing camp for the Southeastern Oregon Expedition that also served as an operations base during the later phase of the expedition. It was a field camp similar to Camps Maury and Dahlgren and directions to the approximate site are given under the entry for the latter camp.

Post at Grand Ronde Agency. *Fort Lafayette.*

Fort Harney. 1867-80. *Camp on Rattlesnake Creek, Camp Steele, Camp Crook.* This was the military headquarters for southeastern Oregon's expeditions against the Piutes and Bannocks, sometimes having more Indians in custody than men in its garrison. All traces of the elaborate post have disappeared except for two civilian graves at the site of the post cemetery. From Burns, go east on US 20 for 12 miles. Turn left at gravel road. Go north 2 miles where Harney City ghost town – private property – is at the left (west). Continue 2 miles more to the north up the valley road where the fort site fills Rattlesnake Canyon, presently owned by the Catterson Ranch.

Fort Hays. 1855-56. Built in 1852 as a stage station and tavern, this building was nicknamed Fort Hays after the family occupying it when volunteers and miners fought off Indians beseiging it in 1856. From Grants Pass, go west on US 199 for 18.6 miles where the Anderson Stage Station is on the right (north) side. This was the Fort Hays of the Rogue River Indian War.

Fort Henrietta. 1855-56. The 1st Oregon Mounted Rifles established this stockade on the Umatilla Indian reservation after the agency buildings were burned by the Indians. The site has been inundated by the Umatilla river at Echo (2 miles from the Echo exit on I-80N, 17 miles west of Pendleton).

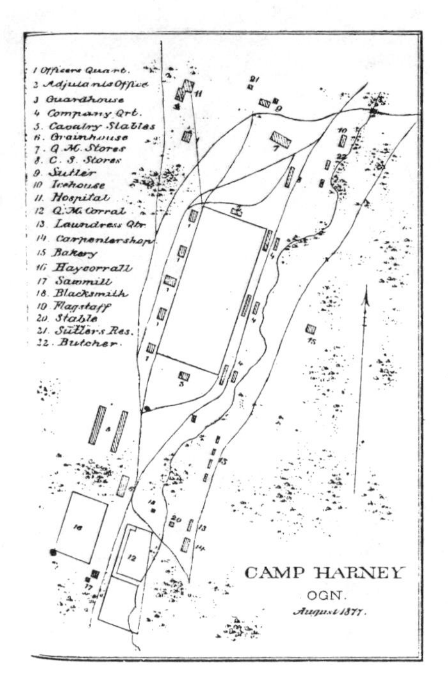

FORT HARNEY *(1)*

Fort Hoskins. 1856-66. Contrary to some records, there was only one Fort Hoskins, a post manned by regulars under Captain C.C. Augur before the Civil War and by unhappy Oregon Volunteers during the war. Several buildings and many local legends remain. From Corvallis, go west on US 20 for 11 miles to the intersection with Oregon 223. Turn right (north) about 5 miles to the turnoff left (west) to Hoskins, 1 mile. The near-ghost town is next to the fort site, on private property on the slight rise behind Main street.

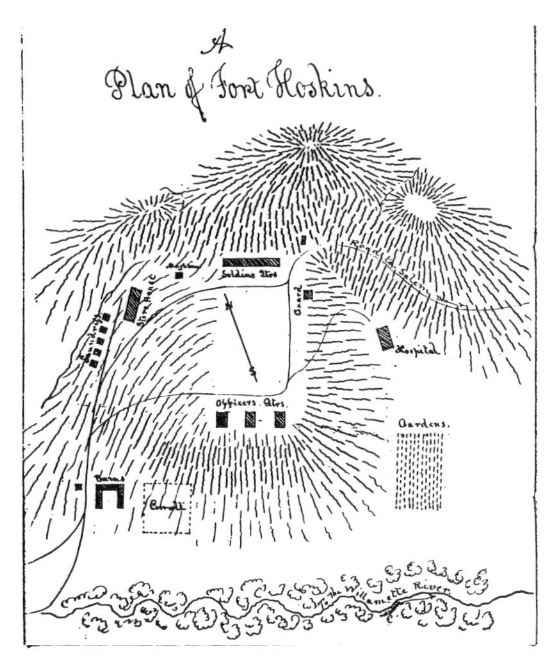

Camp Humbug. *Camp McDowell.*

Fort Klamath. 1863-90. Major permanent military post of southwestern Oregon, Fort Klamath fielded troops for the Modoc War and was the place of execution and burial of the leading Indian participants. The Klamath County Museum, housed in a replica of the fort guardhouse, is on the site. Graves of the Indians are in the cemetery, protected by heavy fences from souvenir hunters. From Klamath Falls, go north on US 97 for 25 miles to Oregon 62. Turn left onto Oregon 62 for 11 miles to the fort site, left (west) side, in a park.

Fort Lafayette. 1863. *Post at Grand Ronde Agency.* A small detachment of Oregon Volunteers manned this outpost of Fort Yamhill and gave it this unofficial designation. The detachment was at the agency headquarters. From Salem, go west 33 miles on Oregon 22 to the approximate site.

Fort Lamerick. 1856. Oregon Volunteers manned this low breastwork during the Rogue River war's final few months. The post was in Big Meadows, 2 miles from where Grave Creek joins the Rogue River. From Grants Pass go north on I-5 for 14 miles to the Sexton Mountain Pass exit. Take the Grave Creek road west from here about 13 miles to the general location of Fort Lamerick in Big Meadows.

Fort Lane. 1853-56. In the shadow of majestic Table Rock, Fort Lane was commissioned to keep the peace treaty signed there during the period of the Rogue River wars. Nothing is left on the meadow that once housed 60 dragoons in a dozen rough buildings; nearby is a splintered dead tree, the so-called "signal gun tree," supposedly blown off by the firing of Fort Lane's howitzer. From Medford, go north on I-5 to the Blackwell junction 3.5 miles north of Central Point. Bear right (east). At Gold Ray Dam road, 1.7 miles, turn right. In .5 mile, note the Tolo railroad sign on the right side of the road; the stone marker for Fort Lane is on the left, 200 yards from the actual site of the fort.

Fort Lee. *Fort Dalles.*

Fort Leland. 1855-56. When Harkness and Twogood built a tavern on Grave Creek and surrounded it with a stout stockade, unknowingly they were providing what would be called Fort Leland during the Rogue River war. From Grants Pass, go north on I-5 for 14 miles to the Sexton Mountain Pass exit. Take the Grave Creek road west from here to the Grave Creek bridge, about 15 miles, general location of Fort Leland.

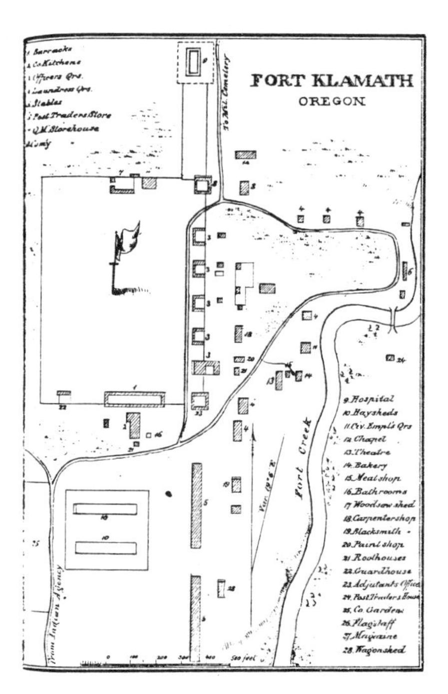

Battery Lewis. This was an Endicott period 10-inch position at Fort Stevens.

Camp Lincoln. 1864. *Camp on the South Fork of John Day's River.* Lieutenant James A. Waymire and 25 Oregon Cavalrymen set up this field depot in order to protect the military road and the settlers. Taking his orders literally, he joined with a citizen group to launch two unsuccessful attacks on an Indian stronghold in Harney Valley and, upon returning to Camp Lincoln, found that the rearguard left to protect the camp had been overpowered by Indians and the horse herd captured.

The general site of the camp is in the vicinity of Dayville on U.S. 26 about 30 miles west of its junction with US 395.

Camp Logan. 1865-66. Forty Oregon Volunteers wintered over at this rough hut field camp near the Roger Kent ranch while they protected the military road. From John Day, go east on US 26 for 13 miles to Prairie City. Turn right (south) at Prairie City. Continue straight on the road when it turns to the left in 1 mile. In about 6 miles from Prairie City the road will meet Strawberry Creek, the general vicinity of Camp Logan.

Camp Maury. 1864. This was the first of three field camps established for the 1864 Southeastern Oregon Expedition. It was given up when the grass for foraging the horses gave out. See Camp Dahlgren item for directions to the site.

Camp McDowell. 1865. *Camp Humbug.* Company F, 1st Oregon Infantry, spent the first six weeks of the summer of 1865 at this field camp, keeping an eye on the local Indian situation and taking full advantage of the fishing in Camas Creek. The troops spent a week at one site, then crossed the river to a second location one-half mile away. Brush huts were sufficient protection despite the usual cool temperatures of Oregon June nights. From John Day, go west on US 26 for 6 miles to US 395. Turn right (north) for 72 miles to Oregon 244. Turn right (east) about 6 miles to the approximate location of both McDowell sites on opposite sides of Camas creek.

Camp Medill. 1858. This was a temporary camp in the vicinity of the Grave Creek bridge, the same location as the so-called Fort Leland. See the latter item for directions.

Fort Miner. 1856. This was a citizen fortification at the mouth of the Rogue river. This would place it in the vicinity of Gold Beach on US 101.

Battery Misler. This was an Endicott period 10-inch position at Fort Stevens.

Fort Orford. 1851-56. A bloody siege of 10 men took place for 14 days on picturesque Battle Rock south of this fort in 1851. Two months after the men escaped, the fort was established. During its five years of activity, the fort was the westernmost U.S. military post. There are no traces of the fort in the town of Port Orford on US 101 about 83 miles north of the California border.

Fort Point. 1851. The early settlers of Port Orford built two blockhouses for their protection while Fort Orford was being constructed nearby. As Indian hostilities increased, the citizens built an eight-foot high double wall, with firing ports every few feet, around the town. Port Orford is on US 101 about 83 miles north of the California border.

Camp Polk. 1865-66. Protecting the settlers and travelers was the not uncommon mission of this temporary post, as with the many others in Civil War Oregon. The approximate site is about 5 miles west of Prineville (at the junction of US routes 26 and 126) on the Crooked river.

Battery Pratt. This was an Endicott period 6-inch position at Fort Stevens.

Camp on Rattlesnake Creek. *Fort Harney.*

Fort Rock. 1805-06. This was the "rockfort camp" of Lewis and Clark in the fall of 1805 and spring, 1806. The natural rock formations of this promontory overlooking the Columbia provided protection against Indians but not, as Clark complained, the fleas that infested their clothes there. From downtown The Dalles, follow a marked trail from the Union Pacific station at the north end of Liberty street.

Camp Rogue River. 1856. This was a temporary military camp at the mouth of the Rogue River. Along with civilian Fort Miner, this would place it in the vicinity of Gold Beach on US 101.

Camp Russell. 1864-65. The State Fair Grounds near Salem probably had never seen such activity as when the Oregon Volunteers took them over to serve as a recruiting and training center. The pavilion became barracks and kitchen, the dance hall a drill hall. The State Fair Grounds are at the intersection of 17th street and Silverton road in northeast Salem.

Battery Russell. This was an Endicott period 10-inch position at Fort Stevens.

Siletz Blockhouse. 1858-66. Only a blockhouse, without a fort adjacent, was the Army protection for the Siletz Indian Agency. This is the same blockhouse erected by Phil Sheridan at Yaquina Bay and later floated in pieces up the Siletz river to the agency. There are no traces of the blockhouse. From Newport, take US 20 east 6 miles to Oregon 229. Turn left (north) onto 229 for 9 miles to the hamlet of Siletz, site of the blockhouse.

Fort Smith. 1855-56. William Henry Smith's house probably had a stockade around it during the Rogue River war and its occupancy by Oregon Volunteers was sufficient reason for the unofficial military title. From Grants Pass, take I-5 north to the Glendale exit, 22 miles. At the exit, cross Cow Creek and turn right (north) 1 mile to the approximate site of Fort Smith.

Battery Smur. This was an Endicott period 3-inch gun position at Fort Stevens.

Camp on the South Fork of John Day's River. *Camp Lincoln.*

Camp Steele. *Fort Harney.*

Fort Stevens. 1865-1948. Oregon's only coast defense fort, this powerful establishment watched over the southern mouth of the Columbia during World Wars I and II. Now a state park, it has suffered more at the hands of vandals, souvenir hunters and tourists than it did from the Japanese submarine that landed several 5-inch shells near the fort's Battery Russell in 1942. The fort, and the concrete gun emplacements of Battery Russell, can be reached from Oregon 104, via U.S. 101 about 13 miles west of Astoria. There were eight batteries at the fort, some of which are in the park, others privately owned: Clark, Freeman, Lewis, Misler, Pratt, Russell, Smur, and Walker.

Camp Stuart. 1851-53. One-armed Captain Phil Kearny, 1st U.S. Dragoons, operated out of this field camp before and after the assaults at Table Rock and Evans Creek that ended that portion

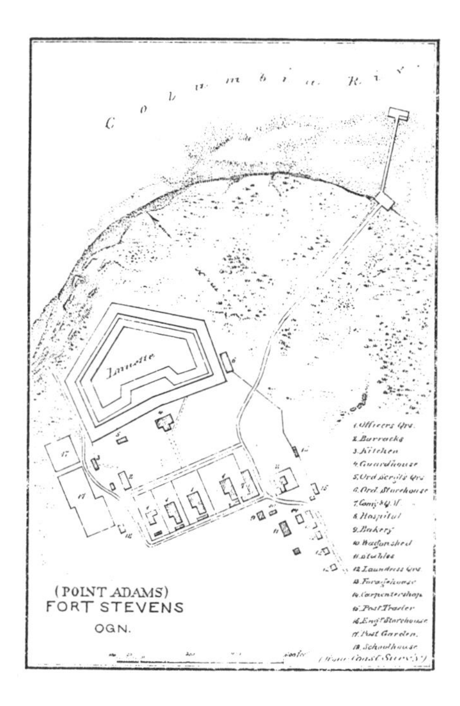

of the Rogue River wars. A marker is on the site southeast of Medford off of I-5.

Fort Trask. 1855. Fur trader turned settler Elbridge Trask built this stockade for protection during periods of unrest, living in it for several years. The site is across from the Sunset Memorial Gardens cemetery in Tillamock.

Fort Umpqua. 1832-50. Indians besieged this fur post for several hours in 1839, but were beaten off by the French trader and his Indian employees. The fort consisted of four log buildings enclosed by 12-foot high pickets with bastions at two corners. The site is about 35 miles east of Reedsport along Oregon 38 on the banks of the Umpqua river.

Fort Umpqua. 1856-62. Shifting sand with which the soldiers had to deal during this post's active days have completely obliterated the site on which the Army quartered a company of artillerymen in a dozen frame buildings plus a log blockhouse. The site is in the triangular corner that faces Winchester Bay on the spit of sand at the northern mouth of the bay across from Reedsport. The nearest road approach is US 101 about 4 miles north of Reedsport. It is a rough sand walk to the site.

Fort Vannoy. 1855-56. The headquarters camp of the volunteers during the Rogue River war, this was a group of log buildings on the right bank of the Rogue River 4 miles west of Grants Pass.

Battery Walker. This was an Endicott period 10-inch position at Fort Stevens.

Fort Wallace. *Fort Champooick.*

Camp Warner 1866-74. *Camp Burbank* (1866). There were two sites for this post. So-called "Old" Camp Warner (1866-67) was located almost by default when the winter closed in and the soldiers set up camp on 7,710-foot high Hart Mountain. When spring and General Crook arrived, he moved the camp to slightly more accessible terrain to the east, building a stone causeway across Hart Lake so that the wagons could be moved.

This camp is near the Order of the Antelope Blue Sky Hotel, reachable by jeep roads atop Hart Mountain, in the Hart Mountain National Antelope Refuge about 50 miles northeast of Lake View. Nothing but a few hollows which may have been fireplaces are at the site; Crook's causeway is still visible, but virtually inundated, at the "narrows" of Hart Lake.

The second Warner, "new" Camp Warner (1867-74) was a permanent-type post of logs with sufficient room for 280 men. It was one of the few at which General Crook resided with his wife, who was usually in the East, and from here he exercised command of the Department of the Columbia for several months.

There are no traces at the site other than some abandoned ranch buildings with doubtful lineage. This is in the Fremont National Forest which has

Hospital billiard room, Fort Umpqua, from the album compiled by Dr. Edward Perry Vollum, dated 1859 *(3)*

CAMP WARNER, 1873 *(1)*

headquarters at the northern edge of Lakeview on US 395. Directions and a map should be requested from the rangers here, who may be able to assist for both fort locations.

From Lakeview, go north on US 395 for 6 miles to Oregon 140. Turn right (east) on 140 as it goes up Warner Canyon. At about 10 miles, take the lumber road to the left (north) up Walker Creek. Stay on this jeep road – if possible – which is numbered 3615 to Sherman Valley where a right turn should be made onto road 3743 and then, shortly, onto road 3720B. This road peters out across the valley from Fort Ranch, site of the second Camp Warner. Without current directions as to road conditions and an updated map, it would be impossible to find this site in view of the many lumber roads that crisscross the entire area.

Fort Wascopam. 1847-48. *Fort Lee, Fort Dalles.* This was a temporary post at The Dalles of Oregon Volunteers for the Cayuse War. The name was carried over unofficially when Fort Dalles was established at about the same site.

Camp Watson. 1864-69. Although this was one of the longest occupied of the temporary posts founded in eastern Oregon during the Civil War, and one of the most active, virtually nothing is left at the site. The post consisted of log huts, a dozen on the north side for the enlisted men, four for the officers along the south side. The west side had a small map house, a hospital, the guardhouse, and a commissary and quartermaster storehouse. Three corrals and stables were on the east side. The cemetery once included 12 dead, including three soldiers first buried at Camp Maury. Although new stone markers were placed by the American Legion in 1932, there is little trace. From John Day, go west on US 26 for 53 miles to a left (south) turn onto an all weather road leading to Rock Creek. About 5 miles south on this road is the site of the camp on the right (south) side, but local directions are essential to insure reaching this difficult but interesting site.

Willamette Post. *Fort Champooick.*

Fort William. 1834-37. This was a trading post built by Captain Nathaniel J. Wyeth on Sauvie Island but, like most western projects of the fur trader, it was unsuccessful. The Hudson Bay Company leased the property as a farm in 1837. The fort was originally on the north end of the island but Wyeth moved it to a rise near the center of the island after spring floods covered the first location. Sauvie Island is about 2 miles northwest of Portland off of US 30.

Camp Wright. 1865-66. Establishing this temporary camp presented more than the usual obstacles to Captain Loren L. Williams, 1st Oregon Infantry, when he led an expedition to Selvie's river near Harney Lake. Having left half of his detachment in camp, he took a dozen men to hunt for a good site – and flushed between 75 to 100 armed Indians. After seven hours and 45 miles of dodging in a great circle route, Williams returned to his camp and decided to make it permanent for the time being. The site was in the area northwest of Malheur Lake now known as Wright's Point. From Burns, go north on US 395 for 2 miles to Oregon 20. Turn right (east) on Oregon 20 for 21 miles to Buchanan, the general area of Camp Wright.

Fort Yamhill. 1856-66. Phil Sheridan was a second lieutenant when he helped to build this post, a collection of log buildings dominated by a blockhouse. Only the blockhouse is left, having been moved in 1912 to the town park in the center of Dayton City, 25 miles southwest of Portland off of US 99W To reach the actual fort site, take Oregon 18 southwest to its intersection with Oregon 22. Three miles from the intersection, on Oregon 22, is the Grand Ronde Agency, site of Fort Yamhill.

Yaquina Bay Blockhouse. 1856-58. Phil Sheridan built this blockhouse to protect the Indian Agent at Yaquina Bay. With a detachment of troops from Fort Yamhill, Sheridan appropriated an Indian burial ground as the site of the blockhouse, something the Indians agreed to only after they were permitted to let the tide take the burial canoes – for the dead were entombed above ground in canoes. In 1858 the blockhouse was dismantled and floated upriver to the Siletz agency where it became Siletz Blockhouse. The site of the Yaquina Bay Blockhouse is in the Olsonville area of Newport (on US 101).

—SOUTH DAKOTA—

FORT PIERRE *(1)*

The Missouri river has left its mark on the sites of the river forts of South Dakota, the Oahe reservoir having inundated many of those of central and northern South Dakota, the Fort Randall reservoir doing likewise for those in the southern part of the state.

Both trading and military posts have been inundated by the Missouri, but the pre-flooding archeological work of the State Historical Society, the National Park Service, and the Smithsonian Institution preserved much of the history and artifacts of the sites. The reports of these projects aided in the compilation of this section.

FT MANUEL LISA 1812
POST GRAND RIVER AGENCY 1870
FT BENNETT 1870
FT SULLY 1866
GALPIN'S CP 1855
FT TECUMSEH 1822
FT LAFRAMBOISE I 1817
CP CHEYENNE 1890
FT MEADE 1878
CP STURGIS 1878
SIDNEY STOCKADE 1876
RAPID CITY BH 1876
CP CROOK 1876
CP COLLINS 1875
GORDON STOCKADE 1874
OGLALA PT 1830
CP MOUTH RED CANYON 1876
CP ROSEBUD AGENCY 1878
LES BELLES PIERRES
Cave
Lodge Butte
EAGLES NEST HILLS
SHORT PINE HILLS
Long Butte
Twin Butte
Saddle Butte
Marked Butte
Hill where the Crows were Killed
Slave Butte
Deers Ears
Owl Butte
Fox Ridge
GRINDSTONE BUTTES
Custer City
Eagle's Nest
Porcupine Tail
RESERVATION FOR DIFFERENT TRIBES

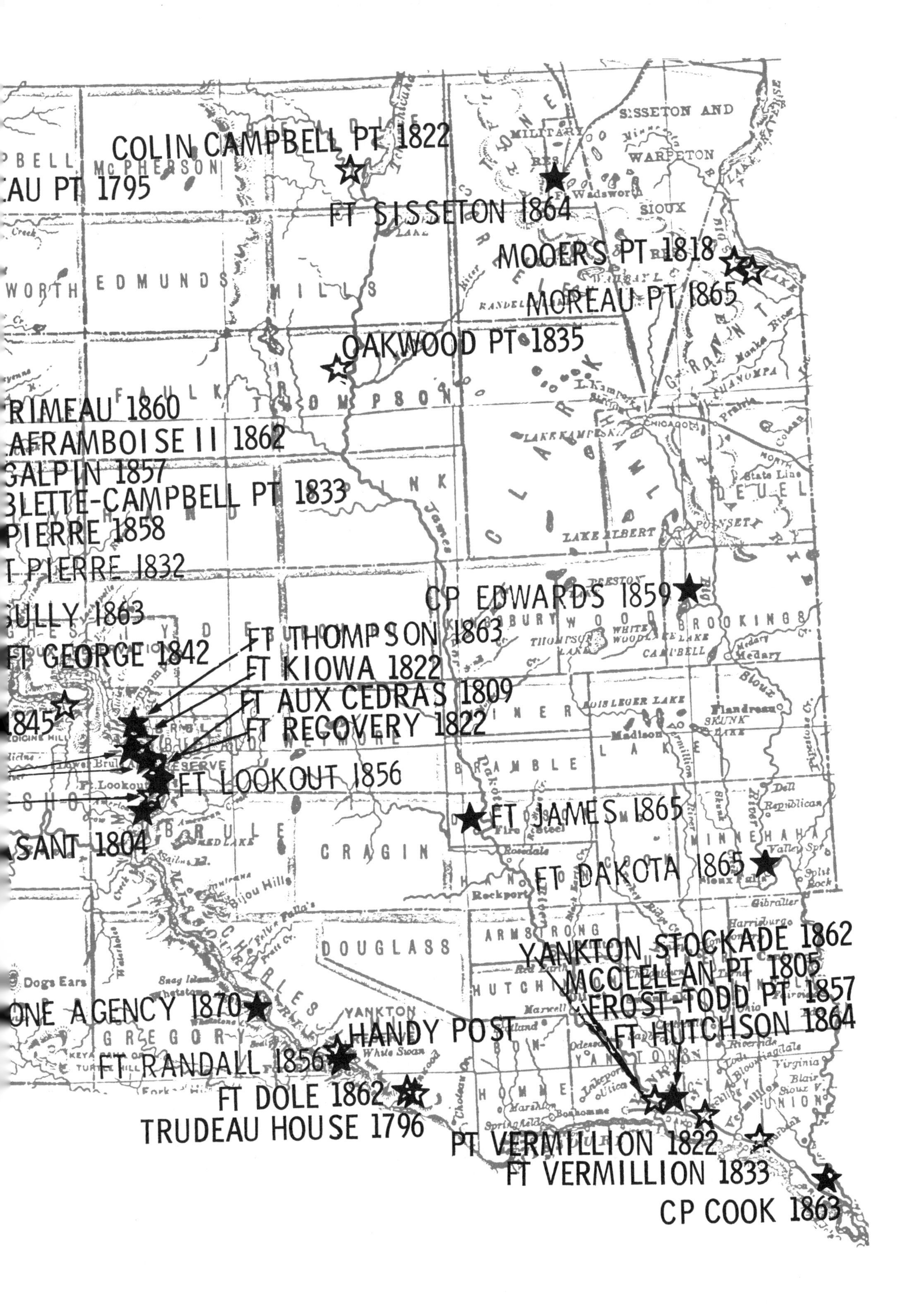

COLIN CAMPBELL PT 1822
FT SISSETON 1864
MOOERS PT 1818
MOREAU PT 1865
OAKWOOD PT 1835
RIMEAU 1860
AFRAMBOISE II 1862
GALPIN 1857
BLETTE-CAMPBELL PT 1833
PIERRE 1858
T PIERRE 1832
SULLY 1863
FT GEORGE 1842
1845
FT THOMPSON 1863
FT KIOWA 1822
FT AUX CEDRAS 1809
FT RECOVERY 1822
FT LOOKOUT 1856
SANT 1804
CP EDWARDS 1859
FT JAMES 1865
FT DAKOTA 1865
YANKTON STOCKADE 1862
MCCLELLAN PT 1805
FROST-TODD PT 1857
FT HUTCHSON 1864
ONE AGENCY 1870
HANDY POST
FT RANDALL 1856
FT DOLE 1862
TRUDEAU HOUSE 1796
PT VERMILLION 1822
FT VERMILLION 1833
CP COOK 1863

Fort aux Cedras. 1809-1822. *Loisell's Post.* This Missouri Fur Company trading post was on American Island—called Cedar Island at the time—in the Missouri river. An important post during its active years, the fort was burned in 1822. Supposedly it was replaced by Fort Recovery, but Smithsonian Institution research indicates that Fort Recovery, although it may have inherited aux Cedras' market, did not occupy the same site. American Island was in the Missouri river about .8 mile south of Chamberlain; it has been inundated by the Fort Randall reservior.

Fort Bartlett. *Old Fort Sully.*

Fort Bennett. 1870-91. *Post at Cheyenne Agency.* A semi-stockade with its open sides on the Missouri river, to the east, and Agency creek to the north, Fort Bennett was intermixed with buildings of the Indian Agency. It occupied three sites, moving as river erosion threatened the various locations, but all within 300 yards of each other. Usually a one-company post, Fort Bennett had a nine-company garrison during the aftermath of the Custer massacre in 1876. The site has the remnants of three buildings about 35 miles northwest of Pierre; although inundated by the Oahe Reservior, it is exposed periodically during low water in the reservoir.

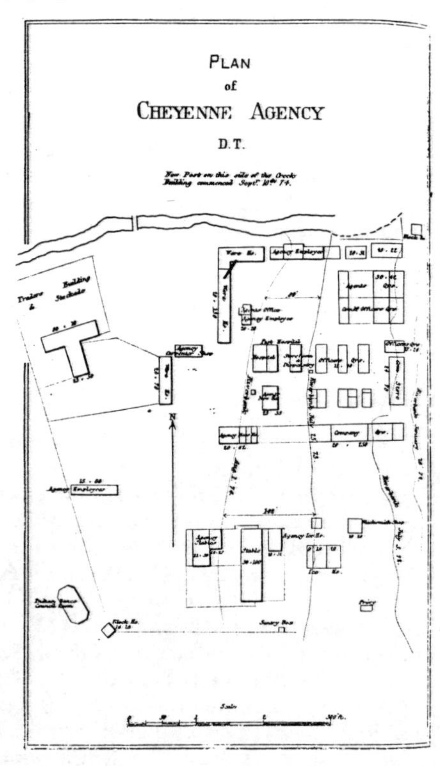

Fort Bouis. *Fort Defiance.*

Fort Brasseaux. *Fort Recovery.*

Fort Brookings. *Fort Dakota.*

Cedar Fort. *Fort Recovery.*

Camp Cheyenne. 1890-91. *Camp of Observation.* Five companies, two Hotchkiss guns, and a detachment of Indian Scouts were stationed at this field camp near the Forks of the Cheyenne rivers during the days leading up to the Messiah War. In addition to the obvious mission described by its alternate and initial name, Camp of Observation, the post was a base of operations for what culminated in the Battle or Massacre of Wounded Knee. From Rapid City, go east on I-90 for 35 miles to Wasta exit. Take a secondary road north from Wasta about 20 miles to Elm Springs. Turn right (east) on a gravel road that passes the approximate site of Camp Cheyenne in 25 miles on the right between the road and the Cheyenne river.

Post at Cheyenne Agency. *Fort Bennett.*

Fort Chouteau. *Fort Pierre.*

Colin Campbell Trading Post. 1822-28. This was a stockaded post built for the Hudson Bay Company. From Aberdeen, go north on US 281 for 17 miles to South Dakota 10. Turn left (west) for 1.2 miles on South Dakota 10 to a dirt road. Turn right (north) for 1.6 miles to a monument on the site of the trading post.

Camp Collier. *Camp at the Mouth of Red Canyon.*

Camp Collins. 1875-76. The Log Cabin Museum in Way City Park on Main street in Custer is reputed to have been built by the Army as the headquarters for a three-company detachment stationed here to keep the miners out of the Black Hills. The cabin is 16 by 20 feet with loopholes. Custer is in the Black Hills National Forest at the junction of US routes 16 and 385.

Camp Cook. 1863. Iowa Volunteers camped at this site for a week in May, 1863. At the time it was located 6 miles west of Sioux City, Iowa, on the west bank of the Big Sioux river. The modern site is about 2 miles north of North Sioux City to the east of US 77.

Camp Crook. 1876. General George Crook established this as his headquarters during the Army attempts to oust prospectors from the Black Hills. From Deadwood, go south on US 85 for 2 miles to US 385. Turn left onto US 385 for 27.3 miles to Pactola recreation area, general site of Camp Crook. The camp has been inundated by the Pactola reservior.

Post at Crow Creek Agency. *Fort Thompson.*

Fort Dakota. 1865-69. *Fort Brookings.* The dozen buildings of Fort Dakota helped bring Indian-wary settlers back to the Sioux Falls area. The fort was so successful in this mission that it was soon all but overrun by homesteaders who wanted to file claims on the military reservation.

FORT DAKOTA, 1866 *(1)*

There are no remains, the site having been swallowed by the city of Sioux Falls, but a marker to the fort is on the exterior wall of the Hollywood theater, 218 North Philips avenue in downtown Sioux Falls. Across the street was the fort site: the barracks was on Philips with the south end of the barracks 125 feet north of 8th street.

Fort Defiance. 1845-49. *Fort Bouis.* When two ex-clerks of the American Fur Company set up a trading post in competition with their former employer, their defiance served as an appropriate name for the fort. A less antagonistic name was Bouis, after a member of the firm. The approximate site was on the west bank of the Missouri near the mouth of Medicine Creek, probably inundated by Lake Sharpe. The general area can be reached from Chamberlain via I-90 west to Reliance. Turn north at Reliance on South Dakota 47W for 8 miles to a fork with a secondary road that heads straight north (47W turns to the right—east—at this point). Go north on this road through Lower Brule; about 7 miles west of Lower Brule the road crosses Medicine Creek and the approximate site of Fort Defiance.

Fort Des Roche. *Fort James.*

Dickson's Post. *Post Vermillion.*

Fort Dole. 1862. Yankton Indian Agent Walter Burleigh took no chances when he heard that the Upper Sioux were on the warpath. He built this double-storied octagonal blockhouse, 26 feet in diameter, of 22-inch thick timbers, loopholed for muskets and defenses by a six-pounder and two three-pounders. The Dole came not from the usual activity with the Indians but from the last name of the Commissioner of Indian Affairs. From Pickstown, next to the Fort Randall Dam, go east on South Dakota 46 for 5 miles to an intersection; turn right (south) through Marty, 5 miles, to Greenwood, an additional 5 miles, once the Yankton Indian Agency and the site of Fort Dole.

Camp Edwards. 1859; 1862; 1864-65. *Cantonment Oakwood, Camp near Preston Lake.* Earthen breastworks five feet high about 100 feet square were erected around a single log hut at this post, occupied in 1859, again after the Sioux Outbreak, and finally by Minnesota Volunteer Cavalry at the end of the Civil War. The outline of the breastworks is in the Oakwood Lakes State Park.

From Brookings, go north on US 77 for 8 miles to County 30. Turn left (west) through Bruce, 4 miles, and after 3 more miles turn right (north) into the Oakwood Lakes.

Follow marked road north between three lakes to the site of Camp Edwards, indentified by a marker intitled "Breastworks;" the Camp Edwards name had been lost until unearthed in National Archives research of regimental records.

Camp near Firesteel Creek. *Fort James.*

French Post. *Fort Lookout II.*

Frost-Todd Trading Post. 1857-61. The firm of Frost and Todd, the latter a cousin of Mary Todd Lincoln who made full use of his connections with the White House, monopolized trade with the Indians and travelers at this post near the Yankton Agency. From Yankton, go east on South Dakota 50 for 3.7 miles to the James river; the site of the trading post is on the left (north) side of the road at the river crossing. The post was moved to Yankton, at the southwest corner of 2d and Walnut streets.

Galpin's Camp. 1855-57. After Charles E. Galpin, serving as the agent of the Chouteau family, engineered the sale of the first Fort Pierre to the Army, he and other former employees from Fort Pierre moved to this site. It appears that they conducted trading operations with the Indians during the winters of 1855-56 and 1856-57 before moving south and establishing Fort Galpin. The site is now inundated on the western edge of the Oahe Reservior about 14 miles directly northwest of Pierre.

Fort Galpin. 1857-59. This trading post was 125 feet square, similar to the first Fort Pierre but without any blockhouses. Two-thirds of the enclosure was a picket stockade and houses closed the remainder. From Pierre, go west across the Missouri river on US 14. Turn right (north) onto South Dakota 514, the Oahe Dam road, for 4 miles. The approximate site of Fort Galpin is to the right (east) of the road, next to the river and just north of the site of the second Fort Pierre.

Fort George. 1842-45. This Fox, Livingston and Company trading post was a stockade 155 by 165 feet with projecting blockhouses at two opposing corners. Smithsonian archaeological excavations in recent years determined that this post was unusual in that the buildings were separated from the stockade walls by an alleyway rather than built against the walls. Liquor and violent competition proved the end of Fort George and it was burned by Indians in the pay of rival traders.

Gordon Stockade. 1874-75. The gold fields of the Black Hills were the targets of the 28 occupants of this 80-foot square, 10-foot high stockade. Their prospecting was successful, even finding it when they dug an eight-foot deep hole in one corner of the stockade. Government policy prohibited incursions in the Black Hills at the time and the U.S. Cavalry was called out to escort the prospectors out of the area after the winter. A replica of the stockade has been erected on the north (left) side of US 16 alternate 3 miles east of Custer.

Post at Grand River Agency. 1870-75. This two-company fort adjacent to the Grand River Agency included 20-some buildings, all of log and mud-chinked construction with plank-and-mud roofs. The nearby Missouri river periodically flooded the post and finally forced the removal of the agency and garrison to Fort Yates. The site finally surrendered to the river with the Oahe Dam project and is inundated about 5 miles north of Mobridge.

Fort Hale. 1870-84. *Post at Lower Brule Agency, Fort Lower Brule.* Protecting the Lower Brule Indian Agency was only part of the mission of Fort Hale. The garrison frequently had to share its commanding officer with the agency because

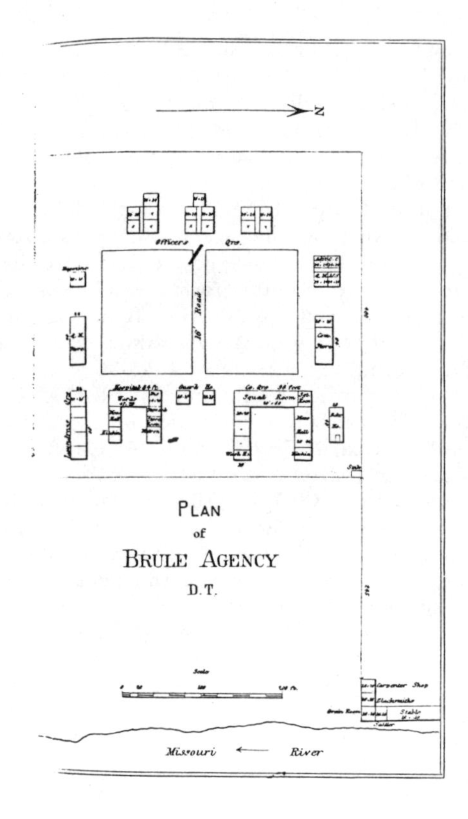

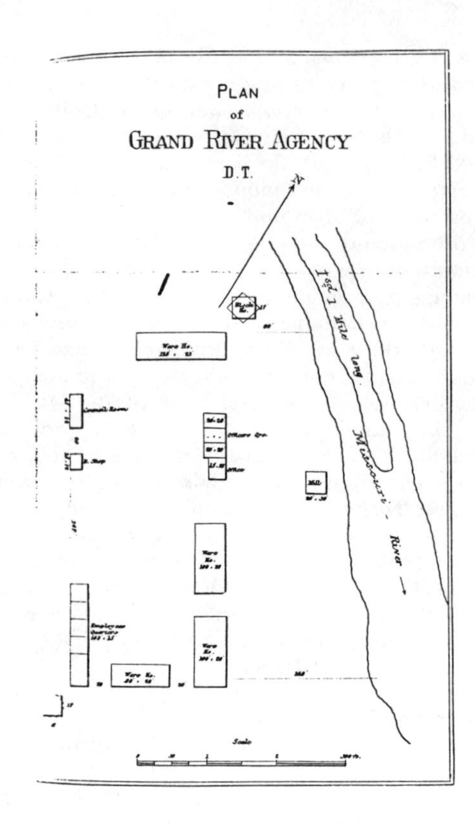

the Army commander served also as the acting Indian Agent. With the commanding officer also serving as the agent at the Crow Creek Agency, this arrangement was less than satisfactory.

The post was originally located near Fort Lookout IV on the west bank of the Missouri but soon was moved 15 miles to the north. Bricks from post buildings were used in the construction of the Chamberlain hotel in Chamberlain; the rest of the post has fallen vicitm to the Missouri river. The final traces, cellar depressions and gravelled walkways, were washed away by the flood of 1952.

From Chamberlain the approximate site can be reached by going north on South Dakota 47 to South Dakota 34, then left on 34 through Fort Thompson town and across the river on the Big Bend dam. The site was south of the dam on the west side of the river.

The site of the first Fort Hale (1870, usually called Fort Lower Brule) is on the west bank of the Missouri almost directly opposite Chamberlain and to the north of US 16 (about 5 miles north of the Oacoma exit on I-90). There are low hammocks on the second terrace above the river which are reputed to be the site.

Handy's Post. On the site of Fort Randall, little is known of this early-day trading post.

Fort Hutchson. 1864. This short-time Civil War Volunteer post was east of Yankton. The approximate site is shown on a state marker at the northeast corner of the intersection of I-29 and South Dakota 50 about 8 miles east of Vermillion.

Fort James. 1865-67. *Camp near Firesteel Creek, Fort Larouche, Fort Des Roche.* This was a quadrangle made of stone and hewn logs that was intended to garrison troops for stage coach protection. It was built by professional stone masons and would have lasted after abandonment except that its materials were of value in other construction. From Sioux Falls, go west on I-90 about 55 miles to Alexandria turnoff. Go west on county road from the north end of town. At 5 miles, turn south for 5.3 miles, then turn east for 2 miles. At bluff, drop down to the first right. Pass through the Hutterite Colony and just past the colony is the fort site on the left side (east) of the road between the road and the James river.

Fort Kiowa. 1822-25. *Fort Lookout I.* Four posts used the Lookout name in South Dakota and the decision to attach the first one with Fort Lookout is based on Smithsonian Institution research in 1950. This was a fur trading fort built by the American Fur Company, consisting of a range of log buildings containing four rooms, a log house and a storehouse forming a right angle, leaving a space of some thirty feet, according to a report quoted by Chittenden. Pickets surrounded the post, including a blockhouse at the south corner and a wooden tower at the north; each side was reported to measure 140 feet. The approximate site is believed to be inundated by the Missouri river directly east of Fort Hale II.

LaBarge's Post. *Fort Lookout II.*

Fort LaFramboise I. 1817-20. *Fort Teton I.* Joesph LaFramboise built this trading post of dead logs which he rescued from the nearby Missouri. The post operated for only a couple of seasons and then was abandoned. The approximate site is

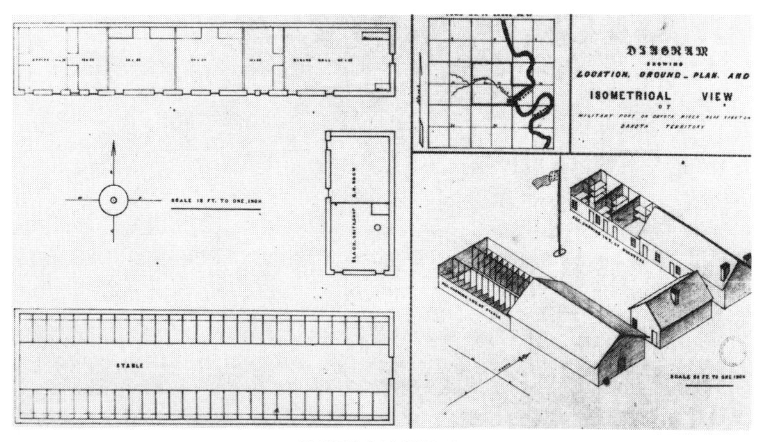

FORT JAMES *(1)*

the same as the modern city of Fort Pierre, across the Missouri river from Pierre.

Fort LaFramboise II. 1862-63. Built by LaBarge, Harkness and Company to oppose the Fort Pierre trading, this post was abandoned within a year. It had no stockade, the buildings themselves making up an enclosure. The approximate site is at the western side of the Oahe Dam off of South Dakota 514 northwest of Pierre.

Fort Larouche. *Fort James.*

Loisell's Post. *Fort aux Cedres.*

Fort Lookout I. *Fort Kiowa.*

Fort Lookout II. 1831-51. *French Post, LaBarge's Post.* Under these three names this site was occupied periodically during the second quarter of the nineteenth century, going under the French Post name in 1833 and with that of the famous St. Louis trading and steamboat LaBarge family between 1840 and 1851.

Smithsonian Institution archeological research in 1950 and 1951 apparently located the site of a rectangular trading post dating from the earlier portion of these dates. This appeared to have fallen into partial ruin and then have been burned after which a second post was built on the same site that suffered the same fate. Both appeared to measure about 70 by 20 feet, consisting of a single building each time and without any evidence of a stockade.

Follow the directions to Fort Lookout IV; at the entrance to the Lower Brule Reservation, where a state marker indentifies the historical sites in the area, the location of Fort Lookout II is to the south about 300 yards in the pastureland along the Missouri river.

Fort Lookout III. The dates of this trading post are as uncertain as whether it is different from Fort Lookout I (Fort Kiowa). It may be that this post, definitely recorded as being in existence in 1833, is the same as that of Fort Kiowa and that is the conclusion accepted by Smithsonian Institution research. All of this is academic, anyway, in that the site is under the Missouri river to the east of the Fort Hale location, making definite determination impossible as to whether it was the same or different from the other Lookout post.

Fort Lookout IV. 1856-57. The only military post of the four—or three, depending upon the authority—Lookouts, this was intended to be an elaborate one. The parade ground was a quarter of a mile long, flanked by barracks and closed by three officers quarters at one end and the guardhouse and headquarters building at the other. After only a season of operation, the post was abandoned and much of its construction moved downriver to Fort Randall.

From Chamberlain, go west on I-90 to Reliance, about 20 miles. Turn right (north) at Reliance to first right turn, 1 mile. Take this dirt road for 11 miles to where it turns south at bluffs overlooking Missouri River. Take primitive road that drops from here to river valley. At end of the road is a marker for the Lower Brule Indian reservation.

The Fort Lookout IV site is to the northeast of the marker, within the reservation and next to the river; slight rises in the ground may be apparent. The site of Fort Lookout II is to the south, 300 yards.

Fort Lower Brule. *Fort Hale.*

Fort Manuel Lisa. 1812-13. Dakota and Wyoming historians disagree on whether Indian girl Sakakawea died and was buried here or at Fort Washakie, Wyoming, with theories as to the ultimate fate of Lewis and Clark's guide drawn upon state loyalties. Regardless, this trading post was the home of Sakakawea's husband during its active period, including December 20, 1812, when at least one contemporary journal notes that his Indian wife died. Whether Sakakawea was the wife in question continues to be debated.

The fort was a stockaded post that supposedly was burned after the traders abandoned when 15 of their number were killed by the Sioux. The stockade was reconstructed by the Civilian Conservation Corps in 1930's. Its deteriorated condition was unchecked by the time the Oahe Reservior was established because the fort stood at the precise high water point of the reservoir, about 30 miles north of Mobridge to the east of Kenel. There is a state marker on the road that provides directions to the site, also identified by another state marker.

FORT MEADE, 1888 *(30)*

McClellan Post. 1805-06. The second trading post on the Upper Missouri, this fort was in operation when Lewis and Clark came downriver in 1806. The site is east of Yankton on South Dakota 50.

Fort Meade. 1878-1944. *Camp Ruhlen.* Meade was the first Army post to play the Star Spangled Banner at retreat ceremonies, later a custom adopted by all Army posts even before it became the national anthem. Many Army buildings are now used by the Veterans Administration Hospital and the post cemetery is now a picturesque national cemetery. From Sturgis, take South Dakota 34 for 2 miles east to a right (south) turn into the Fort Meade VA Hospital.

Mooer's Trading Post. 1818-24. There is nothing but a marker at the site of this early-day trading center which was visited by the Stephen Long expedition in 1823. From Milbank (at the junction of US 77 and 12), go northeast 11 miles on US 12 to Big Stone City. Take South Dakota 15Y north from Big Stone City for 11 miles to Hartford Beach State Park, the site of the trading post.

Moreau-Robar Post. 1865. This trading post was established by Moses Moreau and Solomon Robar for the Missouri river trade. The site is 2 miles south of the Mooers' Trading Post, at Linden Beach.

Camp at the Mouth of Red Canyon. 1876-77. *Camp Collier.* A stockaded affair 125 feet square, bastions at the northeast and southwest corners, this short-term post watched over the Black Hills stage that passed through Red Canyon. Indentations in the pasture and the rotted stump of a stockade picket are at the site. From Edgemont, in southwestern South Dakota, go north on US 18 for 1 mile. Turn left at Red Canyon road for 5 miles to a point just before entering Red Canyon. The camp site is to the right of the road about 50 yards, on privately owned property.

Oakwood Trading Post. 1835-51. Joseph R. Brown established this fort but its manager, Pierre LeBlanc, did not fare too well: he was murdered by an unhappy customer. A DAR marker and a worn doorsill next to it are the only traces of this post in Rondell Park (named after a later operator of the post and a Dakota pioneer). From Aberdeen, go south on US 281 for 16.7 miles to the intersection with a secondary road. Right on this road is the hamlet of Mansfield but left 8 miles is Rondell Park and the site of the Oakwood Trading Post.

Oakwood Cantonment. *Camp Edwards.*

Oglala Post. 1830-34. The American Fur Company erected this fur trading post and it was here that Thomas L. Sarpy was blown up when a candle ignited a barrel of gunpowder. Although part of the fort was destroyed in the explosion, it continued in operation for a few years until the Indians moved to the vicinity of Fort Laramie. The site supposedly was used as a headquarters camp by the 6th Cavalry during the Messiah War in 1890. The site is the same as the ghost town of Link at the mouth of Rapid creek. From Rapid City, go southeast on South Dakota 40 about 35 miles to the Cheyenne river. At this point the site of Oglala Post can be seen to the north on the north side of Rapid creek.

Camp of Observation. *Camp Cheyenne.*

Pawnee House. *Trudeau's House.*

Fort Pierre. 1832-63. *Fort Chouteau.* One of the most important trading posts on the Upper Missouri, this stockaded fort was also the headquarters of General Harney's troops in 1855-57.

When the troops arrived, the American Fur Company employees moved upstream and built a second Fort Pierre, later using timbers from the first fort after the troops left. This second Fort Pierre operated from 1858 to 1863.

After the troops gave up the rotted and in-

FORT PIERRE
From a drawing by Alexander H. Murray *(1)*

adequate first Fort Pierre, it was usually called Fort Chouteau or Fort Pierre Chouteau to differentiate it from the newer post. From Pierre go west on US 14 across the Missouri river. Do not turn into the town of Fort Pierre; instead continue west on US 14 for 1 mile beyond US 83 to a righthand turn onto South Dakota 514. Go north 1.3 miles where the fort site marker, on a large boulder, is .3 mile east (right) of the road in a field at the end of a dirt road that crosses private property. This is the site of the first Fort Pierre.

The second Pierre site is 3 miles to the north and unmarked.

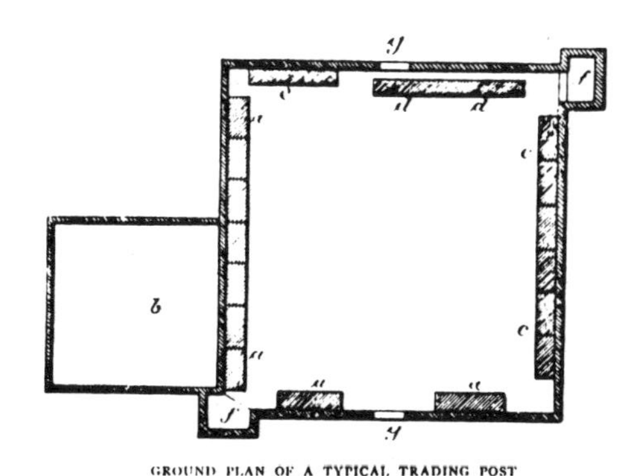

GROUND PLAN OF A TYPICAL TRADING POST
(*Fort Pierre*)
From a drawing by Maximilian

ff. Two-story block-houses. Upper story adapted for use of small arms; lower story for cannon.
gg. Front and back of quadrangle 114 paces in length; other sides 108 paces; inner area 87 by 87 paces.
dd. One-story residence of bourgeois of post.
e. Office and residence of clerk.
aaaa. Residence of other clerks, interpreter, engagés, and their families.
cc. Stores.
gg. Entrance doors to fort.
b. Garden.

Pilcher's Post. *Fort Recovery.*

Camp Pleasant. 1804, 1806. Lewis and Clark used this campsite for two days in September, 1804, on their way to Oregon and stopped overnight in August, 1806, on the way back. It is one of many Lewis and Clark sites along the Missouri river but one of the few marked ones. The marker is on US 16 about 3 miles west of Chamberlain and just north of Oacamoa.

Camp near Preston Lake. *Camp Edwards.*

Fort Primeau. 1860. This was a temporary trading house of LaBarge, Harkness and Company, named for Charles Primeau, one of the firm's partners. It apparently operated in the late 1850's or early 1860's. The site is under the Missouri near the western bank about 1 mile north of the Oahe Dam.

Fort Randall. 1856-84. First in the chain of military forts along the Upper Missouri, Randall was the base of operations for most of the Sioux Expeditions and, during the Civil War, one of the major forts garrisoned by ex-Confederates, so-called "Galvanized Yankees." Remnants of the stone chapel and many marked foundation and cellar outlines are at the site, now a park below the western corner of the Fort Randall Dam. Follow the signs from Pickstown across the dam.

Rapid City Blockhouse. 1876. White settlers who sifted through Army blockades to prospect

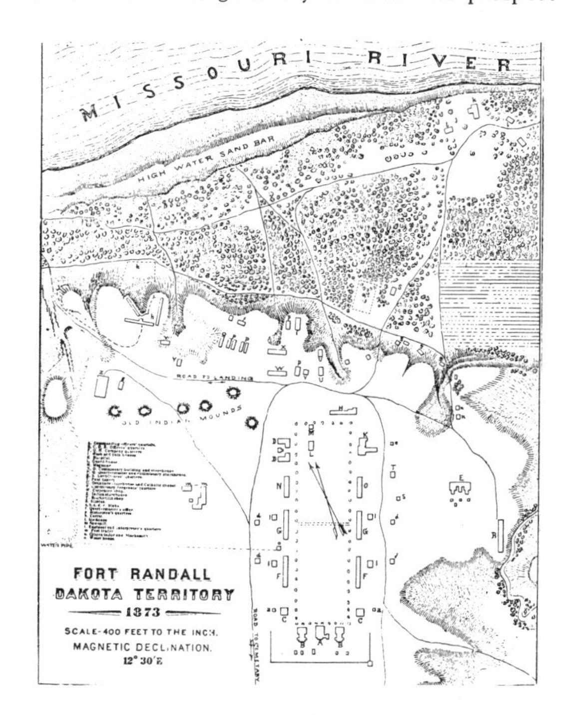

FORT RANDALL *(1)*

the Black Hills had to deal with official government opposition and deadly Indian hostility. After 180 of the original 200 founders of Rapid City abandoned the settlement in the wake of Indian ambushes on the outskirts, the remaining holdouts built this double-story, 30-foot square blockhouse for protection. The group was virtually besieged here for most of September, 1876, until word came through that the government had ceased its opposition to settlement. The site is at the intersection of 5th and Rapid streets in Rapid City.

Fort Recovery. 1822-1830. *Cedar Fort, Pilcher's Post, Fort Brasseaux.* Both the dates and additional names for this important trading post are confusing and uncertain, as uncertain as the site. Most authorities consider that the post was built on the site of Fort aux Cedres when that American Island post burned. Modern Smithsonian Institution archaeological surveys have concluded that it was on the right (west) bank of the Missouri river about even with the southern tip of the island. The matter is academic now: both sides, island or otherwise, have been inundated by the Fort Randall dam project. The fort's most important activity took place in 1823 when it was the base for the Ashley-Leavenworth Expedition against the Arikara Indians. The site would be about 1 mile south of Chamberlain on the western bank of the Missouri river, prior to flooding.

Military Camp at Rosebud Agency. 1878-91. Sixteen companies of soldiers were stationed at this post at the height of its strength to both control and protect the Brule Sioux moved here from the former Spotted Tail Agency in Nebraska.

The cemetery includes the grave of Chief Spotted Tail, marked by a white shaft. The hill above the agency is called Soldier Hill in memory of the rifle pits dug there by the troopers during the Messiah Craze.

The reservation headquarters is at Rosebud which can be reached from the Murdo exit on I-90, then heading south on US 83 for 43 miles to US 18, turning right (west) for 3 miles then heading southwest on a gravel road for 6 miles to Rosebud. The deep cut at the edge of the Agency, nicknamed the "Big Hole," is obvious in contemporary photographs. The cemetery is on the hill to the right.

Camp Ruhlen. This was the first name of the site of Fort Meade, attached to it during the time that Lieutenant George Ruhlen was the quartermaster in charge of the construction of what became Fort Meade.

Fort Sisseton. 1864-90. *Fort Wadsworth.* The peace of the Kettle Lake region of eastern Dakota was kept by this breastwork-surrounded post. The remains of most of the buildings are now at this state park site. From Watertown, take US 81 north to Sisseton, 57 miles. At Sisseton, turn left on South Dakota 10 and go west 25 miles. At gravel road six miles west of Lake City, turn left, go nine miles south. Fort buildings are on the right.

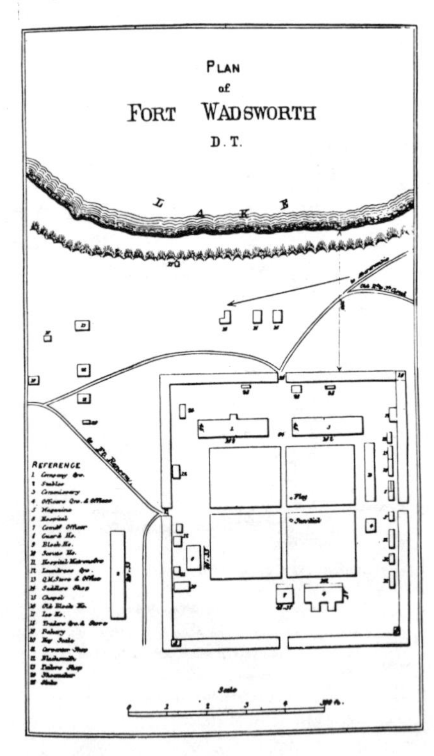

Sidney Stockade. 1876. Guarding the Sidney-Deadwood, Pierre-Deadwood stage lines were stage stations such as this reproduction on the site of the first station north of Rapid City. From Rapid City take I-90 northwest to the exit after Blackhawk. The reproduction is near the highway, right (north) side.

Camp Sturgis. 1878. Here in the shadows of Bear Butte, majestic mountain that dominates

FORT SISSETON
From *Northwest Magazine,* March, 1886

the Sturgis area, troopers constructing nearby Fort Meade encamped. A straight row of a dozen 'A' tents plus officers and supply tents were along Sturgis creek. Custer supposedly camped at the same site in 1874 and a picture of a camp below Bear Butte is variously used to illustrate either camp although local historians insist that it dates from 1878.

Sublette and Campbell's Post. 1833-34. Intended to operate in competition with Fort Pierre, the degree of success of this trading post can be hinted by the fact that it was sold to the American Fur Company after only a year. The site is immediately south of the Fort Tecumseh site.

Old Fort Sully. 1863-66. *Fort Bartlett.* At an unhealthy location of the Missouri river lowlands, this 270-foot square stockade served mainly during the aftermaths of the various Sioux campaigns of General Alfred Sully. A stone post is the only evidence on the site. From Pierre, go east on South Dakota 34 for 4 miles to where the marker is on the side of highway.

New Fort Sully. 1866-94. The direct descendent of Old Fort Sully, this was probably the most active on the Missouri in terms of operations fielded from it during its active years. It started as a stockaded post in which palisades closed the open areas between the buildings, but ultimately it became an expansive spread of buildings surrounded by a picket fence.

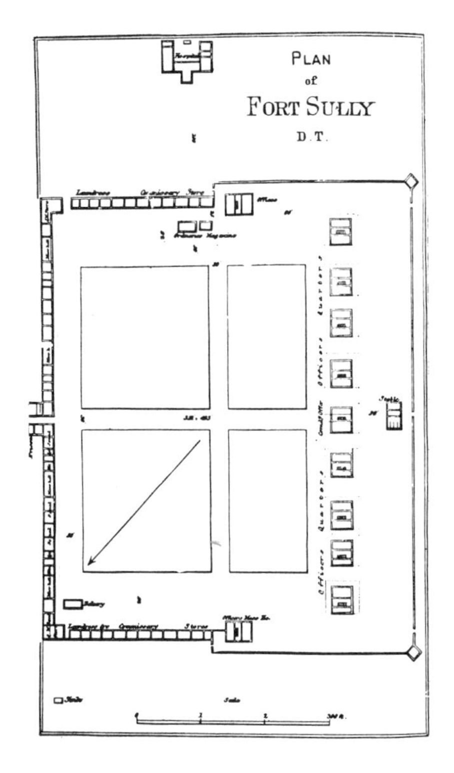

Cellar holes and rock walls marked most building sites and a stone marker was in the center of the parade ground until 1961 when the marker was moved to the Oneida courthouse. It was feared that the Oahe reservior would inundate the site, something finally achieved in 1968 when the reservior water level spread over the Sully table land.

The former hospital is now a granary at a private farm. To reach it from Pierre take US 17 north to the asphalt road at the edge of town. Follow this road to Snake butte, 3 miles. North of the butte bear right onto a gravel road which will pass the hospital building on the left side in 14 miles, in the Okobojo Creek Valley.

Continuing north on this road, turn left in 3 miles at the junction with another gravel road. When the road turns sharply north (right) in 5 miles, stop. From here to the site—or the bluffs overlooking it—is 6 miles along vague traces of a dirt road that can be maneuvered over open range land by a jeep.

Tabeau's Post. 1795-1804. Pierre Antoine Tabeau operated this trading house in or near the Arikara village where he was visited by Lewis and Clark in 1804. Not long after, he left the post for employment with Canadian fur companies. The approximate site is inundated near the east bank of the Missouri about 10 miles north of Mobridge.

Fort Tecumseh. 1822-32. The leading fur post of the Columbia Fur Company in its day, this stockade had the misfortune of being so close

Fort Thompson, on the Upper Missouri River *(19)*

to the Missouri river that it was flooded out annually. It was turned over to the American Fur Company in 1827 and ceased operation five years later after Fort Pierre had assumed all of its functions and taken most of its worthwhile buildings. From Pierre, go west on US 83 toward the city of Fort Pierre. After turning south on US 83 where it makes the junction with US 14, stop at a point 300 yards south of the junction. This is the site of Fort Tecumseh, bisected by US 83.

Fort Teton I. *Fort LaFramboise I.*

Fort Teton II. 1828-30. *Teton Post.* P.D. Papin and Company built this trading post but it was not long before the American Fur Company had taken it over and moved the property to Fort Tecumseh. The site was near the mouth of the Bad river, generally south of the city of Pierre.

Fort Thompson. 1863-71. *Post at Crow Creek Agency.* A stockade 300 by 400 feet surrounded two dozen buildings manned by two companies of Iowa Volunteers, Fort Thompson was the first military habitation north of Fort Randall during the Civil War. It was turned over to the Indian Agency in 1871. When the stockade was torn down in 1878, its dimensions had expanded to 450 by 650 feet. From Chamberlain go north on South Dakota 47 to a gravel road in about 12 miles that forks to the left (northwest) along the Missouri. About 5 miles along this road is a picnic area which is the easternmost edge of Fort Thompson's area but the post itself has been taken away by the Missouri. Some plumbing pipes from the post hang grotesquely over the water from the eroded banks. This site is about 2 miles south of the new town of Fort Thompson at the intersection of South Dakota 34 and 47W where a marker gives the area's history.

Trudeau's House. 1796-97. *Pawnee House.* This was a trading post operated by school teacher Jean Baptiste Trudeau and 10 men. It was the first house built in South Dakota. The site is uncertain, authorities placing it between four miles north of Pickstown to 15 miles south, due to the erosion and flooding of the Missouri.

Fort Vermillion. 1833-1851. The American Fur Company established this post somewhere to the east of the modern city of Vermillion. Flooding of the Missouri and the passage of time has eliminated all traces but there is a state historical marker on the county road between Elk Point and Vermillion at Burbank. This marker places the trading post to the south on the river bank.

Post Vermillion. 1822-50. *Dickson's Post.* Originally a Columbia Fur Company fort, Vermillion was absorbed by the American Fur Company. It was a small stockade and should not be confused with Fort Vermillion to the east of Vermillion. A marker on South Dakota 50 (south side) to the east of Gayville, 18 miles east of Yanton, tells the story of the post and points to the approximate location, 6 miles south on the Missouri on so-called Audubon Point.

Fort Wadsworth. *Fort Sisseton.*

Post at Whetstone Agency. 1870-72. This was a cottonwood picket stockade with buildings against the inside walls of the stockade and blockhouses at two opposite corners. An estimated 4,500 Indians were at the agency during the active period of the Army post. After the troopers left, the post became a supply depot for the other agencies. Not only has the site been frequently flooded by the Missouri, it is now permanently underwater. The site is about 18 miles northwest of the Fort Randall Dam, in midstream opposite Whetstone creek.

Yankton Stockade. 1862. The Sioux Uprising of 1862 caused the citizens of Yankton to build this 450-foot square stockade at 3d and Broadway. Residents of both Sioux Falls—which became a ghost town at the time—and Yankton gathered at the stockade until the threat was over. The center of the stockade would be modern 3d street and Broadway. At the northeast corner of this junction is the hotel which was the headquarters of General Custer when he was stranded at Yankton by a blizzard in 1873. The city was the location of an Army supply forwarding detachment during the days of the Missouri river posts.

TEXAS

FORT INGE, 1867 *(1)*

Texas divides its military and political history into the periods of occupation by the French, Spanish, Mexicans, Texas Republic, Confederate, and United States, presenting the fort researcher with a bewildering array of military, trading and settler posts that usually date from at least two of those eras.

To present a full listing of Texas forts and fort-type places would include at least 500 names and sites, a production beyond the capability of this guide to handle. Complicating this is the fact that many of these sites are either vague or unknown.

In order to keep this guide within space limitations, this listing of Texas forts is restricted to the permanent posts of the United States and the more prominent ones of the other periods, usually the ones about which there is no argument as to the site and at which there are some visible remains or markers.

Pierce's *Texas Under Arms* (Waco, 1969) is a prerequisite for the researcher looking into the forts and camps of the Texas Republic. This book provides exhaustive treatment of more than 200 posts of the period, some of which are noted in the following list.

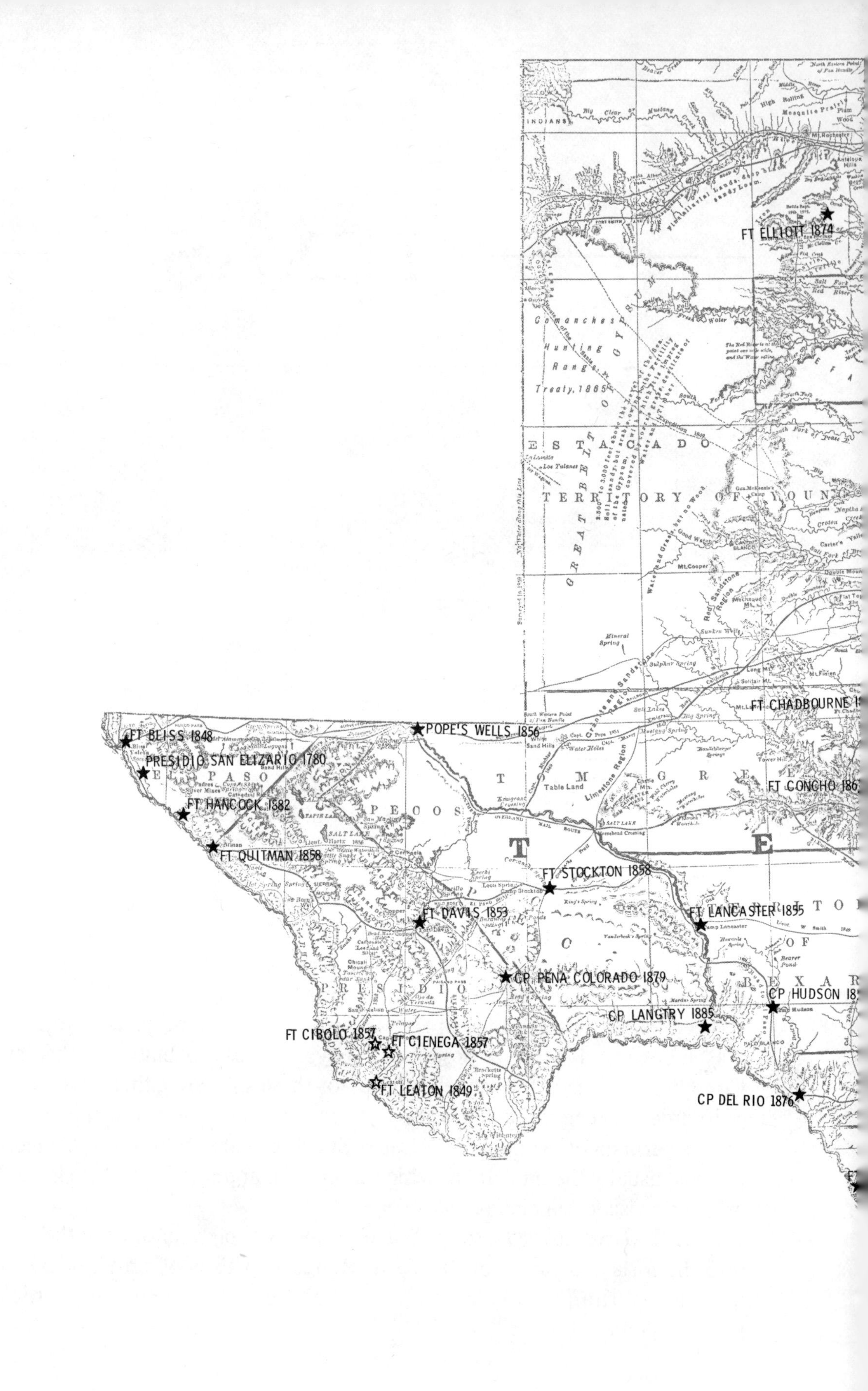

FT ELLIOTT 1874
Comanches Hunting Range Treaty, 1865
GREAT BELT OF GYPSUM
ESTACADO
TERRITORY OF YOUNG
FT CHADBOURNE
FT BLISS 1848
POPE'S WELLS 1856
PRESIDIO SAN ELIZARIO 1780
EL PASO
FT HANCOCK 1882
PECOS
FT QUITMAN 1858
FT CONCHO
FT STOCKTON 1858
FT DAVIS 1853
FT LANCASTER 1855
CP PENA COLORADO 1879
PRESIDIO
BEXAR
CP HUDSON
CP LANGTRY 1885
FT CIBOLO 1857
FT CIENEGA 1857
FT LEATON 1849
CP DEL RIO 1876

FT INGLISH 1837
FT RICHARDSON 1867
FT BELKNAP 1851
BIRD'S FT 1841
FT GRIFFIN 1867
FT WORTH 1849
CP FORD 1862
FT PHANTOM HILL 1847
FT GRAHAM 1849
CP COLORADO II 1858
PARKER'S FORT 1836
CP COLORADO I 1857
FT GATES 1849
CP CROGHAN 1849
FT MASON 1851
CAMP AUSTIN 1845
FT ANAHUAC 1830
CP VERDE 1856
FT SAM HOUSTON 1845
THE ALAMO 1836
FT LINCOLN 1849
FT INGE 1849
FT GOLIAD 1749
INDIANOLA 1851
FT MERRILL 1850
FT EWELL 1852
CP CASA BLANCA 1849
SCALE OF STATUTE MILES
FT McINTOSH 1849
ENGRAVED AND PUBLISHED BY
RAND, McNALLY & CO., MAP ENGRAVERS,
CHICAGO, 1876.
FT RINGGOLD 1848
BRAZOS SANTIAGO 1849
FT POLK 1846
FT BROWN 1846

The Alamo *(20)*

The Alamo. 1863-79. *Post at San Antonio, Camp Almus.* Texas' most historic site, this fortified chapel was where an entire garrison of Texas Republic troops and civilians died to the last man in opposing the onslaughts of Mexican General Santa Ana. The U.S. Army used the building and several adjacent before and after the Civil War. The restored Alamo is in downtown San Antonio on Alamo Plaza at East Houston and Alamo Streets.

Camp Almus. *The Alamo.*

Fort Anahuac. 1830-32. Controlling immigration, preventing smuggling, and collecting customs fees were the primary functions of this Mexican government post, first located in the border town then in the fort after it was built in 1831. Measuring 85 by 55 feet, it had four-foot thick adobe walls, mounted two cannon, had an underground tunnel to a magazine, and a well within the enclosure. It was given up in 1832 and dismantled bit-by-bit beginning in 1836 by settlers who needed the bricks. From Houston, go east on I-10 for 45 miles to Texas 61. Turn right (south) 4 miles, then right (west) again 3 miles to Anahuac. The fort was on a bluff immediately south of the town.

Camp Austin. 1845-54; 1865-75. *Post of Austin, Austin Arsenal, Camp Sanders.* Protection for the state capital was provided by the first U.S. soldiers stationed in Austin. After the Civil War, troopers under General George Custer encamped at the Post of Austin to provide protection from lawless elements, most of whom were white. There are no traces of any of the camps, but two sites are fairly well established. The Post of Austin site is at 1214 West 6th street, an area which includes an automobile agency and a vacant field. The Austin Arsenal was near the Palm Elementary School, 700 East 1st street.

Fort Belknap. 1851-61; 1865-67. This important stone complex fell into ruins during the Civil War and the Army tried after the war to rebuild it. The work that they abandoned in 1867 finally was accomplished by the Texas State Parks Board which now has the restored buildings as

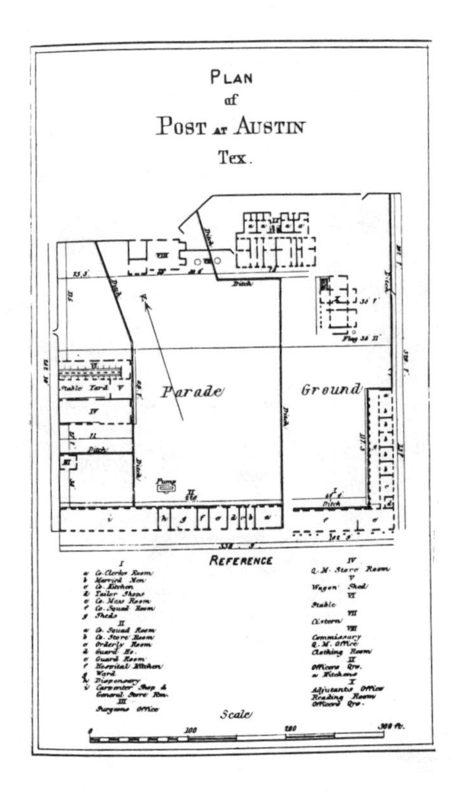

a park. From Newcastle, take Texas 251 south for 2 miles until it ends at the fort.

Fort Big Springs Cibolo. *Fort Cibolo.*

Bird's Fort. 1841-42. *Fort Bird.* Started as a garrison by the Texas Militia, this fort saw more service as a settler fort after the Volunteers were disbanded in 1842. This was a stockade with a blockhouse, enclosing three huts. From Fort Worth, go northeast about 18 miles to Euless. Turn right (south) onto Main street and go south 4 miles to where a marker identifies the fort's site.

Fort Bliss. 1848—. *Camp at Franklin; Military Post of El Paso; Camp at Concordia; Post at Smith's Ranche; Post Opposite El Paso, New Mexico; Military Post Opposite El Paso, Texas.* The varying dates and locations of Fort Bliss and its forebearers began in 1848 with the establishment of the post at Franklin, the site of Smith's ranch and now part of downtown El Paso, at about the intersection of Main and Santa Fe streets.

Absent from the site from 1851 to 1854, the garrison was reestablished on January 11, 1854, a short distance to the southeast of the first post. This would be in the area of Magoffin and Octavia streets in modern El Paso. Here the Fort Bliss title was designated on April 30, 1854. This was then known as Maggoffinsville, after the ranch owner.

Bliss was given up to the Confederates on March 31, 1861, used by them as an assembly area occasionally until California Volunteers arrived in June, 1862, to find the place had been burned. During the times that troops were in El Paso during the Civil War they bivouaced at either the old Franklin location or at Hart's Mill on the western edge of town. The Magoffinsville buildings were rebuilt and reoccupied in October, 1865, but abandoned in March, 1868, because the post was eroding into the Rio Grande.

The third site was three miles to the northeast, occupied as Camp Concordia until 1869 and under the Fort Bliss name until troops were withdrawn from El Paso in January, 1877. This site is now Concordia cemetery, adjacent to I-10 one block from its junction with US 54.

Disorders resulted in a return of the Army to El Paso on January 1, 1878. Rented quarters were used, with the plaza turned into a parade ground, until construction was finished at Hart's Mill in 1880. This permanent post was not as permanent as its construction, sturdy brick buildings still in use as apartments, because the Army had to move again in 1894 after the railroad tracks were laid across the parade ground. This site is reached by taking Paisano drive west to Hart court, a left (west) turn after the viaduct. The buildings on the right after the turn once were Fort Bliss.

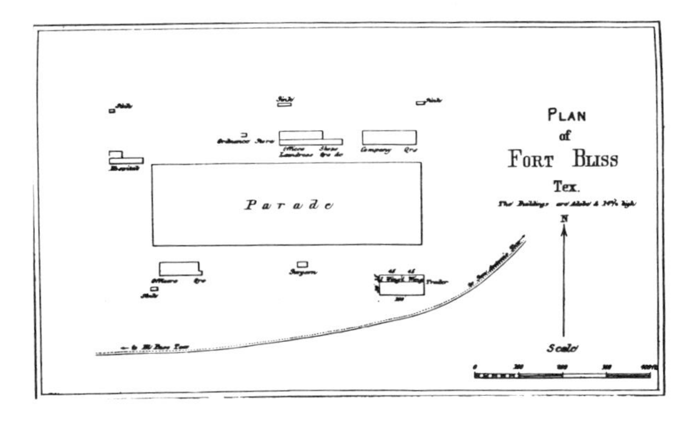

The modern Fort Bliss has been occupied since 1894 and can be reached from I-10 via US 62 (Copia street) to US 54 (Pershing drive) into the post. To reach the Fort Bliss replica within the modern post, turn right (south) at Sheridan after entering the post and follow this around to Pleasanton.

Post at Brazos. *Fort Phantom Hill.*

Brazos Santiago Depot. 1849-61; 1867. Supplies for Forts Brown and Ringgold were brought ashore here and then sent by steamer up the Rio Grande. Three civilians were employed and a three-man guard detachment rotated on a temporary basis to guard the eight-building complex. From Brownsville, go east on Texas 4 about 22 miles to Boca Chica, on Brazos Island. Inquire locally for the means to go north about 4 miles on the landward side. The site of the depot is at this point, facing Point Isabel across the water.

Fort Brown. 1846-1946. *Fort Taylor.* An earthwork fort at first, Fort Brown was involved with Robert E. Lee's Mexican bandit chasing expeditions, had a minor role in the Indian wars, and was a base of operations against the border disturbances in 1914-16. Many buildings are left next to the city of Brownsville at the southern end of S.E. Elizabeth street. The so-called

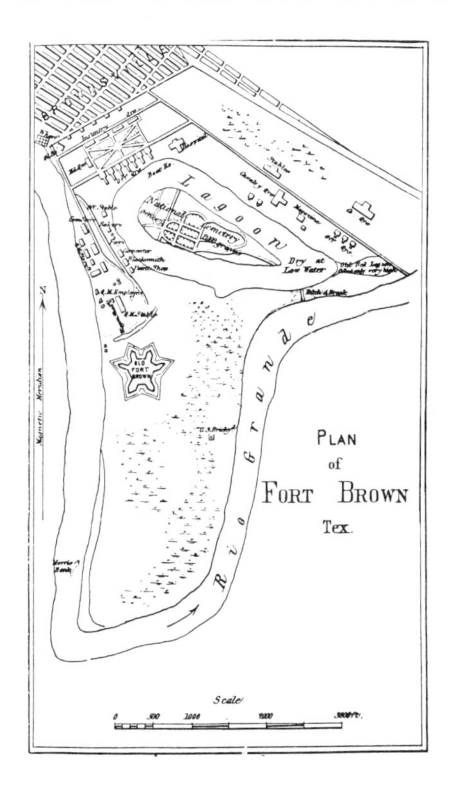

FORT BROWN, 1876 *(1)*

FORT BROWN, Barracks & Commissary Storehouse *(1)*

"Quartermaster's Fence," built in 1850 to separate the city and the post, was torn down in 1950 to widen International boulevard, but its location is marked in cement in the boulevard.

Camp Bugle. *Camp Drum.*

Captain Pope's Wells. *Pope's Camp and Wells.*

Camp Casa Blanca. 1849; 1852. *Camp Merrill.* This temporary regular Army post on the Nueces river became the site of the town of Casa Blanca but not before it was used by a detachment from nearby Fort Merrill as a sub-post. The sub-post went by the Merrill name at the Casa Blanca site. The town came later. Now all are gone along the Nueces river about 15 miles south of the Fort Merrill site.

Castolon Army Depot. 1903-1911. *Camp Santa Helena.* Adobe buildings are still left at this pre-World War I border post in Big Bend National Park.

Fort Chadbourne. 1852-64; 1867; 1870. The Indians harassed this post continually regardless of whether U.S. or Confederates were manning it. After the post was officially closed, it was occupied temporarily after the war as a base of operations during the Kiowa and Comanche campaigns. There are many buildings either in use or in ruins on the privately owned C.O. Richards ranch off of US 277 about 32 miles southwest of Abilene. The ranch is not open to visitors.

Fort Cibolo. 1857. *Fort Big Springs Cibolo.* Milton Faver built this fortified headquarters in the Big Bend country of Texas. Of the usual adobe, the walls were three to four feet thick, spaced with gun posts, and there were circular watchtowers at two of the corners. The fort was used frequently by Army detachments, for storage or a patrol base or way stop, and it appears that a small cannon was loaned to Faver by Fort Davis. The fort is in good condition, presently in use as a bunkhouse and storeroom. From Marfa, on US 90 at the entrance to the Big Bend, go southwest on US 67 for 41 miles to the hamlet of Shafter. Fort Cibolo is northwest of Shafter; obtain directions locally to this hot, desolate site.

Fort Cienaga. 1857. This quadrangular adobe fortress, rectangular double-storied bastions at two corners, was built by Milton Faver to protect his ranch and the nearby spring. He also built Fort Cibolo and had an unfortified ranchhouse at La Morita. In addition to solid gates and high walls, Cienaga had no connecting rooms inside, thus denying additional passage to any Indian who could force his way into a room. The fort was bought in 1924 by the Greenwood family and is occupied by them—after remodeling and putting connecting doors between the rooms. From Marfa, on US 90 at the entrance to the Big Bend, go southwest on US 67 for 41 miles to the hamlet of Shafter. As is specified in the Fort Cibolo item, local directions to Fort Cienaga should be obtained in Shafter.

Fort Clark. 1852-62; 1866-1949. *Fort Riley.* General Ranald Mackenzie led his "Mackenzie Raiders" from this long-active and important fort. Before the Civil War Robert E. Lee was stationed here. Buildings dating from the early days are intermixed with those of more modern vintage at what is now a residental development near Brackettville, about 30 miles east of Del Rio and 40 miles northwest of Uvalde. Now owned by North American Towns of Texas, Inc., the fort

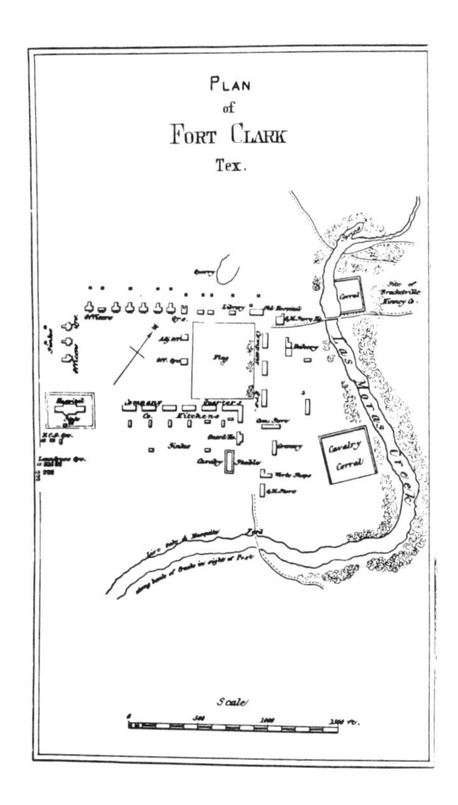

FORT CLARK *(l)*

FORT CLARK

property includes a museum to the Army past. The site is on US 90 at Brackettville.

Post on the Clear Fork of the Brazos. *Fort Phantom Hill.*

Camp Colorado. 1857-61; 1869. First built on Mulewater creek 23 miles south of its ultimate location, the Colorado garrison was forced to move after a year because of too much malaria and mosquitos and not enough water. The second location was manned by U.S. regulars, then Texas Militia until after the Civil War.

There is a replica of the headquarters in the city park in Coleman and several original buildings at the site.

To get to the camp site, go north from Coleman on US 283 for 2 miles, turn right on Texas 206. After 5.5 miles turn right on farm road 2382. In 2.2 miles the route will turn to the left but do not follow it; instead continue straight ahead for 4.3 miles more. Site is on the immediate left side. Historical plaques tell the story on the headquarters building.

Fort Concho. 1867-89. *Camp Kelly, Camp Hatch, Fort Griffin.* This well-maintained post is an example of what a local civic group can do with the proper motivation and talent. Most of the stone buildings of this important Indian Wars fort are at their original locations and can be toured for a token fee that helps maintain them. From downtown San Angelo, take Oakes avenue south across the North Concho river about 5 blocks to East Avenue C. Turn left. The street runs beside the parade ground; headquarters building (museum) is at the dead end, 3 blocks.

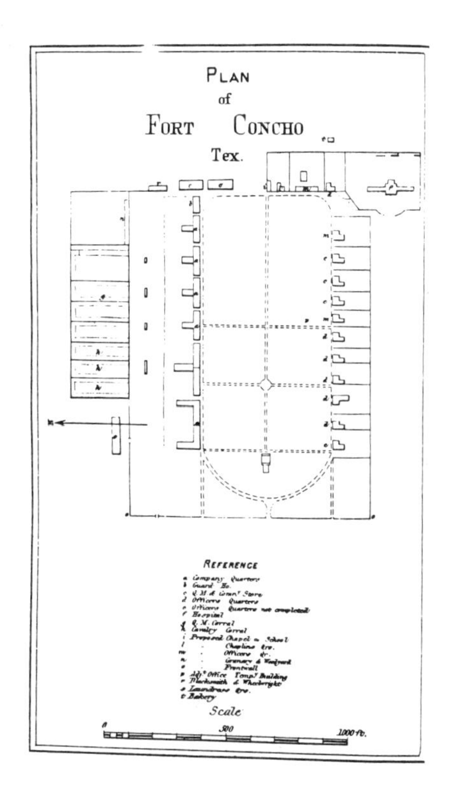

FORT CONCHO, 1886 *(1)*

Camp Concordia. *Fort Bliss.*

Camp Cooper. 1856-61. Robert E. Lee was the most famous commander of this isolated but active post, facing both Indians and vigilantes alike. When the Civil War started and Texas Militia demanded it surrender, the commanding officer agreed—after he burned it down. From Albany, take US 283 north 13 miles to road intersection with farm road (2 miles south of Fort Griffin State Park). Sign for Matthews ranch is at this point; turn left. Follow signs for 8 miles, turn right to Putman ranch, 5 miles. At Putman ranch house, it is a 1 mile hike west, including wading the hip-deep Clear Fork of the Brazos. A marker is where the parade ground once was. Permission should be requested. Beware of rattlesnakes.

Camp Crawford. *Fort McIntosh.*

Fort Crockett. This was an Endicott period (1898 era) coast defense that was active until after World War II. Its three early batteries, Izard, Hampton, and Laval, have been leveled to become a seawall with a playground atop it. Battery Hoskins of the World War I use is privately owned, sitting alone in a field behind the seawall. The fort is on Seawall boulevard in Galveston at City Beach.

Battery Croghan. This was a 3-inch Endicott period gun position at Fort San Jacinto.

Camp Croghan. 1849-55. *Camp Hamilton.* Contrary to local tales, Robert E. Lee was not a commander of this key post on the inner defense line. It was another Lee—Arthur T. Lee, a Union at Gettysburg. One commander who became a Confederate general was H.H. Sibley who later led the invasion of New Mexico. The parade ground and several buildings of this log post are maintained in a city park in Burnet. From I-35 about 22 miles north of Austin at the Georgetown exit, head west on Texas 29 for 36 miles to Burnet. Continue west on Texas 29 from the center of town for 5 blocks to where the fort marker can be seen, left side. Fort park is 100 yards down road behind this sign.

Battery Davis. This was an 8-inch Endicott period gun position at Fort Travis.

Fort Defiance. *Fort Goliad.*

Camp Del Rio. 1876-91; 1914-22. *Post of San Felipe.* Under the latter name this border post was established in the San Felipe river valley and functioned as an independent post. It was made a sub-post of nearby Fort Clark and renamed in early 1881. The post was at the city of Del Rio at the junction of US 277 and 90 near the Rio Grande.

Camp Drum. 1851-52. *Camp Bugle.* The latter designation was supposed to be attached to this border camp of the 2d U.S. Dragoons but for reasons unrecorded the other musical instrument won out. The site is at the town of Zapata, 49 miles south of Laredo on US 83.

Fort Duncan. 1849-61; 1868-83; 1886-1927. *Camp Eagle Pass, Camp near Eagle Pass, Camp on the Rio Grande.* Confederates and Federals fought around and through the buildings of Fort Duncan during the Civil War. The post was abandoned by the Army in 1883 when the owner refused to settle on a firm rental or sale price. Soldiers returned to the site three years later but used the name "Camp at Eagle Pass." Stables, magazine, headquarters, and other buildings are left at this post where, in 1873, General Ranald Mackenzie was told by the Secretary of War and General Phil Sheridan to pursue Indians into Mexico—the start of legendary "Mackenzie's Raiders." From downtown Eagle Pass, go south on Adams street to Fort Duncan Park where the fort buildings are now used for recreation purposes.

Camp at or near Eagle Pass. *Fort Duncan.*

FORT ELLIOTT *(1)*

El Fortin. *Fort Leaton.*

Fort Elliott. 1874-90. *Camp on the North Fork, Red River; Cantonment North Fork, Red River; New Post on the Sweetwater.* This adobe and frame post was arranged around a 450- by 650-foot parade ground, had five barracks and was officially planned for six companies. Among the Western names that frequented this postion of the Texas Panhandle was Bat Masterson who participated in an Elliott scout in spring, 1876. There is a marker at the fort site but no remains. From Amarillo, go east on I-40 to Shamrock, about 90 miles. Turn north on US 83 toward Wheeler, 15 miles. At Wheeler, turn left (west) on Texas 153 for 12 miles to the site of Fort Elliott near Mobeetie.

Engineer's Camp. *Pope's Camp and Wells.*

Battery Ernst. This was a 3-inch Endicott period gun position at Fort Travis.

Fort Davis. 1853-62; 1867-91. *Painted Camp on the Limpia.* Many a western tale can be traced to this post, one of the most important, elaborate and picturesque on the frontier. The National Park Service has been working since 1963 to restore the fort to its post-Civil war appearance. The expansive site is to the immediate east of the town of Fort Davis on Texas 17 in the Davis mountains of West Texas.

Military Post of El Paso; Post Opposite El Paso, New Mexico; Military Post Opposite El Paso, Texas. *Fort Bliss.*

Fort Ewell. 1852-54. The area of Fort Ewell probably is little changed from its heydey when the five-building installation housed the troopers who protected the strategic Nueces river crossing on the San Antonio road.

Though the fort buildings served as the start of the town of LaSalle after the post was abandoned, and LaSalle was the county seat until 1882, there are no traces at the site except for some mounds and slight excavations.

A state marker is the only evidence that this is the spot in the center of the vast Coquat cattle ranch near Cotulla. Permission to visit this privately owned site must be requested at which time directions can be obtained; the site is impossible to find without directions.

Camp at Faver's Ranch. 1879. This was one of the several occasions in which troops were stationed at so-called Fort Cibolo, the headquarters ranch-

FORT DAVIS *(36)*

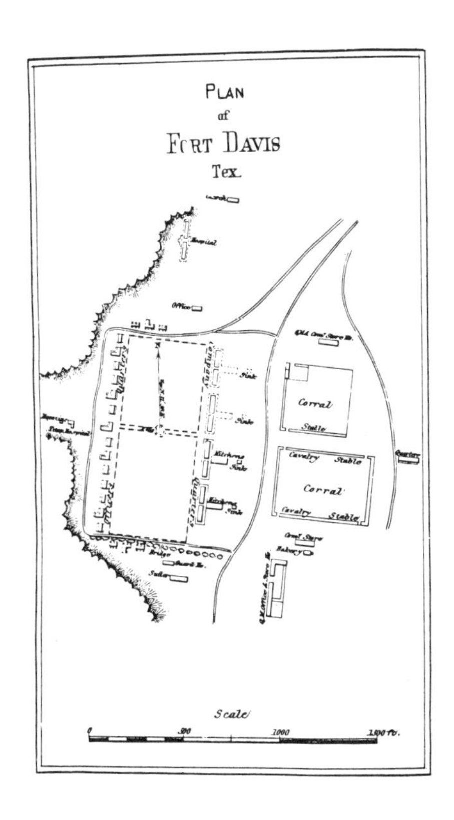

fort of Milton Faver. See Fort Cibolo item for directions.

Camp Ford. 1862-65. At first a Camp of Military Instruction for Confederates training at Tyler, in 1863 the camp became a prison for Union soldiers. Its peak population was 4,800 Federals in July, 1864, confined within the 10-acre stockade. Only a marker at a Highway Department roadside park is left to identify the site along US 271 on the outskirts of Tyler. The actual post location is 25 paces from the marker, away from the highway; this places the visitor in the middle of the post's west wall.

Camp at Franklin. *Fort Bliss.*

Fort Goliad. 1749-1842. *Fort Defiance, Fort LaBahia, Presidio LaBahia.* From its early days as a presidio and mission, through its capture in 1812 by American volunteers, the 1817 massacre of 50 American volunteers, the 1821 capture of the post by Mississipians, the 1836 capture of the post from the Mexicans by Texas Militia and the later massacre of the 330 Texas prisoners after their loss of the Battle of Perdido, Goliad witnessed a good portion of early Texas history, even U.S. troops being stationed in the town in 1867. It is now a state park. From San Antonio, go southeast on U S 181 for 61 miles to Kenedy. Turn left (east) for 2 miles on Texas 72 to Texas 239, then left (south) on 239 for 30 miles to Goliad.

Fort Gates. 1849-52. The 17 or 18 frame buildings at Fort Gates included a one-story octagonal shaped barracks that boasted a fireplace at each of its eight sides. Now only the post cemetery is left at the site. Graves dating to the 1870's are still tended by descendents of soldiers stationed at Gates who remained or returned to settle permanently in the area. From Gatesville, go southeast on Texas 36 for 3 miles to the tiny settlement of Nothinsville. The name is prominently displayed on the grocery, left side of highway. Turn left, continue 1.5 miles to railroad tracks. Post cemetery is down tracks 200 yards on right; post site, with marker, is behind the farmhouse, 100 yards to the left from the railroad crossing.

Fort Graham. 1849-53. Most of Fort Graham's buildings were shingle-sided log cabins built amidst an old Indian village. Stone from the original fort was used in a partial reconstruction of the barracks, although ground plans do not indicate that the barracks were made from anything but log pickets. The building is a recreation clubhouse on Lake Whitney. From Whitney (12 miles west of the Hillsboro exit from I-35W about 50 miles south of Fort Worth), take farm road 933 north in the direction of Blum. Turn left on second paved road. At next road, turn right, then left, then back right again. Follow signs to Fort Graham Hunting and Fishing club on the northeastern bank of Lake Whitney.

Fort Griffin. *Fort Concho.*

Fort Griffin. 1867-81. *Camp Wilson.* Many were the operations fielded from this active post—and many were the adventures recorded of the activities in the hog ranch of the same name on the flat below the Fort Griffin bluff. Picturesque ruins of most of the fort buildings are in Fort Griffin State Park, but watch for rattlesnakes.

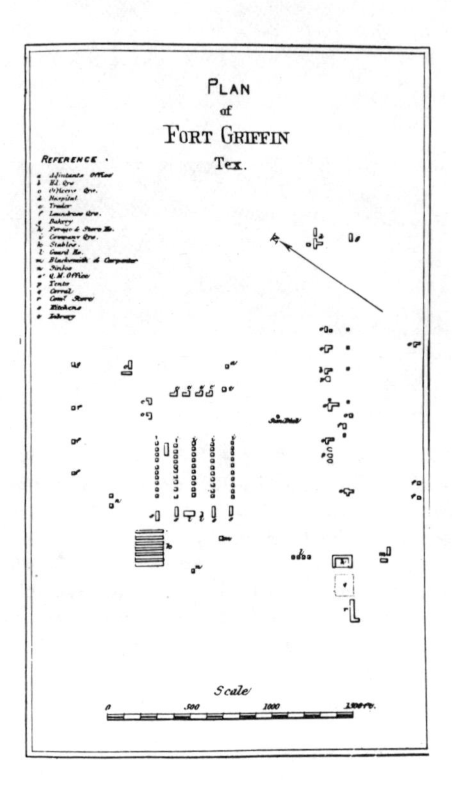

From Albany, take US 283 north about 15 miles. Fort Griffin State Park straddles the highway; entrance to the fort site is through the stone arch at left. North of the site and below the bluff is the site and ghost town of Fort Griffin town, also approachable from US 283.

A thousand yards north of the fort site entrance, on the right side of the road, is headquarters for Fort Griffin State Park, a double-story building dating from 1874. Camping facilities available.

Camp Hamilton. *Camp Croghan.*

Battery Hampton. This was an Endicott period 10-inch gun position at Fort Crockett, destroyed for a seawall.

Fort Hancock. 1882-95. *Camp Rice.* Three sites appear to have involved this latter-day Texas fort. As Camp Rice, the post was established six miles northwest of abandoned Fort Quitman on April 15, 1881. On July 9, 1882, that desolate area was abandoned in favor of a location on the Southern Pacific railroad. Six weeks later, the camp moved to higher ground to the west but still along the railroad. Four years later the Hancock name was selected for what became a substantial post until abandoned. Several buildings and a marker are at the site which straddles US 80 about 52 miles southeast of El Paso.

Camp Hatch. *Fort Concho.*

Battery Heilman. This was a 10-inch gun position of the Endicott period at Fort San Jacinto.

FORT INGE, 1867 *(1)*

Battery Hogan. This was a 6-inch gun position of the Endicott period at Fort San Jacinto.

Battery Hoskins. This was a World War I 12-inch gun position at Fort Crockett, now privately owned to the rear of the seawall.

Camp Houston. *Fort Martin Scott.*

Camp Hudson. 1854-63; 1867-68; 1871. *Camp on San Pedro.* A camel expedition from San Antonio used Hudson as its objective in 1859; the camels made it in better condition than the men and mules that were tending them. The post also was the base for another 1859 expedition, this time a 600-mile foray into Mexico that almost resulted in international complications. Today the site is desolate and rock strewn. From Del Rio, take US 90 north to Comstock. Turn right on Texas 163. The site is 20 miles north on the right side immediately after crossing the Devil's river.

Depot and Post of Indianola. 1851-69. Army tenancy at this important shipping point was not continuous, fluctuating with the manning of the inland posts that it supported and with a change in loyalties during the Civil War.

This depot was the scene in 1856 when the first load of Jefferson Davis' camels arrived in the United States and one camel was loaded with 1,256 pounds of hay and walked calmly away. If true, this was one of the few times a camel was calm during the pre-Civil War experiment, according to less enthusiastic participants in the test.

Indianola included six rented sheds, several shops, a two-story office, and, for the camel experiment, a shed 200 feet by 20, and 12 feet high. There are no modern traces of the depot, the entire port of Indianola having been destroyed by a hurricane in 1875.

From Victoria, go southeast on US 87 to Port Lavaca, 23 miles. Inquire locally for the dirt road that leads to the site of the old town of Indianola, today only a scattering of excavations and rubble.

Infantry Barracks, San Antonio. *Fort Sam Houston.*

Fort Inge. 1849-61; 1866. *Camp Leona.* Whitewashed rough shanties, called jacals, made up Fort Inge on the shore of the Leona river. It was supposed to keep peace along the trail but was established and abandoned so many times that more time was devoted to keeping the post in shape. A marker and a flagpole are at the site.

From Uvalde, take US 83 (Getty street) south

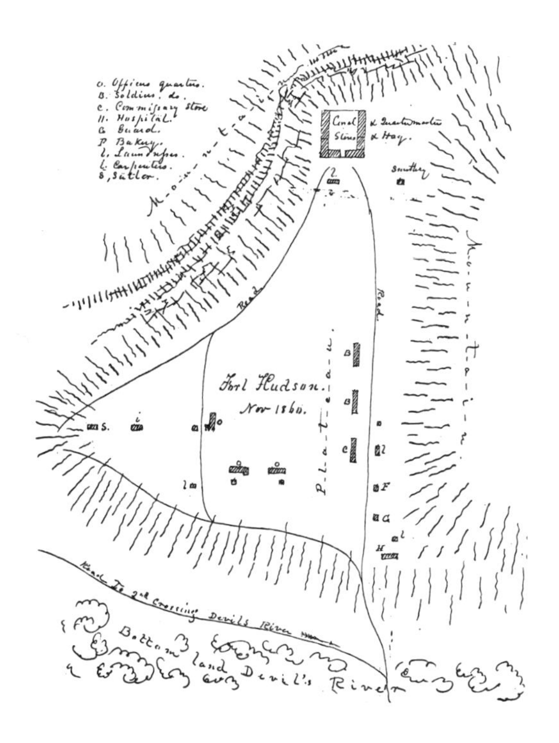

Fort Lancaster *(20)*

from the center of the city to a fork with Texas 117.

Follow this to a left turn on Farm Road 140. One mile and a half east is a sign to the fort on the right (south) side of the road. A high mound-like hill, so-called "Mount Inge," is prominent to the right. Follow the dirt road about one mile into the fort site at the base of the hill.

Fort Inglish. 1837. A single blockhouse, 16 feet square on the ground floor with an overhanging second story 24 feet square, Fort Inglish was a settler post built by Bailey Inglish. Settlers forted up here at the first word of Indian activity and the fort served as the jumping off point for a number of militia and regular military forces. A replica of the blockhouse is in the city of Bonham—the town that grew up around the fort in the 1840's—next to the Bailey Inglish cemetery, East 6th and Linn streets.

Battery Izard. This was an Endicott period 12-inch gun position at Fort Crockett, destroyed for a seawall.

Camp Kelly. *Fort Concho.*

Battery Kimble. This was a 12-inch Endicott period gun position at Fort Travis.

Fort or **Presidio LaBahia.** *Fort Goliad.*

Fort Lancaster. 1855-65; 1867. The site of this post still has many large rock ruins scattered around the former parade ground. The fort was important protection for the pre-Civil War stages, and was occupied during the war by a Confederate force. From Sheffield, take US 290 for 10 miles north to where there is a marker on the right of the road after crossing Live Oak Creek. The fort's chimneys can be seen to the distant left of the highway near the foothills. There is a visitors center and other facilities at this state park.

Camp Langtry. 1885. Judge Roy Bean named this town after Lily Langtry, the actress who finally visited the town but after the judge—so-called "Law West of the Pecos"—had died. Troops were stationed here to protect the rail-

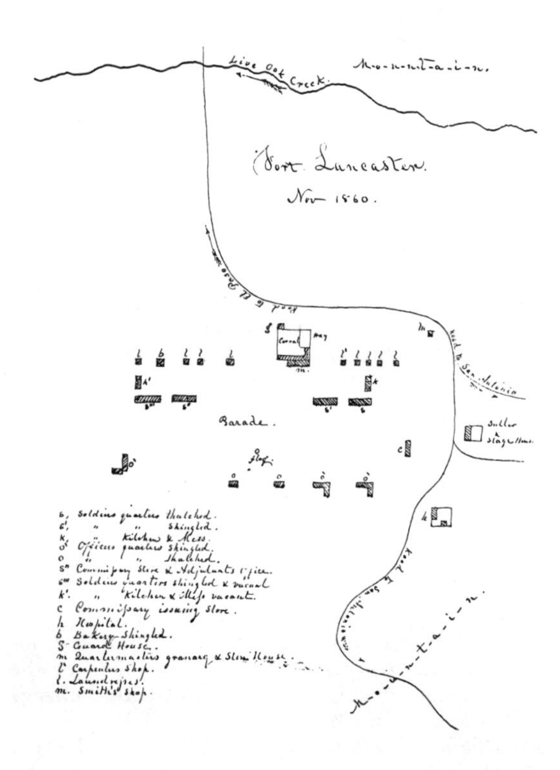

road construction crews. In addition to the Lily Langtry Opera House and Judge Bean's law offices, both in the center of the near-ghost town, the army site is on a slight rise to the northeast of the center of town. Directions should be obtained in town.

Battery Laval. This was an Endicott period 3-inch gun position at Fort Crockett, destroyed for a seawall.

Fort Leaton. 1849. *El Fortin, Leaton's Fort.* Ben Leaton built this 200-foot square adobe trading post amidst Indian country next to the Rio Grande. It was a trade and military center until almost the turn of the century. The elaborate adobe remains of 40-some rooms now belong to the State of Texas. From Presidio, at the end of US 67 in the Big Bend country of West Texas, go south on Farm Road 170 for 3.7 miles. The ruins are next to the road on the right (west) side.

Camp Leona. *Fort Inge.*

Fort Lincoln. 1849-52. Low rock walls and one reconstructed building are the scattered remains of this fort next to a state marker near D'Hanis, Texas. The Army kept the peace here for awhile and the Texas Rangers occupied the post for a short time after the Army left. From D'Hanis, a hamlet on US 90 about 50 miles west of San Antonio, take Farm Road 1296 north 2.2 miles to where it meets Seco river (left). Dirt road on the left goes through gate, across river ford, and winds up the opposite bank onto the side of the fort. This is private property.

Camp Lugubre. *Fort Terrett.*

Fort Martin Scott. 1848-53; 1861-66. *Camp Houston.* Sometimes the fighting was hotter between the soldiers and the settlers of nearby Fredericksburg, than with the Indians. In its later years, the post was occupied by Confederates and Texas Rangers. From the courthouse in Fredericksburg, go west on East Main (US 290) for 2.4 miles to where there is a marker on the left side of the highway. There is one limestone building at the site, said to have been constructed from remnants of the army post.

Fort Mason. 1851-54; 1856-61; 1866-69. Robert E. Lee was stationed at Fort Mason, as were Albert Sidney Johnston, George H. Thomas and Earl Van Dorn. As with other Texas posts it was active against the hostile Indians until it was evacuated by Union troops at the start of the Civil War. Today there is a marker near several low stone wall remnants. From Mason, go south 1 mile to a state marker.

Fort McIntosh. 1849-61; 1865-1945. *Spanish Presidio, Camp Crawford.* The original post, on the site of a Spanish presidio, was a star-shaped earthwork but this was replaced after the Civil War with the usual frame buildings which in turn were replaced by permanent buildings late in the 19th century. The buildings now are used for government and city purposes, including a junior college. From downtown Laredo, go west on Victoria street about 15 blocks until it runs into

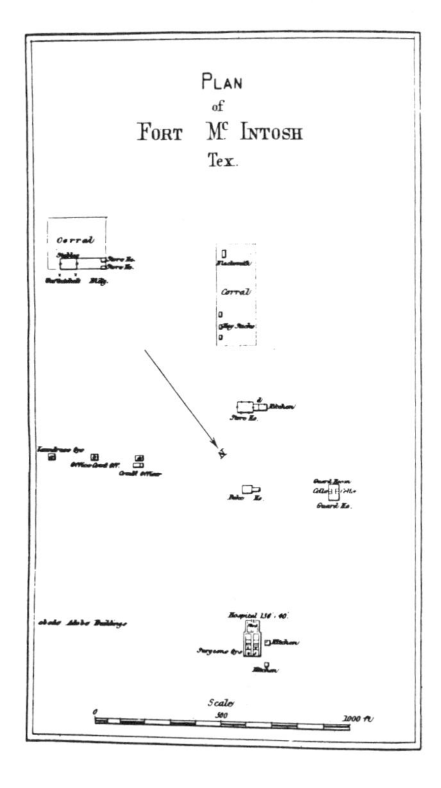

FORT MCINTOSH, guardhouse

the Fort McIntosh reservation. Recent buildings and a parade ground are near the entrance. Older buildings are mainly to the right (north) of the parade ground. The original fortifications can be reached by going north on a dirt road that parallels the river at the far side of the post. The mounds of the star-fort are in the northwestern corner of the reservation.

Fort McKavett. 1852-58; 1868-83. *San Saba River Post.* General Ranald Mackenzie rebuilt this post as a center of operations against hostile Indians after the Civil War. The massive stone buildings were occupied long after the Army left and even today there are several buildings still used as residences. The town of Fort McKavett, which consists primarily of old Army buildings, is reached from Menard. Take Texas 29 from Menard for 16 miles. Turn left (south) on Farm Road 864. In 6 miles this road runs into Fort McKavett.

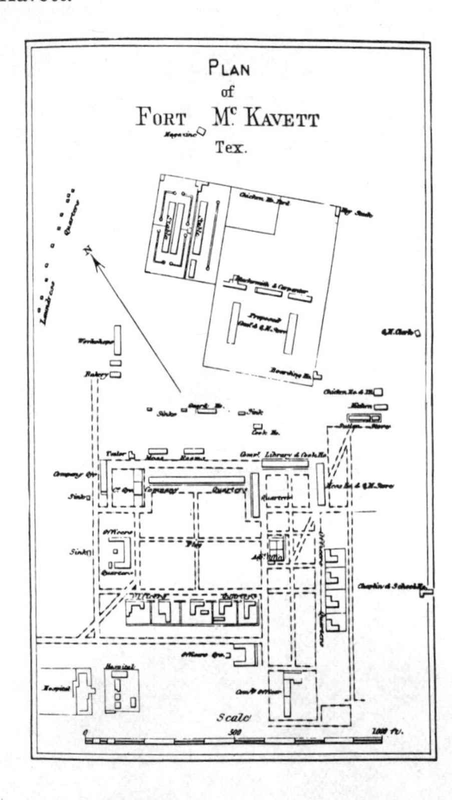

Battery Mercer. This was a 12-inch gun position at Fort San Jacinto during the Endicott period.

Fort Merrill. 1850-55. Indians and disease were the main scourges of this post on the Nueces river bottomlands; the records show that in one two-month period in 1854 every single officer, soldier and laundress at the fort was on the malaria list.

From George West, take US 59 east and turn right on the blacktop after crossing three bridges. Take this south 1 mile to a right turn and a dirt road which shortly crosses Nueces river. Cross railroad tracks in a third of a mile. A hundred yards after passing through deserted Mikeska community, take left fork of the road just below crest of the rise.

This dirt, sand-drifted road crosses Fort Merrill creek—the only formal trace of the fort—in about 1½ miles. When the road reaches the top of the hill, site of Fort Merrill can be seen to left front (north); it is a 400 yard walk through private rangeland but there are no remains. Fair weather driving only.

Post of North Fork of the Llano River. *Fort Terrett.*

Cantonment and Camp on North Fork, Red River. *Fort Elliott.*

Painted Camp on the Limpia. *Fort Davis.*

Parker's Fort. 1834-36. Members of the Parker family were the obvious builders of this settler fort that protected a settlement of eight or nine families. Several hundred Indians attacked it in May, 1836, killing five settlers, wounding a sixth, and kidnapping five more. One of the kidnapped was Cynthia Ann Parker, then nine years old, who grew up as a captive and became the mother of Quannah Parker. The fort was not used after families returned to the area. It has been reconstructed in a state park that encloses the area. From Waco, go east on US 84 for 32 miles to Mexia. At Mexia, turn right (south) 8 miles on Texas 14 to Fort Parker State Park, right (west) side.

Camp Pena Colorado. 1879-93. *Camp Rainbow Cliffs.* Although never considered as more than a camp, this cluster of frame buildings was the only Army post in the desolate West Texas country during the final years of its activity. By this time the main mission was to protect railroad construction gangs. Much of the post is left, used as a ranch headquarters.

From Marathon, which is on US 90, turn west across the tracks at the railroad depot. Follow this gravel road about 4 miles. At the point where the road crosses a small bridge, look to the right. Pena Colorado site is a quarter of a mile from the road on the privately owned property of the Combs Cattle Company. A half a mile further on the gravel road is the site of the original post within a picnic and swimming area, identified by a marker.

Fort Phantom Hill. 1847; 1851-54. *Post on the Clear Fork of the Brazos; Post at Brazos, Texas.* The "Clear Fork" name really was the official designation of this post, but seldom was it used. The ghostly, hovering chimneys and half-overgrown stone ruins make the unofficial name seem even more appropriate. Robert E. Lee never was stationed here, but he did conduct a patrol to the post in 1856, after it had been burned. From Anson, 24 miles north of Abilene, take US 180 to the intersection with Farm Road 600, about 10 miles. Turn right to Nugent, about 5 miles, and go 3 miles further south. Sentinel-like chimneys are scattered along east side of the road, heavily covered with underbrush on private property. Watch for rattlesnakes.

Pope's Camp and Wells. 1856-60. *Post Pecos River; Camp at Pope's Well; Camp Pope; Captain*

Pope's Wells; Engineer's Camp. The Army tried unsuccessfully to find water at several sites near the New Mexico border as part of the pre-Civil War development of a southern stage route to the Pacific. Later, the headquarters camp was a Butterfield stage station.

It is virtually impossible to find the locations without a guide even though there are stone remains at the sites of the camp and the third well.

To get to the well site, from Orla, Texas, (18 miles south of the New Mexico line on US 285) take the dirt road east in the direction of Jal, N.M. 15 miles to a cattle guard of Ohio Camp. From Ohio Camp, take the unimproved road north toward old Ross Ranch, turning left in 7 miles on rough trail. Take this to where oil well site has been cleared, then turn again and head south about 2 miles. Follow trail to the right until it circles right, then left and ends on top of Pope's Hill where there are several low walls.

To get to Pope's Camp from Orla, go north on US 285 about 3 miles to the turnoff to right to Red Bluff Dam. After turning right, proceed about 4 miles to Red Bluff Dam recreation area office where permission to enter should be requested and, if required, a nominal fee paid. Directions can be obtained here to site (or, as it is sometimes called, "Engineer's Camp"). Site is about 3 miles north of Red Bluff Dam on right side of reservoir. Rock building and corral outlines are left.

Post Pecos River. *Pope's Camp and Wells.*

Fort Quitman. 1858-62; 1868-77; 1880-81. This post easily qualified as one of the most uncomfortable forts of the west, located as it was in the sand wastes within a few hundred yards of the Rio Grande. It was active before the Civil War and then later was re-activated for the various wars with the Apaches.

There are no traces at the site; the Quitman cemetery still is in partial use 4 miles from the site.

To get to the actual fort site, from El Paso take I-10 east 55 miles to McNary. Continue on highway for 10 more miles, turning right at "Lower Valley Road." Follow this south 5½ miles to Quitman cemetery on the right; Fort Quitman was 4 more miles south.

A full scale replica of Fort Quitman, accurate except for adobe walls added for anti-vandal protection, is at "Tommy's Town" on I-10 about 20 miles west of Sierra Blanca. This is a commercial tourist stop owned by Tommy Powell.

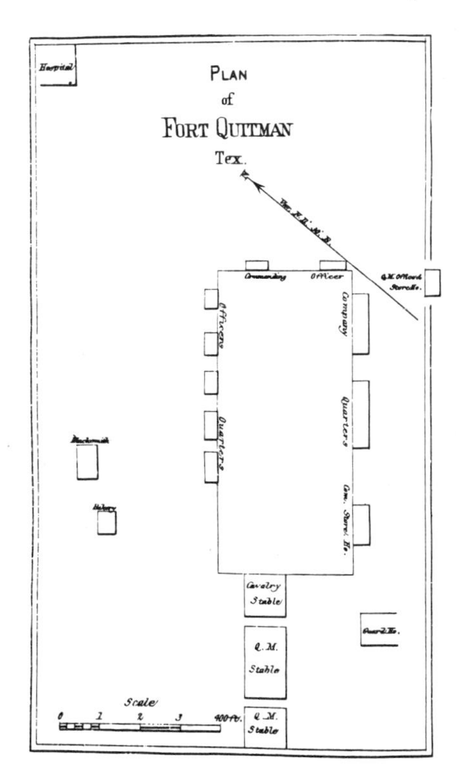

Camp Rainbow Cliffs. *Camp Pena Colorado.*

Camp Rice. *Fort Hancock.*

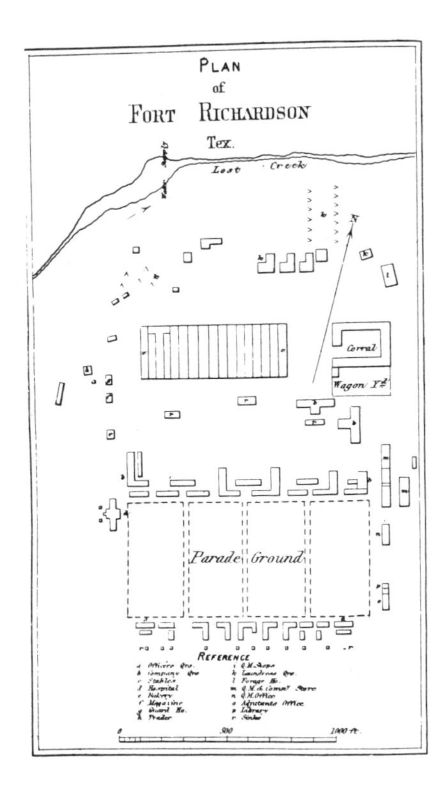

Fort Richardson. 1867-78. Post-Civil war reconstruction duties kept Richardson especially active as both bandits and Indians did not go along with the reestablishment of Federal authority. The troops operated from this permanent-type cluster of stone buildings, now restored as a park. From Jacksboro (northwest of Fort Worth on Texas 199), go south a half mile on US 281. The restored buildings are under the care of a custodian and the former hospital is a museum. There are other fort buildings outside of the restored area, including a stable on the other side of the railroad track.

Fort Riley. *Fort Clark.*

FORT RICHARDSON *(1)*

FORT RINGGOLD *(1)*

Fort Ringgold. 1848-61; 1865-1906; 1917-44. *Ringgold Barracks.* The final defeat of the Mexican bandit Cortinas was accomplished by a combined force of Texas Rangers and Ringgold troopers. Robert E. Lee arrived at Ringgold after the military victory but in time to assure that it was also a political success. Several buildings remain, now used for school purposes by the school district. Fort Ringgold's buildings are immediately adjacent to Rio Grande City (on US 83 near the Mexican border).

Camp on the Rio Grande. *Fort Duncan.*

Fort Sam Houston. 1845-46; 1849-53; 1857-61; 1865–. *Post of San Antonio; Camp Almus; Camp at the Alamo; Infantry Barracks, San Antonio.* The Sam Houston name did not become official for this post until 1890, but the U.S. Army was in San Antonio for a long time before that at camps of various names. Most of the activity was centered in the Alamo vicinity in downtown San Antonio until the Infantry Barracks, San Antonio was established on a 3,300 acre plot two miles to the northeast in 1879. That is where Fort Sam Houston is today. From downtown San Antonio take East Houston

FORT RINGGOLD
Commander's Quarters *(1)*

FORT SAM HOUSTON *(1)*

from the Alamo and turn left on New Braunfels, about 20 blocks to the east. Fort Sam Houston is at the north end of New Braunfels.

Post of San Antonio. *Fort Sam Houston.*

Camp Sanders. *Camp Austin.*

Fort San Jacinto. This was an Endicott period (1898 era) coast defense that included Batteries Mercer, Heilman, Hogan, and Croghan. These batteries, at Fort Point, are visible from Seawall Boulevard extended but the Corps of Engineers is using the area for fill purposes at Galveston.

Presidio of San Elizario. 1847; 1849-51; 1862. *Post San Elizario, Camp at Presidio de Elizario.* Dating from the Spanish presidio of 1780, the buildings at San Elizario claim to be the first U.S. military post. The claim to being a part of the U.S. Army cannot go back earlier than 1847 when elements of Doniphan's Mexican War force set up a camp in the old presidio. The hamlet of San Elizario still has portions of the presidio and chapel and other buildings dating from mid-nineteenth century. From El Paso, take I-10 about 27 miles southeast to the Clint exit. Go west 3 miles to San Elizario where the chapel and adobe headquarters building face the square.

Post of San Felipe. *Camp Del Rio.*

Camp on San Pedro. *Camp Hudson.*

San Saba River Post. *Fort McKavett.*

Post at Shafter. 1916-20. Two adobe structures and crumbling ruins are left of this National Guard camp that housed upwards of 50 soldiers protecting the mining area from border raids. Shafter is a mining hamlet on US 67 about 40 miles south of Marfa and 19 miles north of Presidio.

Post at Smith's Ranche. *Fort Bliss.*

Spanish Presidio. *Fort McIntosh.*

Fort Stockton. 1858-86. Protecting the mail and the settler was the mission of Fort Stockton that became superfluous when the railroad left it 63 miles off of the main route. The guardhouse and several officers quarters, now used as residences, are left around the former parade ground. Fort Stockton, the town, is at the intersection of US routes 285, I-10, and 385 in west Texas. From the intersection of US 385 and I-10, go south on Spring drive to the site and remaining buildings between 5th and 2d streets.

New Post on The Sweetwater. *Fort Elliott.*

Fort Taylor. *Fort Brown.*

Fort Terrett. 1852-54. *Camp Lugubre, Post on North Fork of Llano River.* Almost all of this relatively quiet post is left today as the headquarters and out buildings of a private ranch. One story is that the post was abandoned because of the intemperate habits of the garrison in what must have been a lonely region in the mid-nineteenth century. From Junction, Texas (96 miles southeast of San Angelo), take US 290

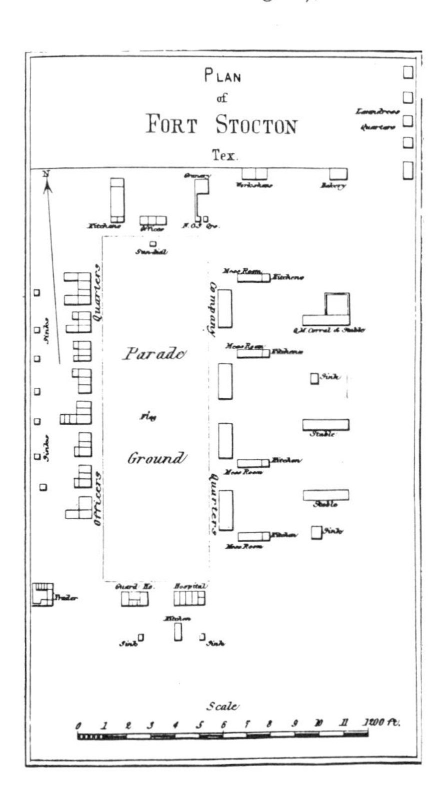

west 26 miles to the intersection with a dirt road beyond Roosevelt. This is River road and also has a sign for Fort Terrett. Go north 1 mile to Noel ranch, the site of the fort where the buildings still are in use.

Fort Travis. This is an Endicott period (1898 era) coast defense at Bolivar Point, Galveston, that included Batteries Davis and Ernst. It was active through World War II when two more batteries, Kimble and No. 236, were added. This is now a county park with the batteries in good shape.

Camp Verde. 1856-67. This was the home of the pre-Civil War camel experiment and the site of probably the only specially designed camel khan (or stable) in Western Army history. Builders' stone in the restored barracks confirms its 1857 construction date. From San Antonio go northwest on Texas 16 for 48 miles to Bandera. Turn right (north) at Bandera onto County 689 for 14 miles to Camp Verde hamlet.

Camp Wilson. *Fort Griffin.*

Camp Wood. 1857; 1860-61. Located at the intersection of several major Indian trails and next to the site of an old mission, Camp Wood was a one-company garrison housed in tents. The company was too depleted by other assignments—such as monthly patrols along the trails it was guarding—to improve its living conditions before the post was abandoned when the Civil War began. The site is now the town of Camp Wood 40 miles north of Uvalde on Texas 55.

Fort Worth. 1849-53. A far cry from the modern city that now occupies the site, early Fort Worth was a cluster of leaky log cabins around a rectangular parade ground. An unusual feature to this parade ground was that a palisade stables, 150 feet long and 30 wide, made up the northeast side of the parade – but the odors usually pervaded the entire post. When settlers began to crowd out the soldiers, it became obvious that there was no need for the post and it was abandoned in 1853. The site of the post is now the courthouse at Houston and Belknap streets.

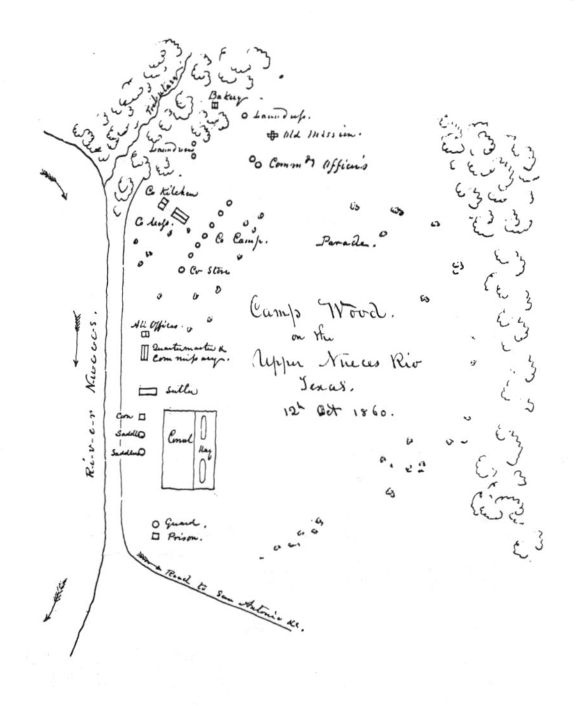

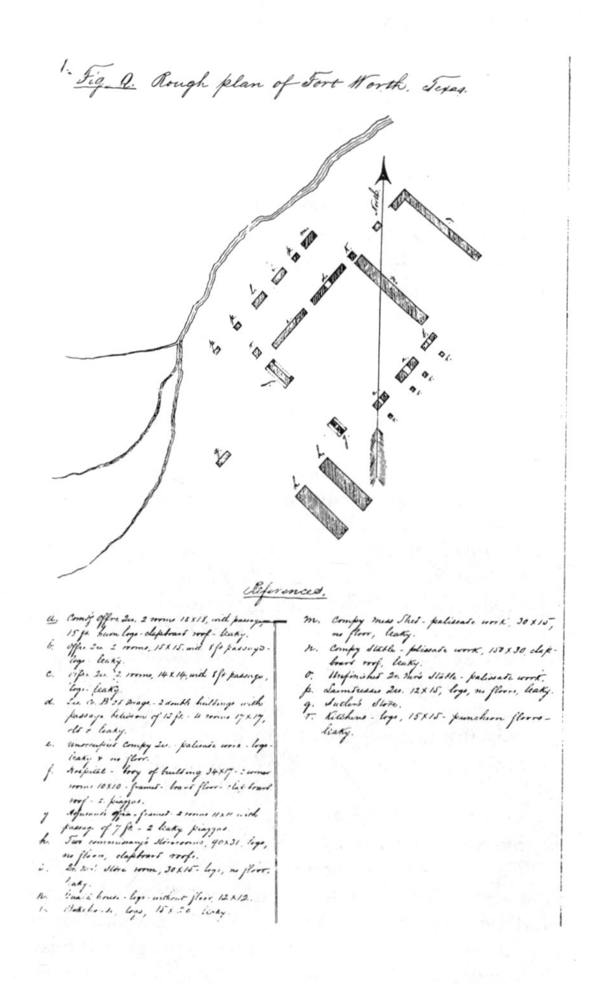

UTAH

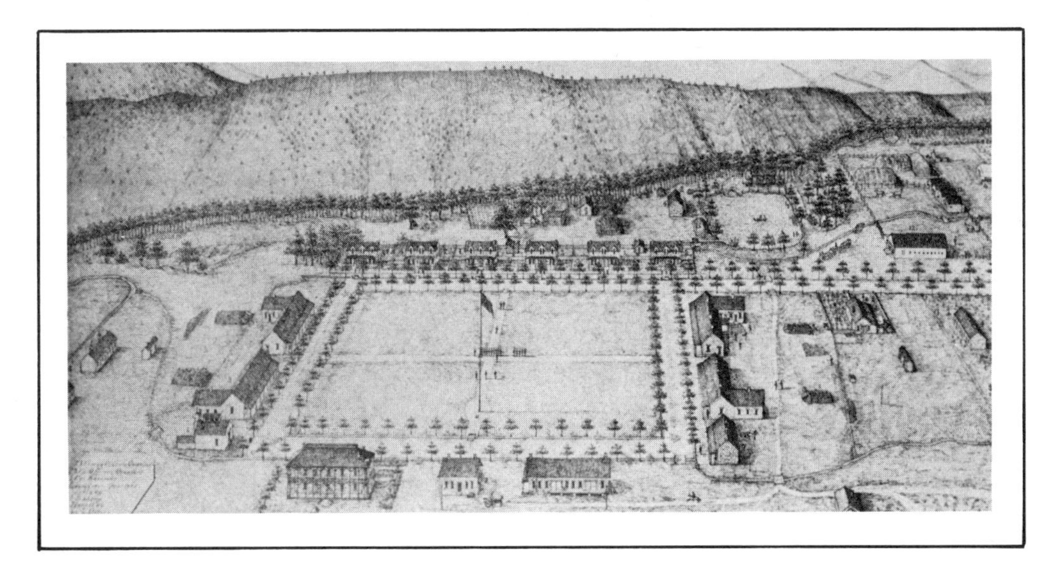

FORT CAMERON *(1)*

Brigham Young's dictate that all new settlements be protected by a fort, usually only a cluster of buildings arranged closely enough together that a defense could be stood against attack, complicates any attempt to locate and list Utah's forts. Many of the so-called forts from 1852 through the Civil War were forts only because their Mormon settler builders chose to call them forts.

The Utah Expedition for the Mormon War brought much of the U.S. Army to Utah before the Civil War. The regular Army camps, and some occupied by the Mormons in initial defense against the Army, were so temporary in tenure and nature that precise site location is impossible.

These factors have been considered in this listing of Utah's forts. Only those sites which seem to have a claim on the title of fort or that were fort-type in appearance, are included if it had been possible to provide some degree of accuracy in locating them.

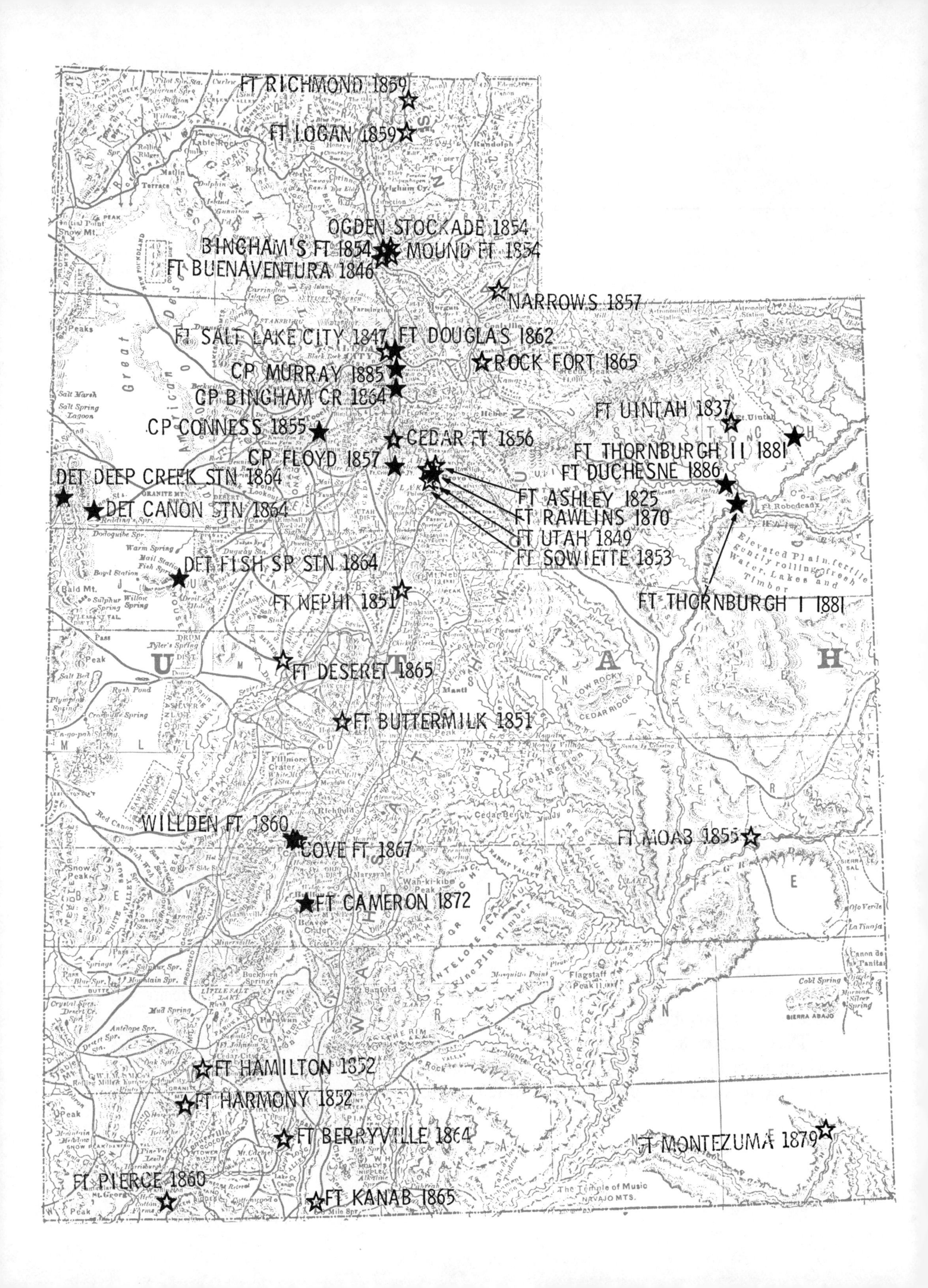
FT RICHMOND 1859
FT LOGAN 1859
OGDEN STOCKADE 1854
BINGHAM'S FT 1854
MOUND FT 1854
FT BUENAVENTURA 1846
NARROWS 1857
FT SALT LAKE CITY 1847
FT DOUGLAS 1862
ROCK FORT 1865
CP MURRAY 1885
CP BINGHAM CR 1864
FT UINTAH 1837
CP CONNESS 1855
CEDAR FT 1856
FT THORNBURGH II 1881
CP FLOYD 1857
FT DUCHESNE 1886
DET DEEP CREEK STN 1864
FT ASHLEY 1825
DET CANON STN 1864
FT RAWLINS 1870
FT UTAH 1849
FT SOWIETTE 1853
DET FISH SP STN 1864
FT NEPHI 1851
FT THORNBURGH I 1881
FT DESERET 1865
FT BUTTERMILK 1851
WILLDEN FT 1860
FT MOAB 1855
COVE FT 1867
FT CAMERON 1872
FT HAMILTON 1852
FT HARMONY 1852
FT BERRYVILLE 1864
FT MONTEZUMA 1879
FT PIERCE 1860
FT KANAB 1865

Ashley's Fort. 1825. This was a temporary trading post listed in Chittenden's *History of the American Trade of the Far West* as having been founded at the site of Provo by William H. Ashley. Bancroft's *Works* describes this as lasting "two or three years, collecting $180,000 worth of furs, and then being sold in 1826 to the Rocky Mountain Fur Company."

Post of Beaver. *Fort Cameron.*

Fort Berryville. 1864. This Mormon settler fort consisted of log cabins built into a square enclosure with large doors at two opposite ends. It was built by the founders of what became Glendale, but first was named Berryville, and was occupied by new families arriving in the town until into the 1870's. From Kanab, go north on US 89 for 26 miles to Glendale, modern version of Berryville.

Bingham's Fort. 1854. This was a settler enclosure at Ogden during the early days of establishing this city 30 miles north of Salt Lake City on I-15.

Camp at Bingham Creek. 1864. Company L, 2d California Cavalry Volunteers camped here during July, 1864. The approximate site is on Bingham Creek south of Midvale, south of Salt Lake City on I-15. The town of West Jordan is at the mouth of Bingham creek and the Jordan river.

Fort Buenaventura. 1846. This half acre square stockade was the first settlement in what is now Utah. It was built by Miles Morris Goodyear as a trading post and sold to the Mormons a year later to serve as the foundation of the city of Ogden. The post was of pickets with a log house at each corner and corrals outside of the walls. The site is in modern Ogden east of the Weber river and slightly south of where 28th street would intersect with the river. Goodyear's original log cabin, part of the fort and the oldest building in the state, is now in the State Relief Society building in Tabernacle Park, on Washington boulevard between 21st and 22d streets.

Fort Buttermilk. 1851. This was the settlers' fort built when the Mormons arrived at what became the town of Holden. Holden is on I-15 about 10 miles north of Fillmore.

Fort Cameron. 1872-83. *Post at Beaver.* The only regular Army permanent post in southern Utah, Fort Cameron was an aftermath of the Ute Black Hawk war, 1865-68, and the fear of more hostilities in the area. The post was built of locally quarried basaltic lava stone, laid out around a rectangle 700 by 620 feet. When completion of the railroad made the fort unnecessary, it was sold for educational purposes; today the site is used for recreational purposes by the citizens of Beaver. Two Army buildings are left. From the center of Beaver (on I-15 about 52 miles north of Cedar City), take a gravel road east for 2 miles to a race track on the left (north) side of the road. The fort's two buildings are next to the track.

Camp Conness. 1855; 1858-69; 1864; 1866. *Camp Rush Valley, Government Reservation in Rush Valley.* This name was attached to the Rush Valley camp by California Volunteers who manned this grazing area during the Civil War and thus honored the governor. Earlier, in 1855, the valley was the site of a two-week camp of Lieutenant Colonel Edward Steptoe. Then when Camp Floyd was in operation, horses were grazed here and a major confrontation with the Mormons generated. Camp Douglas' animals found the grass equally filling during and after the Civil War and the presence of soldiers in the valley resulted in a number of mining attempts. From Tooele go south on Utah 36 for 7 miles to Stockton. The camp and military reservation

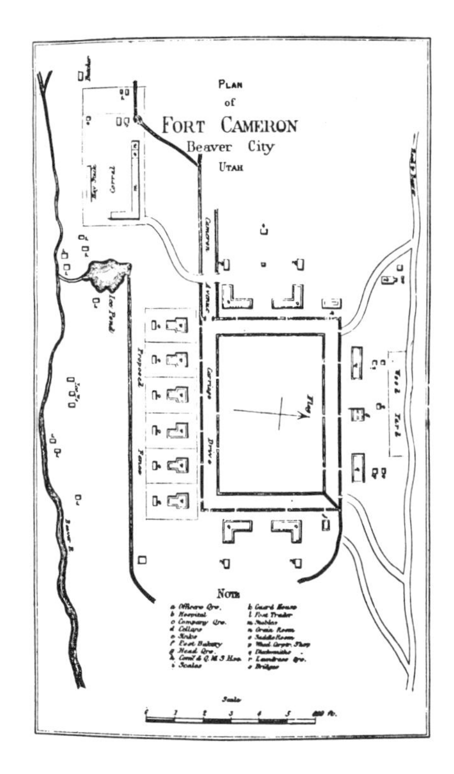

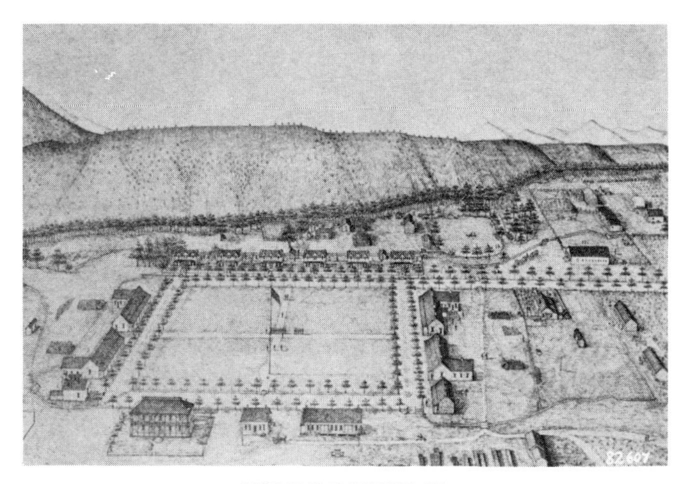

FORT CAMERON *(1)*

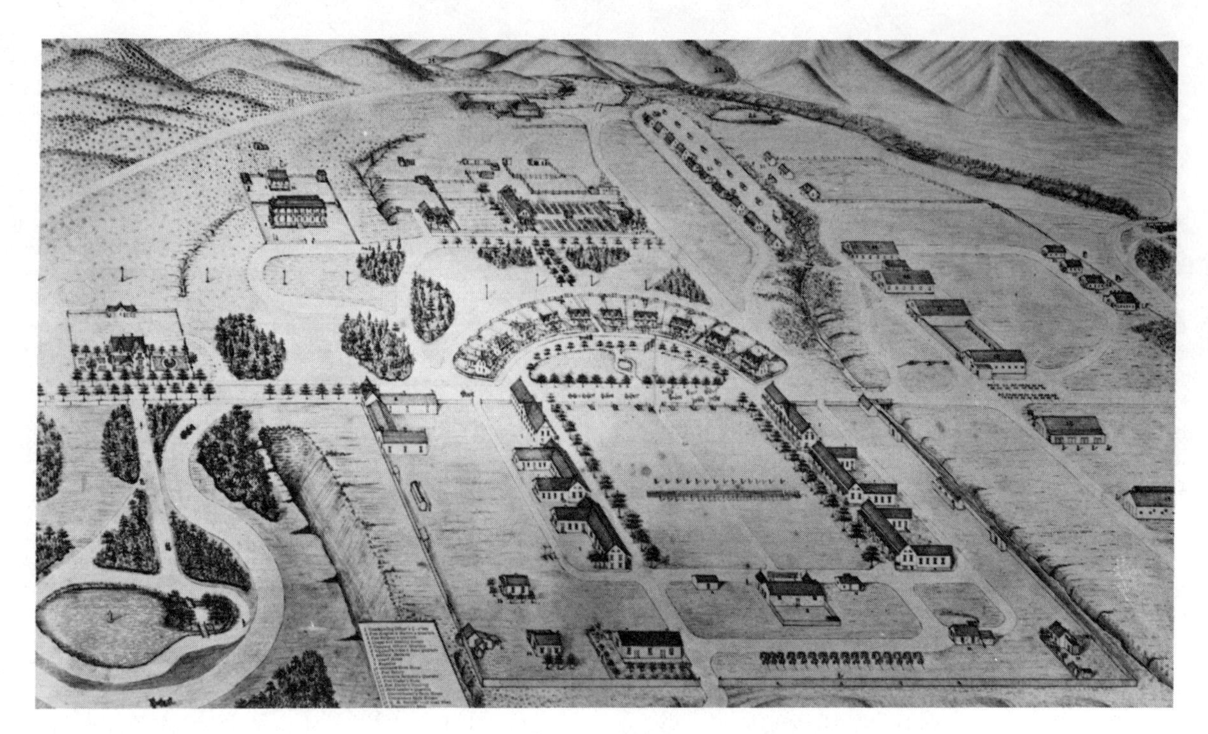

FORT DOUGLAS *(1)*

were in this area, encompassing the Rush Lakes near Stockton.

Detachment at Canon Station. 1864. Troopers from Camp Ruby, Nevada, provided protection at this Overland Stage station, either by riding with the coaches or on them. Remains of the station are marked west of Callao, the location of the Willow Springs station, the first east of Canon Station. From Tooele, go south on Utah 36 about 15 miles to a right (west) turn to Clover, Willow Springs, and the Dugway Proving Ground. About 20 miles west and just before entering the Dugway Army reservation, turn left (south) on a gravel road that follows the Overland and Pony Express routes through rough terrain. Maps and local directions should be obtained to continue to Callao; observe precautions for desert travel. At Callao, obtain directions on how to proceed west to Canon Station.

Cedar Fort. 1856. This Mormon settler fort became the scene of a raid by Camp Floyd soldiers in 1858 in retribution for the alleged killing of a sergeant by other Mormons. Some property damage took place but casualties were prevented by the swift application of Army discipline. Cedar Fort is a town on Utah 73 about 5 miles north of Fairfield (or 14 miles west of the Lehi and Utah 73 exit on I-15).

Cove Fort. 1867-77. *Willden Fort.* A hundred feet square and 18 high, Cove Fort was built to guard the telegraph lines constructed by the Mormon church at the time of the Ute Black Hawk War. The fort is of black volcanic rock; the 12 rooms were built of the same rock against the inside of the enclosure. The walls of the stockade are four feet thick at the bottom, tapering to two feet at the top. Two gateways had thick wooden gates filled with sand to minimize the danger from burning arrows. Catwalks and portholes provided defenders the means to observe and fire on attackers. The building has been occupied by the Kesler family since 1903 and restoring and maintaining this excellently preserved post has been successfully achieved by them. Cove Fort is 22 miles north of Beaver on I-15.

Fort Crittenden. *Camp Floyd.*

Detachment at Deep Creek Station. 1864. This unit had the same mission as the Detachment at Canon Station, the next station on the Overland Stage route to east. Follow directions to Canon Station; ask locally for data on Deep Creek Station, marked site in the vicinity of Ivapah.

Fort Deseret. 1865. Mormons of all ages cooperated to build this 550-foot square adobe post for protection in the Ute Black Hawk war. The builders were formed into competing teams, each charged with the construction of a wall and a bastion, and the post was completed in 10 days. The 10-foot high walls were three feet thick at the base, 1.5 at the top. Most of the fort has crumbled away but the still impressive ruins are now the Fort Deseret State Park. From Delta, on US 6-50, go southwest on US 6-50 for 4 miles to Hinckley. Turn left (south) on US 140-257 to the town of Deseret, 3 miles, on then right (west) on a dirt road for 1.6 miles to the park.

Fort Douglas. 1862-1965. General P. Edward Connor kept his eyes on the Indians and the Mormons, especially the Mormons, from this post overlooking Brigham Young's stronghold. The permanent post is in an inactive status, its

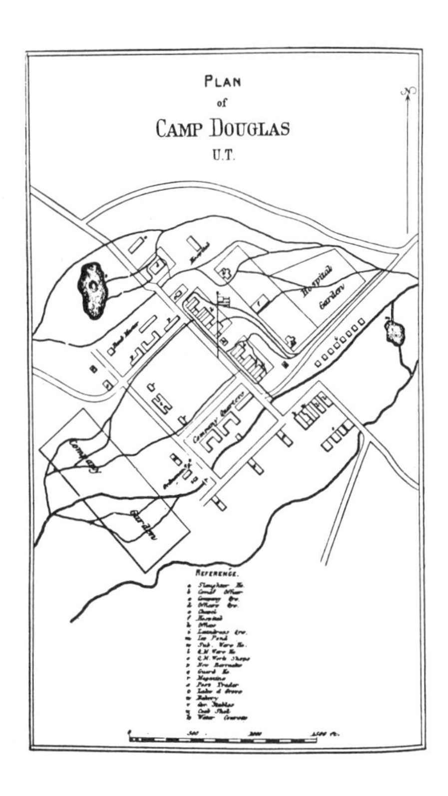

stone and brick buildings used variously by reserve and other military activities and for educational purposes. From downtown Salt Lake City take US Alternate 40 to Fort Douglas at the eastern edge of the city.

Fort Duchesne. 1886-1912. Protecting the Ute Indians and their annuities was the major task of the Duchesne garrison, a mission still accomplished by the Indian Agency that is now at the site. Several frame buildings, a stone magazine, and the sites of other buildings are evident. Take US 40 west from Vernal for 23 miles; turn left (south) 1 mile to the Fort Duchesne Agency.

Detachment at Fish Springs Station. 1864. This garrison had the same mission as the ones defending the Overland Stage stations at Canon and Deep Creek to the west. Fish Springs Station's site has some marked traces. It is on the primitive route (originally used by the Pony Express and Overland Stage) beyond Dugway Proving Ground toward Callao, Cannon and Deep Creek. See Canon item for directions.

Camp Floyd. 1857-61. *Fort Crittenden.* The Army that came to Utah to subdue the Mormons found it had little to do along that line but it was kept in the West just in case. Some critics have suggested that the western location was found

FORT DUCHESNE, Officer's Quarters *(1)*

FORT DUCHESNE *(1)*

FORT DUCHESNE, Officers' Quarters, 1886 *(1)*

convenient to Southern sympathizers in key roles in the U.S. government prior to the Civil War. Several hundred tents and buildings sheltered the largest Army garrison in the country, numbering upwards of 3,000 men on occasion. Several buildings and the post cemetery are at the site. From Salt Lake City go south on I-15 to the Lehi exit, about 30 miles. Go west on Utah 73 about 20 miles to Fairfield, the site of Camp Floyd now a State Park.

Government Reservation, Rush Valley. *Camp Conness.*

Fort Hamilton. 1852. Mormon settlers built this primitive structure for protection in the early days of southwestern Utah. The town of Hamilton Fort is 5 miles south of Cedar City on I-15.

Fort Harmony. 1852-53; 1855-62. Mormon pioneer John D. Lee, of the Mountain Meadows Massacre infamy, established this fortified post in 1852, abandoned it a year later at the start of the so-called Walker War over the question of Indian slave trading, and rebuilt it two years later. The second Fort Harmony collapsed in a 28-day rainstorm, killed two of the Walker children when a wall fell. The settlement was abandoned and the colonists moved four miles northwest to establish the town of New Harmony. From Cedar City, go south on I-15 about 16 miles to Utah 144 and the New Harmony turnoff. Go west on Utah 144 for 5 miles to New Harmony. Go southeast on local roads 4 miles to the site of Fort Harmony.

Fort Kanab. 1865-66; 1870. New arrivals at Kanab usually occupied the log huts of this Mormon fort until farm sites could be assigned and cabins built. This was a headquarters fort for the area's security although abandoned for a short period after 1866. It consisted of six to 10 cabins on one side, five to seven on the other, and two on the third, all facing into a 112-foot square enclosure across which a cedar post stockade provided protection. A stone building, 20 by 30 feet, was also inside the enclosure. A kerosene-turpentine explosion in December, 1870, destroyed part of the fort and killed six occupants. The town of Kanab is on US 89, almost in Arizona. From downtown Kanab, go north on US 89 to the northern edge of town. On the west (left) side of the town is a double marker indicating that Fort Kanab was to the west behind the sign, where a wash has eroded the site.

Fort Logan. 1859. The Mormon settlers of Logan organized a volunteer militia and built their first cabins in a double line. This protection was dubbed Fort Logan. Logan is on US 89-91 about 80 miles north of Salt Lake City.

Fort at Moab. 1855. Forty-one Mormons were sent to the site of Moab in 1851 to establish a mission and, fortunately for their well-being, constructing a stone fort was one of their first accomplishments. In September, 1855, the fort was tested by a series of Indian attacks. After three of the settlers had been killed, the fort was hurriedly abandoned and it was 20 years before another attempt was made to settle at Moab. The city of Moab is in southeastern Utah on US 160 about 30 miles south of I-70.

Fort Montezuma. 1879-80. Mormon attempts to settle the inhospitable and empy southeastern corner of the state, the valley of the San Juan, were preceded by the establishment of this settler fort at the mouth of Montezuma creek. Two families were left at the fort in 1879. In December, 1879, the main group of 200 Mormons headed out for the fort on a trip that took four months because of high snows. From Moab, go south on US 160 for 54 miles to Monticello. Continue south from Monticello on Utah 47 about 48 miles to Bluff. At Bluff, inquire locally for the road to the east to the mouth of Montezuma creek, 15 miles to the east. An historical marker on this road tells the story of the area; the hamlet of Montezuma Creek is the vicinity of the settler fort.

Mound Fort. 1854. The founders of Ogden built this temporary fort for security during the early days of establishing the city 30 miles north of Salt Lake City on I-15.

Murray Camp of Instruction. 1885. Companies from the 6th, 9th, and 21st U.S. Infantry regiments used this maneuver post for three weeks in September, 1885. The town of Murray is 5 miles south of Salt Lake City east of I-15.

Breastworks at the Narrows. 1857-58. These rock works were manned by Mormon Volunteers to oppose the "invasion" of Utah Territory by U.S. Troops. Diplomacy settled the question without bloodshed and these defenses were silent as the Federal troops marched toward Salt Lake City. From Salt Lake City, take I-80 to Echo where it turns to the northeast up Echo Canyon. About 4.5 miles beyond Echo, the road is flanked by the breastworks.

Fort Nephi. 1851. The original Mormon settlement at Nephi had a moated wall around it. It was near here that Brigham Young and Chief Wakara made peace and ended the Walker War. From Provo, go south on I-15 to Nephi, about 44 miles.

Ogden Stockade. 1854. Indian hostilities during the establishing of Ogden caused its settlers to erect walls around the new town. Two temporary forts, Bingham's and Mound, also were built. Ogden is 30 miles north of Salt Lake City on I-15.

Fort Pierce. 1860's. This unfinished rock structure apparently was intended as a stop on the stage road between Virgin Valley and the Pierce ferry on the Mojave. The absence of traffic eliminated the need to complete the work. The building is 14 miles southeast of St. George by dirt road. Obtain latest directions and road conditions at St. George (on I-15 27 road miles from the Arizona border).

Fort Provo. *Fort Utah.*

Fort Rawlins. 1870-71. Two companies of the 13th U.S. Infantry garrisoned this temporary tent camp post from July, 1870, to June, 1871. The site is 2 miles from Provo on the north bank of the Timpanogos river near the base of the Wasatch mountains.

Fort Richmond. 1859. The Mormon settlers at this northern Utah town erected this log fort along with log cabins and dugouts in the early days of the colony. Richmond is 13 miles north of Logan on US 91.

Fort Robidoux. *Fort Uintah.*

Rock Fort. 1865. *Fort at Rockport.* The settlers of Rockport were cautioned to leave the town in 1865 because of Indian hostitlites but were permitted to remain if they built a fort for protection. This stone fortress, eight feet high with walls two feet thick, is the result. From Salt Lake City take I-80 east to Winship and US 189. Go east on US 189 for 2 miles to Rockport Reservoir State Park, the site of the Rock Fort.

Camp Rush Valley. *Camp Conness.*

Fort Salt Lake City. 1847. Seventeen log and adobe houses and a fort were the first construction of the Mormons after they arrived at Salt Lake City in the summer of 1847. Pioneer Park at 3d South and 2d West streets is the site of the fort and living quarters.

Fort Sowiette. 1853. *Fort Utah II.* When the Indians under Chief Walkara threatened the Mormons at the new settlement of Provo, the principal war chief of the Utes, Chief Sowiette, moved his warriors into this fort and prepared to defend it with his white friends. The hostile Indians gave up after a night of whopping around the stockade. The site is now Sowiette Park at 5th West and 5th North streets in Provo.

Old Fort Thornburgh. 1881. Four companies of the 6th U.S. Infantry set up a tent camp here in August, 1881, in the aftermath of the Ute war. The Indian Agent feared that placing the Army this close to the Agency might produce more trouble than it would prevent and the camp was moved 35 miles to the northeast. The site is on Milk creek near Ouray. From Vernal, go west on US 40 for 14 miles to Utah 209. Turn left (south) for 7 miles to the junction with Utah 88. Continue south on Utah 88 to Ouray, 10 miles.

New Fort Thornburgh. 1881-84. Tents had to suffice for the first winter after the Army moved here; the second winter the troopers stayed at other posts because no money had been allocated for construction. Eight adobe buildings finally went up in 1883, but by this time it was too late. Squatters had moved into the area, making it too costly to obtain a clear title so the Army decided to abandon the site after the winter of 1883-84. There are no traces at the site other than the spring which once watered the camp, and from which military artifacts occasionally are salvaged. From Vernal, go west on Utah 245 to Maeser, 3 miles. Turn right on an improved road to the north. After the road crosses Ashley creek, about 3 miles, the site of the camp is on the left (west) side of the road.

Fort Utah. 1849-58. *Fort Provo.* This cluster of log cabins with a cannon mounted atop a platform provided the first defense of the Mormon settlers as they founded Provo. Fifty families were in the first group that established what was then the southernmost Mormon settlement in Utah. A second fort, nicknamed *Fort Sowiette,* was built near or at the same location in 1853.

Fort Uintah. 1837-44. *Fort Robidoux, Fort Wintey.* Antoine Robidoux founded this trading post about 1837 on the south bank of the Uinta river near its junction with the Whiterocks. No descriptions of it appear to exist although one traveler's diary has critical commentary on the "wickedness of the people and the debauchery of the men among the Indian women." Another diary notes the profitable trading exchanges carried on with the trapping parties and the nearby Snake and Ute Indians. It appears that Indians destroyed the fort in 1844, killing a half dozen of its occupants. From Vernal, go west on US 40 for 22 miles to Utah 246. Turn right (north) 7 miles to Utah 121. Turn left (west) about 6 miles to a point where the road parallels the Unita river to the right (northeast), the approximate site of the fort. A marker describing the fort is south on US 40 about 5½ miles west of Roosevelt.

Willden Fort. 1860-6. This was a dugout and three rooms occupied by Charles Willden at the site of what was to become *Cove Fort* when the Mormons bought it in 1867.

Fort Wintey. *Fort Uintah.*

WASHINGTON

FORT SPOKANE *(1)*

Washington's forts included not only those of the regular Army from mid-nineteenth century to slightly into the twentieth century, but a vast variety of posts established by the Washington Territorial Volunteers and by settlers.

To complicate matters, the Washington forts also include a number of fur and trading posts, but not as many as other states along the lanes of Indian trade.

This listing draws heavily on J. S. Whiting's *Forts of the State of Washington*, published by him in 1951, but even that detailed listing was inadequate when it came to locating many of the posts of settlers and volunteers in the wars of the 1850's. The fact that these blockhouses were at the crossing of a certain river was insufficient site location in view of the many crossings on record and for this reason it was impossible to pinpoint a number of camps.

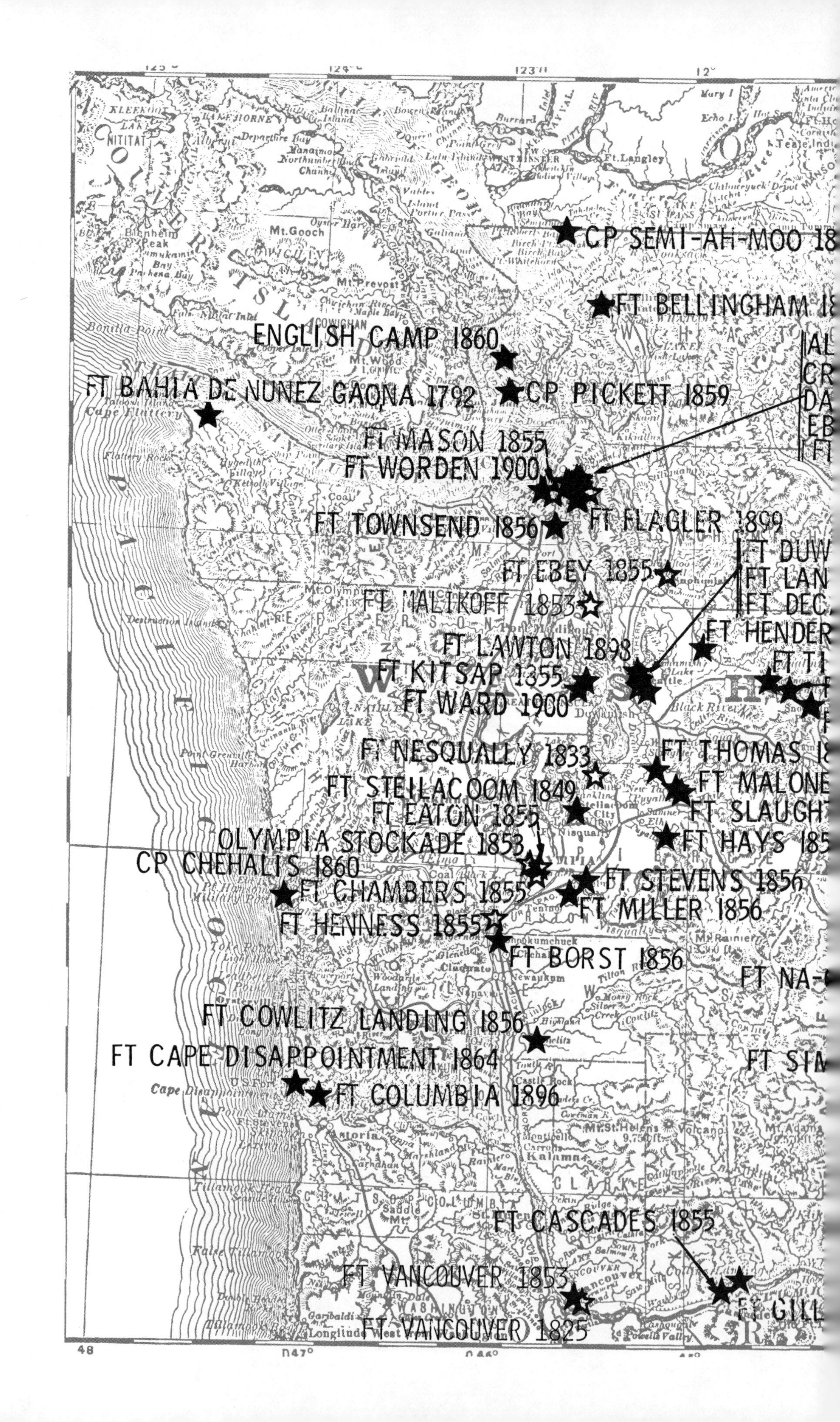
CP SEMI-AH-MOO 18
FT BELLINGHAM 18
ENGLISH CAMP 1860
CP PICKETT 1859
FT BAHIA DE NUNEZ GAONA 1792
FT MASON 1855
FT WORDEN 1900
FT TOWNSEND 1856
FT FLAGLER 1899
FT EBEY 1855
FT MALIKOFF 1853
FT LAWTON 1898
FT KITSAP 1855
FT WARD 1900
FT HENDER
FT NESQUALLY 1833
FT STEILACOOM 1849
FT EATON 1855
FT THOMAS
FT MALONE
FT SLAUGHT
FT HAYS
OLYMPIA STOCKADE 1853
CP CHEHALIS 1860
FT CHAMBERS 1855
FT STEVENS 1856
FT MILLER 1856
FT HENNESS 1855
FT BORST 1856
FT COWLITZ LANDING 1856
FT CAPE DISAPPOINTMENT 1864
FT COLUMBIA 1896
FT CASCADES 1855
FT VANCOUVER 1853
FT VANCOUVER 1825
Mt.Gooch
Mt.Prevost
Cape Flattery
Bonilla Point
Mt.Olympus
Cape Disappointment
Mt.St.Helens
Astoria
Mt.Rainier
Ft.Langley
Mt.Adams
Mt.Wood
COWICHAN
Vancouver

FT COLVILE 1826
FT COLVILLE 1859
FT OKANOGAN 1811
FT SPOKANE 1882
FT SPOKANE 1812
SPOKANE HOUSE 1810
CP WASHINGTON 1853
FT GEORGE WRIGHT 1895
CP CHELAN 1879
FT YAKIMA VALLEY 1856
FT TAYLOR 1858
CARTER'S STOCKADE
FT WALLA WALLA 1856
FT NEZ PERCES 1818
FT WALLA WALLA II 1856
FT BENNETT 1855
FT WALLA WALLA 1858
FT WATERS 1848
FT MASON 1856
Longitude West from Greenwich
PLATEAU OF SPOKANE
GREAT PLATEAU
These Plains cover an area of more than 25,000 square miles, and constitute an immense grazing ground

Fort Alden. 1856. *Fort Alder.* Washington Territory Volunteers built this blockhouse 60 feet south of the Suoqualmie river and 2½ miles above the falls. That would place it at the modern town of Suoqualmie.

Fort Alder. *Fort Alden.*

Alexander Blockhouse. 1855. Settler protection against Indian attack was provided by this double-storied log fort surrounded by a 10-foot high double stockade. Broken glass and jagged metal fragments were imbedded in the top of the stockade for added insurance. The blockhouse has been moved from its original site on the John Alexander claim to Coupeville, on Whidbey Island.

Battery Allen. This was an Endicott period 6-inch gun position at Fort Canby.

American Camp. *Camp Pickett.*

Battery Ash. This was an Endicott period 12-inch position at Fort Worden.

Fort Bahia de Nunez Gaona. 1792. *Spanish Fort at Neah Bay.* A half dozen buildings and a six-cannon defense were planned for this post by Salvador Fidalgo when the Spanish frigate Princesa arrived at what is now Neah Bay on May 29, 1792. Within four months the decision to build a fort was changed and the Princesa sailed with construction partly completėd. Tiles and other traces still are occasionally dug up at the site. Neah Bay is at the end of Washington 112 overlooking the Strait of Juan de Fuca.

Fort Bankhead. This was an Endicott period 12-inch position at Fort Flagler.

Basket Fort. *Fort Na-Chess.*

Fort Bellingham. 1856-60. George Pickett and Haida Indian wife lived in the one officers quarters still remaining at the site of this stockaded fort, once the Army's main fortification on northern Puget Sound. From the center of the city of Bellingham, take West Holly north to E street. Turn right, go 2 blocks east up the hill. Turn left at Bancroft street. The Pickett house is at 910 Bancroft street, right hand side in the middle of the block.

Fort Bennett. 1855-56. Apparently the first site of this field camp of the Oregon Volunteers was a stockade at or near the site of the former Whitman Mission. It was named after Captain Charles Bennett, killed in a battle with the Indians on December 8, 1855, and buried in the stockade. After four days of fighting in the area ended on December 10, the stockade was abandoned and the troops moved 2 miles away where better forage was available. The Whitman Mission, a National Historic Site, is 6 miles west of Walla Walla on US 410. The second Fort Bennett site is 2 miles east of the mission on the north bank of the Walla Walla river.

Battery Benson. This was an Endicott period 10-inch position at Fort Worden.

Fort Borst. 1856. *Blockhouse on Chehalis River Below Mouth of Skookum Chuck, Borst's Fort.* Oregon Volunteers founded this log fort which served to protect the nearby Chehalis river crossing and also as a forwarding and storage point for supplies during the Yakima war. Originally near the junction of Skookumchuch creek and the Chehalis river near Centralia, the blockhouse is now in Fort Borst Park immediately southwest of the intersection of I-99 and Harris avenue in Centralia.

Battery Brannon. This was an Endicott period 12-inch position at Fort Worden.

Battery Calwell. This was an Endicott period 6-inch position at Fort Flagler.

Camp at the Cabins. *Fort Gilliam.*

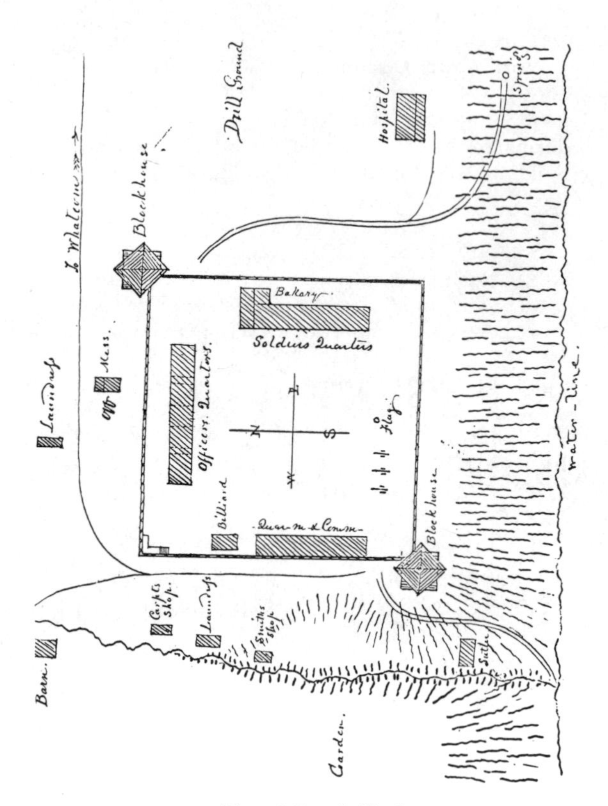

Plan of Fort Bellingham

FORT BELLINGHAM, blockhouse *(26)*

Fort Canby. *Fort Cape Disappointment.*

Fort Cape Disappointment. 1864-1950. *Fort Canby.* It was under the latter less picturesque name that this coast artillery post was known during most of its active carreer. Several Army buildings remain at the headquarters location in Baker Bay; deteriorating coast artillery Batteries Allen, O'Flying, and Guenther, from the Endicott period of World War I, observation platforms and magazines dot the seaward sides of the hills behind the main post. The Coast Guard has a station here but the remainder of the area is the Fort Canby State Park for campers and picnicers. Take US 101 north from Astoria, Oregon. After crossing the Columbia river into Washington, continue on US 101 for 11 miles to Ilwaco. In Ilwaco, follow a marked but unnumbered road 2.4 miles to the state park.

Carter's Stockade. Late 1870's. This was a 100-foot square stockade at the John Carter ranch to which settlers rushed at the first hint of Indian troubles. No hostilities took place, but the security promised by the stockade was sufficient reassurance to keep settlers in the area. The site is ½ mile from Anatone, 26 miles south of Clarkston on Washington 129.

Fort Cascades. 1855-61. *Fort Rains* (applied only to Middle Blockhouse). Rapids in the Columbia, the so-called "Cascades," forced traffic to make a lengthy portage and the Army provided protection from Indian ambush from this fort. Actually it had three simultaneous sites.

The main fort was at the foot of the Cascades where traffic was loaded into wagons and, 1.5 miles eastward, into a horse railway that went as far as the falls.

The Middle Blockhouse was on a rock cliff from which it could command the horse railway unloading point below the falls. The Upper Blockhouse was at the steamer landing at the head of the Cascades. Inspected in 1858, this blockhouse was described as being in the shape of a cross, two stories high with sufficient room for one company. It had a 6-pounder cannon and was manned by 11 privates commanded by a sergeant. A frame officers quarters was nearby.

The Middle Blockhouse, nicknamed Fort Rains after Major Gabriel Rains whose troops fought near here in 1858, was a squat, double-story building housing a corporal and eight privates and armed with a 6-pounder in the second story.

The main post included one small blockhouse that was used as a store room, two officers quarters, a barracks for the 79-man garrison, and other buildings. This site is in the vicinity of the Bonneville Dam, 40 miles east of Vancouver on US 830.

Fort Rains, reconstructed from the original timbers by the Skamania County Historical Society, is on the left (north) side of the highway ½ mile west of the dam.

Fort Casey. 1897-1950. This was one of three coast defense forts at the entrance to Admiralty Inlet. Although the government took title to the site in 1858, it was almost 40 years before the

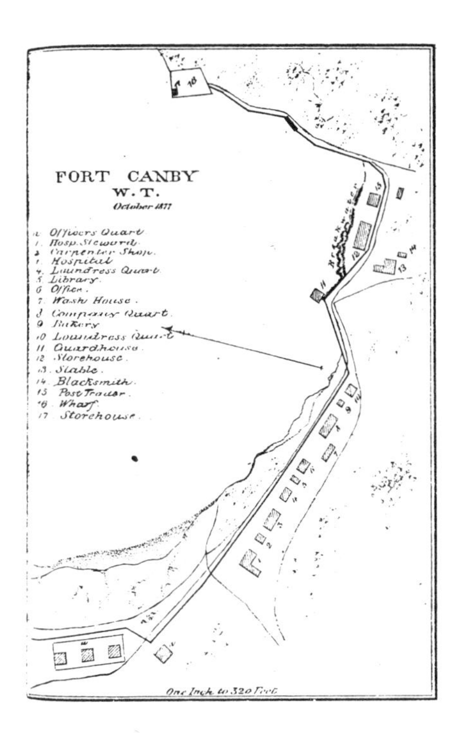

FORT CANBY *(1)*

Middle Blockhouse, Cascades

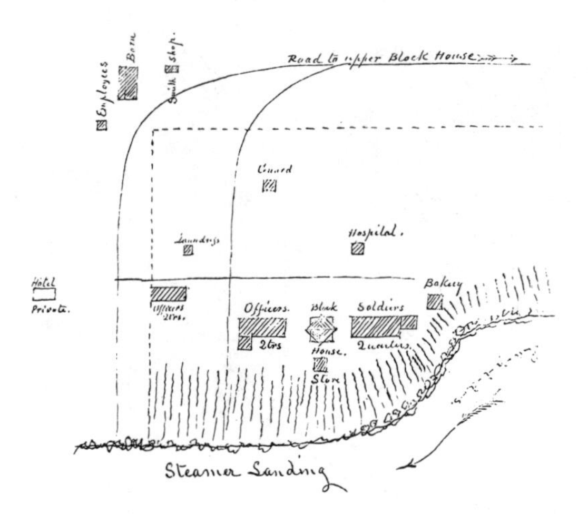

post was established. The site has nine concrete firing batteries, headquarters and fire control bunkers, and magazines in what is now a state recreational park. Four guns, two 10-inch and two 3-inch, formerly at Fort Winton in the Phillippines, are mounted in Batteries Worth and John Trevor as exhibits. The other Endicott batteries are Seymour, Schenck, Moore, Kingsbury, Valleau, Parker, Turman, and Van Horne. The site is on Whidbey Island at the end of Washington 113 – which is also the terminal for the ferry from Port Townsend.

Fort Chambers. 1855. Adjacent to the David Chambers house, this was a stockade and blockhouse that protected the family for three months during the Indian wars. The site is at the Mountain View Golf Club where the remodeled Chambers house still is in use; the other buildings no longer exist. The site overlooks Lake Chambers near Olympia.

Camp Chehalis. 1860-61. This official Army post never attained the dignity of the term "fort," probably because by the time its five buildings were completed the garrison was withdrawn with the start of the Civil War. Although many records suggest that the site was at the mouth of the Chehalis river—and therefore near Aberdeen—actually the post was on the southern spit of sand at the entrance to Grays Harbor. This is now the resort town of Westport, 2 miles north of Washington 105.

Blockhouse on Chehalis River Below Mouth of Skookum Chuck. *Fort Borst.*

Camp Chelan. 1879-80. This post was originally at the junction of Foster creek and the Columbia river but after one season it was moved to higher ground nearby. In the short time that Chelan was in existence, it included barracks, officers quarters, and a sawmill. The site is a mile southeast of the city of Chelan to the right (south) side of Washington 151.

Post at Chinook Point. *Fort Columbia.*

Fort Columbia. 1896-1950. *Post at Chinook Point.* Along with Forts Cape Disappointment (across Baker Bay) and Stevens (across the Columbia), this coast defense post protected the mouth of the Columbia river. The site was acquired in 1864, but construction did not start until 1896; caretaker troops arrived in 1898 and the regular garrison reported in 1903.

The Fort Columbia State Park now includes Endicott-period Batteries Ord, Murphy, and Crenshaw and more than a dozen frame buildings, some of them of the elaborate turn-of-the-century barracks style. A museum is maintained in one former barracks; the DAR maintains the post commander's quarters with furniture of the period.

From Astoria, Oregon, go north across the Columbia river on US 101. Turn left after leaving the bridge (remaining on 101). In 3 miles, and almost immediately after going through a short tunnel, turn left (southwest) at sign into Fort Columbia State Park.

Columbia Barracks. *Fort Vancouver.*

Fort Colvile. 1826-71. This was a leading Hudson Bay Company trading post throughout its existence. Named for Andrew W. Colvile, an officer of the company, the fort had a stockade of more than 200 feet square. The site has been inundated by the Franklin D. Roosevelt Lake. The general area can be reached from Spokane via US 395, going

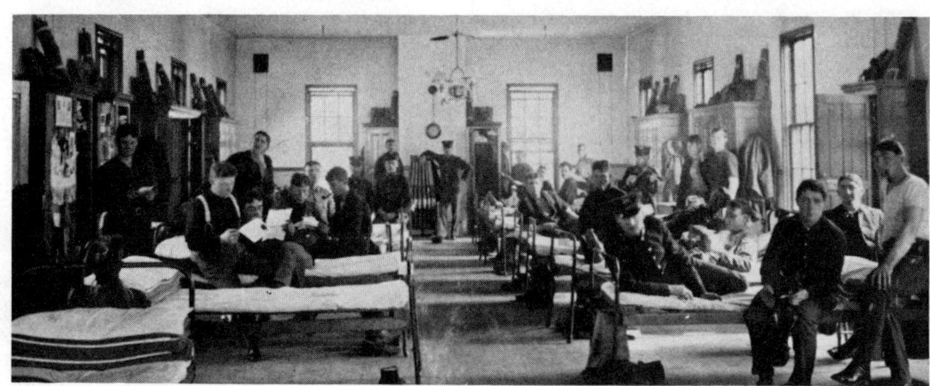

FORT COLUMBIA *(24)*

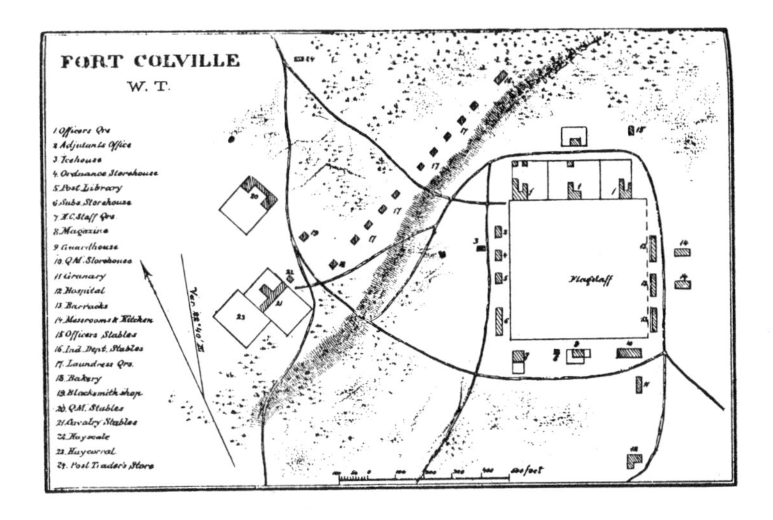

Crockett Blockhouse *(22)*

north on it 92 miles to the junction with Washington 25 about 1 mile west of Kettle Falls. Turn right (north) onto Washington 25 for about 6 miles. On the left (west) at this point is the approximate location of the fort.

Fort Colville. 1859-82. *Harney's Depot.* When the military arrived in northwest Washington, the strategic location of the Hudson Bay Company's Fort Colvile was the obvious point at which the Army should be located. Fourteen miles east of the trading post was selected to be the Army site. At first called Harney's Depot, the camp soon appropriated – and misspelled – the older fur fort's name. It included three double sets of officers quarters, four barracks, and the usual collection of additional buildings, all of logs. There are slight surface remains at the site on the north (left) side of Washington 294 about 3 miles east of the city of Colville (on US 395 about 80 miles north of Spokane).

Connell Prairie Blockhouse. *Fort Hays.*

Cook Blockhouse. *Davis Blockhouse.*

Fort at Cowlitz Landing. 1856. Washington Territorial Volunteers built this stockaded blockhouse at the highest point of navigation on the Cowlitz river. Now called Toledo, the town is about 20 miles south of Chehalis via I-5 and 3 miles east of the interstate on Washington 505 (but the blockhouse probably was about where the interstate crosses the river on the north bank).

Battery Crenshaw. This was an Endicott period 3-inch gun position at Fort Columbia.

Crockett Blockhouse. 1855. Two blockhouses were built at the Crockett farm on Whidbey Island and apparently were instrumental in scaring off Indians who were preparing to attack the family of Governor Isaac I. Stevens, visiting the Crocketts. One blockhouse was moved in 1909 to the Seattle Alaska-Yukon Pacific Exposition. The other one was restored by the WPA and now can be seen next to Washington 113 about ½ mile from Fort Casey entrance.

Davis Blockhouse. 1855. *Cook Blockhouse.* One of the largest of an estimated 11 blockhouses built on Whidbey Island, this settler post was one of the few that included a fireplace. The blockhouse has been restored. From Prairie Center, at the southern edge of Coupeville on Whidbey Island, go west 1 block to deadend at Ebey road. Turn left (south) 1 block to Cook road. Turn right (west) 1 block to deadend at Sherman road which leads to Sunnyside Cemetery, location of Davis Blockhouse.

Fort Decatur. 1855-56. *Seattle Blockhouse.* Marines from the USS Decatur manned this double-storied log building during the siege of Seattle. It was 14 feet high, 25 by 40 feet, had a firing parapet along the interior walls so that muskets could be fired from loopholes under the roof. Two 9-pound cannon were mounted inside. After the Seattle battle, a stockade was built across the open base of the Seattle peninsula and a second blockhouse erected in the city. The first blockhouse, nicknamed Fort Decatur, was at what is now the corner of First avenue and Cherry street in Seattle. The stockade ran west from the point to the bay, also south to modern day Main street, the site of the southern blockhouse.

Battery Downes. This was an Endicott period 3-inch position at Fort Flagler.

Fort Duwamish. 1855-56. Settlers built and occupied this two-story log blockhouse. The ground floor was 22 feet square; the second floor was set even with the first, but had an overhang on all four sides. The blockhouse site is in Seattle, about 60 feet south of the northeast corner of the Puget Sound Power and Light Plant.

Fort Eaton. 1855-56. Protection against Indian attack was provided settlers at Chambers Prairie, near Olympia, when they built their 16 log buildings in a square facing inward. There is a marker at the site. From Olympia, go north on I-5 to the Lacey exit. Take Washington 510 east from this exit to a right (southwest) turn to Lake St. Clair. The site is at the northeast corner where this road deadends.

Fort Ebey. 1855-56. The Washington Territorial Volunteers built this single story blockhouse on Ebey Island in the Snohomish river east of Everett. Apparently the building was left unfinished when the Volunteers moved to Fort Alden.

Ebey Blockhouse. 1855. One of four blockhouses at the Ebey place on Whidbey Island, this is the only one left, mainly through the restoration efforts of an interested owner. A 12-foot high stockade once connected the four bastions. Follow the directions to Davis Blockhouse; at Sunnyside Cemetery, continue on Sherman road to Pratt farm, 1.5 miles. Permission should be requested to visit the blockhouse in a field nearby.

English Camp. 1860-72. Royal Marines maintained the Queen's claim to San Juan Island, but the engagements with the American forces also on the island were more social than militant. The original blockhouse, several buildings, and the Royal Marine cemetery still are at the site, part of the National Park Service. San Juan Island can be reached by way of the auto ferry from Anacortes. Upon landing at Friday Harbor, take the English Camp road from 2d and Spring streets. Go 8.8 miles to marker; turn left on gravel road .7 mile to parking area. The site is .2 mile from the parking area; the cemetery is the same distance near the top of the hill.

Fort Flagler. 1899-1952. This was the third coast artillery fort at Admiral Inlet. After the nine-battery fort was completed in time for World War I, the post was deactivated to caretaker status in 1921 and most of the buildings demolished in 1937. It returned to the active rolls in 1940 for World War II and the Korean War. After abandonment in 1954, it became the Fort Flagler Historical State Park with 20 buildings on the site and Endicott Batteries Wilhelm, Bankhead, Revere, Rawlins, Calwell, Grattan, Lee, Downes, and Wansboro. From Port Townsend, take Washington 113 south for 7 miles to Four Corners. Turn left (east) through Hadlock, 3 miles, Nordland, 7 miles, to the park at the northern tip of Marrowstone Island, 3 miles beyond Nordland.

Fort George Wright. 1895-1941. *Military Post at Spokane.* Military activities in northeast Washington were consolidated at this two-battalion permanent post on a plateau west of Spokane at which the Battle of Spokane Plains was fought in 1858. The solid brick buildings were turned over to the Army Air Corps in 1941 and, after a succession of Air Force roles, became Fort Wright College of the Holy Names, the Spokane Community College of Liberal Arts and the Spokane Lutheran School. From downtown Spokane take Sunset boulevard to Government Way. Follow Government Way northwest to Fort George Wright drive, right turn, into the site of the fort.

Fort Gilliam. 1848. *Camp at the Cabins.* Oregon Volunteers adopted this group of log cabins as a supply depot and base of operations during the Cayuse war. The site is in the vicinity of the main post of Fort Cascades; follow those directions.

Battery Grattan. This was an Endicott period 6-inch position at Fort Flagler.

Battery Guenther. This was a World War I position at Fort Canby that mounted four 12-inch guns previously located at Fort Stevens, Oregon, Battery Clark.

Harney's Depot. *Fort Colville.*

Battery Harrison. This was an Endicott period 6-inch gun position at Fort Whitman.

Fort Hays. 1856. *Connell Prairie Blockhouse.* This cedar log structure was one of two blockhouses built by Washington Territorial Volunteers, this one acquiring the formal designation in honor of the commander of the Central Battalion headquartered there. From Tacoma, go southeast on Washington 410 for 18 miles to the blockhouse, right (south) side, on the brow of a hill overlooking Connell Prairie.

Fort Henderson. 1856. *Fort Patterson.* Washington Territorial Volunteers from Fort Tilton built this outpost blockhouse at the mouth of a small stream entering the Snoqualmie river below Fall City. From Seattle, go east on I-90 for 15 miles to the exit before Issaquah. From the exit go northeastward to Washington 522, about 6 miles. Turn right (east) for 2 miles to the crossing of Patterson creek. About 1.5 miles north is the mouth of Patterson creek on the Snoqualmie, site of the fort.

Fort Henness. 1855-56. Mound Prairie settlers built this large stockade, blockhouses on two corners, with buildings inside for shelter. Although named after a captain of Washington Territorial

Volunteers, the fort had no military connection. From Centralia, go north on I-5 one exit to US 12. Take US 12 to the west 2.1 miles to a right turn (north). The site of Fort Henness is .9 mile from this turn; a stone marker is at the location across from Grand Mound cemetery.

Battery Kingsbury. This was an Endicott period 10-inch position at Fort Casey.

Battery Kinzie. This was a Taft period 12-inch position at Fort Worden.

Fort Kitsap. 1855-56. Volunteer troops built this temporary fort across Puget Sound from Seattle. It was at Port Madison which can be reached from Seattle via the Seattle-Winslow ferry, then north on Washington 305 for 4 miles to the right turn to Port Madison, 2 miles.

Fort Lander. 1856. The blockhouse for this Volunteer post was built in Seattle and moved up the Duwamish river where it was finished and then expanded by a 98- by 58-foot stockade, complete with bastions. In modern Seattle the site is ¼ mile south of the administration building of the King's County Airport on the south bank of the Duwamish river.

Fort Lawton. 1898-1967. Seattle citizens gave the site of this permanent post to the Army and numerous buildings were constructed for various occupants.

First a coast artillery post, Lawton passed successively through the hands of the infantry (1902-27), the engineers (1927-41) and, finally, the transportation corps for use as an embarkation and debarkation center, and once again, the artillery as a support center for Puget Sound Air Defense activities. With the latter function phased out in 1967, the fort was closed as a fully active facility, but some support activities remain.

The post is 3 miles from downtown Seattle, on Puget Sound south of the mouth of the Lake Washington Canal. Take Elliott avenue West in a northwesterly direction from downtown to the Magnolia Bridge and West Garfield street. Across the bridge, pick up Magnolia boulevard West which deadends at Fort Lawton on West Emerson street. Turn left 1 block to the fort entrance.

Battery Lee. This was an Endicott period 5-inch position at Fort Flagler.

Fort Malikoff. 1853. A small fort was built at Port Gamble by settlers to protect their sawmill and, for reasons not quite clear, the name Fort Malikoff was attached to it. From Bremerton, go north on Washington 3 for 26 miles to the toll bridge across the Hood Canal. Instead of crossing the bridge, turn right (east) 1 mile to the hamlet of Port Gamble.

Fort Maloney. 1855-56. The regular Army built this typical blockhouse similar to the one at Fort Bellingham though with only a 6½ foot high overhead on the ground floor. The site is in Puyallup (southeast of Tacoma) on East Meridian across the Puyallup river bridge where a cobblestone monument with four plaques marks the site of what the inscription spells: Malone.

Fort Mason. 1855. Indian outrages in the Puget Sound area caused the pioneers at Port Townsend to built this blockhouse and to organize the Port Townsend Home Guards. The area never was threatened, perhaps because of the number of settlers or, even more so, the efforts of friendly Indians in keeping the hostiles away. The blockhouse stood at Point Wilson, now the location of Point Wilson light and the State Diagnostic Center (the Fort Worden reservation of later year) at the northeast edge of the city of Port Townsend at the end of Washington 113.

Fort Mason. 1856. After the four-day battle with the Indians and subsequent establishment of temporary Fort Bennett in late 1855, the Army spent a year in southeastern Washington settling on a site for a permanent fort. Fort Walla Walla was the ultimate choice, but not before the troops had first settled at Mason – after leaving Bennett – and then moving to the various Walla Walla military sites. The actual location of Mason is uncertain other than the fact that it was in the vicinity of the final Fort Walla Walla site "on a little tributary of Mill Creek and about a mile from it." Follow the directions to military Fort Walla Walla.

Fort Miller. 1856. *Blockhouse on Tenalquot Prairie.* This was a Washington Territorial Volunteers blockhouse and corral, used as a quartermaster's depot, on the Tenalquot Plains southeast of Olympia. The location is vague, perhaps in the vicinity of Ranier, southeast of Olympia between the Deschutes and Nisqually rivers.

Battery Mitchell. This was an Endicott period 3-inch gun position at Fort Ward. It is the only battery at the Middle Point section of the fort, across Rich Passage from Bainbridge Island.

Battery Moore. This was an Endicott period 10-inch position at Fort Casey.

Camp on Muckleshoot Prairie. *Fort Slaughter.*

Battery Murphy. This was an Endicott period 6-inch position at Fort Columbia.

Fort Na-Chess. 1856. *Camp on Nechess River, Fort Naches, Basket Fort.* The 9th U.S. Infantry established this temporary field post, using it as a base of operations during the expedition of 1856. The settlers nicknamed it the Basket Fort because it was a large rectangle of wickerworks of willow filled with earth, officially termed gabions. It served as a depot until the close of the campaign. From Yakima, go north on Washington 14 for 9 miles to Esbach, the approximate site of the camp – although it is likely that it was on the opposite bank of the Naches river at this point.

Battery Nash. This was the largest Endicott period position at Fort Ward, mounting three 8-inch disappearing guns.

Fort Nesqually. 1833-43. The Hudson Bay Company built this stockaded trading post on a bluff overlooking Puget Sound. In 1843 the post was moved 2 miles to the north and the name changed to Fort Nisqually. The site of this first fort is near the main entrance of the Dupont Powder Company on the beach near Dupont (at the Dupont exit from I-5 about 15 miles southwest of Tacoma).

Fort Nez Perces. 1818-56. *Old Fort Walla Walla.* A 20-foot high, 200-foot square enclosure of 6-

FORT NISQUALLY
James M. Alden sketch 1857

inch thick planks, Nez Perces handled the fur business of Donald McKenzie and the Northwest Company in southeastern Washington. It came to be better known by the name of the river nearby, Walla Walla, which now flows over the site as a result of the backup of the Columbia river after completion of the McNary Dam. From the city of Walla Walla, go west on US 410 for 28 miles to the Columbia river and the mouth of the Walla Walla river. The site of the trading post was directly north about 1 mile, now inundated.

Fort Nisqually. 1843-69. This is a continuation of the original Hudson Bay Company trading post, Fort Nesqually, two miles to the southwest, and the better known. The post has been reconstructed in Point Defiance park in Tacoma where a log stockade encloses the original granary and factor's house and replicas of several others. To visit the reconstructed Fort Nisqually, take 6th avenue West from downtown Tacoma to Pearl street (in the 6000 series), turn north (right) and continue north until street deadends at park (on 6000 series north). Follow marked road inside park to the fort.

Battery O'Flyng. This was an Endicott period 6-inch gun position at Fort Canby.

Fort Okanogan. 1811-59. From a 16- by 20-foot trading post built of drift wood, Fort Okanogan passed from the Pacific Fur Company to the Northwest Company and then to the Hudson Bay Company. It was moved a half mile from the original location in 1816 and expanded into a 15-foot high stockade with bastions surrounding four buildings. There is a marker at the site of the first post and a state museum nearby that tells the story of both. From Chelan, go north of US 97 for 27 miles to Brewster. About 3 miles east of Brewster, take a gravel road to the right (south) which leads to Fort Okanogan Historical Museum.

Olympia Stockade. 1853-54. Oregon's territorial capital was protected by this 15-foot stockade erected around the town for a year. After things settled down, the settlers found another use for the planks in the stockade – as sidewalks in the town.

Battery Ord. This was an Endicott period 8-inch position at Fort Columbia.

Battery Parker. This was an Endicott period 6-inch position at Fort Casey.

Fort Patterson. *Fort Henderson.*

Camp Pickett. 1859-72. *Camp Reynolds, Camp San Juan Island, Camp Steele, American Camp.* United States forces manned this cluster of frame buildings on the southern point of San Juan Island during the arbitration with the British on ownership of the island. This was the only western post garrisoned solely by regular Army troops throughout the Civil War. The earthwork fortress still is obvious at what is now a part of the National Park system. From Friday Harbor (see *English Camp* for initial directions), go south on marked road from the intersection of Spring and Argyle streets for 6.6 miles to the site.

CAMP PICKETT

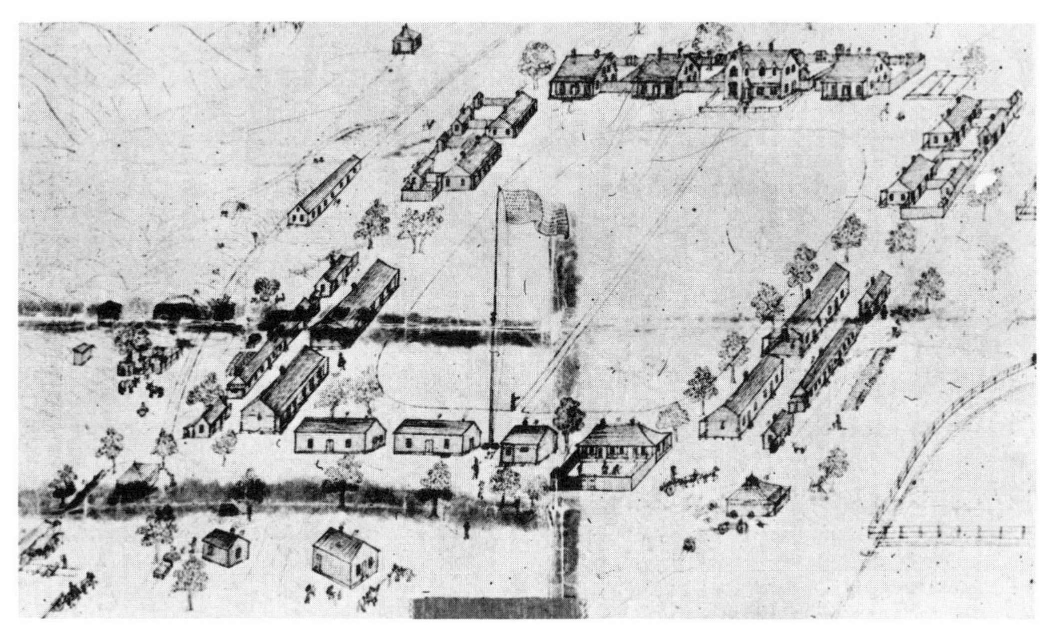

FORT SIMCOE *(25)*

Battery Powell. This was an Endicott period 12-inch position at Fort Worden.

Battery Putnam. This was an Endicott period 3-inch position at Fort Worden.

Battery Quarles. This was an Endicott period 10-inch position at Fort Worden.

Fort Rains. *Fort Cascades'* Middle blockhouse.

Battery Randol. This was an Endicott period 10-inch position at Fort Worden.

Battery Rawlins. This was an Endicott period 10-inch position at Fort Flagler.

Battery Revere. This was an Endicott period 10-inch position at Fort Flagler.

Camp Reynolds. *Camp Pickett.*

Camp San Juan Island. *Camp Pickett.*

Seattle Blockhouse. *Fort Decatur.*

Battery Schenck. This was an Endicott period 12-inch position at Fort Casey.

Camp Semi-ah-moo. 1858-59. The escort of the Boundary Commission camped here at a site on Semiahmoo Bay that is uncertain as to location and allegiance – it is probably in Canada but its nearness to the border is sufficient excuse to include it here. Inspected in 1858, the temporary post was found to consist of rough sheds and two blockhouses. The camp was listed as being at latitude 49°00'43" and longitude 122°47'19", placing it on the northern beach of Semiahmoo Bay in the vicinity of White Rock, British Columbia. Take I-5 north from Seattle through Bellingham toward Vancouver, B.C.; White Rock is the first exit in Canada north of the Peace Arch.

Battery Seymour. This was an Endicott period 12-inch position at Fort Casey.

Fort Simcoe. 1856-59. This picturesquely designed post, by Louis Scholl, the same architect as Fort Dalles, consisted of frame and log buildings and four blockhouses around a 420-foot square

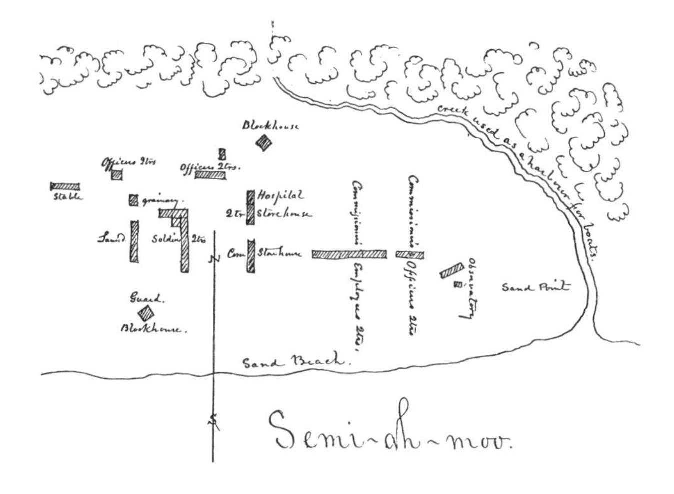

parade ground. Several buildings are left, including the restored and refurnished commander's residence, as part of the Washington State Park system. From Yakima, take I-82 south to the Toppenish exit, about 18 miles. Turn west at the exit on Washington 220 to White Swan, 20 miles. Follow signs for 8 miles beyond White Swan to the Fort Simcoe State Park.

Fort Slaughter. 1855-57. Camp on Muckleshoot Prairie. A stockade and two blockhouses comprised this regular Army temporary camp that was first commanded by Lieutenant William A. Slaughter, 4th U.S. Infantry, and then named in his memory after he was killed. From Tacoma, go north on I-5 for 9 miles to the exit to Auburn. From Auburn (christened Slaughter in memory of the lieutenant but rechristened by squeemish residents), go southeast on Washington 164 for 6 miles. The site of Fort Slaughter is on the right (southwest) side of the road.

Fort Smalley. 1856. This was another outpost of Fort Tilton built by Washington Territorial Volunteers. The site is ½ mile west of the town of North Bend, about 28 miles east of Seattle.

Spanish Fort at Neah Bay. *Fort Bahia de Nunez Gaona.*

Military Post at Spokane. *Fort George Wright.*

Spokane House I. 1810-13. The Northwest Company founded this rough but strategically located fur trading post and for one year had a monopoly on business with the Indians.

In 1812 the Pacific Fur Company built a competition post nearby, Fort Spokane, and the two traded side-by-side until the new post was sold in 1813 to the owners of the Spokane House. At this point the first Spokane House was abandoned and the Northwesterners moved into Fort Spokane which they rechristened Spokane House. Later additions to the second Spokane House (Spokane House II) apparently absorbed Spokane I's site.

From the city of Spokane, go north on US 395 for 3 miles to Washington 291, left (west) turn. Pass Nine Mile Falls in, appropriately, 9 miles; 1 mile beyond is the site of the two Houses, marked by a state sign behind which logs are arranged in the layout of Spokane House II.

Spokane House II. 1812-26. *Fork Spokane* was the name of this post until 1813 it was taken over by the Northwest Company. They brought with them the name Spokane House from their nearby trading post. In 1821 the post became part of the Hudson Bay Company's chain, but was abandoned five years later. The pine log stockade measured 130 by 122 feet and included buildings attached to the inner walls. Archaeological excavations indicate that the post overlapped the site of the first Spokane House. See *Spokane I* for directions to the site.

Fort Spokane. This was the first name of *Spokane House II.*

Fort Spokane. 1882-99. Not to be confused with the fur post near the city of Spokane (the *Spokane Houses*), this was a military post about 50 miles northwest of the city. Six infantry and cavalry companies occupied its frame and brick buildings until the Spanish American War called the garrison and the post was turned over to the Indian Service.

Unoccupied since 1929, there are a few buildings left at the site, now used as the Fort Spokane Recreation Area overlooking Franklin D. Roosevelt Lake. The buildings and other sites are marked with photographs of their appearance when the post was active.

From Spokane, go west on US 2 to Davenport, 32 miles. Turn right on Washington 22 for 23 miles north to the town of Miles, right (east) side. On the left is the site of the fort. Beyond, a half mile, is the recreational area on the right side of the road.

Camp Steele. *Camp Pickett.*

Fort Steilacoom. 1849-68. At the Pacific end of the cross-Washington military road from Fort Walla Walla, Steilacoom occupied a strategic location during pre-Civil War Indian hostilities. Only the officers' row is left of 15 buildings once within this 600-foot square post. From the city of Steilacoom, southwest of Tacoma, take Steilacoom boulevard south 4 miles to the Western State Hospital, present occupants of the site and of the remaining officers quarters.

Fort Stevens. 1856. Washington Territorial Volunteers built this temporary post on Yelm Prairie. The site is in the vicinity of the town of Yelm at the junction of Washington routes 510 and 507 southeast of Olympia.

FORT SPOKANE *(1)*

FORT STEILACOOM, 1857 *(23)*

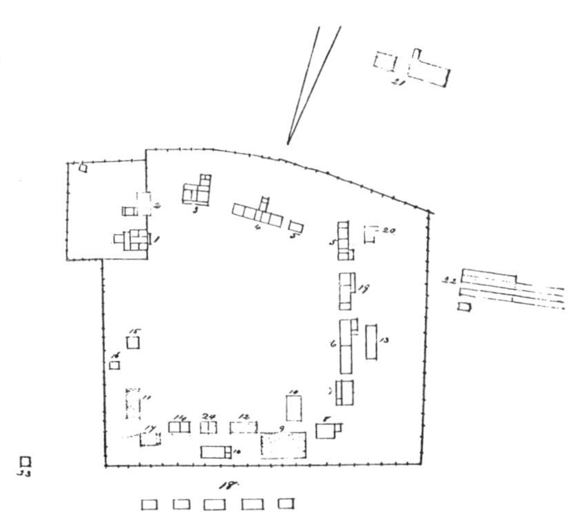

Plan of Fort Steilacoom

FORT TOWNSEND, guardhouse *(1)*

Battery Stoddard. This was an Endicott period 6-inch position at Fort Worden.

Fort Taylor. 1858. Colonel George Wright conducted the 1858 campaign from this six-week post, constructed of basalt rock with hexagonal bastions of alder. From Walla Walla, go north on US 12 for 44 miles to Delaney. Turn left (west) for 9 miles to Starbuck. About 2 miles beyond Starbuck the road passes under the mouth of Tuncannon river on the Snake. The post was on the Snake at the mouth of the Tuncannon.

Blockhouse on Tenalquot Prairie. *Fort Miller.*

Fort Thomas. 1857. The U.S. Army built this temporary field post along the same design as the blockhouse at Fort Bellingham. It was 26 feet square, of notched logs with a shake roof, the second floor offset 45 degrees from the first. From Tacoma, go north on I-5 for 9 miles to the Auburn turnoff. From Auburn, go north on Washington 167 for 6 miles to the crossing of the Green river. Fort Thomas was on the south bank of the Green, about 100 yards to the right (east) of the road.

Battery Thornburgh. This was an Endicott period 3-inch gun position at Ford Ward.

Fort Tilton. 1855-56. Headquarters and principal depot of the Northern Battalion of Washington Territorial Volunteers, Fort Tilton included a blockhouse and other out buildings. It commanded a number of outpost forts in the area and has been described as being from 1½ to 3 miles below Snoqualmie Falls. From Seattle, go east on I-90 for 28 miles to Snoqualmie. Take Washington 203 west from Snoqualmie to a point beyond the falls 1½ to 3 miles, depending upon driver's choice as the site is uncertain.

Battery Tolles. This was an Endicott period 6-inch position at Fort Worden.

Fort Townsend. 1856-95. This permanent Army post was intended to keep the peace of the western portion of Puget Sound, a mission not difficult to accomplish because of the small population in that area – even today. Its troops were called out for the confrontation with the British in the San Juan Islands but had little else to do until the post was abandoned after fire destroyed the barracks. Nothing is left at the modern site other than historical markers and recreational facilities at Fort Townsend State Park. From Port Townsend, go south on Washington 113 for 5 miles to the park, left (east) side.

Battery Trevor. This was an Endicott period 3-inch position at Fort Casey.

Battery Turman. This was an Endicott period 6-inch position at Fort Casey.

Battery Valleau. This was an Endicott period 6-inch position at Fort Casey.

Fort Vancouver. 1825-60. This was the Hudson Bay Company's main post on what was to become the Western coast of the United States. It was a stockade 600 by 525 feet, 12 foot high bastions at two corners, with numerous log buildings within and without the enclosure. The U.S. Army moved next to it in 1849 and the trading post was bought by the United States in 1860. The site is now part of the National Park Service as Fort Vancouver National Monument; the trading post has been excavated and its story is told on the ground and in a museum and several reconstructed buildings.

Fort Vancouver. 1848-1947. *Columbia Barracks.* A hundred years of military occupation of this Army post did not really end in 1947: reserve units and other government agencies continue to use this semi-active installation that once was the Army headquarters in the Pacific Northwest. Several buildings are left on the hill above the Hudson Bay Company's trading post, including an officers' quarters claimed to have been occupied by U.S. Grant when he was quartermaster here. Follow directions to the Fort Vancouver trading post; the military post is passed between the gate and the Park Service buildings.

Battery Van Horne. This was an Endicott period 3-inch position at Fort Casey.

Battery Vicars. This was an Endicott period 5-inch position at Fort Worden.

Battery Vinton. This was an Endicott period 3-inch gun at Fort Ward.

Battery Walker. This was an Endicott period 3-inch position at Fort Worden.

Old Fort Walla Walla. *Fort Nez Perces.*

Fort Walla Walla I. 1856. Not counting the efforts at Forts Bennett and Mason (and the trading post nicknamed Walla Walla), this was the first of three attempts to establish Fort Walla Walla. From September 19, 1856, until sometime in October, 1856, troops under Colonel Edward J. Steptoe built a blockhouse and stockade but did not stay long. In October, 1856, they moved to the present site of the city of Walla Walla and built their second fort. The site of Walla Walla I is probably in the vicinity of Fort Mason.

Fort Walla Walla II. 1856-58. Regular Army troops built this collection of huts with a blockhouse in time to celebrate Christmas, 1856, in them. Unlike most forts of the time and area, there was no stockade. The growth of the town of Steptoeville, later named Walla Walla, around the post, and the need for water to run their sawmill caused the garrison to move to its final location next to Mill Creek in 1858. The second site is in downtown Walla Walla at the intersection of 1st and Main streets.

FORT VANCOUVER
MILITARY RESERVE
W. T.

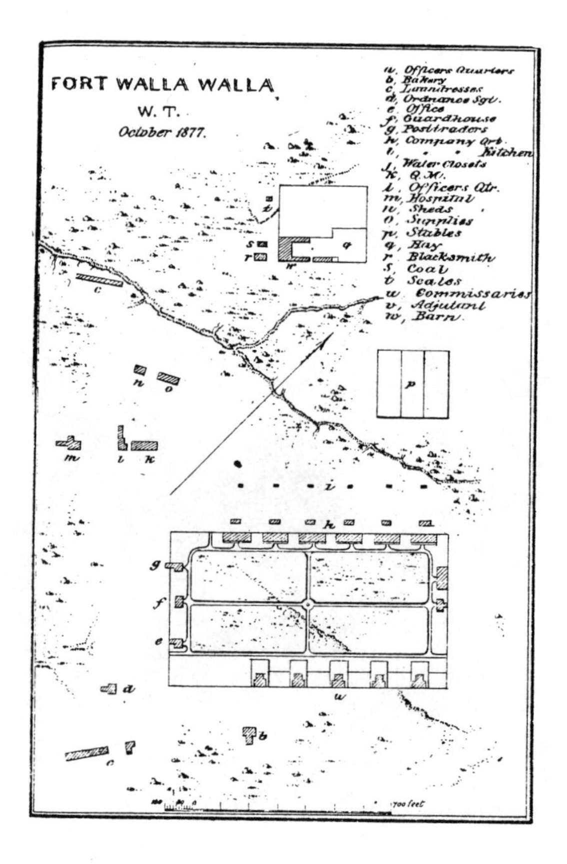

FORT WALLA WALLA *(1)*

Fort Walla Walla III. 1858-1911. Here for 53 years, discounting periods of vacancy, the Army watched over the security of southeastern Washington. This permanent post included five double sets of officers quarters and sufficient barracks and other buildings for six companies of troopers. The post was turned over to the Veterans Administration in 1921. Many buildings are left at the VA Hospital south of the city of Walla Walla. The post cemetery is now part of a city park south of the post; graves in the cemetery represent every period in the fort's history, including the fatalities of the Nez Perce campaigns.

Battery Wansboro. This was an Endicott period 3-inch position at Fort Flagler.

Fort Ward. 1900-34. This coast artillery fortification occupied 375 acres of Bainbridge Island and a like number on the opposite mainland, mounting Endicott period Batteries Nash, Warner, Vinton, Thornburgh, and Mitchell. The fort guarded Rich's Passage and Port Orchard, both of which lead to the Bremerton Naval Yard. The post was abandoned as a coast defense fort in 1934 and the sites turned over to the Navy in 1938 (which maintains a facility on the southern portion, north of Manchester and Washington 160). To reach the site of Fort Ward proper, go by ferry from Seattle to Winslow. Follow secondary roads and local directions to Port Blakely, once a lively port and now only a post office. Go 1.4 miles beyond Port Blakely to a gravel road which terminates in 1.6 miles at the remaining buildings of Fort Ward.

Battery Warner. This was an Endicott period 5-inch gun position at Fort Ward.

Camp Washington. 1853. Not a military post, this was the first camp of Isaac L. Stevens, territorial governor, upon arrival in Washington Territory. There is a monument at the site. From Spokane, go west on US 2 for 17 miles to Coulee Hite road. Turn right (north) on this gravel road for 7 miles, then right (east) again for 1.8 miles to the Camp Washington monument. Three quarters of a mile southwest of this point, at the forks of Coulee creek, is the actual site of the camp.

Fort Waters. 1848. The Oregon Volunteers who arrived at the Whitman Mission in March, 1848, after the November, 1847, massacre of Marcus Whitman, his family and associates, used remains of the mission buildings for Fort Waters. The Cayuse War was directed from a base of operations as this temporary post. The fort consisted mainly of trenches, earthworks, and some reconstructed quarters. The site is now the Whitman Mission National Historic Site of the National Park Service, 6 miles west of Walla Walla on US 410.

Fort Whitman. 1909-1944. This Goat Island post included a commanding officer's quarters, headquarters, two 20 by 100 foot barracks, kitchen and mess hall and other utility buildings plus a four 6-inch Battery Harrison. It was transferred to the state as a wildlife refuge in 1947. The island is 2 miles southwest of La Conner, which is about 30 miles south of Bellingham.

Fort Wilhelm. This was an Endicott period 12-inch position at Fort Flagler.

Fort Wilson. *Fort Worden.*

Fort Worden. 1900-53. *Fort Wilson.* At the northern finger of the left side of Puget Sound's

Admiralty Inlet, Fort Worden was part of the Fort Casey and Fort Flagler triumverate of coast defense fortifications. It was given up in 1953 and the site is now the State Diagnostic Center north of downtown Port Townsend. It is a historic district consisting of 69 buildings, including a dozen batteries that once mounted 41 guns: Kinzie, of the Taft period, and the remainder from the Endicott era, Brannon, Powell, Ash, Benson, Randol, Quarles, Stoddard, Tolles, Vicars, Walker and Putnam.

Battery Worth. This was an Endicott period 10-inch position at Fort Casey.

Fort Yakima Valley. 1856. Washington Territorial Volunteers erected a blockhouse and storehouse here to serve as a base of operations in the Yakima Valley. The site is in the vicinity of modern Yakima (on I-82).

FORT WRIGHT, guardhouse

WYOMING

FORT BRIDGER *(1)*

Cattlemen provided Wyoming with a war that was a little different from that of the other Western states and the camps of the Johnson County War are included in this listing, in addition to those of the military, traders and settlers throughout the nineteenth century.

The geography of Wyoming called for posts along the trails and in the mining camps that could be independent when weather or warfare dictated. This geography also meant an isolation that has preserved the sites of many of the posts and many of the remnants, but it is not uncommon to come upon a lone marker standing amidst sage brush many miles from civilization, vague surface indentations nearby serving as the sole evidence of early occupancy.

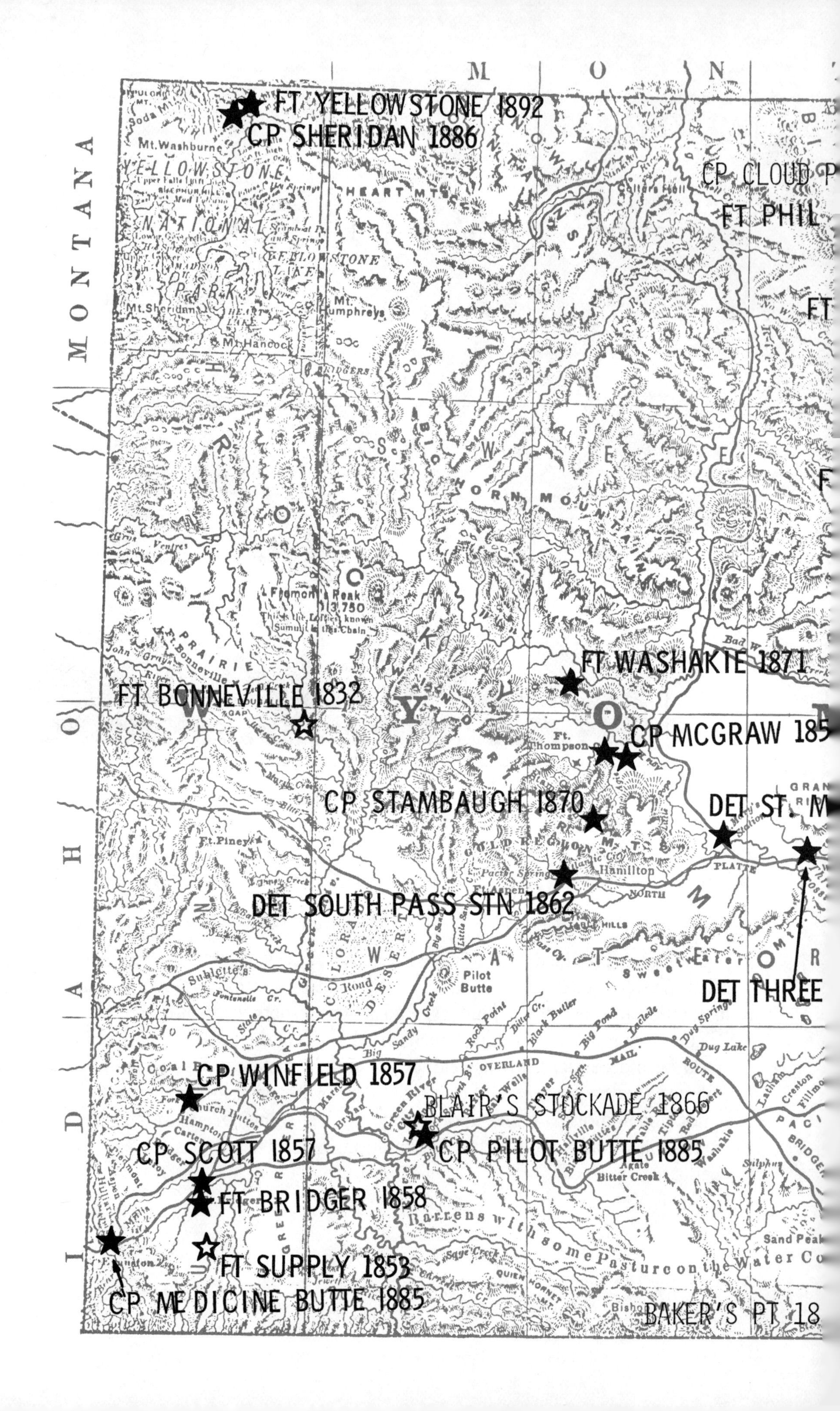

MONTANA
IDAHO
FT YELLOWSTONE 1892
CP SHERIDAN 1886
CP CLOUD P
FT PHIL
FT
F
FT WASHAKIE 1871
FT BONNEVILLE 1832
CP MCGRAW 185
CP STAMBAUGH 1870
DET ST. M
DET SOUTH PASS STN 1862
DET THREE
CP WINFIELD 1857
BLAIR'S STOCKADE 1866
CP PILOT BUTTE 1885
CP SCOTT 1857
FT BRIDGER 1858
FT SUPPLY 1853
CP MEDICINE BUTTE 1885
BAKER'S PT 18
YELLOWSTONE NATIONAL PARK
Mt. Washburne
Mt. Sheridan
Mt. Hancock
Mt. Humphreys
HEART MTS.
YELLOWSTONE LAKE
BIG HORN MOUNTAINS
Fremont's Peak 13,750
PRAIRIE
Ft. Piney
Ft. Thompson
Hamilton
Pilot Butte
Sublette's Road
Fontenelle Cr.
OVERLAND MAIL ROUTE
Dug Lake
Bitter Creek
Sand Peak
Barrens with some Pasture on the Water Co

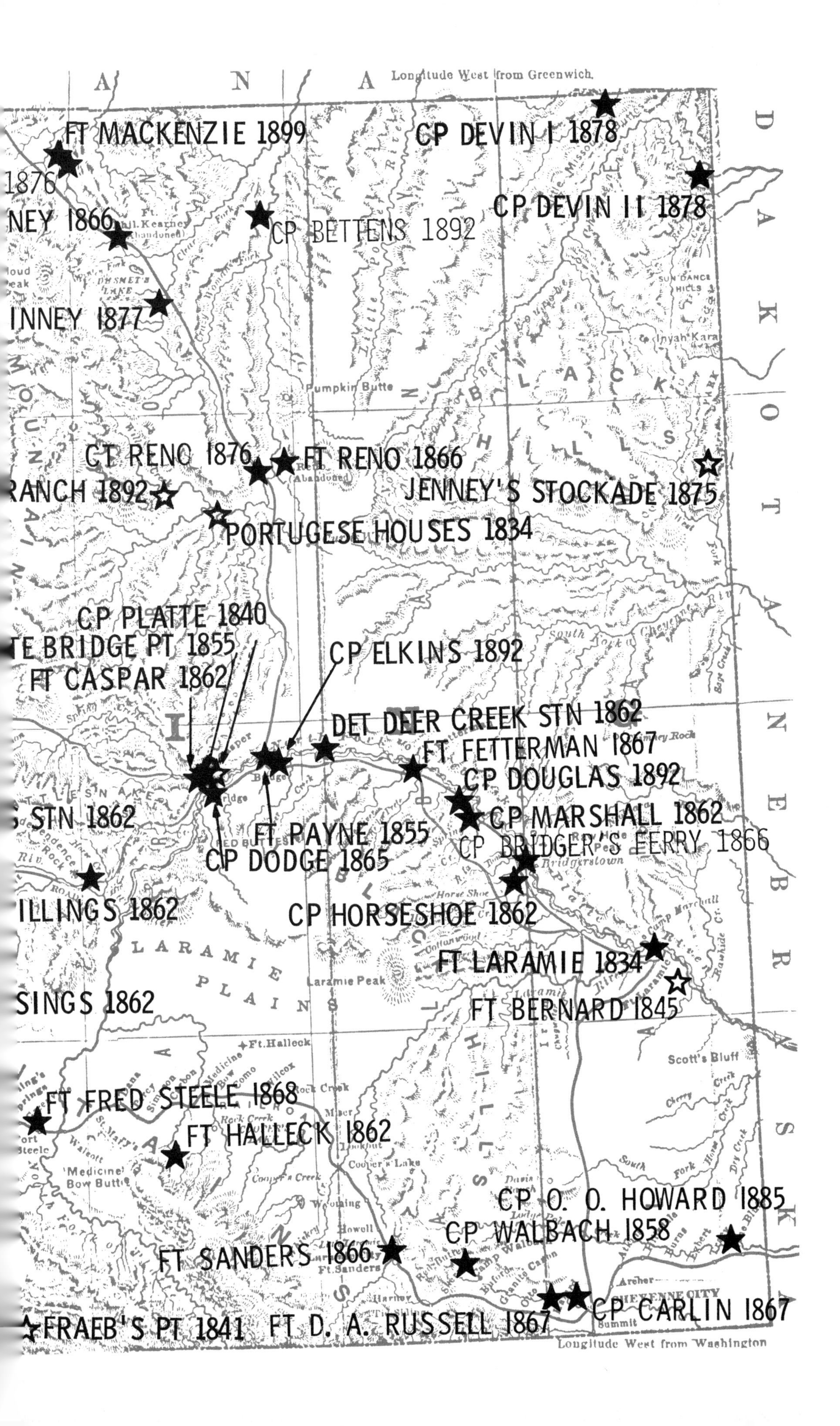

Longitude West from Greenwich
FT MACKENZIE 1899
CP DEVIN I 1878
1876
NEY 1866
CP BETTENS 1892
CP DEVIN II 1878
INNEY 1877
CT RENO 1876
FT RENO 1866
RANCH 1892
JENNEY'S STOCKADE 1875
PORTUGESE HOUSES 1834
CP PLATTE 1840
TE BRIDGE PT 1855
CP ELKINS 1892
FT CASPAR 1862
DET DEER CREEK STN 1862
FT FETTERMAN 1867
CP DOUGLAS 1892
S STN 1862
CP MARSHALL 1862
FT PAYNE 1855
CP BRIDGER'S FERRY 1866
CP DODGE 1865
ILLINGS 1862
CP HORSESHOE 1862
FT LARAMIE 1834
SINGS 1862
FT BERNARD 1845
FT FRED STEELE 1868
FT HALLECK 1862
CP O. O. HOWARD 1885
CP WALBACH 1858
FT SANDERS 1866
CP CARLIN 1867
FRAEB'S PT 1841
FT D. A. RUSSELL 1867
Longitude West from Washington

Camp Augur. 1869-71. *Camp Brown.* Log cabins with sod roofs were surrounded by a ditch within an enclosure 175 feet by 125 at Camp Augur. The post was intended to protect both Indians and settlers in the Sweetwater mining district. It was renamed Camp Brown in 1870 and moved to Little Wind river where it would ultimately be known as Fort Washakie. The site is within the city of Lander (at the US routes 26 and 287) on Main street near 3d street. A block of granite marks the spot.

Baker's Post. 1873. Not a trading post, this three-story blockhouse was the retirement home of Mountain Man James Baker, one of the survivors of the battle at Fraeb's Post, 10 miles to the east in 1841. The building was moved to Frontier Park in Cheyenne in 1917, about 30 years after Baker's death. The site is in a field 1.2 miles south of Savery (see Fraeb's Post item for detailed directions).

Fort Bernard. 1845-46. *Richards Post.* Whiskey and price-cutting were the tools used by John Baptiste Richard to compete with nearby Fort Laramie. This trading post was the successor to Fort Platte and, because it had inherited Platte's inventory, its trade was brisk even before construction was finished on the rough log and brick building. Bernard's accommodations were termed "far inferior to those of an ordinary stable" but this was not the reason for its short life. Apparently Richards' methods and illicit whiskey trade were sufficient reason for the post to be burned, whether by competition or drunken patrons has never been settled. From Fort Laramie town, go southeast on US 26 for 7.3 miles; across the river from here (to the right) is the site of Fort Bernard.

Camp Bettens. 1892-95. Six companies of the 6th Cavalry were deployed here temporarily from Fort Robinson in the later days of the so-called Johnson County War. They were at the camp from mid-June to mid-November, 1892, and returned for portions of the next three summers when the site served as a Camp of Instruction. The site is near Arvada. From Sheridan, go southeast on US 14 for 59 miles to a right (south) turn to Arvada, 3 miles.

Blair's Stockade. 1866-70. This was a trading post of Archie and Duncan Blair, now virtually impossible to locate because of time and construction. From Rock Springs, go north on US 187 for .7 mile to a dirt road. Turn left .2 mile to the site on the west side of Killpecker creek at the foot of the chalk bluffs.

Fort Bonneville. 1832. *Fort Nonsense.* Captain Benjamin L.E. Bonneville spent several weeks and considerable effort in building this log enclosure, blockhouses at two diagonally opposite corners. The post was hardly finished before he moved to a succession of temporary camps in this area of fur trade rendezvous sites. The wasted work won for the abandoned fort the second name listed. From Rock Springs go north on US 187 for 110 miles to the intersection with US 189 north of Daniel. Head straight west 4 miles to point where marker stone and information sign tell the story of Fort Bonneville at the left (south) side of the road.

Fort Bridger. 1842-57. This was the trading post of Jim Bridger until he left in 1853 and, beginning in 1854, of Mormon traders representing Brigham Young. Bridger's original post was the usual collection of log huts connected by mud daubed pickets. In 1855 the Mormons erected a 400 foot square cobblestone wall and added some log buildings within the fort, all of which they destroyed when the U.S. Army and the Utah Expedition arrived in 1857. Remnants of the Mormon cobblestone wall are part of the Fort Bridger State Monument next to the town of Fort Bridger on I-80 about 32 miles east of Evanston.

Fort Bridger. 1858-90. After a cold winter in nearby Camp Scott, the Army moved on to Utah but left a detachment to rebuild a new Fort Bridger, by 1858 designated an official Army post. Log buildings were erected around a parade ground and gradually the post became an expansive cluster of military buildings for traveler protection. Fort Bridger State Monument has restored some buildings, maintained or marked the others, and provided a museum that tells the

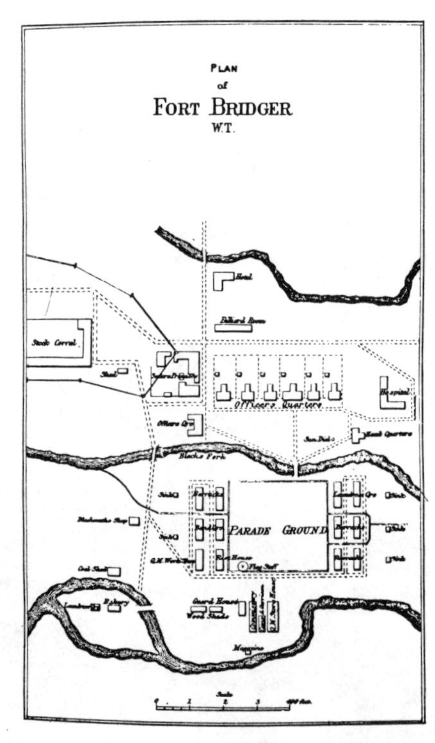

story of the three phases of the post's life: trading post, Mormon fort, and Army garrison.

Detachment at Bridger's Ferry. 1866. Galvanized Yankees of Company I, 11th Ohio Cavalry, spent the summer of 1866 at this field camp guarding Benjamin Mills' ferry across the North Platte river. Howitzers were placed at each landing. With 21-man detachment, the post stopped the raids on the ferry while it was used to supply and reinforce the expeditions and new posts to the north.

From Douglas, go southeast on I-25 to a point 1.5 miles south of Orin. There is a marker indicating that the ferry site is on the river banks north of the railroad tracks.

Camp Brown. *Camp Augur, Fort Washakie.*

Camp Carlin. 1867-88. *Cheyenne Depot, Quartermaster Depot near Cheyenne.* Adjacent to the Fort D.A. Russell reservation, Camp Carlin was the supply center for the posts to the north and west. It had wooden quarters for one company, a guardhouse, three officers quarters, and 16 portable store houses. From Cheyenne, take Randall avenue west 1 mile from the capitol. Obtain pass to Warren Air Force Base at the gate, then turn left at 1st street. A granite marker near the railroad marks the site.

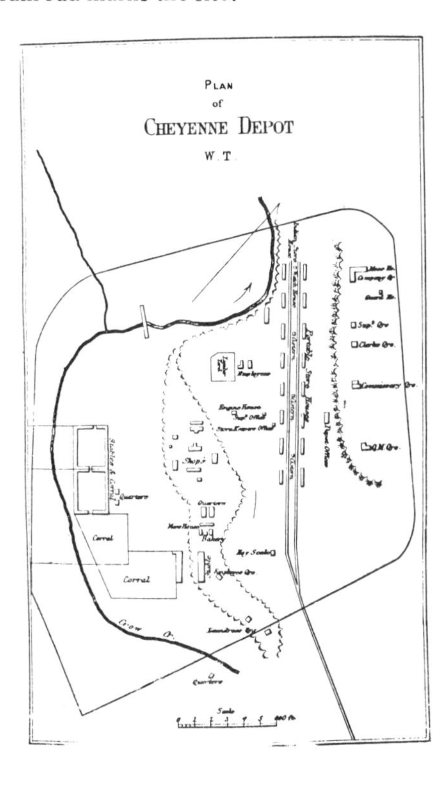

Fort Caspar. 1862-67. *Platte Bridge Station.* Troops were assigned here to guard the 1,000-foot bridge across the Platte during and after the Civil War. This was at a crossing 5 miles above John Richard's bridge (see Camp at Platte Bridge). After Lieutenant Caspar Collins was killed in a battle with Indians, the post was renamed in his honor. Portions of the log fort have been reconstructed on the original foundations and are maintained by the city of Casper (named, but with altered spelling, after the fort). From Casper, take 13th street west 1.5 miles to the fort. Pilings from the bridge are north of the fort.

Camp Clay. *Fort Paine.*

Camp Cloud Peak. 1876. *Crook Supply Camp.* General Crook camped here from June 10 to 16, 1876, on his way to the Battle at the Rosebud and also on his way back after the battle. The site is now within the city of Sheridan where it is marked in the city park.

Fort Connor. *Fort Reno.*

Crook Supply Camp. *Camp Cloud Peak.*

Camp Davis. *Fort Paine.*

Fort D.A. Russell. 1867-1948. *Fort Francis E. Warren, Post of Crow Creek.* An unusual diamond shaped parade ground flanked by 11 wooden barracks and 15 officers quarters was a feature of this headquarters fort. Measuring 1,040 by 800 feet, the parade ground and many of the buildings, rebuilt with brick in 1880, are still in use at Warren Air Force Base, 1 mile west of Cheyenne. The post cemetery has graves removed from many abandoned forts.

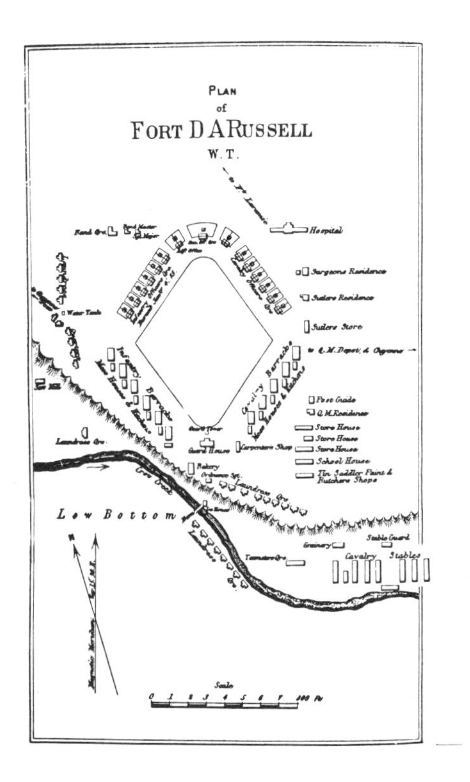

FORT CASPAR (Platte Bridge) *(1)*

FORT D.A. RUSSELL

Detachment at Deer Creek Station. 1862-66. Details of troopers watched over the Oregon Trail travel at this station and, when the telegraph was in operation, protected both the construction crews and line tenders. From Casper, take I-25 for 18 miles east to Glenrock. At Glenrock, take a gravel road from the Deer Creek bridge .3 mile to Glenrock Park. The site of the station is in this park.

Camp Devin. 1878. Building the telegraph line to Fort Keogh meant two temporary field sites for this summer post. The first post was established on June 30, 1878, on the Little Missouri river.

On August 10 the post was moved to Oak Creek south of the Belle Fourche river where the five companies of the 3d U.S. cavalry were headquartered until September 22. The locations of both sites are only approximate.

To visit both camps, go north on I-90 for 13 miles to the intersection with road number 0603 to Alladin, 9 miles. Camp Devin I can be reached by turning left (west) on Wyoming 24 at this point for 25 miles to Hulett. At Hulett, inquire locally for dirt road that goes north to the Little Missouri and the site near the Montana border.

Camp Devin II can be reached from Alladin by inquiring locally for the road to the junction of Oak Creek on the Belle Fourche, about 10 miles north of Alladin.

Camp Dodge. 1865. The spring attacks by the Indians on most of the Oregon Trail stage and telegraph stations caused the 11th Kansas Cavalry to be deployed along the line with headquarters at this temporary post southeast of Platte Station on the east side of Upper Garden Creek. Between April 19 and June 28, 1865, several patrols were fielded from here until the headquarters was shifted to Camp Marshall. Follow directions to Fort Caspar; four miles southeast of Caspar is the site of Camp Dodge.

Camp at Douglas. 1892. Troops A and K, 6th Cavalry, were stationed near Douglas for a short time in the fall, 1892, as an aftermath of the Johnson County War. Douglas is north of I-26 and 48 miles east of Casper.

Camp Elkins. 1892. Six companies of the 6th Cavalry, permanently stationed at Fort Niobrara, Nebraska, established this temporary field camp on June 20, 1892, during the final days of the Johnson County War. These troops were part of the overall plan by the Wyoming cattle barons against the small independent ranchers. The barons had attempted to obtain a declaration of martial law, something the White House refused to do, so President Harrison appeased his political friends by moving troops into the area. The site is between Fort Fetterman and Casper. Inquire locally at Casper for directions.

Fort Fetterman. 1867-82. The four barracks and seven officers quarters of this key fort were originally surrounded by a high plank fence but this gradually disappeared.

Were it not for the isolated position at the jumping off point for the Bozeman Trail, Fetterman would have been highly prized for assignment – at least for the officers who found the quarters particularly good. Apparently the post commanders kept building themselves new quarters, the rejected ones being turned over to the less senior officers. General Crook had his camp north of the fort prior to his 1876 expedition. From Douglas, take I-25 west one exit to road 0502, about 2.7 miles. Go north on 0502 for 6.8 miles to the fort site, marked on the right side (east) of the road where several buildings are left in a state park.

Fort Fred Steele. 1868-86. The unusual arc-shape layout of this railroad post is still obvious in the building foundations of the deserted hamlet of Fred Steele, once the garrison's quarters. The last building burned on New Year's Eve 1976. The site is a state park and preservation is planned. From Rawlins, go east on I-80 for 14 miles to a left (north) turn onto a gravel road just before reaching the North Platte river. The fort site is at the end of this road, about 2.5 miles, on the other side of a road under the railroad.

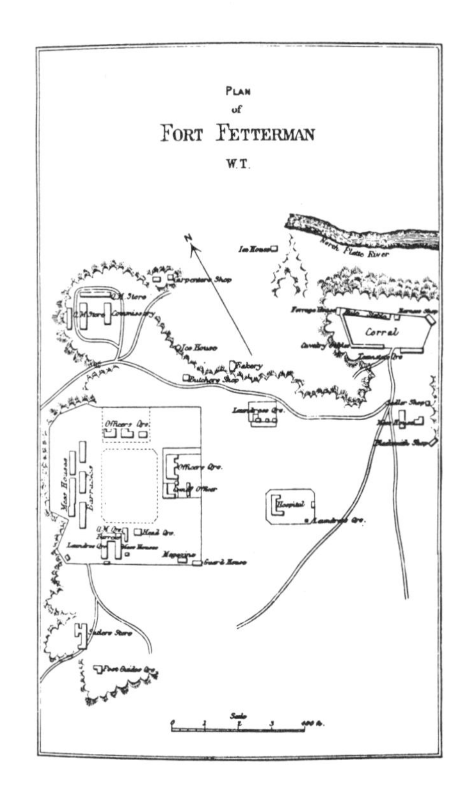

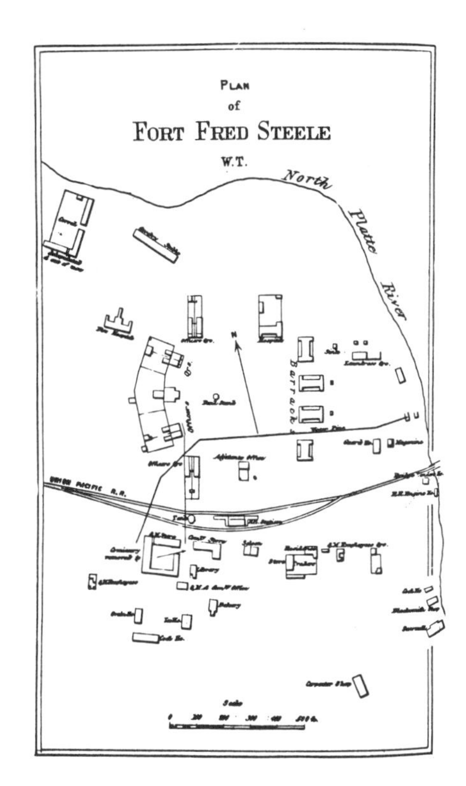

FORT FRED STEELE *(1)*

Fraeb's Post. 1841. Mountain man Henry Fraeb was one of five men killed at this site by Sioux and Cheyennes who resented his attempts to build a trading post here. The fighting took place amidst the logs felled to build the fort. The defenders were able to hold off the several hundred warriors even though Fraeb, mortally wounded, did much of his fighting sitting against a stump until he died. The site is within Battle Mountain State Game Preserve. From Rawlins, go west on I-80 for 26 miles to Wyoming 789. Go south on 789 the 51 miles to Baggs. Turn left (east) at Baggs through Dixon, 7 miles and the site of *Baker's Post,* to Savery, 4 miles. At Savery inquire locally for the unimproved road to the site, 4 miles to the east and just north of the Colorado border.

Fort Halleck. 1862-66. Elk Mountain looks down on the site of this protector for the railroad where several original buildings and the post cemetery are left. From Rawlins, go east on I-80/US 30 for about 40 miles to the turnoff to Hanna. Turn right (south) 10.5 miles to a dirt road. Turn right (west) 4 miles to another dirt road. Turn right (north) 1.7 miles to the entry road to the Quealy Ranch which presently owns and occupies the site and buildings of Fort Halleck.

Camp on Ham's Fork. *Camp Winfield.*

Camp Hat Creek. 1876-77. *Camp on Sage Creek.* This was a stockaded sub-post of Fort Laramie for protection of the Black Hills stage route. It was at the site of Camp on Sage Creek occupied in 1875 as part of the perimeter guard-

FORT HALLECK, from a drawing by bugler C. Moellman, CO. G, 11th Ohio Cavalry in 1863 *(1)*

ing the Black Hills from civilian miners. The site is next to the Hat Creek stage station on US 85 about 14 miles north of Lusk.

Camp Horseshoe. 1862-66. *Detachment at Horseshoe Station.* A lieutenant and 38 men were assigned to guard travelers and telegraph at this important station, the first stopping place for most stages from Fort Laramie. The stockade became a ranch in 1868. When the occupants fired on a passing group of Indians led by Crazy Horse, killing two, the Indians attacked and burned the place. The ranchers were spared because they hid in a root cellar. To reach the site go southeast on I-25 from Douglas to Glendo, 27 miles. Continue south 2.5 miles. At this point, the station site is on the left (east) where there is an historical marker.

Jenney's Stockade. 1875. An expedition into the Black Hills with neither military nor settler objectives was the geological survey led by government geologist Walter P. Jenney in 1875.

Correctly viewing the survey as the first step in a government plan to buy the Black Hills from the Sioux and open them to prospecting, miners were pleased to help Jenney put up this stockade to protect his scientists.

The site of the stockade is on a ranch near Newcastle in northeastern Wyoming. From Newcastle, go southeast on US 16 for 5.2 miles to the Stockade Beaver creek, site of Jenney's Stockade where there is an historical marker.

The stockade was moved in 1933 to Newcastle where it was rebuilt as a pioneer museum in the courthouse yard on Warren avenue.

Fort John. *Fort Laramie.*

Fort John Buford. *Fort Sanders.*

Detachment at La Bonte Station. *Camp Marshall.*

Fort Laramie. 1834-49. *Fort John, Fort John on the Laramie, Fort William.* This was one of the leading trading posts in the northwest, founded in 1834 as Fort William by the firm of William Sublette, Robert Campbell and others. It was a palisade 18 feet high, bastions on two diagonally opposite corners, with a few adobe buildings inside. After it was sold to Milton Sublette and James Bridger, the post was rebuilt of adobe and

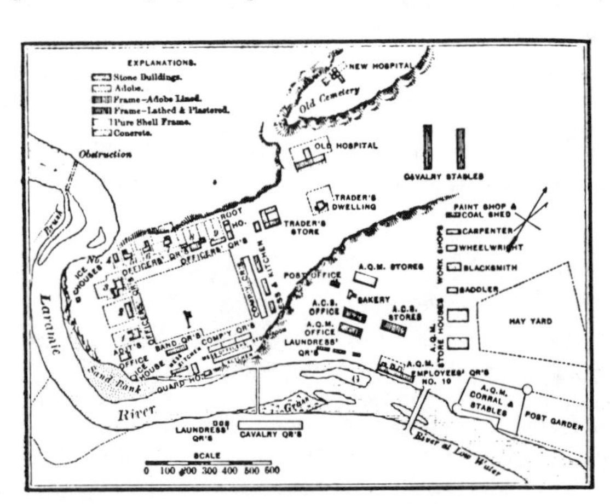

renamed Fort John. Despite all of this, the names of Fort Laramie or Fort John on the Laramie were used frequently because of their geographical description made it obvious what fort was concerned. The buildings were sold in 1849 and became the military post of Fort Laramie.

Fort Laramie. 1849-90. The Grattan Massacre that precipitated the Indian Wars of the 1850's took place near this critical military fort of the plains. From the stockaded trading post purchased in 1849, this fort became a large, rambling affair of more than 150 buildings. It is part of the National Park Service and the buildings have been restored, rebuilt, stabilized or site marked for visitor viewing. From Cheyenne, go north on I-25 for 82 miles to US 26. Turn right (east) for 27 miles to the town of Fort Laramie. A marked gravel road goes 2 miles to the Fort Laramie National Monument.

Fort Mackenzie. 1899-1918. Sheridan's military tradition amidst the forts of the Bozeman Trail and subsequent events became permanent with the establishing of this major fort at the end of the 19th century. The first troops arrived in 1899 but it was not until 1905 that the post was fully garrisoned. Although given up by the Army during the final week of World War I, the fort continues to serve the armed forces as a Veterans Administration hospital specializing in psychiatric care. The former fort is 2 miles northwest of Sheridan off of I-90.

Camp Marshall. 1862-66. *Detachment at La Bonte Station.* Under the La Bonte name, this post was guarded by detachments of troops until 1864 when Captain Levi G. Marshall, 11th Ohio Cavalry, supervised the construction of a more permanent fort. This was little better, being nothing more than a crude square of stables, barracks, and a stockade surrounding the telegraph station. A pair of mountain howitzers provided artillery defense. The site can be reached from Douglas by taking the road across the Platte to Esterbrook. At about 10 miles, when the road crosses La Bonte creek, is the site of Camp Marshall on the left (east) side of the road.

Camp McGraw. 1857-58. Fort Thompson. This temporary field camp was built by a detachment of troops from Fort Kearny, Nebraska, who were surveying a road to Oregon that would miss the Utah Territory. There is a marker at the site on Wyoming 789 about 2 miles northeast of Lander.

Depot Fort McKinney. *Cantonment Reno.*

Fort McKinney. 1877-94. *Cantonment Reno, New Fort Reno.* The lineage of this permanent-type post is scrambled into its use of the Reno names in its early days, and the use of the McKinney name for awhile at the second Fort Reno. It was a direct descendent of Cantonment Reno when it was established in 1877 and for that reason the two alternate names were attached to the new fort until McKinney became official.

Seven double-story barracks, 14 officers quarters, and other frame buildings made up this large post by the time it was completed. In addition to Indian fighting, the garrison was critically involved in the nearby Johnson County War in 1892.

Several buildings remain, including part of the hospital and a stable, at what is now the Wyoming Soldiers and Sailors Home, 3 miles west of Buffalo and south of US 16.

Camp Medicine Butte. 1885-87. Two infantry companies were deployed to Evanston in September, 1885, immediately after the anti-Chinese riot in Rock Springs. The rioting having spread to the property of the Union Pacific railroad, the garrison was ordered to protect the U.S. mail aboard the

FORT LARAMIE
Officers' Quarters, about 1891

railroad trains. The issue was over the hiring of Chinese laborers in the mines, including those owned by the U.P., and the troops in Evanston were close enough to reinforce those at Camp Pilot Butte, if required. Evanston is on I-80 in the southwest corner of Wyoming; the camp was within the town.

Fort Nonsense. *Fort Bonneville.*

Camp O.O. Howard. 1885. This was a temporary Camp of Instruction 1 mile from Pine Bluffs, occupied by eight companies from the 4th, 7th, 9th and 21st U.S. Infantry from September 3 to 21, 1885. Pine Bluffs is 40 miles east of Cheyenne on I-80.

Fort Payne. 1855-59. *Camp Davis, Camp Clay, Camp of Platte Bridge.* John Baptiste Richard of Fort Bernard trading infamy, turned his talents to toll bridge operation from 1851 to 1865 with a small trading post on the side. At Richard's bridge seven miles east of Platte Bridge, two dozen soldiers guarded the bridge during the winter of 1855-56. During the Utah Expedition two companies of the 4th Artillery were garrisoned here in a small adobe fort. The location was nicknamed Camp or Fort Payne by the soldiers, possibly because of the "pain" they felt by having to spend the winter of 1855-56 at this desolate spot. From Casper, go east on I-25 to the next exit, Evansville. South of Evansville on the river are the archeological remains at the site of the blacksmith shop, cabin and trading post at which Fort Payne was located.

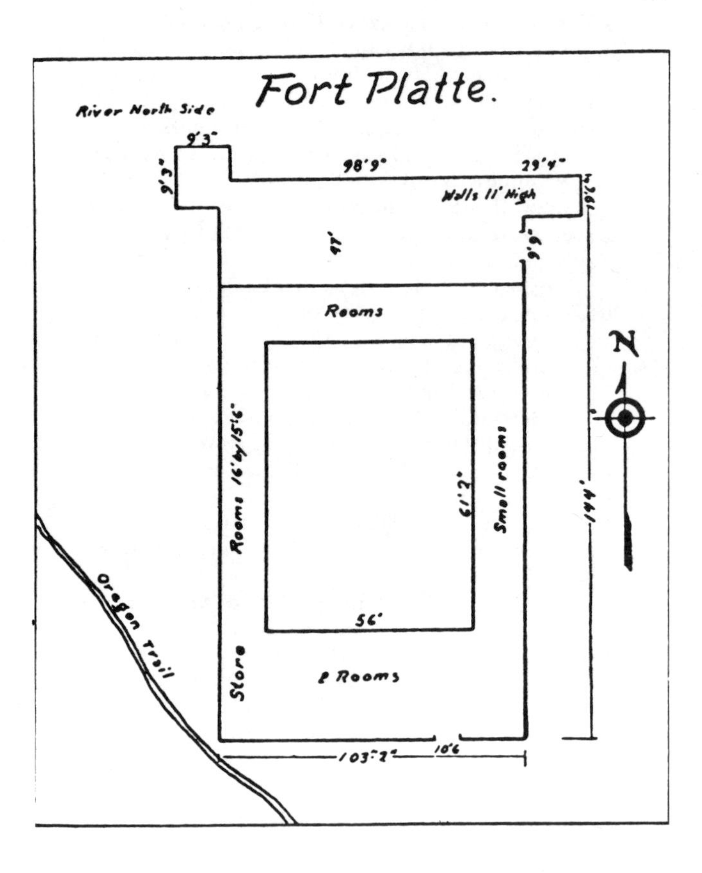

FORT PHIL KEARNY *(I)*

Fort Phil Kearny. 1866-68. *New Fort Reno.* Colonel Henry B. Carrington built this post to be the keystone of the Bozeman Trail, but most of the time it was under virtual siege. It was intended to be a replacement for Fort Reno, instead it was the headquarters of the Bozeman Trail forts of Reno, Phil Kearny, and C.F. Smith.

From this 42-building log palisade, Brevet Lieutenant Colonel William Fetterman led 81 men to their deaths in the Fetterman Massacre nearby. A year later, revenge of sorts was exacted near the fort in the Wagon Box Fight in which the Indians suffered surprising losses when the troopers answered an Indian ambush with new breech-loading rifles.

There is a log cabin and partial stockade wall at the fort's site, neither of authentic origin. From Buffalo, go north on I-90 to Story, 14 miles. Turn west on Valley road, a short distance, to the Portugee Phillips marker (memorializing fort's guide who rode 236 freezing miles to warn of the Fetterman Massacre). On the left (south) of the road is a plateau, the site of Fort Phil Kearny.

Camp Pilot Butte. 1885-99. *Camp Rock Springs.* After a score of Chinese laborers were killed during a strike at the mines around Rock Springs on September 2, 1885, the government rushed troops into the city on September 5. Two companies remained behind when the bulk of the force was withdrawn a month later, and the post continued to be manned until the end of the century. The site of the camp still has several Army buildings in use. The parochial school building of the Church of Saints Cyril and Methodius was a barracks, since rebuilt and refaced with brick. Across the street are former barracks, now apartments, that retain their Army appearance. Rock Springs is on I-80 midway between Evanston and Rawlins.

Camp Platte. 1840-47. This was a camp site on the Platte river used by Oregon Trail trains. The ferry crossed the river at this point, later the location of Fort Caspar. For directions see Fort Çaspar item.

Platte Bridge Station. *Fort Caspar.*

Camp at Platte Bridge. *Fort Payne.*

Portugese Houses. 1834-40. *Fort Antonio.* More legend than fact appears to have been written about this fur trade post established by Antonio Montero, a Portugese Mountain Man. A cluster of solidly built hewn log huts and a stout stockade 200 feet square provided protection in the hostile Powder River country.

According to tales the protection was enough for Montero to hold off an Indian siege for 40 days, but not enough for him to keep out 300 fellow trappers who descended on his area for the winter of 1836-37 and gradually absconded with everything movable.

From Casper, go north on I-25 to Kaycee, 72 miles. Turn right (east) at Kaycee on a gravel road that arrives in 11 miles at a marker for the site of the Portugese Houses.

Fort Reno. 1865-68. *Fort Connor, Old Fort Reno.* General P. Edward Connor led his troops from this new post on the Powder River Expedition of 1865.

Later when the Bozeman Trail was opened, Connor was to be abandoned but Colonel Henry B. Carrington decided to keep and remodel it after he led his 500-man expedition to it. The open post was enclosed with a stockade and renamed Reno on November 11, 1866. The post was abandoned when the Army withdrew from the Bozeman Trail in 1868.

From Casper, go north on I-25 to Kaycee, 72 miles. Turn right (east) at Kaycee on route 1002, going east 17 miles to Sussex schoolhouse. A quarter of a mile past the school, turn north on a gravel road. The Fort Reno (and Connor) site is on the right (east) side of the road, about 10 miles. A sign is beside the road, a marker in the pasture behind the marker and on a bluff overlooking the Powder.

Cantonment Reno. 1876-77. *New Fort Reno, Reno Station, Depot Fort McKinney.* Connected with the earlier Fort Reno only because of the similarity of names and geographical proximity, this post was three miles south and active only for nine months at the time of the Little Big Horn Sioux Expeditions of 1876. Consisting mainly of cottonwood log cabins and dugouts, it lasted into 1878 under the McKinney depot name while the garrison officially moved northward to newly established Fort McKinney. Only parched remains of building sites are left next to the Powder river. Although in the vicinity of Fort Reno, the unmarked privately owned site is impossible to find without local assistance.

Richards Post. *Fort Bernard.*

Camp Rock Springs. *Camp Pilot Butte.*

Detachment at Rocky Ridge. *Detachment at St. Mary's Station.*

Detachment at St. Mary's Station. 1862-65. *Detachment at Rocky Ridge.* As with the other stage station posts, the tiny garrison was responsible for the security of occupants and travelers, a task severly challenged on May 27, 1865, when the post was attacked. The occupants were able to hide on June 1 when the post was burned down and 400 yards of telegraph wire cut. From Lander, go south on US 287 for 38 miles to Sweetwater Station (a crossroads, not the historic Sweetwater Station further east). From this point where the highway crosses the Sweetwater river, St. Mary's Station is about 10 miles to the southwest on the banks of the Sweetwater.

Fort Sanders. 1866-82. *Fort John Buford.* This four-company post was arranged around a 400- by 235-foot parade ground when first built, then enlarged to a 600- by 500-foot parade when two more companies were assigned to the permanent garrison. Two buildings are left at the site, both of stone for obvious reasons: guardhouse and maga-

OLD FORT RENO *(1)*

zine. I-80 cuts right across the parade ground south of the city of Laramie. From the downtown area, take US 287 south 2 miles. A stone marker is at the junction of the highway and a dirt road which leads to the guardhouse ruins, 100 yards east. The magazine is on the other side of the interstate highway in front of the Laramie Country Club clubhouse.

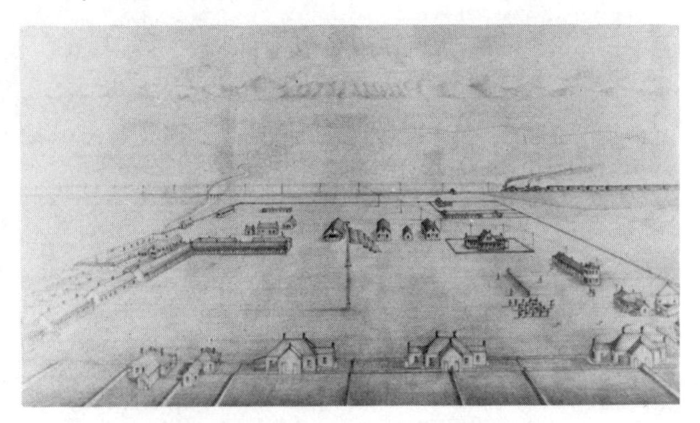

FORT SANDERS, 1875 *(9)*

Camp on Sage Creek. *Camp Hat Creek.*

Camp Scott. 1857-58. When the Utah Expedition arrived at Fort Bridger, they found that the Mormons had burned both it and Fort Supply to the south. The winter found the expedition quartered in rude huts, leantos, dugouts, and tents at Camp Scott 2 miles from the scorched remnants of Fort Bridger. Follow directions to Fort Bridger; turn south for 2 miles past the post to the approximate site of temporary Camp Scott.

Camp Sheridan. 1886-91. When the Army was directed to take over the security of Yellowstone Park, their first camp was this post, a number of wooden buildings sufficient for one cavalry troop. This was temporary, however, and when the permanent buildings of Fort Yellowstone were completed, Sheridan's site was abandoned. The camp site is south of the Yellowstone National Park headquarters at Mammoth Hot Springs and on the south side of Capitol Hill (in front of the hotel). The last remaining building of Camp Sheridan burned down in 1964.

Detachment at South Pass Station. 1862-66. Indians twice burned this station, giving it the name of "Burnt Ranch." Troops operated from it in protecting the entrance to South Pass.

In spring, 1865, three ex-Confederates serving here with the 11th Ohio Cavalry as Galvonized Yankees were shot to death for mutiny. Previously they had been in the Fort Laramie guardhouse for the same offense; their resistance to his authority was sufficient basis for the officer commanding the detachment to take the ultimate action warranted by field conditions.

From Lander, go south on US 287 for 6 miles to Wyoming 28. Turn right (southwest) for 24 miles to a left (southeast) turnoff to Atlantic City. A marker is on the highway 1.5 miles before the turnoff. At 2.3 miles turn right (southwest) toward South Pass City. Pass through South Pass City ghost town and in about 3 miles turn left (southeast) for 6 miles to Burnt Ranch site on the Sweetwater river, site of South Pass Station. This is a rough, fair weather road; local directions should be obtained.

Camp Stambaugh. 1870-78. Two hewn log barracks, 80 by 32 feet, with an L, 48 by 20 feet, four sets of married soldiers quarters, four officers quarters, and other wooden buildings comprised this military protection for the miners in the Sweetwater district. By mid-1870 the drop in local population made the post unnecessary.

The modern site has traces of most of the buildings, now no more than mounds or outlines on the surface of the ground, and a historical marker nearby.

From Lander, go south on US 287 for 6 miles to Wyoming 28. Turn right (southwest) for 24 miles to a left (southeast) turnoff to Atlantic City. This is 1.5 miles past a marker to Atlantic City on the highway. At 2.3 miles turn left (southeast) to Atlantic City. Out of Atlantic City, follow the Micro Wave Tower road about 2.8 miles to a dirt track entering from the left (north). Follow this dirt track across the plain to the marker; the site and the surface traces are beyong the marker. This is a rough, fair weather road; local inquiry is essential.

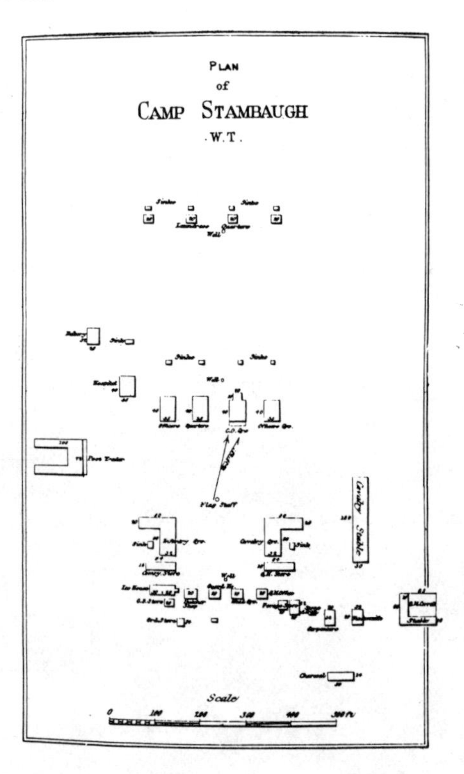

Camp Stillings. 1862-66. *Detachment at Sweetwater Station.* Forty Arapahoes attacked this garrison in June, 1865, but were beaten off by the 14 soldiers who lost one trooper killed, one wounded. Only excavations are left where the buildings once stood. From Casper, go west on Wyoming 220 about 55 miles to the crossing of the Sweetwater river. Turn left (west) 1 mile to the site of Sweetwater Station and Camp Stillings.

Fort Supply. 1853-57. Not really a military fort, this was the site to which the Mormons sent representatives in an attempt to establish a farm to support emigrating Mormons. A high stockade surrounded the cluster of buildings, all of which was burned when the Mormons abandoned the area upon the approach of the Utah Expedition. This post represents the first effort at farming in Wyoming, as the plaque at the site points out. Follow directions to Fort Bridger, then turn south through Mountain View to Robertson, 12 miles. One mile west of Robertson is a marker at the site of Fort Supply.

Detachment at Sweetwater Station. *Camp Stillings.*

Fort at TA Ranch. 1892. The Johnson County war between the cattle barrons and the independent cattle ranches reached its highpoint here when forces of the barons started to storm this tiny defensive work at the TA ranch. The "fort" was on top of a knoll, deep trenches enclosing a space 12 to 14 feet square surrounded by a wall of heavy timbers with firing portholes. The permanent buildings of the ranch were logged up for protection, the main ranchhouse also has a series of trenches around it. The attackers were behind a moving barricade but before it had a chance to challenge the defenders, regular Army troopers from Fort McKinney arrived to suspend the conflict. The TA ranch location is south of Buffalo about 13 miles on the east side of I-25 (US 87).

Fort Thompson. *Camp McGraw.*

Detachment at Three Crossings. 1862-66. It was a true cavalry finish when the troopers stationed at this stage station were surrounded by an estimated 300 to 500 Indians on May 20, 1865. Troops from other stations arrived just in time to rescue the garrison. This site also was the headquarters post for Company I, 3d U.S. Volunteers, Captain A. Smith Lybe, which provided the details for three other posts. This company marched farther and had more casualties than any other company in the regiment. It was known also as Galvanized Yankees because of their former Confederate allegiance. From Lander, go south on US 287 for 58 miles to where the highway nears the site of the station on the left (north) side.

Camp Walbach. 1858-59. Protecting the dangerous crossing through Cheyenne Pass was the mission of Camp Walbach, described in 1866 by a passing traveler: "A small military post that had been entirely destroyed by Indians years before, vividly reminding us of the deadly foe, not far away." Whether destroyed by Indians or firewood-hungry travelers, the questions of who destroyed the post is academic since anything untended was fair game at the time. The camp was manned by two companies of the 4th U.S. Artillery between September, 1858, and April, 1859. From Cheyenne, take I-25 north 7 miles to the exit to Federal. Take this exit to the west about 16 miles to Federal. Inquire here for directions to Cheyenne Pass and Camp Walbach, about 4 miles to the west.

Fort Washakie. 1871-1909. *Camp Brown.* A rarity, this fort was named after an Indian chief, Shoshone leader Chief Washakie who was also the leading resident at this permanent stone garrison in the Wind River area. A number of buildings still are in use at the Wind River Indian Agency. From Lander, go northwest on US 287 for 17 miles to the town of Fort Washakie. The fort buildings can be seen from the road on the left (west) side. The post cemetery, with the grave of Chief Washakie in it, is about 4 miles south of the former post.

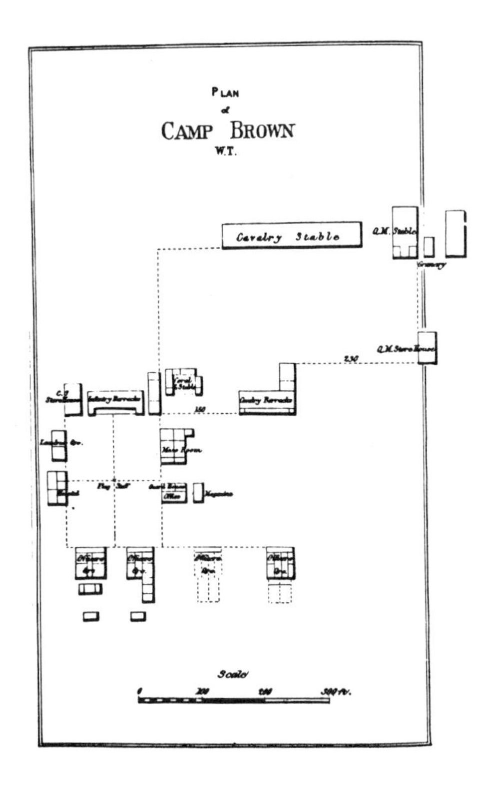

Fort William. *Fort Laramie.*

Camp Winfield. 1857. *Camp on Ham's Fork.* Upon arriving at Fort Bridger and finding it burned, Colonel E.B. Alexander took his forces about 30 miles to the northwest and made camp at this point. Much indecision and correspondence with Brigham Young followed before the troops left the camp on a northwesterly route, intending to descend upon Salt Lake City from the north.

Six days later the seven mile long column ground to a halt 35 miles from Winfield. It turned around and returned to Winfield after another 16 days, having spent from October 11 to November 2, 1857, making a great circle without accomplishing anything. By this time, General Albert S. Johnson had arrived and ordered the column to begin moving on November 6 for the site of what became Camp Scott, 35 miles to the south.

From Fort Bridger on I-80, go northeast on I-80 to US 30W. Turn to the northwest on US 30W through Granger. Twenty miles from the interstate – which is about 15 from the junction of Ham's Fork and Black's Fork – is the site of Camp Winfield.

Fort Yellowstone. 1892-1918. Upwards of four troops of cavalry and one machine gun platoon garrisoned this permanent post designed for the protection of Yellowstone Park before the organization of the National Park Service. This post succeeded and was just north of Camp Sheridan. The buildings are now used by the administration staff of the National Park Service at Yellowstone in the Mammoth Hot Springs area.

Chief Washakie talking to a group at Fort Washakie *(1)*

FURTHER READING

If this volume has planted or increased an interest in the military history of the American West, it has been a success. These short entries cannot pretend to be definitive treatments of a thousand-some frontier posts, camps, and installations of the Army, Navy, and Marines in the 19th century, but there are sources where further information is available.

The reader who is interested in researching deeper has several places to go. The first would be the historical offices of each service, all of which are in Washington, D.C. The name of the office and a zip code are adequate for an address.

The Army's Center of Military History is at zip 20314; the Air Force at 20332; the Naval Historical Center, 20374; and the Marine Corps Historical Center, 20380.

The Navy and Old Branch of the National Archives and Records Service also is in Washington at zip 20408. The Army's Military History Institute at Carlisle Barracks, Pennsylvania 17013, has a vast collection of publications and documents and can be of considerable help. The Air Force's Albert E. Simpson Historical Research Center is at Maxwell Air Force Base, Alabama 36112.

All of the Western states have excellent historical society staffs and collections and often can respond on specific installations or help during a research visit. Several also have regional historical societies and there are many oriented to single localities or cities. Staffs usually are small, often consisting of volunteers, so this should be recognized in placing demands on their resources: they do not have to assist and if the request is unreasonable, probably are unable to do so. The fact that a "taxpayer" is asking has little effect on an office that receives no tax support.

There are three national military history organizations which are supported by dues and bequests.

The American Military Institute is the oldest. It was founded as the American Military History Foundation in 1933 by military historians of the Army War College and the National Archives. Later, it absorbed The Order of Indian Wars of the United States. As AMI, it has expanded to include military historians of all persuasions, publishes a quarterly journal, *Military Affairs*, which includes European history in its mixture, and can be contacted through the Department of History, Kansas State University, Manhattan, Kansas 66506.

The Company of Military Historians and Collectors was founded in 1951 with the plan to publish a journal of military antiquities and a companion series of military uniform plates. It had been informally publishing "Military Collector & Historian" for two years and this January 13, 1951, meeting was the occasion of its formal incorporation.

The name suggested that there was a dual reason for the society: collections and history. Even though it dropped "and Collectors" from its corporate name in 1962, the quarterly publication is still titled "Military History and Collector: Journal of The Company of Military Historians." It can be reached through The Company of Military Historians, North Main Street, Westbrook, Connecticut 06498.

The Council on Abandoned Military Posts was incorporated in Arizona in 1966 to "identify, locate, restore, preserve, and memorialize old military installations and their history and traditions." It has members in every state and territory and emphasizes American and Canadian military history. It also is involved in historic preservation on the premise that it must be part of this ethic in order to carry out the objectives. A quarterly "Periodical, Journal of the Council on Abandoned Military Posts" is published along with a monthly newspaper, "Headquarters Heliogram." This carries articles of timely interest in the areas of military history and historic preservation and has received several honors for its work. CAMP can be reached through Post Office Box 171, Arlington, Virginia 22210.

As years pass, these addresses might become out-dated but the official historical offices of the services should be able to supply information on the status and locations of these organizations.

The same offices should be able to suggest the best histories of their respective services. This question was posed to each office as this book was going to print, and several volumes were suggested.

The Army recommended its own official publication *American Military History*, published in 1973 under the general editorship of Maurice Matloff, chief historian. It also suggested Russell F. Weigley's *History of the United States Army*, part of the Macmillan "Wars of the United States" series, discussed below.

The Air Force recommended *History of the U.S. Air Force, 1907-1957*, by Alfred Goldberg (editor) with expectation that an overall history soon would be printed under the authorship of Colonel Alfred Hurley, USAF, Air Force Academy. This was to be part of the Macmillan series.

The Marine Corps has two recent histories to draw from. *The U.S. Marines, The First Two Hundred Years 1775-1975* was published first in England in 1974 and then in the United States two years later. It is the first overall definitive updated history since before World War II and is by Brigadier General Edwin H. Simmons, USMC (Retired), Director of Marine Corps History and Museums. In 1977 J. Robert Moskin appeared with *The U.S. Marine Corps Story*, a thicker, more detailed, and more expensive recounting.

The Navy could not point to a new record other than the 1948 revision of Dudley W. Knox's *A History of the United States Navy*. A coffee table history appeared in 1977, *U.S. Navy: An Illustrated History*, with text by Nathan Miller.

Hawthorn published its "Compact" histories of the services in the early 1960s: the *Army* by Colonel R. Ernest Dupuy, the *Air Force* by Carroll V. Glines, Jr., the *Navy* by Fletcher Pratt, *Marines* by Howard V. L. Bloomfield. The series even included the Red Cross, by Charles Hurd.

One of the earlier attempts to summarize the topic of American forts was published in 1915, *Quaint and Historic Forts of North America*. Unfortunately this volume by John Martin Hammond depended more on nostalgia than research for its content. It visits 50-some posts and sites, the approximate count necessary because it groups some, such as a few Western forts, into single chapters.

Four volumes in the "Forts of the Old West" series appeared between 1963 and 1967. By the author of this *Tour Guide to Old Western Forts*, Herbert M. Hart, they were one of the first attempts to list all of the posts and stations of the Western frontier and, in each volume, to tell the stories of 60 to 70 of them. Titled *Old Forts of the Northwest*, *Old Forts of the Southwest*, *Old Forts of the Far West*, and *Pioneer Forts of the West* the contents are based on research in the primary holdings of the National Archives and actual visits to the sites. Each volume also has a listing of sites in the western states covered by the book. A fifth addition to the set, *Frontier Forts of the West*, was projected but has yet to be completed.

One of the most useful compilations of forts is Rev. Francis Paul Prucha's *Guide to Military Posts of the United States* published in 1964. Concentrating on the official forts of the regular Army, Prucha gives such basic data as active dates and location. He is also the editor of *Army Life on the Western Frontier* (1958) drawn from the reports of Colonel George Croghan's inspection trips 1826-1845, and the author of *Broadax and Bayonet: The Role of the United States Army in the Development of the Northwest 1815-1860*, published in 1953.

Forts of the West is the helpful coverage by Robert W. Frazer published in 1963, who also edited *Mansfield on the Condition of the Western Forts 1853-54* (1963) and *New Mexico in 1850: A Military View* (1968), drawn from the reports of former Army Inspectors-General Joseph K. F. Mansfield and Archibald McCall.

Kent Ruth followed in 1963 with *Great Days in the West: Forts, Posts, and Rendezvous Beyond the Mississippi* which covered a total of 147 "important frontier sites," several per Western state. Sixteen years later in 1979 Irvin Haas followed in similar style with *Citadels, Ramparts & Stockades: America's Historic Forts*, but this included only 100 "historic monuments" throughout the country.

The National Park Service presented an overview of military sites in the West in *Soldier and Brave, Historic Places Associated with Indian Affairs and the Indian Wars in the Trans-Mississippi West*. This was edited by Robert G. Ferris in its most recent edition, published in 1971, and based on the original edition of 1963.

Two guides to Army and Air Force installations appeared in the mid-1960s. Army Times published *Guide to Army Posts* in 1966, giving photographs and data on both active and inactive activities of the period. Stackpole published *Air Force Bases, A Directory of U.S. Air Force Installations, Both in the Continental U.S. and Overseas, with Useful Information on Each Base and Its Nearby Community* in 1965.

Mrs. Alice Cromie is the author of a work that includes many Western posts, published in 1976 as *Tour Guide to the Old West*. Howard R. Lamar is the editor of *The Readers Encyclopedia of the American West* (1977) a hefty 1,306 pages in which almost 200 contributors include many Western forts among the 2,400 entries.

No search into historic sites would be complete without looking into the classic state guides prepared under the Federal Writers project before World War II. Many of these have been reprinted, some even updated, but all are interesting in conducting a mile-by-mile coverage of a state. Do not depend solely on the index of each volume; it leaves out more fort and camp sites than it includes.

Between 1954 and 1962 Leroy R. Hafen's 15-volume *Far West and the Rockies* series was published by the Arthur H. Clark Company. It was quickly followed by his 10-volume *Mountain Men and the Fur Trade* series. Each has considerable coverage of posts in the West.

Even more specific to the military subject are two series that seem to have ceased with the deaths of their editors. prentice Hall had Stewart H. Holbrook at the helm of its "American Fort Series" and Macmillan had Louis Morton as general editor of its "Wars of the United States" set.

The Prentice Hall collection published in the mid-1960s includes *Guns at the Forks* regarding Fort Pitt, Pennsylvania, in the French and Indian Wars, by Walter O'Meara; *Louisbourg: Key to a Continent*, by Fairfax Downey; *Sutter's Fort: Gateway to the Gold Fields*, by Oscar Lewis; *Three Flaggs at the Straits: The Forts of Mackinac*, by Walter Havighurst; *Fort Laramie and the Sioux Indians*, by Remi Nadeau; and *Forts of the Upper Missouri*, by Robert G. Athearn.

The Macmillan series included, in chronological sequence of the contents, *Arms for Empire, A Military History of the British Colonies in North America, 1607-1763*, by Douglas Edward Leach; *The War of American Independence, Military Attitudes, Policies, and Practice, 1763-1789*, by Don Higginbotham; *The Sword of the Republic: The United States Army on the Frontier, 1783-1846*, by Father Prucha, noted above; *The Mexican War, 1846-1848*, by K. Jack Bauer; *Frontiersman in Blue: The United States Army and the Indian, 1848-1865* and *Frontier Regulars, The United States Army and the Indian, 1866-1891*, both by Robert M. Utley; *Blood on the Border, The United States Army and the Mexican Irregulars*, by Colonel Clarence C. Clendenen, USA (Retired), about the border problems before World War I; and *President Wilson Fights His War: World War I and the Mexican Intervention*, by Harvey A. DeWeerd.

Russell F. Weigley authored both *The American Way of War, A History of United States Military Strategy and Policy* and *History of the United States Army*. This was the only service history published in the series although preparations continued on others for publication by different presses: Colonel Alfred Hurley, USAF, on the Air Force; Raymond G. O'Connor, the Navy; and Lieutenant Colonel Allan R. Millet, USMCR, Marine Corps.

Another series that has been in preparation for several years is *Guardians of the Western Frontier*. Edited by Herbert M. Hart, it is to include monographs on forts by a number of contributors, similar to the format of Hafen's *Mountain Men and the Fur Trade* series. Upwards of nine volumes are planned with between 15 to 20 fort histories per book.

The non-military side of forts is covered in Brigadier General Hiram M. Chittenden's *American Fur Trade of the Far West*, first published in 1902 and made available again through a 1954 reprint. This provides mini-histories of many fur trading posts and forts, many of which had a military connection.

Edited by John S. Billings, Surgeon General Circular No. 4, *Reports on Barracks & Hospitals with Descriptions of Military Posts*, 1870, and No. 8, *Report on the Hygiene of the U.S. Army with Descriptions of Military Posts*, 1875, were reprinted in 1974. Each reprint has a 15-page Introduction by Herbert M. Hart that includes a biography of Billings and updated status reports on the 250 posts described in the two volumes. The original reports go into considerable detail on the history, appearance, and activities of the posts, based on the submissions of the surgeons stationed at them.

Another reprint is that of Lieutenant General Philip H. Sheridan's *Outline Descriptions of the Posts in the Military Division of the Missouri*, 1876, reprinted by Old Army Press in 1969. This provides data on 90 posts from the Canadian border to the Gulf of Mexico with ground plans of many of them.

A volume that is occasionally available, especially in Western libraries, is Brigadier General Richard Orton's *California Men in the War of the Rebellion*. Published in 1890, this book describes the activities and locations of the California volunteers in places all over the West.

The Western military frontier's campaigns are covered in a limited-printing *Indian Battles and Skirmishes on the American Frontier, 1790-1898*, compiled by Joseph D. Peters in 1966. A portion of it, based on War Department records, was reprinted in 1879 by Old Army Press under the title, *Chronological List of Actions, &c with Indians from January 15, 1837, to January 15, 1891*.

One of the most successful attempts to put the Army's frontier role in perspective, showing that it contributed far more than just military security, is Henry Beers' *Western Military Frontier*. This was published in 1935 but copies sometimes are available in libraries.

Fairfax Downey first wrote of the frontier in 1941 with *Indian-Fighting Army* and then in 1963 with *Indian Wars of the United States Army*. Paul Wellman covered the same general topic in 1954 with *Indian Wars of the West*. All three volumes are most useful.

Others covering the frontier era include Averam B. Bender's *The March of Empire: Frontier Defense in the Southwest, 1848-1860* (1952); William H. Goetzmann, *Army Explorations in the American West, 1803-1863* (19623); George F. Price, *Across the Continent with the Fifth Cavalry*, (1883 but later reprinted); R. Settle, *March of the*

Mounted Riflemen (1940); R. Calvin, *Lieutenant Emory Reports*, regarding the Corps of Topographical Engineers (1951); R. P. Bieber, *Marching with the Army of the West* (1936); John M. Carroll, *The Black Military Experience in the West* (1971); Dr. Lonnie J. White edited the *Chronicle of a Congressional Journey, the Doolittle Committee in the Southwest, 1865*, covering several posts (1976).

Two books with similar titles should not be confused. Odie B. Faulk appeared in 1974 with *Crimson Desert, the Indian Wars of the American Desert* while in 1972 S. L. A. Marshall's *Crimsoned Prairie, the Indian Wars on the Great Plains* was published. Only Faulk's work should be taken seriously. Marshall, the chroniclor of the the European and Korean battlegrounds, was far more proficient there than in the familiar grounds of the frontier West.

The final days of the frontier were brought to the twentieth century with Craham Cosmas' *An Army for Empire: The United States Army in the Spanish-American War*, published in 1975 and an outstanding discussion of the problems of expanding a frontier military force into one with the administrative and logistical capabilities to fight in a broader, world-wide amphitheater.

Two more books with similar titles covered the general subject in the West: S. E. Whitman's *The Troopers* in 1962 and Ray Brandes' *Troopers West* in 1971. A classic in describing the frontier soldier was Don C. Rickey's *40 Miles a Day on Beans and Hay*, published in 1963 and based on interviews with veterans of service in the late 19th century.

The Potomac Corral of the Westerners published *Great Western Indian Fights* in 1960 and twenty years later it was still earning royalties in paperback reprints.

Two official Army publications of significance to the study of the frontier are Erna Risch's *Quartermaster Support of the Army*, 1961, and the Center of Military History's official *Army Lineage* series that began in 1973.

The personnel who served on the frontier have left a number of good accounts of that service. This applies particularly to the generals and, especially, to George Armstrong Custer and his wife Elizabeth Custer. Custer wrote *My Life on the Plains*, his wife *Boots and Saddles*, *Following the Guidon*, and *Tenting on the Plains*. All were reprinted in a single set by the University of Oklahoma Press in 1976.

John Scholfield appeared with *46 Years in the Army* in 1897; U. S. Grant paid off many debts with his two-volume *Personal Memoirs* in 1885; Philip H. Sheridan issued a two-volume *Personal Memoirs* in 1888; William T. Sherman came out with his two-volume *Memoirs* in 1875; and Nelson A. Miles split his autobiography into two separate appearances: *Personal Recollections* in 1898 and *Serving the Republic* in 1911.

General George Crook, His Autobiography, appeared in 1960 under the editorship of Martin Schmitt while, earlier, John G. Bourke, Crook's aide, had authored several volumes on the general.

George Forsyth wrote two volumes that were somewhat autobiographical but included much general information on the Army on the frontier: *Story of a Soldier* and *Thrilling Days of Army Life*, both published in 1900.

Books about generals are even more plentiful with Ezra Warner devoting two volumes of attention to those who served in the Civil War. They were *Generals in Gray*, 1959, and *Generals in Blue*, 1964, both with valuable biographies of every officer who wore generals' stars during the war.

Stephen Perry Jocelyn's story in the Pacific Northwest is told by his son in *Mostly Alkali*, 1953, while Donald Smythe recounts the pre-World War I Army days in the Southwest in *Guerrilla Warfare: the Early Life of John J. Pershing*, 1973.

Memories of Major General George H. Thomas appeared in 1881 by R. Johnson while William Johnson wrote *Life of General Albert Sidney Johnston* in 1878. Roger Nichols was the author of *General Henry Atkinson: Western Military Career* in 1965 and J. King told of *War Eagle: the Life of General Eugene A. Carr* in 1963. Robert G. Athearn wrote *William Tecumseh Sherman and the Settlement of the West* in 1956. Carl Coke Rister discussed two Civil War opponents' early years in *Border Command: General Phil Sheridan in the West* (1944) and *Robert E. Lee in Texas* (1946).

Merrill J. Mattes used the papers of Brigadier General Reynolds Burt to tell of the Burt family's frontier days on the Bozeman Trail and elsewhere in the West. This appeared in 1960 as *Indians, Infants, and Infantry*. It is especially interesting regarding Fort C. F. Smith, Montana.

Lawrence Frost has completed several books heavy with text and illustrations including the *Custer Album* (1964), *U. S. Grant Album* (1966), *Phil Sheridan Album* (1968), and *General Custer's 'Libbie'* 1976.

Great Plains Command, William B. Hazen in the Frontier West tells of this general who once commanded several posts in the West. It is by Marvin E. Kroeker and was published in 1976.

Edward K. Eckert and Nicholas J. Amato were the co-editors of *Ten Years in the Saddle: The Memoirs of William Woods Averell 1851-1862*, published in 1979 and telling particularly good accounts of pre-Civil War New Mexico.

In *No Tears for the General*, published in 1974, Langdon Sully draws on his grandfather's 315 letters to tell of the career of Alfred Sully in California and the Dakotas.

Medal of Honor winner Cornelius Cole Smith's story is told by his son in *Don't Settle for Second*, published in 1976. Smith won the medal at Pea Ridge in the Dakotas as a corporal, later commanded troops and posts in the Southwest as a colonel.

Diaries and letters have provided the meat for a number of second hand accounts skillfully put together by editors. One example is Sandra L. Myres' editorship of *Cavalry Wife: The Story of Eveline M. Alexander, 1866-1867*, published in 1977 and telling of posts in New Mexico and Colorado. Robert C. and Eleanor R. Carriker edited *An Army Wife on the Frontier: The Memoirs of Alice Blackwood Baldwin, 1867-1877* with accounts of assignments at Plains posts and in Montana. This was published in 1975.

Robert M. Utley edited *Life in Custer's Cavalry: Diaries and Letters of Albert and Jennie Barnitz, 1867-1868*, of the post Civil War activities that long preceded the Battle of the Little Big Horn. This was published in 1977.

The end of the Civil War in the Plains, having more to do with Indians than Confederates, was told by Lieutenant Charles Springer through the editorship of B. Frank Cooling in *Soldiering in Sioux Country, 1865*, published in 1971.

The Oregon Trail and Wyoming is the setting for *Tending the Talking Wire: A Buck Soldier's View of Indian Country, 1863-1866*, taken from the letters of Private Hervey Johnson by William E. Unrau in 1979.

Patricia M. Stallard looked to a number of accounts by officers' wives for *Glittering Misery; Dependents of the Indian Fighting Army*, telling of the families of the posts. This was published in 1978.

Probably one of the best, at least most reprinted, wives' accounts is *Vanished Arizona* by Martha Summerhayes, a first person account of life on the Arizona frontier in the 1870s. This was first published in 1911 and reprinted several times since.

Lydia Lane wrote *I Married a Soldier* of her life as the post commander's wife in New Mexico, published in 1893, and Ellen Biddle, *Reminiscenses of a Soldier's Wife* in the Pacific Northwest area, published in 1907 and reprinted. One of the rarest, as it does not appear to have been reprinted, is *Letters from an Officer's Wife 1871-1888* by Frances Roe, published in 1909. This is particularly interesting because of accounts of life in obscure Kansas camps.

Frontier life of a different sort is described by Stacy C. Hinkle in *Wings and Saddles: The Air and Cavalry Punitive Expedition of 1919*, telling how the last days of the frontier were conquered by the Army Air Service. This autobiographical monograph was published in 1967 as part of the Southwestern Studies of the University of Texas at El Paso.

Posts of the Western frontier did not follow the usual systems of fortification nor were they in the stockade stereotype portrayed by Hollywood. There were some principles that were followed and a few books usually available can assist in understanding the designs.

Max L. Moorhead published in 1975 on the earliest styles of fortification in North America, the presidios of the Southwest and Baja California. Appropriately, the book is titled *The Presidios.*

The design of stockaded forts and their Eastern and European predecessors is discussed in detail in *American Forts, Architectural Form and Function* by Willard Robinson in 1977. He stops short of the coast artillery defenses of the late 19th century but these are discussed, as part of the entire spectrum of seacoast protection, in E. Raymond Lewis' *Seacoast Fortifications of the United States: An Introductory History*, published in 1970 and republished in 1979. A detailed examination of the theory of fortification as seen from the European viewpoint is in Ian V. Hogg's *Fortress: A History of Military Defence* (1975).

Some of the best sources for state-wide and single coverages of forts lie in the records and publications of the state and local historical societies. Father Prucha's *Military Posts of the United States*, already noted, has an excellent bibliography of short histories in the quarterlies of these societies; the Hart *Forts of the Old West* series also lists many short histories. There are a number of books in print, or available in libraries, that cover the forts of a state, or specific forts, or note them in sufficient detail to be of interest. These are noted here in groupings by each Western state.

In 1960 Ray Brandes published *Frontier Military Posts of Arizona,* a handy roundup of mini-histories of the camps and stations of the Army. In 1975 Stan C. Agnew appeared with *Garrisons of the Regular U.S. Army, 1851-1899, Arizona*, a detailed month-by-month statistical profile of what unit was where at Arizona posts in the latter half of the nineteenth century.

Henry F. Dobyns appeared in 1976 with *Spanish Colonial Tucson: A Demographic History* which tells of the early presidio there.

The specialist on the Apache campaigns, Dan L. Thrapp, has a number of books that draw heavily on the history of Arizona posts, one of which is *Dateline Fort Bowie: Charles Fletcher Lummis Reports on an Apache War*. This is an edited compilation of the published reports of Lummis during the campaign. It appeared in 1979.

Robert M. Utley's prolific output on the West included a number of monographs for the National Park Service. One was *A Clash of Cultures: Fort Bowie and the Chiricahua Apaches* in 1978.

Harold B. Wharfield's account, *With Scouts and Cavalry at Fort Apache*, first appeared in 1965 as edited by John Alexander Carroll. The story of Fort McDowell by Bill Reed was issued in 1977 as *The Last Bugle Call: A History of Fort McDowell, Arizona Territory, 1865-1890.*

California was covered in a general overview but with considerable lapses by Joseph S. Whiting and R. J. Whiting in *Forts of the State of California* (1960) but much of this was drawn from mentions in official records without elaboration.

The Copley Press of San Diego published in the 1960s a five-volume history of Southern California, with the emphasis on the San Diego area. By Richard F. Pourade, the coffee table set starts with the period of exploration and ends with the 20th century.

A number of accounts were written of the Navy and Marine Corps advent onto the California scene in the 1840s and before, but these are not generally available. One that is was edited by Howard Lamar, *The Cruise of the Portsmouth: A Sailor's View of the Naval Conquest of California 1845-1847* from a manuscript by Joseph T. Downey, yeoman in the *Portsmouth*. Yale published it in 1958.

Marines in the War with Mexico, by Gabrielle N. Santelli, was scheduled to be published in 1980 by the Marine Corps History and Museums Division. This will contain considerable discussion of Navy and Marine actions throughout California, suggesting that the state had been conquered before the Army arrived to "act as occupation forces."

Lieutenant Commander Arnold S. Lott is the author of *A Long Line of Ships; Mare Island's Center of Naval Activity in California*, published in 1954 as the history of the Mare Island Naval Shipyard, the first of its type on the West Coast.

Oscar Lewis authored *Sutter's Fort: Gateway to the Gold Fields* in 1966 as part of the "American Forts Series," telling the story of John Sutter and his fort at Sacramento.

Aurora Hunt wrote a series of books in the 1950s that tell of the California Volunteers in the Civil War. They include *Army of the Pacific 1860-1866*, in 1951, and *James H. Carleton, Frontier Dragoon*, in 1958.

A romanticized history based on historical research is *The Boys in Sky Blue Pants*, a history of Camp Independence, published in 1975 by Dorothy C. Cragen, discussing the 1862-1877 period of the post.

J. G. Motheral is the author of a short treatment of Fort Point, the fortress under the Golden Gate at the entrance to San Francisco Bay. Published in 1971, it is entitled *Fort Point, Gibraltar of the Pacific.*

Fort Yuma on the Colorado River, telling of a fort popularly thought to be in Arizona but actually on a bluff across the Colorado River in California, appeared in 1968 under the authorship of Harold B. Wharfield.

Dennis G. Casebier is the prolific writer of the Mojave Desert with *The Battle of Camp Cady*, 1973, *Camp Rock Springs, California*, 1973, *Carleton's Pah-Ute Campaign*, 1972, *Camp El Dorado, Arizona Territory*, 1971, and *The Mojave Road*, 1975.

The story of the immense Marine Corps Base at Camp Pendleton is told in *Marines of the Margarita* by Robert M. Whitty and Neil Morgan in 1970.

Bringing fort history up to World War I is William F. Strobridge's *Golden Gate to Golden Horn: Camp Fremont, California, and the American Expedition to Siberia of 1918*, telling of the training at this San Mateo tent camp.

Military Posts of Colorado by T. Don Brandes was published in 1973 while *Along Colorado Trails* and *Old Forts of Southern Colorado* appeared in 1975 by Raymond M. Bechner. Guy L. Peterson is the author of *Fort Collins: The Post, the Town*, published in 1972.

David Lavender authored *Bent's Fort* in 1951 and Robert A. Murray, *A Citadel on the Santa Fe: The Saga of Bent's Fort* in 1971.

The days of the Indian Agency at Meeker and the establishment of Cantonment on the White River is told in Marshall Sprague's *Massacre: The Tragedy at White River*, published in 1957.

Confederates in the Union uniform, mustering for the Federal government to fight the common Indian foe in the West, are discussed in Dee Brown's *Galvanized Yankees*, published in 1963. The troopers were stationed at posts in Colorado and elsewhere in the Plains states.

Idaho does not seem to have an overall publication on its forts but they are mentioned in many of the autobiographies and biographies noted earlier. No. 63 of the Idaho Historical Society's Reference Series is *Idaho Military Posts and Camps*, published in 1971, with short accounts of the places.

Frank C. Robertson appeared in 1963 with *Fort Hall, Gateway to the Oregon Country*, primarily a story of the trading post.

In 1971 the Kansas State Historical Society published Louise Barry's *The Beginning of the West; Annals of the Kansas Gateway to the American West, 1540-1854.* This provides much data on forts and camps in the state.

Captain William F. Pride is the author of *The History of Fort Riley* in 1926. Elvyn Hunt wrote *The History of Fort Leavenworth, 1827-1927* in 1929 and in 1973 Colonel George Walton came out with a newer version, *Sentinel of the Plains: Fort Leavenworth and the American West.* Another but different sentinel is David K. Strate's *Sentinel to the Cimarron: The Frontier Experience at Fort Dodge, Kansas,* published in 1971.

The Minnesota Historical Society has published numerous short histories of forts in its quarterly but few have been favored with book-length treatments. Fort Snelling is the subject of Marcus L. Hansen's *Old Fort Snelling* in 1958 and Evan Jones' *Citadel in the Wilderness: The Story of Fort Snelling and the Northwest Frontier,* published in 1966.

Robert Orr Baker is the author of *The Muster Roll: A Biography of Fort Ripley, Minnesota,* in 1972.

Montana has had at least two summary treatments: Michael Koury's *Military Posts of Montana* in 1971 and Don Miller and Stan Cohen with *Military and Trading Posts of Montana* in 1978. The State Historical Society published a *Map of Montana Showing Military Sites* in 1976.

Richard Upton is the author of *Fort Custer on the Little Big Horn,* published in 1973, and Michael Koury of *Guarding the Carroll Trail: Camp Lewis* in 1971.

As the location of the Battle of the Little Big Horn, Montana is the setting for many books on the battle, Custer, the Seventh Cavalry, and other assorted actions and individuals. One of the best treatments is John S. Gray's *Centennial Campaign: The Sioux War of 1876,* published in 1976.

Nebraska does not seem to have an overall review of forts but Captain Eugene F. Ware's *The Indian War of 1864* is a good first-hand account of the Civil War camps of the era. This was re-published in 1960. *Fort McPherson, Nebraska; Fort Cottonwood, N.T.: Guardian of the Tracks and Trails* was by Louis A. Holmes but published after his death in 1963.

Colonel Virgil Ney is the author of *Fort on the Prairie, Fort Atkinson on Council Bluff, 1819-1827,* in 1978 and Mrs. Harold Gilman of *Pump on the Prairie, Gilman Ranch, 1859-1868,* of her family's stagecoach stop and sometimes Army camp, in 1975. *The History of Fort Crook 1888, Offutt Air Force Base 1976* is an example of an official Air Force history. It was published at Offutt in 1979.

Nevada's forts are mentioned in many accounts but in no full-length treatment. The best overall summary is by Colonel George Ruhlen in *Early Nevada Forts,* published as a double-issue edition of the Nevada Historical Quarterly in 1964.

In format similar to that of his book on Arizona, Stan C. Agnew published *Garrisons of the Regular U.S. Army, New Mexico, 1846-1899* in 1972.

Probably the best overview of New Mexico's forts was published as a Bicentennial project by the Phelps Dodge Corporation in 1976, *Echoes of the Bugles.* In 32 pages, author Dale F. Giese summarizes the histories of 62 posts.

Andy Gregg appeared in 1968 with *Drums of Yesterday: The Forts of New Mexico.* In 1973, the Council on Abandoned Military Posts published the map by Lee Myers and George F. Caldwell, *Military Installations of New Mexico.*

James Bennett was the original author of *Forts and Forays,* edited by C.E. Brooks and F.D. Reeve for 1948 publication. It includes first-hand accounts of life at several pre-Civil War New Mexico posts.

Ed Bartholomew is the editor of William T. Parker's *Annals of Old Fort Cummings, 1867-1868,* published in 1968. Mrs. Marion Grinstead wrote *Life and Death of a Frontier Fort: Fort Craig, New Mexico, 1854-1885,* published in 1973.

Robert M. Utley prepared a number of reports on Southwestern military posts, but the most unusual must have been a history of Fort Union. It was eight pages long and each page the size of a postage stamp, obviously not designed for library shelves. He also wrote the official National Park Service report on Fort Union in 1962.

Chris Emmett is the author of *Fort Union and the Winning of the Southwest,* published in 1965. Another story of the fort is by Rev. Stanley F.L. Carochiola, *Fort Union,* in 1961. Under the name of F. Stanley, this author-priest prepared many short histories of towns in the Southwest plus *Fort Bascom, Comanche-Kiowa Barrier* (1961), *Fort Craig* (1962), *Fort Fillmore Story* (1961), *Fort Conrad* (1962), and *Fort Stanton* (1964). Obviously the labors of love, these books border on being scrapbooks of reprints from other published material from newspapers and official reports.

The story of the Navajos and their tribulations from one side of New Mexico to the other has been told in L. Bailey's *Long Walk,* 1964; Lawrence Kelly's *Navajo Roundup,* 1971, and Frank McNitt's *Navajo Wars: Military Campaigns, Slave Raids, and Reprisals,* 1972. The Confederate expeditions into the territory are covered by Martin Hardwick Hall's *The Confederate Army of New Mexico,* 1978.

North Dakota's two historical societies have published many short accounts of the state's forts, many of them touching on Custer's Fort Abraham Lincoln, south of Bismarck.

Phillippe R.D. De Trobriand commanded posts in North Dakota after the Civil War, wrote his memoirs in French, and in 1941 the translated version was published as *Army Life in the Dakotas.*

Usher L. Burdick published *Tales From Buffalo Land, the Story of Fort Buford* in 1940, occasionally available in libraries.

Odie B. Faulk, Kenny A. Franks, and Paul F. Lambert are the coeditors lof *Early Military Forts and Posts of Oklahoma,* published in 1979. William Morrison was the author in 1936 of *Military Posts and Camps in Oklahoma* and Vinson Lackey the author and illustrator of a softbound *Forts of Oklahoma,* 1963. Another of the earliler summaries of the state's forts was *Advancing the Frontier,* by Grant Foreman in 1947.

George Shirk, Muriel H. Wright, and Kenny Franks published *Mark of Heritage,* an updated summary of Oklahoma's historic sites, in 1976.

Colonel Wilbur Nye had the unusual situation of writing the first version of *Carbine & Lance,* the history of Fort Sill, in 1937 and its revision in 1969, more than thirty years later.

Robert Carriker is the author of *Fort Supply, Indian Territory, Frontier Outpost on the Plains,* 1970. Edging into Oklahoma when it was known as Indian Territory was Fort Smith. This post now is in modern-day Arkansas, but its first site straddled the border, as described by Edwin C. Bearss and A.M. Gibson in *Fort Smith, Little Gibraltar on the Arkansas,* 1969.

Early days at Civil War Volunteer posts in Oregon are told in Nelson and Onstad's *Webfoot Volunteer,* 1965, while Priscilla Knuth appeared in 1971 with *Picturesque Frontier: The Army's Fort Dalles,* of pre-Civil War activity.

Two books have appeared recently on Fort Klamath: *Fort Klamath, Frontier Post in Oregon,* 1863-1890, by Buena Cobb Stone, in 1964, and *Burnt Out Fires: California's Modoc Indian War,* by Richard H. Dillon in 1973.

Marshall Hanft authored *Cape Forts of the Columbia River,* regarding the coastal defenses in Northern Oregon and Southern Washington at the mouth of that river. This appeared in 1971.

South Dakota's military posts have been covered in a number of historical society articles but no full-length book history is available. Helen White's *Ho! for the Gold Fields,* 1966, tells of a number of camps of both Dakotas. Short histories of trading and military posts appeared in the society's newsletter, "Wi-Iyohi," during its publishing days in the 1950s.

Walter Prescott Webb's two-volume *Handbook of Texas* has considerable coverage of the many posts and camps of the state while Gerald S. Pierce's *Texas Under Arms—The Camps Posts, Forts, & Military Towns of the Republic of Texas, 1836-1846,* tells of the Texas Republic days. This is one of the best books on posts, covering in 200 separate articles 30 military towns, 53 public and private forts, and 130 military camps and posts. It was published in 1969.

Bill Winsor is the author of *Texas in the Confederacy; Military Installations, Economy, and People,* appearing in 1978. The Government Printing Office published Ronnie C. Tyler's *The Big Bend: A History of the Last Texas Frontier* in 1976 with coverage of the border campaigns.

Colonel M.H. Thomlinson was the author in 1945 of *The Garrison of Fort Bliss, 1849-1916,* and Major Richard K. McMaster in 1975 of *Musket, Saber & Missile: A History of Fort Bliss, 1862-1974.*

Oliver Knight wrote in 1953 of *Fort Worth on the Trinity;* Carl Coke Rister in 1956 of *Fort Griffin on the Texas Frontier;* Thomas R. Havins in 1964 on *Camp Colorado: A Decade of Frontier Defense;* Mary O. Handy in 1951 on *History of Fort Sam Houston;* and Margaret Bierschwale in 1966, *Fort McKavett, Texas, Post on the San Saba.*

Barry Schobee first wrote of Fort Davis in *Old Fort Davis* in 1947 and in *Fort Davis, Texas* in 1963. Walter Lord covered the Alamo in *A Time to Stand* in 1961 and Leavitt Corning, Jr., the sites of the Big Bend country in *Private Forts of Presidio County, Texas,* 1967. H. Allen Anderson wrote *Fort Phantom Hill: Outpost on the Clear Fork of the Brazos* in 1977.

J. Evetts Haley is the author of *Fort Concho and the Texas Frontier* in 1952 and Susan Miles the editor of *Fort Concho in 1877,* by Alice Kirk Grierson, wife of the commanding officer, in 1973.

Utah's posts are covered in short versions in historical society publications, especially in the fall, 1964, edition of the "Utah Historical Quarterly" with Thomas G. Alexander and Leonard J. Arrington in *The Utah Military Frontier, 1872-1912, Forts Cameron, Thornburgh, and Duchesne.*

Fred B. Rogers tells of Utah's frontier in *Soldiers of the Overland: Being Some Accounts of the Services of General Patrick Edward Connor & His Volunteers in the Old West,* 1938. Harold D. Langley in 1976 edited the anonymous articles by a recruit called "Utah" to the Philadelphia *Evening Bulletin* to publish *To Utah with the Dragoons with Glimpses of Life in Arizona and California, 1858-1859.* Camp Floyd, Utah, is the main setting for the book.

Joseph Whiting published *Forts of the State of Washington* in 1951, providing brief glimpses of several posts in extracts from official records and newspaper mentions. Albert F. Salisbury's *Here Rolled the Covered Wagons* visits many of the state's sites, plus others on the Oregon Trail. This was first published in 1948.

John A. Hussey is the author of *Fort Vancouver,* 1957, and H. Dean Guie of *Bugles in the Valley: Garnett's Fort Simcoe,* reprinted in 1977.

The subject of National Park Service reports but yet to be covered in book length, the U.S.—British confrontation in the 1860s over the boundary in the San Juan Islands area is in *Pig War Islands* in 1971. V.J. Gregory authored *Keepers of the Gate,* the story of the coast defense of Puget Sound in 1976.

Grace R. Hebard and Earl Brininstool were the co-authors of *The Bozeman Trail,* first published in 1922 and reprinted as a single volume in 1960. This tells the history of the trail and its several forts.

Robert A. Murray wrote *The Army on the Powder River* in 1968, and *Military Posts in the Powder River Country of Wyoming, 1866-1894,* in 1974. He also wrote *Fort Laramie, Visions of a Grand Old Post,* in 1974, as well as *Military Posts of Wyoming,* both published by the Old Army Press.

Fort Laramie also was treated by Leroy Hafen and F. Young in *Fort Laramie and the Pageant of the West* in 1938 and Remi Nadeau in *Fort Laramie and the Sioux Indians* as part of the American Forts Series.

Fort Bridger, Island in the Wilderness, appeared by Fred. R. Gowans and Eugene E. Campbell in 1975 and Dee Brown wrote an informal story of *Fort Phil Kearny, An American Saga* in 1962. Another informal account was *Bugs to Blizzards or An Army Wife at Ft. D.A. Russell* by Martha Fleishman and Carol Joy Justice in 1974.

This listing would be incomplete without taking note of several books for children, especially Harold Peterson's *Forts in America,* published in 1964, and C.B. Colby's *Historic American Forts, From Frontier Stockade to Coastal Fortress,* 1963.

Bruce Grant appeared in 1965 with *American Forts Yesterday & Today* and Edith McCall is the author of two earlier tales, *Log Fort Adventures,* 1958, and *Heroes of the Western Outposts,* 1960.

A last reminder that this is not a bibliography of this book nor of the subject of the posts, forts, camps, and installations of the Army, Navy, and Marine Corps on the Western Frontier. That would draw heavily on documentary and primary resources. What has been listen here is material on the subject that is in print or probably in the local library which can be pursued by anyone wanting to delve more deeply into this fascinating page from the past.